# 2003 SUPPl
# HEALTH LAW
## CASES, MATERIALS AND PROBLEMS
## Fourth Edition

By

**Barry R. Furrow**
*Professor of Law and Director, Health Law Institute*
*Widener University*

**Thomas L. Greaney**
*Professor of Law and Professor of Health Administration and*
*Co-Director, Center for Health Law Studies*
*Saint Louis University*

**Sandra H. Johnson**
*Tenet Professor in Health Care Law and Ethics*
*Professor of Law, Professor of Health Administration and*
*Professor of Law in Internal Medicine*
*Saint Louis University*

**Timothy S. Jost**
*Robert L. Willett Family Professor of Law*
*Washington and Lee University School of Law*

**Robert L. Schwartz**
*Professor of Law and Professor of Pediatrics*
*University of New Mexico*

**AMERICAN CASEBOOK SERIES®**

Mat # 40160143

West Group has created this publication to provide you with accurate and authoritative information concerning the subject matter covered. However, this publication was not necessarily prepared by persons licensed to practice law in a particular jurisdiction. West Group is not engaged in rendering legal or other professional advice, and this publication is not a substitute for the advice of an attorney. If you require legal or other expert advice, you should seek the services of a competent attorney or other professional.

*American Casebook Series* and West Group are trademarks registered in the U.S. Patent and Trademark Office.

COPYRIGHT © 1996 WEST PUBLISHING CO.
COPYRIGHT © 1999 WEST GROUP
COPYRIGHT © 2003 By WEST GROUP
                    610 Opperman Drive
                    P.O. Box 64526
                    St. Paul, MN 55164–0526
                    1–800–328–9352

All rights reserved
Printed in the United States of America
**ISBN** 0–314–14756–X

TEXT IS PRINTED ON 10% POST CONSUMER RECYCLED PAPER

# Acknowledgements

We all thank Mary Ann Jauer at Saint Louis University for her unflagging efforts to prepare this supplement for print.

We thank our research assistants Noreen Ahmed, Heather Bearden, Kelly Dineen, Kallie Dixon and Jeanmarie Montney for their work. We also thank secretary Karla Harris. As always, we appreciate the support of our deans Jeffrey Lewis, David Partlett, Douglas Ray, and Suellyn Scarnecchia.

We also appreciate all of the teachers around the country who are using our casebook and who share their experiences and suggestions with us. We encourage professors to access the West TWEN site for this casebook for syllabi, sample examinations, and further updates.

National Academy of Sciences, Responsible Research: A Systems Approach to Protecting Research Participants. © 2003, National Academy of Sciences.

*

# Table of Contents

|  | Page |
|---|---|
| ACKNOWLEDGMENT | iii |
| TABLE OF CASES | xiii |

| | |
|---|---|
| **Chapter 1. Defining, Evaluating and Distributing Health Care: An Introduction** | 1 |
| I. Defining Sickness | 1 |
| III. The Problem of Medical Error | 1 |
|     B. The Extent of Medical Misadventures | 1 |
|     C. Remedying Quality Problems of Health Care Services | 2 |
|         3. Regulatory Approaches to Medical Errors | 2 |
|             a. The Joint Commission on the Accreditation of Healthcare Organizations | 4 |
|             b. The New CMS Rules on Error | 6 |
|             c. The Pennsylvania Patient Safety Authority | 8 |
| IV. Distributive Justice and the Allocation of Health Care Resources—The Example of Human Organ Transplantation | 11 |
|     B. Rationing of Scarce Human Organs | 11 |
|         1. Geographic Distribution of Organs | 13 |
|         2. Listing Patients for Transplantation | 13 |
|     C. Increasing the Supply of Organs for Transplantation: The Impact of Legal Restraints | 13 |
|         1. Cadaver Organs | 13 |

## PART I. PROMOTING QUALITY

| | |
|---|---|
| **Chapter 2. Quality Control Regulation: Licensing of Health Care Professionals** | 18 |
| I. Discipline | 18 |
| II. Alternative and Complementary Medicine | 21 |
| III. Unlicensed Providers | 22 |
| **Chapter 3. Quality Control Regulation of Health Care Institutions** | 23 |
| I. Introduction | 23 |
| II. Regulatory Systems | 26 |
|     A. Differences Among Institutions | 26 |
|     C. The Regulatory Process | 27 |
|         1. Standard Setting | 27 |
|         2. Survey and Inspection | 30 |
|         3. Sanctions | 30 |
| III. Private Accreditation of Health Care Facilities | 31 |
| **Chapter 4. Liability of Health Care Professionals** | 33 |
| I. The Standard of Care | 33 |

|  |  | Page |
|---|---|---|
| A. | Establishing the Standard of Care | 33 |
| 2. | Expert Testimony | 33 |
| B. | Practice Guidelines As Codified Standards of Care | 34 |
| C. | Other Methods of Proving Negligence | 34 |

- II. Judicial Risk–Benefit Balancing — 34
- IV. Defenses to a Malpractice Suit — 34
  - B. Practice Guidelines as an Affirmative Defense — 34
  - D. Good Samaritan Acts — 35
  - G. Restrictions on the Learned Intermediary Rule — 35
    - *Perez v. Wyeth Laboratories Inc.* — 35
    - Notes and Questions — 44
  - H. Physician Off–Label Prescribing of FDA–Approved Drugs — 46
    - *Richardson v. Miller* — 47
- VI. Damage Innovations — 48
  - B. Increased Risks and Fear of the Future — 48

**Chapter 5. The Professional–Patient Relationship** — 49

Introduction — 49
- I. The Contract Between Patient and Physician — 49
  - A. Express and Implied Contract — 49
  - D. Exculpatory Clauses — 50
- II. Confidentiality and Disclosure in the Physician–Patient Relationship — 51
  - B. Federal Medical Privacy Standards — 51
- III. Informed Consent: The Physician's Obligation — 51
  - B. The Legal Framework of Informed Consent — 51
    - 1. Negligence as a Basis for Recovery — 51
    - 2. Disclosure of Physician–Specific Risk Information — 52

**Chapter 6. Liability of Health Care Institutions** — 53
- I. From Immunity to Vicarious Liability — 53
  - B. Vicarious Liability Doctrine — 53
    - 2. Stretching Vicarious Liability Doctrine — 53
      - e. The Non–Delegable Duty Doctrine — 53
        - *Simmons v. Tuomey Regional Medical Center* — 53
        - Notes and Questions — 59
- II. Hospital Direct Liability — 60
  - E. The Emergence of Corporate Negligence — 60
    - 3. The Duty of a Hospital to Obtain Patient Consent — 60
- III. Reforming the Tort System for Medical Injuries — 61
  - A. The Sources of the Malpractice Crisis — 61
    - 1. The Nature of the Insurance Industry — 61
      - Notes and Questions — 63
    - 2. Insurance Availability and Cost: Some Evidence — 66
  - B. Responses to the Crisis — 67
    - 1. Benchmarks for Evaluating Reforms — 67
    - 2. Improving Insurance Availability for Physicians — 67
      - a. New Sources of Insurance — 67
      - b. Claims-Made Policies — 68
      - c. Stop-Gap State Coverage — 68
      - d. Hospital Provision of Coverage for Staff Physicians — 68
      - e. Selective Insurance Marketing — 68
      - f. Hospital Complaint Profiling — 69

|   | Page |
|---|---|
| 3. Altering the Litigation Process | 69 |
| *Problem: Coping With Reform* | 73 |
| *Problem: Designing State Law Reforms* | 77 |
| C. The Effects of Reform: A Preliminary Assessment | 78 |
| 1. Caps on Awards and Statutes of Limitations | 78 |
| 2. Pretrial Screening Panels | 78 |
| 3. Other Reform Measures | 79 |
| D. Alternative Approaches to Compensation of Patient Injury | 80 |
| 1. The Rationale for an Alternative System | 80 |
| 2. No–Fault Reforms | 85 |
| Abraham, Medical Liability Reform: A Conceptual Framework | 85 |
| 3. Current Federal Proposals | 91 |
| 4. Second–Generation Reforms | 93 |
| a. Medical Practice Guidelines as the Standard of Care | 93 |
| b. Alternative Dispute Resolution (ADR) | 94 |
| c. No–Fault Systems | 94 |
| (1) Medical Adversity Insurance | 94 |
| *Notes and Questions* | 95 |
| (2) Offers to Pay Patient Losses | 95 |
| 4. Administrative Systems | 96 |
| *Notes and Questions* | 98 |
| 5. Enterprise Liability | 99 |
| 6. Conclusion | 101 |

## PART II. ACCESS AND COST CONTROL

Chapter 7. Health Care Cost and Access: The Policy Context ... 104
I. The Problems ... 104
  A. The Problem of Access ... 104
  B. The Problem of Cost ... 104
    1. Recent Developments in Health Care Cost Inflation ... 104
II. Approaches to Health Care Reform ... 105
  A. Options for Expanding Access to Care ... 105
    2. Approaches to Insuring the Uninsured based on Private Insurance ... 105
  B. Cost Control ... 106
    2. Consumer Choice in Purchasing Health Care Services: The Medical Savings Account ... 106

Chapter 8. Private Health Insurance and Managed Care: State Regulation and Liability ... 107
III. Tort Liability of Managed Care ... 107
  D. Repair Team Litigation and RICO ... 107
V. State Regulation of Managed Care ... 112
  A. Introduction ... 112

Chapter 9. Regulation of Insurance and Managed Care: The Federal Role ... 114
II. The Employee Retirement Income Security Act of 1974 (ERISA) ... 114
  A. ERISA Preemption of State Health Insurance Regulation ... 114
    *Rush Prudential HMO, Inc. v. Moran, Et Al.* ... 114
  B. ERISA Preemption of State Tort Litigation ... 126
    *Cicio v. Does 1–8 Et Al.* ... 126
  C. Beneficiary Remedies Provided by ERISA ... 138

|   |   | Page |
|---|---|---|
| | 2. Administrative Claims and Appeals Procedures under ERISA | 138 |
| | D. Provider Fiduciary Obligations Under ERISA | 139 |
| | E. Provider Disclosure Requirements | 139 |
| III. | Federal Initiatives to Expand Private Insurance Coverage: The Health Insurance Portability and Accountability Act of 1996, the Consolidated Omnibus Reconciliation Act of 1995 and the Americans With Disabilities Act | 139 |
| | A. The Health Insurance Portability and Accountability Act of 1996 and Cobra Coverage Requirements | 139 |

### Chapter 10. Public Health Care Programs: Medicare and Medicaid — 140

| | | |
|---|---|---|
| I. | Introduction | 140 |
| II. | Medicare | 140 |
| | B. Benefits | 140 |
| |    1. Coverage | 140 |
| | C. Payment for Services | 142 |
| |    5. Medicare Managed Care | 142 |
| | D. Administration and Appeals | 143 |
| | E. Medicare Reform | 145 |
| III. | Medicaid | 145 |
| | D. Program Administration: Federal/State Relationships | 146 |
| |    *Westside Mothers v. Haveman* | 146 |
| |    *Notes* | 152 |
| V. | State Pharmaceutical Benefit Programs | 154 |

### Chapter 11. Access to Health Care: The Obligation to Provide Care — 158

| | | |
|---|---|---|
| I. | Physicians' Duty to Treat | 158 |
| | B. The Americans With Disabilities Act | 158 |
| II. | Hospitals' Duty to Provide Treatment | 158 |
| | *Problem: Delayed Treatment* | 162 |

## PART III. ORGANIZING THE HEALTH CARE ENTERPRISE

### Chapter 12. Professional Relationships in Health Care Enterprises — 168

| | | |
|---|---|---|
| I. | Staff Privileges and Hospital–Physician Contracts | 168 |
| | *Note on HCQIA Litigation* | 168 |
| | *Mahan v. Avera St. Luke's* | 173 |
| II. | Managed Care Contracts for Professional Services | 180 |
| | *Note on In re Managed Care Litigation* | 182 |
| III. | Labor and Employment | 183 |
| | A. Employment–At–Will | 183 |
| | B. National Labor Relations Act | 184 |
| |    2. Supervisor? | 184 |
| |    *NLRB v. Kentucky River Community Care* | 184 |
| |    *Notes and Questions* | 192 |
| |    *Nurses United for Improved Patient Healthcare and VNA Corporation* | 193 |
| |    3. Concerted Action | 194 |
| |    *Problem: Changing Things, Continued* | 194 |
| IV. | Discrimination Law | 195 |

| | Page |
|---|---|
| Chapter 13. The Structure of the Health Care Enterprise | 198 |
| II. Forms of Business Enterprises and Their Legal Consequences | 198 |
|     B. Governance and Fiduciary Duties in Business Associations | 198 |
|         Note on Actions by State Attorneys General Alleging Breaches of Fiduciary Duties | 198 |
|         Manhattan Eye, Ear and Throat Hospital v. Spitzer | 200 |
|         Notes and Questions | 214 |
|     D. Professionalism and the Corporate Practice of Medicine Doctrine | 214 |
| III. Integration and New Organizational Structures Where's Waldo—Part II | 215 |
|     A. The Changing Structure of the Modern Health Care Enterprise | 215 |
| IV. Tax–Exempt Health Care Organizations | 216 |
|     A. Charitable Purposes: Hospitals | 216 |
|     B. Charitable Purposes: Health Maintenance Organizations | 217 |
|     C. Charitable Purposes: Integrated Delivery Systems (IDSs) | 218 |
|     D. Joint Ventures Between Tax–Exempt and for–Profit Organizations | 218 |
|         St. David's Health Care System v. United States | 218 |
|         Notes and Questions | 224 |
|     E. Relationships Between Physicians And Tax–Exempt Health Care Organizations | 225 |
|         3. Acquisition of Physician Practices by Exempt Organizations | 225 |
| Chapter 14. Fraud and Abuse | 227 |
| I. False Claims | 227 |
|     A. Governmental Enforcement | 227 |
|         United States ex rel. Mikes v. Straus | 227 |
|         Notes and Questions | 235 |
|     B. Qui Tam Actions | 236 |
| II. Medicare and Medicaid Fraud and Abuse | 237 |
|     E. Statutory Exceptions, Safe Harbors and Fraud Alerts | 237 |
|         Note: Staff Privileges as Illegal Remuneration? | 238 |
|         Notes and Questions | 244 |
| III. Stark I & II: A Transactional Approach to Self–Referrals | 244 |
|     B. Exceptions | 244 |
|         Note on Fair Market Value | 244 |
| Chapter 15. Antitrust | 247 |
| Introduction | 247 |
| I. Cartels and Professionalism | 247 |
|     B. Collective Activities With Justifications | 247 |
|         1. Restrictions on Advertising and Dissemination of Information | 247 |
|             Note on Information Dissemination by Physician Groups: Advocacy, Efficiency, or Cartelization? | 248 |
|             Note on Group Purchasing Organizations | 249 |
|         2. Private Accreditation and Professional Standard–Setting | 250 |
| II. Health Care Enterprises, Integration and Financing | 250 |
|     A. Provider–Controlled Networks and Health Plans | 250 |
|         Federal Trade Commission, Advisory Opinion In Re Medsouth, Inc. | 252 |

|  | Page |
|---|---|
| *Notes and Questions* | 262 |
| B. Exclusive Contracting | 263 |
| *Note on Monopolization by Hospitals* | 263 |
| *Note on the FTC's Pharmaceutical Initiative* | 264 |
| D. Mergers and Acquisitions | 266 |
| 1. Hospital Mergers | 266 |

## PART IV. BIOETHICS

Chapter 16. Human Reproduction and Birth ..... 268
  I. When Does Human Life Become a "Person"? ..... 268
    B. Legal Recognition of the Beginning of Human Life ..... 268
      2. Statutory Recognition ..... 268
      3. Common Law Recognition ..... 269
  II. Medical Intervention in Reproduction ..... 270
    A. Limiting Reproduction ..... 270
      3. Abortion ..... 270
      4. Sterilization ..... 271
    B. Assisting Reproduction ..... 272
      3. In Vitro Fertilization, Egg Transfer and Embryo Transfer ..... 272
        *J.B. v. M.B.* ..... 272
      4. Surrogacy ..... 279
        *Prato–Morrison v. Doe* ..... 279
        *Notes on Prato–Morrison v. Doe* ..... 282
      5. Cloning ..... 283
        *Note on Reproductive and Therapeutic Cloning and Stem Cell Research* ..... 283
  III. Fetal Maternal Decisionmaking ..... 284

Chapter 17. Legal, Social and Ethical Issues in Human Genetics ..... 285
  I. Introduction ..... 285
  II. Legal Responses to Privacy, Confidentiality, Consent and Discrimination ..... 285
    A. Focus on Privacy ..... 285
    B. Focus on Discrimination ..... 285
    C. Creating DNA Databases ..... 288
      *Problem: Creating the Treasure Trove* ..... 289
  III. Genetic Screening ..... 290

Chapter 18. Defining Death ..... 292
  III. The "Dead Donor" Rule and Expanding Classes of Organ Donors—Anencephalic Infants and "non–Heart Beating" Donors ..... 292

Chapter 19. Life and Death Decisions ..... 293
  IV. The "Right to Die"—Patients Without Decisional Capacity ..... 293
    B. Determining the Patient's Choice ..... 293
      2. Decisionmaking in the Absence of a Governing Statute ..... 293
        b. The Role of the Courts and the Burden of Proof in Cases Involving the Decision to Forego Life–sustaining Treatment ..... 293
          *Conservatorship of Wendland* ..... 293
          *Notes and Questions on the California Supreme Court opinion in Wendland* ..... 302
  V. The "Right to Die"—Children and Newborns ..... 304

|  | Page |
|---|---|
| B. Newborns | 304 |
| *HCA, Inc. v. Miller* | 304 |
| Notes and Questions on *HCA, Inc. v. Miller* | 309 |
| VII. Physician Assisted Death | 310 |
| B. Legislation to Support Physician Assisted Death—"Death with Dignity" Initiatives | 310 |
| Fifth Annual Report on Oregon's Death With Dignity Act | 310 |
| VIII. Regulation of End–of–Life Care: The Case of Medical Marijuana | 314 |
| *United States v. Oakland Cannabis Buyers' Cooperative* | 314 |
| Notes and Questions on *United States v. Cannabis Buyers' Cooperative* | 319 |
| Problem: Drafting Medical Marijuana Legislation | 323 |

Chapter 20. Interdisciplinary Decisionmaking In Health Care: Regulation of Research Involving Human Subjects, Ethics Committees, and Advisory Committees ............ 324

| I. Regulation of Research Upon Human Subjects | 324 |
|---|---|
| C. Current Regulation of Research Upon Human Subjects in the United States | 324 |
| Note: Liability Arising out of Research Involving Human Subjects | 325 |
| D. Reforming the System to Protect Research Participants | 325 |
| Committee on Assessing the System for Protecting Human Research Participants of the Institute of Medicine, Responsible Research: A Systems Approach to Protecting Research Participants | 326 |
| Notes and Questions on Proposed Reform | 333 |
| Problem | 334 |

# Table of Cases

The principal cases are in bold type. Cases cited or discussed in the text are roman type. References are to pages. Cases cited in principal cases and within other quoted materials are not included.

Advocate Health Care, United States ex rel. Obert–Hong v., 211 F.Supp.2d 1045 (N.D.Ill.2002), 245

Alcalde, Estate of v. Deaton Specialty Hosp. Home, Inc., 133 F.Supp.2d 702 (D.Md. 2001), 60

Alexander v. Sandoval, 532 U.S. 275, 121 S.Ct. 1511, 149 L.Ed.2d 517 (2001), 164, 165

Alivio, State v., 275 Kan. 169, 61 P.3d 687 (Kan.2003), 21

American Lithotripsy Soc. v. Thompson, 215 F.Supp.2d 23 (D.D.C.2002), 245

Antrican v. Odom, 290 F.3d 178 (4th Cir.2002), 146

Ardoin v. Mills, 780 So.2d 1265 (La.App. 3 Cir.2001), 33

Arrington v. Wong, 237 F.3d 1066 (9th Cir. 2001), 160

A Woman's Choice–East Side Women's Clinic v. Brizzi, ___ U.S. ___, 123 S.Ct. 1273, 154 L.Ed.2d 1026 (2003), 271

A Woman's Choice–East Side Women's Clinic v. Newman, 305 F.3d 684 (7th Cir.2002), 271

A Woman's Choice–East Side Women's Clinic v. Newman, 132 F.Supp.2d 1150 (S.D.Ind. 2001), 271

A.Z. v. B.Z., 431 Mass. 150, 725 N.E.2d 1051 (Mass.2000), 277, 278

Baby M, Matter of, 109 N.J. 396, 537 A.2d 1227 (N.J.1988), 276, 277

Banker v. Hoehn, 278 A.D.2d 720, 718 N.Y.S.2d 438 (N.Y.A.D. 3 Dept.2000), 46

Barker v. International Paper Co., 993 F.Supp. 10 (D.Me.1998), 181

Barmak, United States ex rel. v. Sutter Corp., 2002 WL 987109 (S.D.N.Y.2002), 235

Barnes v. Gorman, 536 U.S. 181, 122 S.Ct. 2097, 153 L.Ed.2d 230 (2002), 152, 153, 158

Barragan v. Providence Memorial Hosp., 2000 WL 1731286 (Tex.App.-El Paso 2000), 60

Bell v. UNUM–Provident Corp., 222 F.Supp.2d 692 (E.D.Pa.2002), 125

Benson v. Tkach, 30 P.3d 402 (Okla.Civ.App. Div. 2 2001), 34

Berg v. Shapiro, 36 P.3d 109 (Colo.App.2001), 169

Berlin v. Sarah Bush Lincoln Health Center, 179 Ill.2d 1, 227 Ill.Dec. 769, 688 N.E.2d 106 (Ill.1997), 214, 215

Beverly Health & Rehabilitation Services, Inc. v. N.L.R.B., 317 F.3d 316, 354 U.S.App.D.C. 414 (D.C.Cir.2003), 192

Beverly Health & Rehabilitation Services, Inc. v. Thompson, 223 F.Supp.2d 73 (D.D.C. 2002), 28, 30

Bixler v. Central Pennsylvania Teamsters Health & Welfare Fund, 12 F.3d 1292 (3rd Cir.1993), 111

Blanks v. Southwestern Bell Communications, Inc., 310 F.3d 398 (5th Cir.2002), 158, 195

Board of Trustees of University of Alabama v. Garrett, 531 U.S. 356, 121 S.Ct. 955, 148 L.Ed.2d 866 (2001), 19

Bragdon v. Abbott, 524 U.S. 624, 118 S.Ct. 2196, 141 L.Ed.2d 540 (1998), 158, 195

Brown v. Glaxo, Inc., 790 So.2d 35 (La.App. 1 Cir.2000), 46

Brumley v. Pfizer, Inc., 149 F.Supp.2d 305 (S.D.Tex.2001), 45

Burlington United Methodist Family Services, Inc. v. Atkins, 227 F.Supp.2d 593 (S.D.W.Va.2002), 153

Buspirone Patent Litigation, In re, 185 F.Supp.2d 363 (S.D.N.Y.2002), 266

California Dental Ass'n v. F.T.C., 526 U.S. 756, 119 S.Ct. 1604, 143 L.Ed.2d 935 (1999), 247

Caracci v. Commissioner, 118 T.C. 379 (U.S.Tax Ct.2002), 225

Carter–Shields, M.D. v. Alton Health Institute, 201 Ill.2d 441, 268 Ill.Dec. 25, 777 N.E.2d 948 (Ill.2002), 214

Cather v. Catheter Technology Corp., 753 F.Supp. 634 (S.D.Miss.1991), 45

Chevron U.S.A. Inc. v. Echazabal, 536 U.S. 73, 122 S.Ct. 2045, 153 L.Ed.2d 82 (2002), 197

Ching v. Methodist Children's Hosp., 2003 WL 943740 (Tex.App.-Amarillo 2003), 169

**Cicio v. Does,** 321 F.3d 83 (2nd Cir.2003), **126**

# TABLE OF CASES

Circuit City Stores, Inc. v. Adams, 532 U.S. 105, 121 S.Ct. 1302, 149 L.Ed.2d 234 (2001), 182

Clackamas Gastroenterology Associates, P. C. v. Wells, ___ U.S. ___, 123 S.Ct. 1673 (2003), 197

Clark v. Columbia/HCA Information Services, Inc., 117 Nev. 468, 25 P.3d 215 (Nev.2001), 169

Colorado State Bd. of Medical Examiners v. Ogin, 56 P.3d 1233 (Colo.App.2002), 20

Columbia/HCA Healthcare Corp., United States ex rel. McCready v., 2003 WL 912738 (D.D.C.2003), 236

Conant v. Walters, 309 F.3d 629 (9th Cir.2002), 19, 321, 322

**Conservatorship of Wendland,** 110 Cal. Rptr.2d 412, 28 P.3d 151 (Cal.2001), **293,** 302, 303

Cook County, Ill. v. United States ex rel. Chandler, ___ U.S. ___, 123 S.Ct. 1239, 155 L.Ed.2d 247 (2003), 236

Dallas County Medical Society v. Ubinas Brache, 68 S.W.3d 31 (Tex.App.-Dallas 2001), 169

Daubert v. Merrell Dow Pharmaceuticals, Inc., 509 U.S. 579, 113 S.Ct. 2786, 125 L.Ed.2d 469 (1993), 33, 34

Davis v. Davis, 842 S.W.2d 588 (Tenn.1992), 276, 278

Diabetes Treatment Centers of America, Inc., United States ex rel. Pogue v., 238 F.Supp.2d 258 (D.D.C.2002), 235

Dillon v. Evanston Hosp., 199 Ill.2d 483, 264 Ill.Dec. 653, 771 N.E.2d 357 (Ill.2002), 48

Drevenak v. Abendschein, 773 A.2d 396 (D.C. 2001), 33

Duttry v. Patterson, 565 Pa. 130, 771 A.2d 1255 (Pa.2001), 52

Dyer v. Danek Medical, Inc., 115 F.Supp.2d 732 (N.D.Tex.2000), 45

Eddy v. Colonial Life Ins. Co. of America, 919 F.2d 747, 287 U.S.App.D.C. 76 (D.C.Cir. 1990), 111

Edson v. Valleycare Health System, 21 Fed. Appx. 721 (9th Cir.2001), 182

E.E.O.C. v. Waffle House, Inc., 534 U.S. 279, 122 S.Ct. 754, 151 L.Ed.2d 755 (2002), 182

Eidson v. State, Dept. of Licensing, 108 Wash. App. 712, 32 P.3d 1039 (Wash.App. Div. 1 2001), 20

Equality Emergency Medical Group v. Valley Presbyterian Hosp., 2002 WL 1293011 (Cal. App. 2 Dist.2002), 180, 183

**Estate of (see name of party)**

Exeter Hosp. Medical Staff v. Board of Trustees of Exeter Health Resources, Inc., 148 N.H. 492, 810 A.2d 53 (N.H.2002), 172

**Ex parte (see name of party)**

First Healthcare Corp. v. Hamilton, 740 So.2d 1189 (Fla.App. 4 Dist.1999), 26

Florida Convalescent Centers v. Somberg, 840 So.2d 998 (Fla.2003), 26

Fournet v. Roule–Graham, 783 So.2d 439 (La. App. 5 Cir.2001), 33

Frazar v. Gilbert, 300 F.3d 530 (5th Cir.2002), 152, 153

Freilich v. Upper Chesapeake Health, Inc., 313 F.3d 205 (4th Cir.2002), 168, 181

Frye v. United States, 293 F. 1013 (D.C.Cir. 1923), 33

Gant v. Novello, 302 A.D.2d 690, 754 N.Y.S.2d 746 (N.Y.A.D. 3 Dept.2003), 21

Gonzaga University v. Doe, 536 U.S. 273, 122 S.Ct. 2268, 153 L.Ed.2d 309 (2002), 152, 153

Goodstein, United States ex rel. v. McLaren Regional Medical Center, 202 F.Supp.2d 671 (E.D.Mich.2002), 244

Gowesky v. Singing River Hosp. Systems, 321 F.3d 503 (5th Cir.2003), 196

Harris v. New York State Dept. of Health, 202 F.Supp.2d 143 (S.D.N.Y.2002), 20

Harry v. Marchant, 291 F.3d 767 (11th Cir. 2002), 163

Hason v. Medical Bd. of California, 279 F.3d 1167 (9th Cir.2002), 19

**HCA, Inc. v. Miller,** 36 S.W.3d 187 (Tex. App.-Hous. (14 Dist.) 2000), **304,** 309

Health Midwest v. Kline, 2003 WL 328845 (Kan.Dist.Ct.2003), 200

Horn v. New York Times, 2003 WL 443259 (N.Y.2003), 183

Howard v. University of Medicine and Dentistry of New Jersey, 172 N.J. 537, 800 A.2d 73 (N.J.2002), 52

Humana Inc. Managed Care Litigation, In re, 285 F.3d 971 (11th Cir.2002), 182

Humana Inc. Managed Care Litigation, In re, 2000 WL 1925080 (Jud.Pan.Mult.Lit.2000), 183

IHC Health Plans, Inc. v. Commissioner, T.C. Memo. 2001-246 (U.S.Tax Ct.2001), 217, 218

**In re (see name of party)**

Intervest Corp., United States v., 67 F.Supp.2d 637 (S.D.Miss.1999), 235

Jacobo v. Binur, 70 S.W.3d 330 (Tex.App.-Waco 2002), 51

**J.B. v. M.B.,** 170 N.J. 9, 783 A.2d 707 (N.J. 2001), **272,** 278

Kentucky Ass'n of Health Plans, Inc. v. Miller, ___ U.S. ___, 123 S.Ct. 1471 (2003), 125, 126

Kirkhuff v. Lincoln Technical Institute, Inc., 221 F.Supp.2d 572 (E.D.Pa.2002), 125

Kumho Tire Co., Ltd. v. Carmichael, 526 U.S. 137, 119 S.Ct. 1167, 143 L.Ed.2d 238 (1999), 33, 34

Kurr, People v., 253 Mich.App. 317, 654 N.W.2d 651 (Mich.App.2002), 268, 269

Lesley v. Chie, 81 F.Supp.2d 217 (D.Mass. 2000), 161

# TABLE OF CASES

Linton v. Commissioner of Health and Environment, State of Tenn., 65 F.3d 508 (6th Cir.1995), 164

Lipson v. Anesthesia Services, P.A., 790 A.2d 1261 (Del.Super.2001), 171

Luckey v. Baxter Healthcare Corp., 183 F.3d 730 (7th Cir.1999), 235

Madsen v. Audrain Health Care, Inc., 297 F.3d 694 (8th Cir.2002), 168, 179

**Mahan v. Avera St. Luke's,** 621 N.W.2d 150 (S.D.2001), **173,** 244

Maher v. Yoon, 297 A.D.2d 361, 746 N.Y.S.2d 493 (N.Y.A.D. 2 Dept.2002), 270

Managed Care Litigation, In re, 209 F.R.D. 678 (S.D.Fla.2002), 107

Managed Care Litigation, In re, 150 F.Supp.2d 1330 (S.D.Fla.2001), 107

**Manhattan Eye, Ear & Throat Hosp. v. Spitzer,** 186 Misc.2d 126, 715 N.Y.S.2d 575 (N.Y.Sup.1999), **200,** 214

Mateo–Woodburn v. Fresno Community Hospital & Medical Center, 221 Cal.App.3d 1169, 270 Cal.Rptr. 894 (Cal.App. 5 Dist.1990), 173

**Matter of (see name of party)**

Maui Medical Group, Inc., In re, 2002 WL 561329 (N.L.R.B.2002), 193

McCombs v. Synthes, 250 Ga.App. 543, 553 S.E.2d 17 (Ga.App.2001), 45

McCready, United States ex rel. v. Columbia/HCA Healthcare Corp., 2003 WL 912738 (D.D.C.2003), 236

McLaren Regional Medical Center, United States ex rel. Goodstein v., 202 F.Supp.2d 671 (E.D.Mich.2002), 244

Metrahealth Ins. Co. v. Anclote Psychiatric Hosp., Ltd., 1997 WL 728084 (M.D.Fla. 1997), 109

**Mikes, United States ex rel. v. Straus,** 274 F.3d 687 (2nd Cir.2001), **227,** 235

Miller v. Bristol–Myers Squibb Co., 121 F.Supp.2d 831 (D.Md.2000), 46

Moore v. Regents of the University of California, 271 Cal.Rptr. 146, 793 P.2d 479 (Cal. 1990), 290

Nathan Littauer Hospital Ass'n v. Spitzer, 287 A.D.2d 202, 734 N.Y.S.2d 671 (N.Y.A.D. 3 Dept.2001), 200

National Ass'n. of Chain Drug Stores v. Thompson, 241 F.Supp.2d 29 (D.D.C.2003), 141

Nelson v. Glynn–Brunswick Hosp. Authority, 257 Ga.App. 571, 571 S.E.2d 557 (Ga.App. 2002), 195

Newman v. Sathyavaglswaran, 287 F.3d 786 (9th Cir.2002), 13, 14

New York v. United States, 505 U.S. 144, 112 S.Ct. 2408, 120 L.Ed.2d 120 (1992), 321

Nguyen v. State, Department of Health Medical Quality Assurance Commission, 144 Wash.2d 516, 29 P.3d 689 (Wash.2001), 20

N.L.R.B. v. Health Care & Retirement Corp. of America, 511 U.S. 571, 114 S.Ct. 1778, 128 L.Ed.2d 586 (1994), 192

**N.L.R.B. v. Kentucky River Community Care, Inc.,** 532 U.S. 706, 121 S.Ct. 1861, 149 L.Ed.2d 939 (2001), **184,** 192

**Nurses United for Improved Patient Healthcare,** 338 NLRB No. 113 (N.L.R.B. 2003), **193**

**Oakland Cannabis Buyers' Co-op., United States v.,** 532 U.S. 483, 121 S.Ct. 1711, 149 L.Ed.2d 722 (2001), 19, **314,** 320, 321, 322, 323

Obert–Hong, United States ex rel. v. Advocate Health Care, 211 F.Supp.2d 1045 (N.D.Ill. 2002), 245

O'Byrne v. Santa Monica–UCLA Medical Center, 114 Cal.Rptr.2d 575 (Cal.App. 2 Dist. 2001), 168

Oliveras–Sifre v. Puerto Rico Dept. of Health, 214 F.3d 23 (1st Cir.2000), 181

O'Neil v. Unum Life Ins. Co. of America, 2002 WL 31356453 (N.D.Ill.2002), 125

Orchard Park Health Care Center, Inc., In re, 2003 WL 430502 (N.L.R.B.2003), 195

Oregon v. Ashcroft, 192 F.Supp.2d 1077 (D.Or. 2002), 313

PacifiCare Health Systems, Inc. v. Book, ___ U.S. ___, 123 S.Ct. 1531 (2003), 182, 183

Pathfinder Healthcare, Inc. v. Thompson, 177 F.Supp.2d 895 (E.D.Ark.2001), 30

Pediatric Neurosurgery, P.C. v. Russell, 44 P.3d 1063 (Colo.2002), 215

Pegram v. Herdrich, 530 U.S. 211, 120 S.Ct. 2143, 147 L.Ed.2d 164 (2000), 139

**People v. _____ (see opposing party)**

**Perez v. Wyeth Laboratories Inc.,** 161 N.J. 1, 734 A.2d 1245 (N.J.1999), **35**

Perna v. Pirozzi, 92 N.J. 446, 457 A.2d 431 (N.J.1983), 79

Petriello v. Kalman, 215 Conn. 377, 576 A.2d 474 (Conn.1990), 48

Petrosky v. Brasner, 279 A.D.2d 75, 718 N.Y.S.2d 340 (N.Y.A.D. 1 Dept.2001), 49

Pharmaceutical Research and Mfrs. of America v. Concannon, 249 F.3d 66 (1st Cir.2001), 154, 157

Pharmaceutical Research and Mfrs. of America v. Thompson, 313 F.3d 600, 354 U.S.App. D.C. 150 (D.C.Cir.2002), 157

Pharmaceutical Research and Mfrs. of America v. Thompson, 251 F.3d 219, 346 U.S.App. D.C. 158 (D.C.Cir.2001), 156

Pogue, United States ex rel. v. Diabetes Treatment Centers of America, Inc., 238 F.Supp.2d 258 (D.D.C.2002), 235

Potvin v. Metropolitan Life Ins. Co., 95 Cal. Rptr.2d 496, 997 P.2d 1153 (Cal.2000), 182

**Prato–Morrison v. Doe,** 126 Cal.Rptr.2d 509 (Cal.App. 2 Dist.2002), **279**

Printz v. United States, 521 U.S. 898, 117 S.Ct. 2365, 138 L.Ed.2d 914 (1997), 321

Redlands Surgical Services v. Commissioner, 113 T.C. 47 (U.S.Tax Ct.1999), 224

Reed v. Bojarski, 166 N.J. 89, 764 A.2d 433 (N.J.2001), 49

**Richardson v. Miller,** 44 S.W.3d 1 (Tenn.Ct. App.2000), **47**

## TABLE OF CASES

Riley v. St. Luke's Episcopal Hosp., 252 F.3d 749 (5th Cir.2001), 236
Rivera v. Wyeth–Ayerst Laboratories, 121 F.Supp.2d 614 (S.D.Tex.2000), 46
Roe v. Wade, 410 U.S. 113, 93 S.Ct. 705, 35 L.Ed.2d 147 (1973), 270, 271
Rolland v. Romney, 318 F.3d 42 (1st Cir.2003), 27
Rosenbaum v. Unum Life Ins. Co. of America, 2002 WL 1769899 (E.D.Pa.2002), 125
**Rush Prudential HMO, Inc. v. Moran,** 536 U.S. 355, 122 S.Ct. 2151, 153 L.Ed.2d 375 (2002), **114,** 125, 126

Sattler v. Northwest Tissue Center, 110 Wash. App. 689, 42 P.3d 440 (Wash.App. Div. 1 2002), 15
Scheidler v. National Organization for Women, Inc., ___ U.S. ___, 123 S.Ct. 1057, 154 L.Ed.2d 991 (2003), 271
Schoonmaker v. Employee Sav. Plan of Amoco Corp. and Participating Companies, 987 F.2d 410 (7th Cir.1993), 112
Siegel v. CHW West Bay, 2002 WL 31599012 (Cal.App. 1 Dist.2002), 182
**Simmons v. Tuomey Regional Medical Center,** 341 S.C. 32, 533 S.E.2d 312 (S.C. 2000), **53**
Singh v. Blue Cross and Blue Shield of Massachusetts, Inc., 182 F.Supp.2d 164 (D.Mass. 2001), 172
Singh v. Blue Cross/Blue Shield of Massachusetts, Inc., 308 F.3d 25 (1st Cir.2002), 168, 171, 182
Sithian v. Staten Island University Hosp., 189 Misc.2d 410, 734 N.Y.S.2d 812 (N.Y.Sup. 2001), 169
Smith v. Borello, 370 Md. 227, 804 A.2d 1151 (Md.2002), 270
Sprecher v. Aetna U.S. Healthcare, Inc., 2002 WL 1917711 (E.D.Pa.2002), 125
**St. David's Health Care System v. United States,** 2002 WL 1335230 (W.D.Tex.2002), 216, **218**
Stenberg v. Carhart, 530 U.S. 914, 120 S.Ct. 2597, 147 L.Ed.2d 743 (2000), 271
St. Lukes Episcopal–Presbyterian Hospitals, Inc. v. N.L.R.B., 268 F.3d 575 (8th Cir. 2001), 194
**Straus, United States ex rel. Mikes v.,** 274 F.3d 687 (2nd Cir.2001), **227,** 235
Superior Court Trial Lawyers Ass'n v. F.T.C., 493 U.S. 411, 110 S.Ct. 768, 107 L.Ed.2d 851 (1990), 262
Surgical Care Center of Hammond, L.C. v. Hospital Service Dist. No. 1 of Tangipahoa Parish, 309 F.3d 836 (5th Cir.2002), 263
Sutter Corp., United States ex rel. Barmak v., 2002 WL 987109 (S.D.N.Y.2002), 235

Thompson v. Western States Medical Center, 535 U.S. 357, 122 S.Ct. 1497, 152 L.Ed.2d 563 (2002), 45
Toyota Motor Mfg., Kentucky, Inc. v. Williams, 534 U.S. 184, 122 S.Ct. 681, 151 L.Ed.2d 615 (2002), 158, 195
Turkette, United States v., 452 U.S. 576, 101 S.Ct. 2524, 69 L.Ed.2d 246 (1981), 109

Ulrich v. City and County of San Francisco, 308 F.3d 968 (9th Cir.2002), 170, 183
**United States v. _____ (see opposing party)**
**United States ex rel. v. _____ (see opposing party and relator)**

Van v. Anderson, 199 F.Supp.2d 550 (N.D.Tex. 2002), 169
Varity Corp. v. Howe, 516 U.S. 489, 116 S.Ct. 1065, 134 L.Ed.2d 130 (1996), 111
Velazquez v. Jiminez, 336 N.J.Super 10, 763 A.2d 753 (2000), 35
Viazis v. American Ass'n of Orthodontists, 314 F.3d 758 (5th Cir.2002), 247, 250

Waddell v. Bhat, 257 Ga.App. 580, 571 S.E.2d 565 (Ga.App.2002), 195
Waddell v. Valley Forge Dental Associates, Inc., 276 F.3d 1275 (11th Cir.2001), 195
Waters v. Churchill, 511 U.S. 661, 114 S.Ct. 1878, 128 L.Ed.2d 686 (1994), 184
**Westside Mothers v. Haveman,** 289 F.3d 852 (6th Cir.2002), **146**
Westside Mothers v. Haveman, 133 F.Supp.2d 549 (E.D.Mich.2001), 146, 153
Wheeler v. Methodist Hosp., 95 S.W.3d 628 (Tex.App.-Hous. (1 Dist.) 2002), 170
Wilder v. Virginia Hosp. Ass'n, 496 U.S. 498, 110 S.Ct. 2510, 111 L.Ed.2d 455 (1990), 152
Williams v. American Medical Systems, 248 Ga.App. 682, 548 S.E.2d 371 (Ga.App.2001), 45
Wisconsin Dept. of Health and Family Services v. Blumer, 534 U.S. 473, 122 S.Ct. 962, 151 L.Ed.2d 935 (2002), 153
Wyeth–Ayerst Laboratories Co. v. Medrano, 28 S.W.3d 87 (Tex.App.-Texarkana 2000), 46

Young, Ex parte, 209 U.S. 123, 28 S.Ct. 441, 52 L.Ed. 714 (1908), 152

# 2003 SUPPLEMENT TO
# HEALTH LAW
## CASES, MATERIALS AND PROBLEMS
## Fourth Edition

*

# Chapter 1

# DEFINING, EVALUATING AND DISTRIBUTING HEALTH CARE: AN INTRODUCTION

## I. DEFINING SICKNESS

**Add, at p. 17, a new note 3:**

3. Scholars debate the fundamental question of what health policy should be. Can we agree upon basic goals that health care regulation and policy should see to achieve? Are there unified principles and values that underpin health law generally? For a well argued position that no single goal can be found, and that we must settle for more modest goals, see M. Gregg Bloche, The Invention of Health Law, 91 Cal.L.Rev. 247 (2003):

> The law of health care provision is a chaotic, dysfunctional patchwork. It is thus understandable that many commentators and some courts now look to the logic of social-welfare maximization to harmonize health law. But the welfare-maximization premise is not up to the task. Our cognitive limitations and moral disagreements make its logic too blurry in practice. We cannot ask economics—or health law—for clear answers to scientific and moral questions about medical care's efficacy and value that our society has not been able to resolve.

\* \* \*

\* \* \* Courts should resist the allure of a single yardstick of cost and benefit. And when judges choose, as they must, between competing priorities, they should make the normative basis for their choices explicit. By so doing, courts can increase the likelihood that their decisions, over time, will produce wise health policy, responsive to the revolutionary changes American medicine is undergoing.

## III. THE PROBLEM OF MEDICAL ERROR

### B. THE EXTENT OF MEDICAL MISADVENTURES

**Add, at p. 35, a new note 6:**

6. A sophisticated look at the practice of medicine, and how errors occur, is found in Atul Gawande, Complications: A Surgeon's Notes on An Imperfect Science 45–46 (2002). He writes:

... [C]ompassion and technology aren't necessarily incompatible; they can be mutually reinforcing. Which is to say that the machine, oddly enough, may be medicine's best friend. On the simplest level, nothing comes between patient and doctor like a mistake. And while errors will always dog us—even machines are not perfect—trust can only increase when mistakes are reduced. Moreover, as "systems" take on more and more of the technical work of medicine, individual physicians may be in a position to embrace the dimensions of care that mattered long before technology came—like talking to their patients.

The book gives good examples of how young physicians learn medicine, and how errors are dealt with in the hospital setting.

**Add, at p. 64, before Problem: ManageCare, Section 3.**

## C. REMEDYING QUALITY PROBLEMS OF HEALTH CARE SERVICES

### 3. *Regulatory Approaches to Medical Errors*

The Institute of Medicine reports, beginning with **To Err Is Human**, focused attention on medical systems and the level of errors they produced. Hospitals and other providers were asked to respond by developing error tracking systems and strategies for improvement. This approach was first developed by Dr. Ernest Codman, a Boston doctor who wanted hospitals and doctors to track their practices and evaluate outcomes of their patients, an ideal he developed around 1920. He offered an "end-result system" based "... on the common-sense notion that every hospital should follow *every* patient that it treats, long enough to determine whether or not the treatment has been successful, and then to inquire 'if not, why not?' with a view to preventing similar failures in the future." Codman's central idea was a complete patient record that assessed why a treatment was unsuccessful, including discussion of errors of technical knowledge or risk; lack of surgical judgment; lack of care or equipment; lack of diagnostic skill; unconquerable disease; patient's refusal of treatment; calamities of surgery or accidents and complications over which doctors had no control. This detailed record was to serve an auditing function to evaluate, compare and establish benchmarks for the performance of physicians and hospitals. His idea was revolutionary, aiming to assess a hospital's efficiency in therapeutic, outcome-based terms.

To Codman, patient harm due to infections or unnecessary or inappropriate operations was a hospital "waste product". Such performance measurement was a clear threat to physicians, and when the American College of Surgeons (ACS) developed its program of hospital standardization after World War I, the analysis of patient outcomes and reporting of preventable errors was omitted—and these were Codman's most central ideas for error reduction. His work did lay the foundation for the Joint Commission on Accreditation of Health Care Organizations (JCAHO) which has slowly moved toward a more outcome-based accreditation system. See Virgina A. Sharpe and Alan I. Faden, Medical Harm: Historical, Conceptual, and Ethical Dimensions of Iatrogenic Illness 31 (1998).

Quality has only recently become a central goal for health care institutions. Many errors are simply never reported. Reasons may include failure to recognize that an error occurred; liability worries; concerns about job security (especially for nurses); concerns about personal and professional reputation. One study found that 29% of observed errors were not reported. Barker, K.N. & McConnell, W.E., Detecting Errors in Hospitals, 19 A. J. Hosps. 361 (1962). See generally Margaret H. Applegate, Diagnosis–Related Groups: Are Patients in Jeopardy?, in Human Error in Medicine (Marilyn Sue Bogner, Ed. 1994). Given that most errors are not reported, a voluntary system has limited value in detecting errors. A regulatory approach that imposes a mandatory system of detection and disclosure may better promote effective error correction. See generally Elizabeth A. McGlynn and Robert H. Brook, Keeping Quality on the Policy Agenda, 20 Health Affairs 82 (2001); Mark R. Chassin, Robert W. Galvin, and the National Roundtable on Health Care Quality, 280 J.A.M.A. 1000 (1998).

Health care is a large scale corporate team-oriented enterprise, but these enterprises are often chaotic and poorly managed, producing far too many errors that injure patients. Institutions often fail to effectively deliver care. And while individual providers can be faulted, what is more common is the failure of a system, and units within the system, to prevent an otherwise avoidable error. Hospitals too often lack good error management—they are far from the industrial model of continuous quality improvement. The very structure of delivery through a medical staff working with hospital employees like nurses lends itself to diffusion of authority and failures to communicate. And the training of residents by attending physicians often produces errors through failures to adequately supervise beginners in the field. Hospitals have been described as one of the most complex organizations possible, integrating hierarchical bureaucracy and informal professional decision making under one roof. See Odin W. Anderson, Health Services as a Growth Enterprise in the United States Since 1875 309 (1990).

The issue of mandatory versus voluntary reporting has loomed large for health care providers, afraid that disclosure of an error will come to plaintiff lawyers' attention. Voluntary reporting of mistakes has been argued to be the preferable approach to uncovering errors and correcting them. Brian Liang, Promoting Patient Safety Through Reducing Medical Error, 22 J.L.Med & Ethics 564 (2002). States that have mandatory reporting requirements for errors have found that underreporting is the norm. J. Rosenthal et al., Current State Programs Addressing Medical Errors: An Analysis of Mandatory Reporting and Other Initiatives (2001). But the fact that underreporting occurs does not mean that performance cannot be improved. The reasons for such poor performance are several. Mandatory systems lack support from physicians, who are worried about liability, damage to reputation, and the hassle factor of any reporting system.

Mandatory error reporting has several advantages. First, institutional incentives are enhanced by regulation that mandates error reporting. The health care institution has incentives to better track and monitor errors within its walls if required to report at the risk of sanctions. Risk management may be turned into something more than a legal backwater driven by insurance considerations if mandatory reporting becomes the norm for hospitals and other institutions. Assuming that the various mandates have some regulatory teeth, a hospital risks sanctions for its failure to comply; patients learn about errors, and the ventilation of error and the transparency of the processes expose variations among providers.

Second, learning can only happen if root causes are understood. The acknowledgment of near misses and patient injury—that an "error" occurred—is a major part of facilitating learning among individual providers as well as institutional providers. The retreat from blame also risks retreat from responsibility: by neutering the climate of blame, we also weaken a culture in which providers challenge each other to improve. Patients appear to prefer honesty and apology when they have suffered an adverse event, and are less inclined to use litigation as a blaming mechanism, once they have been satisfied that the institution is attentive to error creation and correction. Thomas H. Gallagher et al., Patients' and Physicians' Attitudes Regarding the Disclosure of Medical Errors, 289 J.A.M.A. 1001 (2003).

Third, voluntary reporting is unlikely to function effectively as an alternative to the feared results of mandatory reporting. Providers dread taking responsibility for error, as we would expect highly trained professionals to feel; a "mea culpa" does not come easily in a culture of perfection developed through medical training over many years. If the law does not mandate reporting, and if the tort system were replaced tomorrow by a toothless compensation system free of trial lawyers, we would still be unlikely to see a blossoming of error reporting and a broadcasting of error admission by providers. Good intentions without financial and regulatory incentives to report are unlikely to succeed. Voluntary reporting is unlikely to prove any more effective than mandatory reporting without a complete retooling of incentives.

Fourth, mandatory reporting will reshape leadership within institutions, acknowledging the centrality of error reduction and system failures as intolerable. The connection between disclosure of errors and their correction is primarily fostered by the leadership climate in a health care institution. Within institutions, surgeons are expected to talk about their mistakes, in order to learn from them. Errors and near misses require institutional attention as well, since many mistakes may be due to staffing, resource limitations, poor leadership, and deterioration in skill that peers who have not yet detected or are not yet willing to respond to. A focus on teams within health care systems will facilitate the kind of learning and adaption that can promote error reduction.

Mandatory reporting is resisted by providers. The emphasis has therefore been on voluntary reporting systems. But given the lack of evidence that such voluntary systems reveal most errors, a mandatory model should be developed, as the original IOM report proposed. Several moves in this direction are worth noting: the JCAHO Sentinel Events policy, the new CMS rules on hospital error, and the new Pennsylvania statute that requires disclosure of errors.

*a. The Joint Commission on the Accreditation of Healthcare Organizations*

The JCAHO is a private accreditor, granted authority by federal and state governments to accredit hospitals. See pp. 155–159 in the Casebook. The new JCAHO Sentinel Event Policy has adopted the view of medical errors of the Institute of Medicine report **To Err is Human**. It requires reporting on two levels: first to JCAHO of serious events, and second to patients. It defines a sentinel event as "an unexpected occurrence involving death or severe physical or psychological injury, or the risk thereof," including unanticipated death or major loss of functioning unrelated to the patient's condition; patient suicide; wrong-side surgery; infant abduction/discharge to the wrong family; rape; and hemolytic transfusion reactions. JCAHO, "Sentinel Event Policy and Procedures", online at www.jcaho.org (last visited January 28, 2003).

Hospitals must report serious events to the JCAHO, and if they do not and JCAHO learns of the events form a third party, the hospital must conduct an analysis of the root cause or risk loss of accreditation. Loss of accreditation is rarely exercised, however, leaving accreditation as a modest tool to promote uniformity of hospital systems. Sentinel Event Alert, Joint Commission on Accreditation of Healthcare Organizations, 2002, *www.jcaho.org/about + us/news + letters/sentinel + event + alert/index.htm*.

See generally Timothy Stoltzfus Jost, Medicare and the Joint Commission on Accreditation of Healthcare Organizations: A Healthy Relationship? 57 Law & Contemp. Probs. 15 (1994); Eleanor Kinney, Private Accreditation as a Substitute for Direct Government Regulation in Public Health Insurance Programs: When Is It Appropriate?, 57 Law & Contemp. Probs. 47, 52–55 (1994); Douglas C. Michael, Federal Agency Use of Audited Self–Regulation as a Regulatory Technique, 47 Admin. L. Rev. 171, 218–22 (1995).

The JCAHO disclosure standard also requires that "[p]atients, and when appropriate, their families, are informed about the outcomes of care, including unanticipated outcomes." Joint Commission on Accreditation of Healthcare Organizations, Revisions to Joint Commission Standards in Support of Patient Safety and Medical/Health Care Error Reduction, at www.jcaho.org/standard/fr_ptsafety.html (July 1, 2001)(JCAHO Revisions) at RI.1.2.2. The intent statement provides: "The responsible licensed independent practitioner or his or her designee clearly explains the outcomes of any treatments or procedures to the patient and, when appropriate, the family, whenever those outcomes differ significantly from the anticipated outcomes". Id.

The JCAHO standard suffers from several infirmities. First, the use of "significantly" is not self-defining, and hospitals are likely to adopt a very conservative interpretation to reduce their disclosure obligations. JCAHO indicates that they are the same as "sentinel events" or "reviewable sentinel events". A "sentinel event" is defined in JCAHO standards as: "... an unexpected occurrence involving death or serious physical or psychological injury, or the risk thereof. Serious injury specifically includes loss of limb or function. The phrase 'or the risk thereof' includes any process variation for which a recurrence would carry a significant chance of a serious adverse outcome." Joint Commission on Accreditation of Healthcare Organizations, Hospital Accreditation Standards 53 (2001)(JCAHO Standards).

The second problem is the locus of the disclosure obligation. The intent statement specifies that "the responsible licensed independent practitioner or his or her designee" must clearly explain "the outcomes of any treatments or procedures." This practitioner is someone with clinical privileges, typically the patient's attending physician. Since the attending physician typically has the informed consent responsibility, he or she is the logical person to conduct such a conversation. But physicians are not subject to JCAHO requirements, and they are therefore likely to resist such disclosures out of fear of liability, stigma or other motivations. LeGros and Pinkall note that "[s]ome hospitals already have encountered resistance from medical staff members regarding involvement in the disclosure process ... the Joint Commission has not issued guidance on what is to be done if the physician refuses to make the disclosure. The issue could be a particularly explosive one if the physician was responsible for the error." The disclosure of errors that lead to an increased number of small claims increases the risks to physicians. "The impact of multiple claims on professional credentialing matters likely is one reason why many hospitals are encountering resistance from physicians in participating in the disclosure process." See, e.g. Nancy LeGros and Jason D. Pinkall, The New JCAHO Patient Safety Standards and the Disclosure of Unanticipated Outcomes, 35 J. Health L. 189, 205 (2002).

Third, private accreditation like that provided by JCAHO is notoriously gentle in its approach, slow to develop meaningful standards and reluctant to develop enforcement mechanisms other than the unlikely threat of withdrawal of accreditation. Barry R. Furrow, Regulating the Managed Care Revolution: Private Accreditation and A New System Ethos, 43 Vill. L. Rev. 361 (1998).

### b. *The New CMS Rules on Error*

The Centers for Medicare and Medicaid Services (CMS) (formerly HCFA) have recently issued a final rule that requires hospitals to develop a quality assessment and performance improvement (QAPI) program. This QAPI program is intended to push providers to look at the care delivered to their patients and how the hospital performs. It mandates systematic examination of a hospital's quality and requires the hospital to undertake improvement projects on an ongoing basis, in order to maintain hospital quality of care at what CMS calls "acceptable" levels. The rules list the requirements as including the identification and verification of quality problems and their causes; acting to correct these deficiencies; determining the success of an intervention; and detecting new problems. "Performance improvement activities aim to improve overall performance assuming that there is no permanent threshold for good performance. Under a performance improvement framework, hospitals will continuously study and improve the processes of healthcare and delivery of service." Summary, Medicare and Medicaid Programs; Hospital Conditions of Participation: Quality Assessment and Performance Improvement, 42 CFR Part 482, 8 Fed. Reg. 3425, 3435 (January 24, 2003).

CMS notes in the summary of the rules and review of the comments to the proposed rules that medical error in hospitals has become a major concern for patients and payors. "While both the public and the private sectors have made notable contributions to reducing preventable medical errors, additional and aggressive efforts are needed to further reduce these types of incidents. Therefore, we are publishing this final rule, with some modification in response to comments, to guide improved patient safety in the hospital setting." The comments note that medical errors are sometimes hard to recognize due to patient variation, and providers may not notice that a product or procedure caused a problem, given an already sick patient. Detection is difficult since "medical errors usually affect only a single patient at a time, they are treated as isolated incidents and little attention, if any, is drawn to these problems." Errors are underreported. "All of these factors explain the ongoing invisibility of medical errors despite the existence of research that documents their high prevalence."

CMS has promulgated this new rule to follow up the IOM recommendations in their previous reports: reduction of preventable medical errors; a system of public accountability; a knowledge base system regarding medical errors; and a change in the culture of healthcare organizations to ferret out errors and improve patient safety.

CMS notes that accreditation surveys for deemed status performed by national accrediting organizations such as JCAHO are performed under the authority of CMS, and may provide grounds for enforcement by CMS in some cases. During accreditation surveys, CMS intends that their QAPI program will be evaluated for its hospital-wide effectiveness on the quality of care provided. If a hospital, for example is "... significantly out of compliance with the QAPI Condition of Participation requirements, the hospital will be scheduled for termination from the Medicare and Medicaid programs." A plan of correction could then be submitted and a follow-up survey conducted to see if the hospital can bring itself into compliance. The Quality Improvement Organizations (QIOs) (formally known as Peer Review Organizations (PROs)) are intended to be CMS's "quality improvement agents".

What is the role of medical error reporting? Is a mandatory system required? CMS writes in the comments:

> We agree that hospitals should consider adverse events in the development of its QAPI strategy. We expect hospitals to implement an internal error reduction system. *Adverse event tracking and analysis of underlying causes are an effective way to determine issues involving medical errors.* [Italics added]. We emphasize the need for hospitals to assess processes and systems that affect patient care and quality. Section 482.21(c) requires the hospital(s) to establish priorities, and identify areas of risk that affect patient safety. We believe that the identification of adverse events and analyses of events must be an integral part of the hospital's QAPI program, as the analyses will lead to better protections for patients. Id. at 3438.

The standards of the Joint Commission are consistent with the CMS rule, according to the Comments. Section 482.21(c) of the rules requires hospitals to "consider prevalence and severity of identified problems and to give priority to improvement activities that affect clinical outcomes, patient safety, and quality of care." JCAHO's sentinel events could be one such source, along with external industry data, or government data.

The current rules do not yet require evidence-based performance measures, which are left to a future rule-making process. CMS writes: "In this final rule, we are not setting a requirement for using and reporting on a core set of evidence-based performance measures. Once the evidence and methodologies to support a set of performance measures that can be used nationwide are available, we will assess issues such as commonality of data elements, standardization, and reporting systems. We will inform hospitals and the public of the specifics of and the methods for reporting these performance measures via future rulemaking. This will give the public the opportunity to comment on the core measures before implementation." Id. at 3445 Nor is mandatory reporting required, other than through acknowledgment of JCAHO and its requirements of error reporting.

This CMS rule is quite modest in its ambitions, tracking the JCAHO standards closely, and sounding more aspirational than compulsory in its tone. The rule mentions the possibility that a hospital's Medicare status might be denied if a hospital does not implement proper error detection systems; the lack of explicit mandates for error reporting, however, remove teeth from the rule. CMS, like HFCA before it, has traditionally viewed itself as a funding agency, not a regulatory one, and this rule reflects that tradition of a timid regulatory stance and reliance on the parallel efforts of private accreditation. As Michael Astrue has described CMS and its historical roots, it is a reluctant regulator: "... HCFA [now CMS] has attempted to minimize its role as regulator through liberal use of private contractors and private accrediting agencies." Michael J. Astrue, Health Care Reform and the Constitutional Limits on Private Accreditation as an Alternative to Direct Government Regulation, 57 Law & Contemp. Prob. 75 (1994). Eighty years after Codman developed his model of a result-based outcome system for hospitals, both JCAHO and the federal government are finally beginning to move health care institutions in this direction. It has taken the image of almost 100,000 unnecessary deaths a year, painted by the IOM report, to move us to this point.

### c. *The Pennsylvania Patient Safety Authority*

Pennsylvania passed a new law in 2002 to address patient safety and medical errors, as part of a larger legislative package to reform the malpractice system. The law is Act 13, the Medical Care Availability and Reduction of Error Act, part of a larger legislative enactment with malpractice and insurance reform components. 49 P.S. 1303.301. It has several central features: mandatory reporting to the state of serious events, incidents, and infrastructure failures; mandatory disclosure of serious events to patients; and penalties for failures to report. The centerpiece of this reform legislation is the Patient Safety Authority and accompanying requirements imposed on providers to reduce medical errors. The Authority has eleven members, and is chaired by the Physician General of Pennsylvania. Medical Care Availability and Reduction of Error (MCARE) Act, 49 P.S. 1303.301.

The statute defines "incident" as "[a]n event, occurrence or situation involving the clinical care of a patient in a medical facility which could have injured the patient but did not either cause an unanticipated injury or require the delivery of additional health care services to the patient. The term does not include a serious event. S. 302. It also defines "infrastructure failure": "[a]n undesirable or unintended event, occurrence or situation involving the infrastructure of a medical facility or the discontinuation or significant disruption of a service which could seriously compromise patient safety." A 'serious event' is "[a]n event, occurrence or situation involving the clinical care of a patient in a medical facility that results in death or compromises patient safety and results in an unanticipated injury requiring the delivery of additional health care services to the patient. The term does not include an incident."

Section 303 establishes the new Patient Safety Authority, comprised of eleven members: The Physician General of the Commonwealth; four residents appointed by the legislature; a physician; a nurse; a pharmacist; a health care worker in a hospital; and two residents of the Commonwealth, one of whom is a health care worker and one is not. Among the powers of the Authority is to contract with a for-profit or registered nonprofit entity or entities, other than a health care provider, to do the following:

(i) Collect, analyze and evaluate data regarding reports of serious events and incidents, including the identification of patterns in state facilities;

(ii) Transmit to the authority recommendations for changes in health care practices and procedures, which may be instituted for the purpose of reducing the number and severity of serious events and incidents.

(iii) Directly advise reporting medical facilities of immediate changes that can be instituted to reduce serious events and incidents.

The Authority can issue recommendations to medical facility as to improvements in health care practice and procedures to reduce the number and severity of serious events. A whistleblower provision allows a health care worker to anonymously report a serious event, triggering an investigation unless the facility has already begun its own investigation.

The statute requires the development of a patient safety plan, which must designated a patient safety officer; establish a safety committee, and a system for workers to report "serious events and incidents which shall be accessible 24 hours a day, seven days a week"; prohibit retaliation against workers who report a serious event; and provides for written notification to patients under 308(b). A serious event must under 308 be reported to the state within 24 hours of its discovery.

Providers are granted, under § 311, protection from discovery of documents and materials prepared for compliance with 310(b) "which arise out of matters" reviewed by the patient safety committee pursuant to section 310(b) or the governing board of a medical facility pursuant to section 310(b). Such materials "... are confidential and shall not be discoverable or admissible as evidence in any civil or administrative action or proceeding. Any documents, materials, records or information that would otherwise be available from original sources shall not be construed as immune from discovery or use in any civil or administrative action or proceeding merely because they were presented to the patient safety committee or governing board of a medical facility." This immunity provision is quite extensive and appears to be broader than the current statute for peer immunity generally in Pennsylvania. 63 P.S. § 425.3, Peer Review Protection Act.

A medical facility must report a serious event to the department and the authority within 24 hours of the confirmation that such an event took place, under § 313. Incidents must also be reported, under subsection (b), and subsection (c) mandates a report of the occurrence of an infrastructure failure report within 24 hours of the facility's confirmation of the occurrence or discovery of the failure.

The penalties for failure to report are two fold. The individual physician or nurse may be reported to the state licensing board for a failure to report a serious event, under 313(e). If the medical facility fails to report or notify, or to develop and comply with a patient safety plan under 307 or to notify the patient under 308(b) has a double effect. First, it is treated as a violation of the Health Care Facilities Act and its penalties; second, the new statute allows for an administrative penalty of $1,000 per day imposed by the department.

A patient must be notified if he or she has been affected by a serious event. The statute provides:

> 308(b) Duty to notify patient.—A medical facility through an appropriate designee shall provide written notification to a patient affected by a serious event or, with the consent of the patient, to an available family member or designee, within seven days of the occurrence or discovery of a serious event. If the patient is unable to give consent, the notification shall be given to an adult member of the immediate family. If an adult member of the immediate family cannot be identified or located, notification shall be given to the closest adult family member. For unemancipated patients who are under 18 years of age, the parent or guardian shall be notified in accordance with this subsection. The notification requirements of this subsection shall not be subject to the provisions of section 311(a). Notification under this subsection shall not constitute an acknowledgment or admission of liability.

This provision, like JCAHO's patient notification provision, seems intended to promote candid disclosure of errors by facilities, on the theory perhaps that such disclosure and an apology will reduce litigation.

The new Pennsylvania Patient Safety Authority is unique. No other state has yet created such a regulatory body with a mandate to compel reporting of serious events and incidents ("near misses"), and to mandate disclosure to patients of serious events. The Authority sees itself as assuming a leadership rather than a regulatory role, hoping to build up hospital culture in favor of error reporting and analysis, without fear of retribution. From a regulatory perspective however what is most interesting about the new Pennsylvania law is that error reporting is mandatory, that a hospital can be fined for underreporting and that whistleblower protection is provided to promote detection of underreporting.

These three overlapping regulatory approaches to medical error disclosure illustrate three rather distinct regulatory strategies. The JCAHO sentinel events policy has responded to hospital anxiety by surrounding errors by a cloak of secrecy, even though peer immunity statutes are likely to protect them from disclosure during civil discovery. JCAHO's approach has been a delicate tiptoeing around hospital concerns, as has been the tradition with such a private accrediting body. The CMS rule is too new to evaluate but it clearly is a "go-slow" policy allowing hospitals substantial time to develop reporting systems for errors. Such data collection is strongly urged but the mechanics of it are left up to hospitals during this cycle of the rule. CMS continues its role as reluctant regulator, only slowly moving toward recognition of the magnitude of the medical error problem. Pennsylvania through its MCARE law now has the strongest regulatory approach to properly address error detection and reduction. The concept of mandated reporting—backed by both state immunity from discovery of the reports and sanctions for failures to report—is a strong regulatory strategy with the potential to become a model for other states.

The patient disclosure requirements of JCAHO and the Pennsylvania statute have the potential to not only reduce medical errors but also the frequency of malpractice litigation, if done well. There is evidence that disclosure and apology is desired by patients, and it may even serve to reduce patient inclinations to sue for malpractice when they have experienced a bad outcome. See Thomas H. Gallagher et al., Patients' and Physicians' Attitudes Regarding the Disclosure of Medical Errors, 289 J.A.M.A. 1001 (2003)(finding that patients are troubled by the unwillingness of physicians to discuss the cause and future prevention of medical errors).

## IV. DISTRIBUTIVE JUSTICE AND THE ALLOCATION OF HEALTH CARE RESOURCES— THE EXAMPLE OF HUMAN ORGAN TRANSPLANTATION

### B. RATIONING OF SCARCE HUMAN ORGANS

**Add, at p. 73, at the end of the Problem:**

Assume that Antonia Friedman is HIV-positive, but not in the terminal stages of the disease. Should she be barred from having the transplant? UNOS policy states that asymptomatic HIV-positive patients should not necessarily be excluded from organ transplantation. Halpern, et al., argue that HIV-positive patients who are not in the terminal stages of the disease should have access to organ transplantation. They report that despite UNOS policy, 80% of transplantation centers responding to a 1997 survey stated that they would not consider transplantation for a patient with "asymptomatic HIV-infection who is otherwise a good candidate for transplantation." The authors report that HIV infection does not affect the outcome of transplantation, and that immunosuppressive drugs do not cause the HIV infection to progress.

The authors state the questions to be considered:

There are two distinct ethical questions about efficacy: Does transplantation benefit the individual patients? Would it benefit other patients more? ... The second question—concerning relative efficacy—is rarely addressed in the distribution of plentiful resources, but there is a strong moral basis for posing this question when scarce resources are being allocated. We do not ask whether elderly persons should receive antihypertensive therapy, even though the benefits of long-term treatment are greater for younger persons.

The authors state that if organ transplants provided "substantially" less benefit, "in terms of survival and quality of life," for HIV-positive patients, a policy of "preferential allocation of organs to HIV-negative patients might be tenable."

The authors go further, however, and argue that even if outcomes were worse for HIV-positive patients, they should still be candidates for transplantation. They point to the priority established for patients with prior failed transplant as proving that relative efficacy is not the only ethical value at play. They also argue that transplants are available for other classes of patients, including those with hepatitis C and diabetes, who experience lesser survival rates. Halpern, Ubel, and

Caplan, Solid–Organ Transplantation in HIV-infected Patients, 347 NEJM 284 (July 25, 2002).

Should we confine our arguments about relative efficacy to the question of organ transplantation, as the authors say that we do, or should the same question apply to most health care services, at least of the "expensive" kind? While it is hard to argue that transplantable solid organs are not scarce, can you argue that other types of medical interventions are also scarce?

Do you agree that policies should be consistent in terms of an absolute priority for relative efficacy? If not, what other values might lead us to conclude otherwise? If you do favor departures from relative efficacy, under what terms would you accept them? Whom would you authorize to make those departures? The physician in deciding to list the patient? The individual transplant centers? UNOS? HHS?

The issue of whether individuals convicted of a crime should have access to organ transplants soared across the headlines in 2002 when a man convicted of robbery and serving a 14–year sentence in a California prison received a heart transplant at Stanford University Medical Center. The inmate died about 11 months after the transplant. According to corrections officials, the total cost of his care amounted to up to $2 million, although the transplant itself cost about $200,000. A local donor organization official reported that some individuals called to say they would rip up their donor card unless they could be guaranteed that their organs would not go to a prisoner. UNOS and some ethicists stated in interviews that the distribution of organs is done and should be done on a medical basis only, and does not account for social factors. Another ethicist remarked that only prisoners are guaranteed free transplants. The case stimulated a broader discussion of the cost and benefit of prison health care. The Eighth Amendment prohibition against cruel and unusual punishment, which is often used as a basis for lawsuits concerning prison conditions, applies to medical care where there is "deliberate indifference" to "serious medical needs" of prisoners. How might you apply this standard to the question of organ transplantation?

The Virginia corrections system policy is to provide kidney transplants to inmates because it is considered "standard of care" and is cheaper than dialysis in the long run (which is part of the reason that Medicare pays for kidney transplants for patients with end-stage renal disease regardless of whether the patient is otherwise eligible for Medicare). Virginia does not pay, however, for lung transplants. Nationally, only 956 lung transplants were performed in 2001, although there were nearly 4,000 patients on the waiting list. Is Virginia confusing the scarcity of the organ with "standard of care?" Or is frequency of the procedure relevant to that question?

See American Political Network: American Health Line, January 31, February 5, August 1, December 19, 2002, and November 9, 2001, summarizing media reports.

In what might be considered a related issue, media have reported that increasing numbers of United States citizens have gone to China for organ transplants. China harvests transplantable organs from executed prisoners who are shot to death. (Other countries also allow prisoners to donate organs.) Craig S. Smith, Quandary in U.S. Over Use of Organs Of Chinese Inmates, New York Times, November 11, 2001. Chinese law provides that the prisoners or their families must consent to the procedure, but some report that this is not done in practice. Craig S. Smith, On Death Row, China's Source of Transplants, New York Times, October 18, 2001. In contrast, there is a cultural bias in China against organ donation so that voluntary donors are few. See Craig S. Smith, China Resists Efforts to Make Donations of Organs Feasible, New York Times, December 5, 2001. As you read the materials in the following section in the casebook, consider whether the United States should allow prisoners to donate organs; whether any "donations" should require consent; and whether the issue of allowing prisoners to donate or barring prisoners from receiving transplants is a matter for state or federal control.

### 1. *Geographic Distribution of Organs*

**Add, at p. 74, in section 1:**

Errata: Policy referenced as 3.5.2 should be 3.5.3, and policy referenced as 3.5.2.3.1 should be 3.5.3.3.1.

### 2. *Listing Patients for Transplantation*

**Add, at p. 75:**

Policy 3.6 was modified again in June 2002, but in details not discussed in this note.

## C. INCREASING THE SUPPLY OF ORGANS FOR TRANSPLANTATION: THE IMPACT OF LEGAL RESTRAINTS

### 1. *Cadaver Organs*

**Add, at p. 83, note 2, and on page 85 in the Problem:**

The UAGA of 1987 recognizes presumed consent (Section 4 of the UAGA on pages 80–81 of the casebook), and this type of provision has been adopted, at least for certain tissues, in many states. Most of these states allow the medical examiner or coroner to remove eyes, eye tissue, or corneas. Statutory authority to remove tissue without prior consent does not mean that this is actually done. See Jaffe, cited on page 85 of the casebook.

A few statutes allow for removal under presumed consent in broader circumstances. See, for example, Haw. Rev. Stat. 327–4 and Idaho Code 39–3405 which allow for removal of any body part with presumed consent after attempt to contact next-of-kin. See also, Mo. Stat. 58.770, Ark. Code 12–12–320, and Colo. Rev. Stat. 30–10–621, which allow for the removal of the pituitary gland under presumed consent. These latter statutes do not require that an attempt be made to contact the family.

Should the courts include a duty to make an attempt to contact the family (where the statute is silent on that matter) as an interpretation of the statutory "good faith" immunity accorded persons involved in harvesting organs? (See section 11(b) on page 83 of the casebook.)

The Ninth Circuit Court of Appeals reviewed the constitutionality of California's presumed consent statute for the removal of corneas. Newman v. Sathyavaglswaran, 287 F.3d 786 (9th Cir.2002), cert. den. ___ U.S. ___, 123 S.Ct. 558, 154 L.Ed.2d 444 (2002). The suit was brought by two families against the LA County coroner for removing their children's corneas without having made an effort to secure the parents' consent. Unlike the 1987 UAGA provision, the California statute allowed removal of the corneas if the coroner had no knowledge of an objection by the family but did not require that there be an attempt to contact the family. The Ninth Circuit held that the parents had a property interest in their child's body even though that right is limited due to the prohibition against the sale of organs. The Ninth Circuit remanded to the District Court for further proceedings to decide whether the state of California has interests in the harvesting of corneas without consent significant enough to limit the parents' rights.

The legislature had amended the statute prior to the Ninth Circuit's consideration of this case. As amended, the California statute required that the coroner secure consent by telephone from specified family members prior to removal of the corneas. Do you think it makes a difference to a court in reviewing the constitutionality of a statute that the state has already changed the provision in controversy?

Do you think that the difference between the original California statute and the UAGA is significant? Did the California legislature have to go as far as it did by requiring actual consent? Is the type of tissue or organ relevant? Or, does the Ninth Circuit opinion spell the end of presumed consent?

*Newman* arose after a situation in which the coroner's office in Los Angeles removed the corneas from a young man who had been shot to death where the family specifically objected to organ removal, but three hours after the corneas had been removed. The LA County coroner's office discontinued the practice after several news articles were published. One article covering the issue asked whether the practice would have a disproportionate impact on people of color. In LA at the time, 80% of autopsies were performed on African–American or Latino individuals and only 16% on whites. The UAGA, and the state statutes allowing for presumed consent for cornea removal, give authority to the medical examiner or coroner only rather than hospitals, so removal is likely to occur during forensic autopsies only. Ralph Frammolino, Harvest of Corneas at Morgue Questioned, L.A. Times, Nov. 2, 1997.

**Add, at p. 84, in note 4:**

In June, 2002, the American Medical Association House of Delegates adopted a report from the Association's Council on Ethical and Judicial Affairs (CEJA) recommending that particular financial incentives for the donation of cadaveric organs be tested on an experimental basis. The Report highlights the fact that donations of organs have not kept pace with the need. From 1990–2000, the number of patients on waiting lists increased on an average of 14.1% per year while the number of organs donated increased only 2.9% annually. Cadaveric Organ Donations: Encouraging the Study of Motivation, Report of the Council on Ethical and Judicial Affairs, available in proceedings of the 2002 Annual Meeting of the American Medical Association posted on the AMA's web site at www.ama-assn.org/.

The AMA has supported limited financial incentives for cadaveric organ donation since 1993. (See, Financial Incentives for Organ Donation, Policy E–2.15, AMA Policy Database, available at the AMA web site.) The more recent report recommends rigorous study of the impact of certain financial incentives under the following circumstances: consultation and advice is sought from the population to be studied; written protocols evidencing sound study design are approved by institutional review boards (see discussion of IRBs in Chapter 20) and are available to the public; incentives should be modest and set at the lowest level that can reasonably be expected to increase donations; no study should include payment to living donors; financial incentives should be for cadaveric organs only; and organs donated should be allocated by UNOS under medical need standards so that the purchasing of specific organs does not occur.

The state of Pennsylvania enacted legislation to establish a public trust fund that would supply funds for the families of deceased patients who donated organs. Payments would be limited to $3000 and could be used to cover funeral expenses and incidental expenses borne by the donor's family in relation to the donation. Because of concerns that NOTA prohibits such payments, the plan dropped coverage for funeral expenses and decided to cover only incidental expenses such as food, lodging and transportation for the family. See discussion in John Zen Jackson, When It Comes to Transplant Organs, Demand Far Exceeds Supply, New Jersey Law Journal, December 16, 2002.

For a discussion of the current movement toward allowing payment for organ donations and an argument against such compensation, see Joralemon and Cox, The Case Against Compensating for Transplant Organs, 33 Hastings Center Report 27 (Jan.-Feb. 2003).

**Add, at p. 85, in the Questions:**

In Sattler v. Northwest Tissue Center, 110 Wash.App. 689, 42 P.3d 440 (2002), the court held that although the procuring organization was covered within the immunity provisions of the UAGA, the question of good faith precluded summary judgment in favor of the organization. The husband of the decedent claimed that he gave consent to some tissue retrieval (including bone and skin), but not to any part of the eyes; and the hospital's representative who completed the consent form over the phone with the husband claimed that he had authorized cornea removal but not the entire eye.

Should the question of good faith be decided on summary judgment? If it is not, is the protection of the statute effective? If so, are the rights of the family protected?

**Add, at p. 90, after note 2:**

The author of a recent article proposes that families of persons needing organs be brought together so that those who are willing to donate an organ to a family member but who cannot due to biological incompatibility be matched with family members of other individuals similarly situated. Both individuals would receive organ transplants from unrelated but matched donors. Michael T. Morley, Increasing the Supply of Organs for Transplantation Through Paired Organ Exchanges, 21 Yale Law and Policy Review 221 (2003). Some transplant centers have seen an increase in the number of persons who simply offer to donate a nonvital organ to anyone who needs it. See, Lainie Friedman Ross, Solid Organ Donation Between Strangers, 30 Journal of Law, Medicine & Ethics 440 (2002) for a discussion of the ethical issues in this class of inter vivos donations, including the issue of competition between transplant centers for usable organs.

# Part I
## PROMOTING QUALITY

# Chapter 2

# QUALITY CONTROL REGULATION: LICENSING OF HEALTH CARE PROFESSIONALS

## I. DISCIPLINE

**Add, at p. 98, after note 2:**

For a position advocating that expert testimony requirements depend not on the type of proceeding but the particular facts of each proceeding, see Timothy P. McCormack, Expert Testimony and Professional Licensing Boards: What is Good, What is Necessary, and the Myth of the Majority–Minority Split, 53 Me. L. Rev. 139 (2001).

**Add, at p. 99, after note 3:**

There are indications that disciplinary practices in regard to prescribing controlled substances for the treatment of pain are improving to accommodate a more balanced approach. A recent study of medical boards and their approach to such cases indicates that boards are using guidelines where they are available and do recognize that pain control sometimes requires high doses of medications over a long period of time. Diane Hoffmann and Anita Tarzian, Achieving the Right Balance in Oversight of Physician Opioid Prescribing for Pain: The Role of the State Medical Boards, 31 Journal of Law, Medicine & Ethics 21 (2003). (This article is part of a symposium issue on legal and policy issues in pain management.)

Another indicator of change among the medical licensing boards is the discipline of physicians for the undertreatment of pain. In 1999, the Oregon medical board disciplined a physician for failure to adequately treat multiple patients in pain. This was the first instance of such a proceeding. Oregon brought action against the same physician again in 2002. The complaint states that the doctor continued to withhold narcotics from terminal patients. 11 Health Law Reporter 1222. Recently, California followed suit, and disciplined a doctor for undertreatment.

States have continued to enact intractable pain statutes. At least 23 states have adopted such legislation to date, and the Model Pain Act has been adopted in whole or in part by several of those states. Sandra H. Johnson, Providing Relief to Those in Pain: A Retrospective on the Scholarship and Impact of the Mayday Project, 31 Journal of Law, Medicine & Ethics 15 (2003).

**Add, at p. 99, a new note:**

Several states have enacted legislation to allow patients to use marijuana to relieve pain and other symptoms of chronic and terminal illness. See discussion in this supplement at page 314. The U.S. Supreme Court held that an organization that distributed marijuana could not use the California statute as a defense to federal prosecution under the federal Controlled Substances Act. U.S. v. Oakland Cannabis Buyers' Cooperative, 532 U.S. 483, 121 S.Ct. 1711, 149 L.Ed.2d 722 (2001). The Ninth Circuit later considered the issue of whether a physician could simply advise a patient of the medicinal properties of marijuana, under the California statute, as long as the physician did not distribute the drug to the patient. The Court held that prohibiting the physician from so advising his or her patients would violate the First Amendment rights of the physician. Conant v. Walters, 309 F.3d 629 (9th Cir.2002).

The court in *Conant* enjoined the federal government from even investigating physicians where the sole basis for the government's action is the "physician's professional 'recommendation' of use of medical marijuana." In his concurring opinion, Judge Kozinski quotes an expert concerning the impact of investigations on physicians:

> Physicians are particularly easily deterred by the threat of governmental investigation and/or sanction from engaging in conduct that is entirely lawful and medically appropriate.... [A] physician's practice is particularly dependent upon the physician's maintaining a reputation of unimpeachable integrity. A physician's career can be effectively destroyed merely by the fact that a governmental body has investigated his or her practice....

If this is true, what are the implications for medical discipline? Are disciplinary boards to refrain from investigations? Should the standards for beginning an investigation be higher because of this impact? Or, does the public health demand active investigations? Is there anything in the investigatory process that could diminish this impact?

**Add, at p. 99, after note 4:**

In 2001, 2,708 serious disciplinary actions were taken by state medical boards against physicians in the U.S. (0.34%) This was a slight decrease over the previous year when 2,746 actions were taken. (0.35%) States continued to differ widely. For a state-by-state ranking, see The Public Citizen, Ranking of State Medical Boards' Serious Disciplinary Actions in 2001 available at www.citizen.org/publications. Public Citizen also rated web sites of state medical boards based on user friendliness and content including names of disciplined physicians and detail of the basis for discipline. 11 Health Law Reporter 555.

**Add, at p. 100, after note 7:**

The Ninth Circuit decided in 2002 that a physician with a history of mental illness could bring a claim against the state of California under Title II of the ADA for damages and injunctive relief for the state's refusal to issue a medical license. Hason v. Medical Board of California, 279 F.3d 1167 (9th Cir.2002) The Ninth Circuit distinguished an earlier Supreme Court case that had held that the government has immunity under the Eleventh Amendment for claims under Title I of the ADA. Board of Trustees of Univ. of Alabama v. Garrett, 531 U.S. 356, 121 S.Ct. 955, 148 L.Ed.2d 866 (2001) The Ninth Circuit held that even if the state enjoyed immunity for damages claims, it would still be subject to injunctive relief. In November 2002, the Supreme Court granted *cert.* in *Hason* on the issue of

Eleventh Amendment immunity for Title II claims. ___ U.S. ___, 123 S.Ct. 561, 154 L.Ed.2d 441 (2002). Oral argument was scheduled for March, 2003; however, the case was removed from the Court's calendar in response to a formal petition from the state of California to withdraw the case. The medical board had voted 14–1 to withdraw the appeal of the Ninth Circuit's decision in response to a letter from the Governor at the urging of disability rights groups. In contrast to the Ninth Circuit, a district court in New York held that the New York Department of Health was immune from the ADA claim of a physician who argued that the department failed to account for his learning and attention deficit disorders in revoking his license for professional misconduct. Harris v. New York State Dept. of Health, 202 F.Supp.2d 143 (S.D.N.Y.2002).

A Colorado appeals court recently upheld the decision of the Colorado State Board of Medical Examiners in revoking an anesthesiologist's license to practice medicine. The physician suffered from a sleep disorder and fell asleep several times during the administration of anesthesia. The court held that no reasonable accommodation could be made because the disability posed a significant risk to patients. Colo. State Board of Medical Examiners v. Ogin, 56 P.3d 1233 (Colo.App. 2002).

**Add, at p. 101, after note 10:**

In March, 2002, the U.S. Supreme Court denied *cert.* in Nguyen v. State, Department of Health, 144 Wash.2d 516, 29 P.3d 689, cert. den. 535 U.S. 904, 122 S.Ct. 1203, 152 L.Ed.2d 141. In *Nguyen*, the Washington Supreme Court held that a medical board is required under due process to support its decision to revoke a medical license with clear and convincing evidence, rather than a preponderance of evidence. Three justices from the Washington court dissented. The appellate courts in Washington have distinguished *Nguyen* in subsequent cases. In Eidson v. State Dept. of Licensing, 108 Wash.App. 712, 32 P.3d 1039 (2001), the appellate court held that *Nguyen* did not apply to real estate appraiser licenses. The court in *Eidson* notes that several courts have held that it is appropriate under due process to require a higher burden of proof in attorney disciplinary cases as compared to physician disciplinary cases because the damage done by an attorney can usually be remedied with money. Do you agree? The *Nguyen* opinion cites cases showing a split among the states in the requirement of clear and convincing as compared to preponderance of the evidence, with a trend toward requiring the higher level of proof. Does the requirement of the higher level of proof fairly balance the interests in medical discipline?

**Add, at p. 103:**

California has aggressively disciplined physicians who prescribed medications on line. In January, 2003, the medical board revoked the license of a physician who prescribed various medications, including Cipro in the midst of the anthrax episode last year, and controlled substances such as pain and anti-anxiety medications based on phone interviews and internet questionnaires. The medical board based the revocation on the failure to perform physical examinations as required by a long-standing state law. Ca. Bus. & Prof. Code § 2242. The doctor plans to challenge the revocation, contesting the board's claim that he failed to perform a good faith physical examination of his patients as he limited his phone practice to patients he had previously examined. For a report of the disciplinary action, see 12 Health Law Reporter 158. The Medical Board of California also fined six out-of-state doctors over

$48 million for issuing just under 2,000 prescriptions to California residents over the internet. The prescriptions were primarily for drugs to treat sexual dysfunction, hair loss, and obesity. The medical board has 23 open cases. 12 Health Law Reporter 223. North Carolina also moved to revoke the licenses of physicians for internet prescribing without prior physical exam. 10 Health Law Reporter 1714. See also, State v. Alivio, 275 Kan. 169, 61 P.3d 687 (2003), allowing a default judgment to stand revoking the license of a physician who prescribed Viagra on line for a female government agent without physical examination of the patient.

The fines in the California actions were levied under a California statute enacted in 2000 that provides for civil penalties of $25,000 per occurrence for prescribing over the internet without a good faith prior exam. Ca. Bus. & Prof. Code § 2242.1

Should there be heavier penalties for violations of the state law requiring physical examination of patients when the violation occurs over the internet? Why a fine rather than other disciplinary action?

In 2002, the Illinois Department of Professional Regulation took action against an Indiana-based internet company, My.Docs.com, to prevent it from doing business in Illinois as it was not licensed as a physician or medical corporation in Illinois. The company's general manager claims that the goal of the web site is to make health care accessible to people who cannot go to a physician, and that the site is just an intermediary between these patients and the physicians working under contract with his organization. The site reportedly serves 17,000 patients in Indiana, without contest, and plans to expand nationally. 11 Health Law Reporter 1587.

Ohio requires that out-of-state physicians prescribing medication or treatment for Ohio residents over the internet hold a certificate for the "practice of telemedicine" issued by the medical board. Ohio Rev. Code § 4731.296 The certificate requires that the physician hold a current license in another state and does not allow the physician to practice in any other way in Ohio.

For an argument advocating state regulation and aggressive enforcement against online pharmacies, see Sara E. Zeman, Regulation of Online Pharmacies: A Case for Cooperative Federalism, 10 Ann. Health L. 105 (2001). For a more cautious approach aimed at preserving the benefit to patients, see David B. Brushwood, Responsive Regulation of Internet Pharmacy Practice, 10 Ann. Health L. 75 (2001).

## II. ALTERNATIVE AND COMPLEMENTARY MEDICINE

**Add, at p. 108, after note 3:**

In Gant v. Novello, ___ A.D.2d ___, 754 N.Y.S.2d 746 (App.Div.2003), the New York appellate court rejected a physician's claim that the medical board was required to consult an expert in nonconventional medicine prior to suspending his license for five years for failing to meet the standards of medical practice in New York. The physician was practicing orthomolecular medicine which he described as "straightening out or correcting ... the molecules [and] harmful toxic substances ... that are found to be present in the body." The court also held that there was no requirement to admit testimony from patients.

## III. UNLICENSED PROVIDERS

**Add, at p. 115, after note 1:**

For a discussion of barriers created by inconsistent state regulation of midwifery, see Susan Corcoran, To Become a Midwife: Reducing Legal Barriers to Entry into the Midwifery Profession, 80 Wash. U. L. Q. 649 (2002).

# Chapter 3

# QUALITY CONTROL REGULATION OF HEALTH CARE INSTITUTIONS

**Note:** On June 14, 2001, Secretary of HHS, Tommy Thompson announced that HCFA's name would be changed to the Centers for Medicare and Medicaid Services (CMS) as part of a larger agency restructuring intended to focus the service areas of the agency and provide a more beneficiary friendly environment. The New Centers for Medicare and Medicaid Services, available at http://www.hhs.gov/news/press/2001pres/20010614a.html.

## I. INTRODUCTION

**Add, at p. 127, after Introduction:**

In the last two years, failures in the quality of care in nursing homes have received a great deal of national attention. For example, in November, 2002, the New York Times profiled a Long Island facility allowed to remain in operation despite ongoing citations and strong evidence of poor care to residents. Vivian S. Toy, Not a Place to Leave a Relative, New York Times, 14L1, Nov. 17, 2002. In October, 2002, the St. Louis Post Dispatch ran a week-long series of articles on the state of nursing homes, preventable deaths, abuse, substandard care and proposed solutions. Less than a week later, Governor Holden of Missouri called for sweeping reform and increased funding in response to the investigative reports by the newspaper. Phillip O'Connor, Holden Calls for Action on Nursing Homes, Oct. 21, 2002. A series of reports by the General Accounting Office, referenced later in these materials, called into question federal efforts at quality control regulation and enforcement for nursing homes.

A report compiled from complaint investigations of 1,148 nursing homes in Texas from March, 2001, to August, 2002, found serious deficiencies. Only 14 percent were found to be in full or substantial compliance with federal standards, and 39 percent had violations that placed residents at risk of serious jeopardy or placed them at actual risk of harm. Overall, Texas homes rated 43rd in the nation in hours of nursing care provided each day. The president of the Texas Health Care Association, the nursing home trade association, advocated increased funding to improve nursing home staffing. 11 Health Law Reporter 1582. In responding to such a statement, how would you go about analyzing whether the problem is lack of funds for improvement, excess margins, lack of commitment or training, or intractability of problems?

Staffing levels undoubtedly are crucial to providing good care. Indeed, nursing homes face serious problems of understaffing. According to a study completed in 2000, 90% of nursing homes are not properly staffed. To correct the staffing numbers, between 77,000 to 137,000 registered nurses; 22,000 to 27,000 licensed practical nurses; and 181,000 to 310,000 nurse's aides need to be hired. The industry, however, generally opposes staffing mandates. John Pear, 9 in 10 Nursing Homes in U.S. Lack Adequate Staff, The New York Times, Feb. 18, 2002. Should the focus be on the number of employed or on the quality of their care? If the connection between the two has been proven overall, should the standards revert to such proscriptive standards?

A GAO report that looked at 1999 spending and staffing levels in nursing homes for three states found that staffing level has a great impact on improving quality of care. The study found that the more nursing hours logged, the fewer quality issues surfaced on successive state surveys. Conversely, increased spending alone did not necessarily result in better care as it may not mean more hours of care. GAO, Nursing Homes: Quality of Care More Related to Staffing than Spending (2002). CMS emphasized that the quality of care that residents received was dependent on staffing levels and estimated that appropriate staffing requirements would raise nursing home expenditures by about eight percent. CMS noted that factors other than nursing staffing levels also improved quality, including retention of nurse assistants and creation of single-task workers. 11 Health Law Reporter 521.

Others have noted that part of the problem of nursing home quality is a lack of accountability. See, for example, Reed Abelson, Bringing Discipline and Scorecards to Nursing Homes, The New York Times, July 7, 2002.

A related problem is deficiencies in reporting abuse and adverse events. A GAO study using a sampling of nursing homes in Georgia, Illinois and Pennsylvania found that instances of abuse were seriously underreported and typically were not reported for two days after the facilities first learned of the abuse, making investigation and preservation of evidence difficult. GAO: Nursing Homes: More Can Be Done to Protect Residents From Abuse, GAO 02–312 (2002). See also, Kelly Greene, Study Finds Many Nursing Homes Fail To Promptly Report Abuse Allegations, The Wall Street Journal, B2, March 4, 2002. The Medical Examiner in St. Louis suggests that a procedure for investigation of elderly deaths in nursing homes similar to that for suspected abuse-related deaths of children could increase the accountability of facilities. Phillip O'Connor, Triage Review is Option in Elderly Deaths, St. Louis Post Dispatch, Oct. 25, 2002.

Since 1995, JCAHO has tracked "sentinel events" as an attempt to improve quality. JCAHO defines a sentinel event as "an unexpected occurrence involving death or serious physical or psychological injury, or the risk thereof.... Such events are called 'sentinel" because they signal the need for immediate investigation and response." Joint Commission on Accreditation of Healthcare Organizations, Sentinel Event Policy and Procedures, Revised: July 2002, available at http://www.jcaho.org/accredited+organizations/long+term+care/sentinel+events/se_pp.htm#1. Of the sentinel events recorded by the JCAHO since 1995, 3.6% (70 of 1,595) of them have occurred in long-term care settings. Joint Commission on Accreditation of Healthcare Organizations, Sentinel Events Statistics as of January 29, 2003, available at http://www.jcaho.org/accredited+organizations/long+term+care/sentinel+events/se_stats.htm#5. However, JCAHO acknowledges that sentinel events are underreported, especially in long-term care, and have publicly urged better compliance with reporting. Joint Commission on Accreditation of Healthcare Organizations, Dear Colleague Letter: Underreported Sentinel Events, letter from President Dennis S. O'Leary, available at http://www.jcaho.org/accredited+organizations/ambulatory+care/sentinel+events/underreported+sentinel+events.htm.

Some facilities do a better job at providing quality care. LTCQ, Inc., conducted a study commissioned by JCAHO comparing JCAHO-accredited long-term care facilities with nonaccredited facilities. Upon completion in 2002, the results indicated accredited facilities performed significantly better in terms of medication errors, complaints and substantiated allegations, health related deficiencies and life safety code deficiencies. Joint Commission on Accreditation of Healthcare Organizations, JCAHO Accreditation Helps Nursing Facilities Achieve Better Outcomes, available at, http://cms.hhs.gov/manuals/pub07pdf/part–08.pdf-State Agency quality improvement plan.

Some have argued that families should be allowed to use video surveillance to monitor care. On one side of the issue are families who would like the security of knowing they could check on an elderly loved one remotely in the hope that the cameras would decrease the potential for abuse by workers. Several states are reported to be considering enacting "granny-cam" statutes which would allow families to install a camera at their own cost. On the other side are many facility operators who contend that such surveillance is an invasion of privacy for the residents, may increase insurance premiums, and make it even more difficult to attract workers. Not all owners are opposed, and those that currently utilize video surveillance credit it with an increased ability to attract excellent workers who appreciate the increased accountability, an increase in quality of care, an increased demand for beds in their facilities and a drop in insurance premiums. Kelly Greene, Support Grows for Cameras in Care Facilities, The Wall Street Journal, B1, March 7, 2002.

Are some residents improperly placed in nursing homes while others remain even after functioning improves? A special program out of New Jersey has been successful in removing over 2,500 residents from nursing homes and placing them in assisted living, back in their own homes, or with foster families. For more on the program, see Lucette Lagnado Living and Dying: An Innovative New Jersey Program Offers What May Be a More Humane Alternative to Nursing Homes, The Wall Street Journal, R11, Feb. 21, 2001.

There is hope for real change. For a story in which one physician has made a significant difference as he works tirelessly to promote quality care for the elderly population and serves as medical director for eight Missouri long-term care facilities, see Phillip O'Connor, Doctor Has Cure for Ailing Homes, St. Louis Post Dispatch, Oct. 18, 2002. For a success story of a nursing home using an innovative approach to improving care by personalizing resident needs, see Virginia Young, Innovative Home Lets People Take Control of Their Lives, St. Louis Post Dispatch, Oct. 18, 2003. Crestview Nursing Home allows its residents to sleep late, eat on demand, keep cherished pets, and much more. The facility has done all this while saving money and retaining staff to the point of having a waiting list for nurses' aides. There are many like them.

**Add, at p. 128, after Note 2:**

3. Home health care agencies in New Jersey can no longer avoid regulation by calling the personnel sent into senior's homes "consultants" or "friends." In December, 2001, the governor signed a bill subjecting any agency that arranges for workers to provide in-home health care or personal care to regulation by the state and thus closing the loophole used by many agencies to avoid regulation. 12 Health Law Reporter 28.

4. In Delaware, the governor signed legislation in June of 2002 expanding the definitional scope of home health care services to subject businesses which provide aide services to state licensing requirements. The definition of home health care was expanded to include the provision of personal care such as bathing, feeding, grooming and household services. 11 Health Law Reporter 1075.

## II. REGULATORY SYSTEMS

### A. DIFFERENCES AMONG INSTITUTIONS

**Add, at p. 131, before the Notes and Questions:**

The decision in First Healthcare Corporation v. Hamilton, cited in the casebook at page 130, was overruled by the Florida Supreme Court in Florida Convalescent Centers v. Somberg, 840 So.2d 998 (Fla.2003). The *Somberg* court held that plaintiffs could recover damages (including punitive damages) under both the statute governing the violation of nursing home residents' rights and under the Wrongful Death Act of Florida. The *First Healthcare* court had previously limited the damages to those recoverable under the Nursing Home Act.

Litigation against nursing homes and resulting jury awards have increased substantially over the last several years in Florida and Texas. For example, in 2001 in Florida, negligence or residents' rights lawsuits were filed against 62 percent of nursing homes. Of those involved in suits, 23 percent faced three or more civil actions. A study commissioned by the Florida Health Care Association, the trade association for nonprofit nursing homes, emphasized that just before a statute requiring liability insurance went into effect, 19 percent of facilities were uninsured and another 36 percent were self-insured. 11 Health Law Reporter 29.

In response to the increase in civil suits, nursing home liability rates have increased. Florida and Texas have enacted legislation in response. Punitive damages and attorneys' fees are now capped, and liability insurance is a condition of licensing in Florida. As of September, 2003, Texas will require nursing homes to maintain $3 million in professional liability insurance. Ohio, a state that has not seen the increase in litigation comparable to Florida and Texas, enacted a statute in 2002 limiting the reach of litigation against nursing homes. The legislation shortens the statute of limitations to one year and limits who may bring suit. Additionally, the use of state inspection findings or any statements of deficiencies is now prohibited as evidence in a civil case. 11 Health Law Reporter 1185. For a discussion advocating imposition of tort liability as a catalyst for change in the nursing home industry, see Christine V. Williams, The Nursing Home Dilemma in America Today: The Suffering Must be Recognized and Eradicated, 41 Santa Clara L. Rev. 867 (2001).

Updating another item, the Centers for Medicaid and Medicare Services project that Medicaid will pay for 50.2% of nursing home care and Medicare will pay for 11.1%. Nursing Home Care Expenditures Aggregate and Per Capita Amounts and Percentage Distributions, By Source Funds, http://www.cms.hhs.gov/statistics/nhe/projections-2001/t14.asp.

## C. THE REGULATORY PROCESS

### 1. Standard Setting

**Add, at p. 137:**

1. Under OBRA 87, all facilities have an obligation to provide special services for any resident whose reason for residence is a developmental disability. The obligation was not clear, however, for developmentally disabled residents who require nursing care for other health needs. In Rolland v. Romney, 318 F.3d 42 (1st Cir.2003), the court held that the Nursing Home Reform Amendments of 1987 (OBRA 87) and subsequent regulations required states to provide special services for such "dual need" residents and rejected Massachusetts' argument that HHS's regulatory interpretation requiring the same was unenforceable. The court also confirmed that residents have a private right of action under the statute and that right is enforceable under § 1983.

2. The HHS annual work plan released October 3, 2002, included several nursing home initiatives aimed at improving the accuracy of quality, patient and operation data collected and a focus on the use of minimum data sets in nursing homes as correlated to Medicare compliance. The Office of the Inspector General also plans to look at trends in deficiencies and complaints and the efficacy of enforcement actions mandated by OBRA 87. 11 Health Law Reporter 1419.

3. In November of 2002, CMS implemented the Nursing Home Quality Initiative, a national effort aimed at improving care by sharing data with the public on quality in ten functional areas already provided to CMS. The Agency conducted a pilot of the program in six states in April of 2002. The program has not been without its critics and problems. The public release of the pilot data was delayed in April. 11 Health Law Reporter 615. Shortly after its release, U.S. Senators Waxman and Grassley sent a letter to CMS Administrator Thomas Scully regarding the website, charging that thousands of the most severe violations had been omitted because complaint data was not included, thereby misinforming consumers searching for information on particular nursing homes. 11 Health Law Reporter 346. CMS agreed to include complaint data. 11 Health Law Reporter 624. The General Accounting Office released a report the day following the release of national data saying the roll out of the program by CMS was premature and not backed up by an effective evaluation of the usefulness of the pilot program. 11 Health Law Reporter 1661; GAO: Nursing Homes, Public Reporting of Quality Indicators Has

Merit, but National Implementation is Premature, GAO 03–187 (2002). The data is available at http://www.medicare.gov/NHCompare/home.asp.

**Add, at p. 138, Note 3:**

In Beverly Health and Rehabilitation Services v. Thompson, 223 F.Supp.2d 73 (D.D.C.2002), the court rejected the provider's argument that the survey process was invalid because it did not comport with the APA's notice and comment rulemaking requirements. Rather, the court held that the CMS guidelines are not the type of substantive rules that are subject to the APA's notice and comment requirements.

**Substitute, on p. 144, for HCFA "Guidance to Surveyors:"**

*Guidelines: § 483.13(a)*

The resident has the right to be free from any physical or chemical restraints imposed for purposes of discipline or convenience, and not required to treat the resident's medical symptoms...

Convenience is defined as any action taken by the facility to control a resident's behavior or manage a resident's behavior with a lesser amount of effort by the facility and not in the resident's best interest.

Restraints may not be used for staff convenience. However, if the resident needs emergency care, restraints may be used for brief periods to permit medical treatment to proceed unless the facility has a notice indicating that the resident has previously made a valid refusal of the treatment in question. If a resident's unanticipated violent or aggressive behavior places him/her or others in imminent danger, the resident does not have the right to refuse the use of restraints. In this situation, the use of restraints is a measure of last resort to protect the safety of the resident or others and must not extend beyond the immediate episode.

Physical Restraints are defined as any manual method or physical or mechanical device, material, or equipment attached or adjacent to the resident's body that the individual cannot remove easily which restricts freedom of movement or normal access to one's body.

"Physical restraints" include, but are not limited to, leg restraints, arm restraints, hand mitts, soft ties or vests, lap cushions, and lap trays the resident cannot remove easily. Also included as restraints are facility practices that meet the definition of a restraint, such as:

- Using side rails that keep a resident from voluntarily getting out of bed;

- Tucking in or using velcro to hold a sheet, fabric, or clothing tightly so that a resident's movement is restricted;

- Using devices in conjunction with a chair, such as trays, tables, bars or belts, that the resident cannot remove easily, that prevent the resident from rising;

- Placing a resident in a chair that prevents a resident from rising; and

- Placing a chair or bed so close to a wall that the wall prevents the resident from rising out of the chair or voluntarily getting out of bed.

Side rails sometimes restrain residents. The use of side rails as restraints is prohibited unless they are necessary to treat a resident's medical symptoms. Residents who attempt to exit a bed through, between, over or around side rails are at risk of injury or death. The potential for serious injury is more likely from a fall from a bed with raised side rails than from a fall from a bed where side rails are not used. They also potentially increase the likelihood that the resident will spend more time in bed and fall when attempting to transfer from the bed.

\* \* \*

The same device may have the effect of restraining one individual but not another, depending on the individual resident's condition and circumstances. For example, partial rails may assist one resident to enter and exit the bed independently while acting as a restraint for another...

\* \* \*

The resident's subjective symptoms may not be used as the sole basis for using a restraint. Before a resident is restrained, the facility must determine the presence of a specific medical symptom that would require the use of restraints, and how the use of restraints would treat the medical symptom, protect the resident's safety, and assist the resident in attaining or maintaining his or her highest practicable level of physical and psychosocial well-being...

While there must be a physician's order reflecting the presence of a medical symptom, HCFA will hold the facility ultimately accountable for the appropriateness of that determination. The physician's order alone is not sufficient to warrant the use of the restraint. It is further expected, for those residents whose care plans indicate the need for restraints, that the facility engage in a systematic and gradual process toward reducing restraints (e.g., gradually increasing the time for ambulation and muscle strengthening activities). This systematic process would also apply to recently admitted residents for whom restraints were used in the previous setting.

In order for the resident to be fully informed, the facility must explain, in the context of the individual resident's condition and circumstances, the potential risks and benefits of all options under consideration including using a restraint, not using a restraint, and alternatives to restraint use. Whenever restraint use is considered, the facility must explain to the resident how the use of restraints would treat the resident's medical symptoms and assist the resident in attaining or maintaining his/her highest practicable level of physical or psychological well-being. In addition, the facility must also explain the potential negative outcomes of restraint use which include, but are not limited to, declines in the resident's physical functioning (e.g., ability to ambulate) and muscle condition, contractures, increased incidence of infections and development of pressure sores/ulcers, delirium, agitation, and incontinence. Moreover, restraint use may constitute an accident hazard. Restraints have been found in some cases to increase the incidence of falls or head trauma due to falls and other accidents (e.g., strangulation, entrapment). Finally, residents who are restrained may face a loss of autonomy, dignity and self respect, and may show symptoms of withdrawal, depression, or reduced social contact. In effect, restraint use can reduce independence, functional capacity, and quality of life. Alternatives to restraint use should be considered and discussed with the resident. Alternatives to restraint use might include modifying the resident's environment and/or routine.

In the case of a resident who is incapable of making a decision, the legal surrogate or representative may exercise this right based on the same information that would have been provided to the resident. [ ] However, the legal surrogate or representative cannot give permission to use restraints for the sake of discipline or staff convenience or when the restraint is not necessary to treat the resident's medical symptoms. That is, the facility may not use restraints in violation of the regulation solely based on a legal surrogate or representative's request or approval.

\* \* \*

There are instances where, after assessment and care planning, a least restrictive restraint may be deemed appropriate for an individual resident to attain or maintain his or her highest practicable physical and psychosocial well-being. This does not alter the facility's responsibility to assess and care plan restraint use on an ongoing basis.

Medicare State Operations Manual, Appendix PP–Guidance to Surveyors–Long Term Care Facilities (Sept. 7, 2000), available at http://cms.hhs.gov/manuals/pm_trans/R20SOM.pdf.

### 2. *Survey and Inspection*

**Add, at p. 148, to Notes and Questions:**

1. An owner and operator lost a challenge to the validity of the surveyor protocol after termination of the licensee's contract to participate in Medicare and Medicaid. Beverly Health and Rehabilitation Services v. Thompson, 223 F.Supp.2d 73 (D.D.C.2002). CMS terminated the contract after discovering deficiencies which amounted to immediate jeopardy, and the court determined the Secretary had the power to take such action after findings that the facility was not in compliance with the governing law and regulations. The court also rejected Beverly's argument that the survey process was invalid because it did not comport with the APA's notice and comment rulemaking requirements. Rather, the court held that the CMS guidelines are not the type of substantive rules that are subject to the APA's notice and comment period requirements. In contrast, a U.S. District Court enjoined HHS from terminating the provider agreement with Pathfinder Healthcare, Inc. to allow the facility to complete its administrative appeals process. Pathfinder Healthcare Inc. v. Thompson, 177 F.Supp.2d 895 (E.D.Ark.2001). The judge in the *Pathfinder* case made a distinction based on the hardship to the patients that would be forced to transfer and the fact that the violations were not of the immediate jeopardy type. If the statute does not require immediate jeopardy for the termination of the contract, is the court's decision correct?

### 3. *Sanctions*

**Add, at p. 150, in Note 3:**

Federal criminal sanctions have resulted in a ten-month prison sentence for an LPN who falsified medication records after an error led to the deterioration of a patient. The investigation also led to a civil settlement for billing Medicaid for inadequate services.

False Claims Act suits against nursing home for substandard care have increased dramatically. An Assistant U.S. Attorney has said that those cases which offend the senses or occur at facilities with a history of poor care will be more likely to be prosecuted under the False Claims Act. 11 Health Law Reporter 1180.

In February, 2003, the Elder Justice Act was introduced in the United States Senate. It would impose very serious penalties, including prison time, on staff who abuse residents, and fines in the millions of dollars on facilities that fail to report or that allow abuse. An editorial blamed apathy for substandard care but lauded the potential of this federal legislation as a possible start to improving care. Editorial, A Ray of Hope for Reform, St. Louis Post Dispatch, Feb. 17, 2003.

In February, 2003, the president of a company operating nursing homes in Missouri received the maximum sentence of one year in jail plus a $1,000 fine for failing to report abuse in which an elderly resident was beaten to death by a nurse's aide. The aide was also sentenced to 15 years for elderly abuse. In addition, the company and the facility in which the abuse occurred were ordered to pay $5,000 each in fines. Valerie Schremp, Nursing Home Chief Gets One Year Sentence, St. Louis Post Dispatch, Feb. 7, 2003.

**Add, at p. 151, after Note 3:**

5. For the fiscal year 2004, CMS requested $247.6 million for survey and certification of facilities. The Nursing Home Oversight Improvement Program would be allocated $35.2 million of the overall funding. This program includes increased frequency of inspections of homes with repeat violations; increased efforts targeted at bed sores, dehydration and nutrition; and the imposition of immediate sanctions on facilities found guilty of second offenses causing actual harm to residents. 12 Health Law Reporter 184. What is the difference between this new improvement program and the authority granted by OBRA 87?

6. Beverly Enterprises, Inc., the nation's largest nursing home chain which owns or operates 300 facilities nationwide, agreed to pay more than $2 million to resolve criminal and civil actions alleging substandard practices and elder abuse at its California facilities. Over a three-year period, Beverly facilities in California received over 90 citations for deficiencies including two patient deaths from poor care. An injunction was also issued requiring substantial changes at all 60 facilities in California. In response to the settlement, a company spokesman said that Beverly had performed better than the state average in 2002. 11 Health Law Reporter 1157.

**Add, at p. 155:**

The newest and most substantial initiative from the Joint Commission is its Patient Safety Initiative. A key part of this effort is the Sentinel Event program described earlier in this section. See also, the description of this program in Chapter 1 of this Supplement.

## III. PRIVATE ACCREDITATION OF HEALTH CARE FACILITIES

**Add, at p. 159:**

The Joint Commission's Long Term Care Accreditation Program now accredits more than 2,200 organizations offering long term care and subacute care. Joint Commission on Accreditation of Healthcare Organizations, Long Term Care Accreditation, available at http://www.jcaho.org/accredited+organizations/long+term+care/ltc+accreditation.htm.

As of 2003, long term care facilities are still not eligible for deemed status. However, The Joint Commission has established a pilot project for "deemed status" with Illinois for long term care accreditation and is working with other states interested in long term care deemed status for licensure. Joint Commission on Accreditation of Healthcare Organizations, Long Term

Care, Deemed Status, available at http://www.jcaho.org/accredited+organizations/long+term+care/survey+process/deemed+status/index.htm.

In the last few years, several types of healthcare organizations have gained deemed status, including critical access hospitals and Medicare+Choice organizations licensed as HMOs and PPOs. Joint Commission on Accreditation of Healthcare Organizations, Federal Deemed Status and State Recognition, available at http://www.jcaho.org/about+us/government+relations/fed_st_rec.htm

# Chapter 4

# LIABILITY OF HEALTH CARE PROFESSIONALS

## I. THE STANDARD OF CARE

### A. ESTABLISHING THE STANDARD OF CARE

#### 2. *Expert Testimony*

**Add, at p. 176, a new paragraph to a:**

The weight given to the PDR entries and contraindications listed may on occasion be held to be conclusive of the standard of care, in spite of defendant's experts testimony to the contrary. In Fournet v. Roule–Graham, 783 So.2d 439, 443 (La.App. 5 Cir. 2001), the defendant had prescribed a hormone drug Provera in spite of warnings in the PDR that it was contraindicated for patients with deep vein thrombosis. The defendant's OB/GYN witnesses testified that 70% of OB/GYNs nationwide would find no risk in this situation, contradicting the PDR. The court held that the PDR was an authoritative medical source, that it should not be ignored for any reason, and that "it may very well be the case that a majority of those OB/GYNs are simply unaware of this specific contraindication for Provera, or may simply ignore it."

**Add, at p. 178, at the end of section c:**

State courts are struggling with the applicability of the scientific evidence admissibility tests of *Frye*, *Daubert* and *Kumho* in medical malpractice cases. For example, in Drevenak v. Abendschein, 773 A.2d 396, 418–419(D.C. 2001), the court held that *Frye* and *Daubert* apply only to a "novel scientific test or unique controversial methodology or technique"; where the issue is one of the exercise of clinical judgment based on scientific medical knowledge, reliability can be tested by several relevant factors: "the expert's training, board certification in the pertinent medical specialty, specialized medical experience, attendance at national seminars and meetings, familiarity with published specialized medical literature, and discussions with medical specialists form other geographical regions."

In Ardoin v. Mills, 780 So.2d 1265 (La.App.3 Cir. 2001), a suit against a radiologist, hospital and orthopedic surgeon alleged that the radiologist was negligent in performing an arthrogram causing infection, that hospital breached its duty to provide a sterile environment, and that surgeon was liable for failing to diagnose infection. One issue was experts' testimony as to possibility that gamella morbillorum could colonize on the skin and this could have caused the plaintiff's condition. This testimony satisfied the "flexible" test of *Daubert* and *Kumho*—relevancy and reliability. Louisiana had adopted the *Daubert* requirement that "expert scientific testimony must rise to a threshold level of reliability in order to be admissible". The court noted that the test is flexible, and the *Daubert* factors are not a checklist. The expert testified based his testimony on a textbook on infectious diseases. While the *Daubert* factors may not all have been satisfied, flexibility is the key.

## B. PRACTICE GUIDELINES AS CODIFIED STANDARDS OF CARE

### Add, at p. 181, at end of section B:

For an interesting discussion of the use of empirical evidence to set medical standards of care, see Symposium, Empirical Approaches to Proving the Standard of Care in Medical Malpractice Cases, 37 Wake Forest L. Rev. 663 (2002).

## C. OTHER METHODS OF PROVING NEGLIGENCE

### Add, at p. 181, to note 2:

An extrajudicial statement by a physician that he would not provide necessary treatment because of financial constraints is sufficient to relieve the plaintiff of the need for expert testimony on the standard of care. See Benson v. Tkach, 30 P.3d 402 (Okla. Civ. App. Div. 2 2001) (physician refused to perform additional surgery on patient's infected area to allow it to heal because 'Medicare had his hands tied' and there was no money to pay for the surgery).

# II. JUDICIAL RISK–BENEFIT BALANCING

### Add, at p. 202, at the end of the last paragraph before Section III, add the following:

For a thorough review of the evidence for and against malpractice litigation as an effective deterrent to bad medical practices, see Michelle M. Mello and Troyen A. Brennan, Deterrence of Medical Errors: Theory and Evidence for Malpractice Reform, 80 Texas L. Rev. 1595 (2002).

# IV. DEFENSES TO A MALPRACTICE SUIT

## B. PRACTICE GUIDELINES AS AN AFFIRMATIVE DEFENSE

### Add, at p. 226, at the end of section B:

For a thorough treatment of the role of clinical practice guidelines in malpractice litigation, see Michelle M. Mello, Of Swords and Shields: The Role of Clinical Practice Guidelines in Medical Malpractice Litigation, 149 U.Pa. L. Rev. 645 (2001) (Mello argues that physician compliance is low, so they cannot be said to reflect customary practice; and departing from custom in favor of such guidelines could weaken the deterrent effect of tort law by increasing physician uncertainty about the law's requirements; she concludes that " ... increased reliance on clinical practice guidelines to establish the standard of care in medical malpractice cases would be undesirable whether the guidelines are used in an inculpatory or an exculpatory way.".)

**Sec. IV**  DEFENSES TO A MALPRACTICE SUIT  35

### D. GOOD SAMARITAN ACTS

**Add, at p. 233, a new paragraph to note 2:**

The modern view is that hospital emergencies should not fall within the protection of Good Samaritan statutes. In Velazquez v. Jiminez, M.D., 336 N.J.Super. 10, 763 A.2d 753 (2000), the infant plaintiff suffered brain damage as the result of a complicated and difficult delivery in which several obstetricians were involved in trying to deliver him vaginally, before finally performing a C-section. When confronted with shoulder dystocia, the delivering physician normally attempts a number of standard maneuvers. The nurses and doctor tried several maneuvers to deliver the baby. At the time the decision to operate was made, a second doctor could not be found, and the doctor who was keeping the cord from tightening around the baby was forced to remove her hand from the mother's vagina in order to perform the emergency c-section. Among the defenses raised was the Good Samaritan doctrine, on the grounds that this was a hospital emergency.

The court wrote:

[L]egislatures and courts around the country are split on the wisdom of providing physicians the protection of Good Samaritan laws when responding to an emergency within a hospital. Although the Act is not wholly unambiguous, we adopt the view that the protection of the Good Samaritan Act stops at the door of the hospital. Reuter (a doctor as well as a lawyer), in *Physicians as Good Samaritans, supra* (20 *J. Legal Med.* at 188), persuasively presents arguments in favor of this position. He points out that physicians are already obligated to provide emergency service to patients within the hospital walls through their relationship with the hospital. Thus, immunizing these doctors does not encourage them to treat people who would otherwise go untreated. He also points out that physicians in hospitals have modern diagnostic and therapeutic equipment at their disposal and so they are not disadvantaged in the same way that a doctor trying to treat someone at the roadside would be. Further, immunizing physicians in hospitals might have the adverse effect of lowering the quality of medical care in those hospitals without justification.

**Add, at p. 248, new sections G and H.**

### G. RESTRICTIONS ON THE LEARNED INTERMEDIARY RULE

#### PEREZ v. WYETH LABORATORIES INC.
Supreme Court of New Jersey, 1999.
734 A.2d 1245.

O'HERN, J.

Our medical-legal jurisprudence is based on images of health care that no longer exist. At an earlier time, medical advice was received in the doctor's office from a physician who most likely made house calls if needed. The patient usually paid a small sum of money to the doctor. Neighborhood pharmacists compounded prescribed medicines. Without being pejorative, it is safe to say that the prevailing attitude of law and medicine was that the "doctor knows best." [ ]

Pharmaceutical manufacturers never advertised their products to patients, but rather directed all sales efforts at physicians. In this comforting setting, the law created an exception to the traditional duty of manufacturers to warn consumers directly of risks associated with the product as long as they warned health-care providers of those risks.

For good or ill, that has all changed. Medical services are in large measure provided by managed care organizations. Medicines are purchased in the pharmacy department of supermarkets and often paid for by third-party providers. Drug manufacturers now directly advertise products to consumers on the radio, television, the Internet, billboards on public transportation, and in magazines. For example, a recent magazine advertisement for a seasonal allergy medicine in which a person is standing in a pastoral field filled with grass and goldenrod, attests that to "TAKE [THE PRODUCT]" is to "TAKE CLEAR CONTROL." Another recent ad features a former presidential candidate, encouraging the consumer to "take a little courage" to speak with "your physician." The first ad features major side effects, encourages the reader to "talk to your doctor," and lists a brief summary of risks and contraindications on the opposite page. The second ad provides a phone number and the name of the pharmaceutical company, but does not provide the name of the drug.

The question in this case, broadly stated, is whether our law should follow these changes in the marketplace or reflect the images of the past. We believe that when mass marketing of prescription drugs seeks to influence a patient's choice of a drug, a pharmaceutical manufacturer that makes direct claims to consumers for the efficacy of its product should not be unqualifiedly relieved of a duty to provide proper warnings of the dangers or side effects of the product.

I

THE NORPLANT SYSTEM (NORPLANT)

This appeal concerns Norplant, a Food and Drug Administration (FDA)-approved, reversible contraceptive that prevents pregnancy for up to five years. The Norplant contraceptive employs six thin, flexible, closed capsules that contain a synthetic hormone, levonorgestrel. The capsules are implanted under the skin of a woman's upper arm during an in-office surgical procedure characterized by the manufacturer as minor. A low, continuous dosage of the hormone diffuses through the capsule walls and into the bloodstream. Although the capsules are not usually visible under the skin, the outline of the fan-like pattern can be felt under the skin. Removal occurs during an in-office procedure, similar to the insertion process.

We have no doubt of the profound public interest in developing new products for reproductive services. We intend no disparagement of the product when we recite plaintiffs' claims concerning the efficacy of Norplant. The procedural posture that brings this case before us requires that we accept as true plaintiffs' version of the facts. The motion to dismiss was in the nature of a motion for judgment on the pleadings.

According to plaintiffs, Wyeth began a massive advertising campaign for Norplant in 1991, which it directed at women rather than at their doctors. Wyeth advertised on television and in women's magazines such as *Glamour, Mademoiselle* and *Cosmopolitan*. According to plaintiffs, none of the advertisements warned of any inherent danger posed by Norplant; rather, all praised its simplicity and convenience. None warned of side effects including pain and permanent scarring attendant to removal of the implants. Wyeth also sent a letter to physicians advising them that it was about to launch a national advertising program in magazines that the physicians' patients may read.

Plaintiffs cite several studies published in medical journals that have found Norplant removal to be difficult and painful. One study found that thirty-three percent of women had removal difficulty and forty percent experienced pain. Another study found that fifty-two percent of physicians reported complications during removal. Medical journals have catalogued the need for advanced medical technicians in addition to general surgeons for Norplant removal. Plaintiffs assert that none of this information was provided to consumers.

In 1995, plaintiffs began to file lawsuits in several New Jersey counties claiming injuries that resulted from their use of Norplant. Plaintiffs' principal claim alleged that Wyeth, distributors of Norplant in the United States, failed to warn adequately about side effects associated with the contraceptive. Side effects complained of by plaintiffs included weight gain, headaches, dizziness, nausea, diarrhea, acne, vomiting, fatigue, facial hair growth, numbness in the arms and legs, irregular menstruation, hair loss, leg cramps, anxiety and nervousness, vision problems, anemia, mood swings and depression, high blood pressure, and removal complications that resulted in scarring.

Class action certification was denied. All New Jersey Norplant cases were consolidated in Middlesex County. Eventually, twenty-five New Jersey Norplant cases involving approximately fifty Norplant users were pending in the Superior Court in Middlesex County.

After a case management conference, plaintiffs' counsel sought a determination of whether the learned intermediary doctrine applied. Pursuant to that conference, five bellwether plaintiffs were selected to challenge defendant's motion for summary judgment concerning the learned intermediary doctrine.[ ] The trial court dismissed plaintiffs' complaints, concluding that even when a manufacturer advertises directly to the public, and a woman is influenced by the advertising campaign, "a physician is not simply relegated to the role of prescribing the drug according to the woman's wishes."[ ] Consequently, the court held that the learned intermediary doctrine applied. [ ] According to the court, the physician retains the duty to weigh the benefits and risks associated with a drug before deciding whether the drug is appropriate for the patient. [ ] Because *N.J.S.A.* 2A:58C–4 of the Products Liability Act [ ] measures warning adequacy based on the knowledge and characteristics of the health-care provider, the court was not "concerned with the effect that a warning had on the ... consumer-plaintiff." [ ] The court found, however, that plaintiffs failed to provide expert testimony to rebut the statutory presumption under *N.J.S.A.* 2A:58C–4, that the manufacturer's warning is adequate when it has been approved by the FDA, as is the case here. The court found that plaintiffs failed to rebut the presumption by demonstrating that the manufacturer's warnings to the physicians were inadequate or that a warning as to the difficulty of removal would have altered the health-care providers' decisions to implant Norplant. [ ] * * *

\* \* \*

Plaintiffs appealed. Plaintiffs challenged the court's failure to hear expert testimony on the adequacy of the warnings and the decision concerning proximate cause because "it was specifically agreed that the production of expert testimony would await the outcome of the decision on the issue of the learned intermediary doctrine." The Appellate Division affirmed the trial court's grant of summary judgment in favor of defendants and its determination that the learned intermediary doctrine applied. 313 *N.J.Super.* 511, 713 *A.*2d 520 (1998). The court supplemented the trial court's opinion, comparing Section 6d of the *Restatement (Third) of Torts: Products Liability* (1997) (*Restatement*) to *N.J.S.A.* 2A:58C–4, the similar provision of New Jersey's Products Liability Act. Section 6(d) of the *Restatement* provides:

> (d) A prescription drug or medical device is not reasonably safe due to inadequate instructions or warnings if reasonable instructions or warnings regarding foreseeable risks of harm are not provided to:
>
> (1) prescribing and other health-care providers who are in a position to reduce the risks of harm in accordance with the instructions or warnings; or
>
> (2) the patient when the manufacturer knows or has reason to know that health-care providers will not be in a position to reduce the risks of harm in accordance with the instructions or warnings.

As noted by the Appellate Division, the new *Restatement* is similar to *N.J.S.A.* 2A:58C–4, which defines an adequate warning as

> one that a reasonably prudent person in the same or similar circumstances would have provided with respect to the danger and that communicates adequate information on the dangers and safe use of the product, ... in the case of prescription drugs, taking into account the characteristics of, and the ordinary knowledge common to, the prescribing physician.

The court noted that Section 6(d)(2) of the *Restatement* may require a warning when the physician or health-care provider has a "diminished role as an evaluator or decision maker," in which case the manufacturer would have a duty to warn patients directly. [ ] Consequently, the court agreed with the trial court that if the warning was "legislatively deemed adequate and has been given to the proper party," no warning defect under *N.J.S.A.* 2A:58C–4 had been established. [ ]

We granted plaintiffs' petition for certification. 156 *N.J.* 410, 719 *A.*2d 642 (1998).

II

[The Court considered its prior caselaw involving the relationship between products liability law and pharmaceutical products, concluding that "a pharmaceutical manufacturer generally discharges its duty to warn the ultimate user of prescription drugs by supplying physicians with information about the drug's dangerous propensities. [ ] This concept is known as the "learned intermediary" rule because the physician acts as the intermediary between the manufacturer and the consumer." Exceptions to the learned intermediary recognized by New Jersey law include direct warnings about the risks of vaccines administered in mass immunization clinics and oral contraceptives. "The question in this appeal is whether sufficient reasons exist to warrant its application under these facts. Norplant appears to be a hybrid prescription medical device exhibiting characteristics both of a medical device implanted in the body and of a drug. For convenience, most of our discussion will use the terminology relevant to prescription drugs, the context in which most such claims may arise."]

### III

#### DIRECT-TO-CONSUMER ADVERTISING

It is paradoxical that so pedestrian a concern as male-pattern baldness should have signaled the beginning of direct-to-consumer marketing of prescription drugs. Upjohn Company became the first drug manufacturer to advertise directly to consumers when it advertised for Rogaine, a hair-loss treatment. Jon D. Hanson & Douglas A. Kysar, *Taking Behavioralism Seriously: Some Evidence of Market Manipulation,* 112 Harv. L.Rev. 1420, 1456 (1999). The ad targeted male consumers by posing the question, "Can an emerging bald spot . . . damage your ability to get along with others, influence your chance of obtaining a job or date or even interfere with your job performance?" [ ] A related ad featured an attractive woman asserting suggestively, "I know that a man who can afford Rogaine is a man who can afford me." [ ].

Advertising for Rogaine was the tip of the iceberg. Since drug manufacturers began marketing directly to consumers for products such as prescription drugs in the 1980s, "almost all pharmaceutical companies have engaged in this direct marketing practice." [ ] * * *

Pressure on consumers is an integral part of drug manufacturers' marketing strategy. From 1995 to 1996, drug companies increased advertising directed to consumers by ninety percent. [ ] In 1997, advertising costs of pharmaceutical products surpassed the half-billion dollar mark for the first time, "easily outpacing promotional efforts directed to physicians." Lars Noah, *Advertising Prescription Drugs to Consumers: Assessing the Regulatory and Liability Issues,* 32 Ga. L.Rev. 141, 141 (1997) * * * . These efforts are not just an essential part of manufacturers' marketing plans; they are an extremely successful one. As of December 1998, "because of its testimonials" in print and broadcast media by renowned personalities, sales of a product that treats male impotence had increased to $788 million, with approximately 7.5 million prescriptions having been written. [ ]

* * *

The American Medical Association (AMA) has long maintained a policy in opposition to product-specific prescription ads aimed at consumers. A 1992 study by the Annals of Internal Medicine reports that a peer review of 109 prescription ads found 92 per cent of the advertisements lacking in some manner. [ ] The difficulties that accompany this [type of advertising] practice are manifest. "The marketing gimmick used by the drug manufacturer often provides the consumer with a diluted variation of the risks associated with the drug product." Even without such manipulation, "[t]elevision spots lasting 30 or 60 seconds are not conducive to 'fair balance' [in presentation of risks]." Given such constraints, pharmaceutical ads often contain warnings of a general nature. However, "[r]esearch indicates that general warnings (for example, see your doctor) in [direct-to-consumer] advertisements do not give the consumer a sufficient understanding of the risks inherent in product use." Consumers often interpret such warnings as a "general reassurance" that their condition can be treated, rather than as a requirement that "specific vigilance" is needed to protect them from product risks. [ ]

## IV

### How Has the Law Responded to These Changes?

A. The new *Restatement (Third) of Torts* has left the issue to "developing case law."

Parallel to the developments in drug marketing, the American Law Institute was in the process of adopting the *Restatement (Third) of Torts: Products Liability* (1997). The comment to Section 6 explains that subsection (d)(1) sets forth the traditional rule of the learned intermediary that drug and medical device manufacturers are liable for failing to warn of a drug's risks only when the manufacturer fails to warn the health-care provider of risks attendant to a specific drug. *Restatement, supra,* § 6(d) comment a. That same comment also notes that subsection (d)(2) reflects decisional law and provides limited exceptions to the traditional rule by requiring manufacturers to warn patients in certain circumstances. [ ] Because situations may exist when the health-care provider assumes a "much-diminished role as an evaluator or decisionmaker," it is appropriate to impose a duty on the manufacturer to warn the patient directly. *Id.* at § 6d comment b. Despite the early effort to provide an exception to the doctrine in the case of direct marketing of pharmaceuticals to consumers, the drafters left the resolution of that issue to "developing case law." * * *

This is an entirely appropriate resolution. * * *

B. The New Jersey Products Liability Act does not legislate the boundaries of the learned intermediary doctrine.

* * * We believe that the part of the provision establishing "a presumption that a warning or instruction is adequate on drug or food products if the warning has been approved or prescribed by the Food and Drug Administration," [ ] will provide the benchmark for this decision.

* * *

C. Direct advertising of drugs to consumers alters the calculus of the learned intermediary doctrine.

* * *

A more recent review summarized the theoretical bases for the doctrine as based on four considerations.

> First, courts do not wish to intrude upon the doctor-patient relationship. From this perspective, warnings that contradict information supplied by the physician will undermine the patient's trust in the physician's judgment. Second, physicians may be in a superior position to convey meaningful information to their patients, as they must do to satisfy their duty to secure informed consent. Third, drug manufacturers lack effective means to communicate directly with patients, making it necessary to rely

on physicians to convey the relevant information. Unlike [over-the-counter products], pharmacists usually dispense prescription drugs from bulk containers rather than as unit-of-use packages in which the manufacturer may have enclosed labeling. Finally, because of the complexity of risk information about prescription drugs, comprehension problems would complicate any effort by manufacturers to translate physician labeling for lay patients. For this reason, even critics of the rule do not suggest that pharmaceutical companies should provide warnings only to patients and have no tort duty to warn physicians. [Noah, *supra,* 32 *Ga. L.Rev.* at 157–59 [ ].]

These premises: (1) reluctance to undermine the doctor patient-relationship; (2) absence in the era of "doctor knows best" of need for the patient's informed consent; (3) inability of drug manufacturer to communicate with patients; and (4) complexity of the subject; are all (with the possible exception of the last) absent in the direct-to-consumer advertising of prescription drugs.

First, with rare and wonderful exceptions, the " 'Norman Rockwell' image of the family doctor no longer exists." [ ]. Informed consent requires a patient-based decision rather than the paternalistic approach of the 1970s. [ ] The decision to take a drug is "not exclusively a matter for medical judgment." [ ].

Second, because managed care has reduced the time allotted per patient, physicians have considerably less time to inform patients of the risks and benefits of a drug. Sheryl Gay Stolberg, *Faulty Warning Labels Add to Risk in Prescription Drugs,* N.Y. Times, June 4, 1999, at A27. "In a 1997 survey of 1,000 patients, the F.D.A. found that only one-third had received information from their doctors about the dangerous side effects of drugs they were taking." [ ].

Third, having spent $1.3 billion on advertising in 1998, [ ] drug manufacturers can hardly be said to "lack effective means to communicate directly with patients," [ ]when their advertising campaigns can pay off in close to billions in dividends.

Consumer-directed advertising of pharmaceuticals thus belies each of the premises on which the learned intermediary doctrine rests.

First, the fact that manufacturers are advertising their drugs and devices to consumers suggests that consumers are active participants in their health care decisions, invalidating the concept that it is the doctor, not the patient, who decides whether a drug or device should be used. Second, it is illogical that requiring manufacturers to provide direct warnings to a consumer will undermine the patient-physician relationship, when, by its very nature, consumer-directed advertising encroaches on that relationship by encouraging consumers to ask for advertised products by name. Finally, consumer-directed advertising rebuts the notion that prescription drugs and devices and their potential adverse effects are too complex to be effectively communicated to lay consumers. Because the FDA requires that prescription drug and device advertising carry warnings, the consumer may reasonably presume that the advertiser guarantees the adequacy of its warnings. Thus, the common law duty to warm the ultimate consumer should apply. [ ].

When all of its premises are absent, as when direct warnings to consumers are mandatory, the learned intermediary doctrine, "itself an exception to the manufacturer's traditional duty to warn consumers directly of the risk associated with any product, simply drops out of the calculus, leaving the duty of the manufacturer to be determined in accordance with general principles of tort law." [ ] * * *

Concerns regarding patients' communication with and access to physicians are magnified in the context of medicines and medical devices furnished to women for reproductive decisions. * * * In MacDonald v. Ortho Pharmaceutical Corp., [ ], the plaintiff's use of oral contraceptives allegedly resulted in a stroke. The Massachusetts Supreme Court explained several reasons why contraceptives differ from other prescription drugs and thus "warrant the imposition of a common law duty on the manufacturer to warn users directly of associated risks." [ ] For example, after the patient receives the prescription, she consults with the physician to receive a prescription annually, leaving her an infrequent opportunity to "explore her questions and concerns about the medication with the prescribing physician." [ ]. Consequently, the limited participation of the physician leads to a real possibility that their communication during the annual checkup is insufficient. [ ] The court also explained that because oral contraceptives are drugs personally selected by the patient, a prescription is often not the result of a physician's skilled balancing of individual benefits and risks but originates, instead, as a product of patient choice. [ ] Thus, "the physician is relegated to a ... passive role." [ ]

Patient choice is an increasingly important part of our medical-legal jurisprudence. New Jersey has long since abandoned the "professional standard" in favor of the objectively-prudent-patient rule, recognizing the informed role of the patient in health-care decisions. [ ] Accordingly, a patient must be informed of material risks, which exist "when a reasonable patient, in what the physician knows or should know to be the patient's position, would be 'likely to attach significance to the risk or cluster of risks' in deciding whether to forego the proposed therapy or to submit to it." [ ] When a patient is the target of direct marketing, one would think, at a minimum, that the law would require that the patient not be misinformed about the product. It is one thing not to inform a patient about the potential side effects of a product; it is another thing to misinform the patient by deliberately withholding potential side effects while marketing the product as an efficacious solution to a serious health problem. Further, when one considers that many of these "life-style" drugs or elective treatments cause significant side effects without any curative effect, increased consumer protection becomes imperative, because these drugs are, by definition, not medically necessary.

* * *

D. Prescription drug manufacturers that market their products directly to consumers should be subject to claims by consumers if their advertising fails to provide an adequate warning of the product's dangerous propensities.

[The Court considered the role of FDA approval of prescription drugs and whether this should relieve manufacturers of exposure to state tort liability. The Court noted that "FDA regulations are pertinent in determining the nature and extent of any duty of care that should be imposed on pharmaceutical manufacturers with respect to direct-to-consumer advertising." Compliance with federal labeling creates a rebuttable presumption that a duty to warn has been met by the manufacturer.]

V.

[The Court then considered proximate cause–whether the patients in the case were actually affected by drug misinformation and, if so, whether the intervention of the treating physician breaks the causal chain. The first issue is left to the jury to resolve. As to the physician's role in possibly breaking the chain of causation, the Court observed that "the physician's role in deciding which prescription drug is selected has been altered."]

Although the physician writes the prescription, the physician's role in deciding which prescription drug is selected has been altered. With the arrival of direct-to-consumer advertising, patients now enter physicians' offices with "preconceived expectations about treatment because of information obtained from DTC [direct-to-consumer] advertisements." [ ] Consequently, [p]hysicians may relent to patient pressure, even if it is not in the best interest of the patient. In fact, physicians state that they are increasingly asked and pressured by their patients to prescribe drugs that the patient has seen advertised. For example, the diet drug combinations known as fen- phen was prescribed despite little hard scientific evidence of its potential side-effects. Physicians are under attack for prescribing the pills too often and too readily to inappropriate patients. Physicians argue that it is not their fault; rather, they claim pushy patients, prodded by DTC advertisements, pressed, wheedled, begged and berated them for quick treatments. This scenario comes at a time when physicians cannot afford to lose patients, because their income is already strained by managed care cost cutting. Physicians complain that it is impossible to compete with pharmaceutical companies' massive advertising budgets, and resign themselves to the fact that if consumers make enough noise, they will eventually relent to patient pressure. [ ]

* * *

* * * In the case of direct marketing of drugs, we believe that neither the physician nor the manufacturer should be entirely relieved of their respective duties to warn.

VI

To sum up, the dramatic shift in pharmaceutical marketing to consumers is based in large part on significant changes in the health-care system from fee-for-service to managed care. Managed care companies negotiate directly with pharmaceutical companies and then inform prescribers which medications are covered by the respective plans. Because managed care has made it more difficult for pharmaceutical companies to communicate with prescribers, the manufacturers have developed a different strategy, marketing to consumers.

* * *

The direct marketing of drugs to consumers generates a corresponding duty requiring manufacturers to warn of defects in the product. The FDA has established a comprehensive regulatory scheme for direct-to-consumer marketing of pharmaceutical products. Given the presumptive defense that is afforded to pharmaceutical manufacturers that comply with FDA requirements, we believe that it is fair to reinforce the regulatory scheme by allowing, in the case of direct-to-consumer marketing of drugs, patients deprived of reliable medical information to establish that the misinformation was a substantial factor contributing to their use of a defective pharmaceutical product.

Before concluding, we acknowledge that the procedural posture of this case casts defendant's product in an unfair light. Because the case arises on a motion for summary judgment, we are obliged to view the issues in the light most favorable to the claimants. We have no doubt that substantial proofs will be marshaled to show that Norplant is a safe and efficacious product and that Wyeth's advertising, if any, was fairly balanced. An agreed statement of facts submitted to the trial court suggested as much. And Norplant probably does not afford the best context in which to address the general question whether direct-to-consumer marketers of pharmaceutical products are unqualifiedly relieved of a duty to warn consumers of the dangerous propensities of a product. After all, in the case of Norplant, the role of the physician can never be insubstantial because only a physician may implant the device. Just as it is difficult to legislate a rule for every foreseeable circumstance, so too it is difficult to create a special rule of law for a hybrid product such as Norplant.

We are called upon, however, to resolve a question of law that will apply equally as well to an unprincipled marketer of pharmaceutical products as to a principled marketer. To place the issue in context, consider if prescription diet drugs were heavily advertised without warning of a known potential for heart damage.

* * *

That is the normative situation for which we must decide if a pharmaceutical manufacturer is free to engage in deceptive advertising to consumers. We believe that the answer in such a case should be no. Any question of fairness in imposing on the direct marketer of a product such as Norplant a duty to warn the targeted consumers will be resolved in the proximate cause analysis.

Finally, we return briefly to the main theme of the dissent [ ], that our decision is inconsistent with legislative mandate. We are certain that legislative codification of the learned intermediary doctrine—which generally relieves a pharmaceutical manufacturer of an independent duty to warn the ultimate user of prescription drugs, as long as it has supplied the physician with information about a drug's dangerous propensities—does not confer on pharmaceutical manufacturers a license to mislead or deceive consumers when those manufacturers elect to exercise their right to advertise their product directly to such consumers.

The judgment of the Appellate Division is reversed and the matter is remanded to the Law Division for further proceedings.

Pollock, J, filed a dissenting opinion in which Garibaldi, J., joined .

### *Notes and Questions*

1. The Learned Intermediary Rule provides protection for pharmaceutical manufacturers by shifting responsibility to physicians to properly prescribe drugs,

warn of their uses and side effects, and generally protect patients. As one court has stated, "the cornerstone of the learned intermediary doctrine is the ability of the physician to intervene between the drug and the patient, and to make an informed decision as to the course of treatment based on the physician's knowledge of the drug as well as the propensities of the patient." Cather v. Catheter Technology Corporation, 753 F.Supp. at 639. The assumption is that the treating physician is best situated to know the propensities of a drug and to know the needs and characteristics of his patient.

2. The aggressive marketing by drug companies directly to consumers has changed the environment in which physicians prescribe medications. The massive increase in direct-to-consumer advertising has become obvious over the past four years, as every popular magazine is full of ads for drugs to ailments that we may have, or that have been constructed to make us imagine we have them. Rosenthal et al., Promotion of Prescription Drugs to Consumers, 346 N.E.J.M. 498 (2002). See Breyer, dissenting in Thompson v. Western States Medical Center, 535 U.S. 357, 378–390, 122 S.Ct. 1497, 152 L.Ed.2d 563 (2002) (noting off label problems and aggressive advertising by the drug industry).

3. The increase in marketing means that more patients are prescribed new drugs, and may suffer adverse drug reactions (ADRs). Patients are exposed to new drugs with unknown toxic effects; nearly 20 million patients took at least 1 of 5 drugs withdrawn form the market between September 1997 and September 1998. Three of these five drugs were new, having been on the market for less than 2 years. The authors of one study concluded that "[m]any serious ADRs are discovered only after a drug has been on the market for years. Only half of newly discovered serious ADRs are detected and documented in the Physicians' Desk Reference within 7 years after drug approval." See Karen E. Lasser et al, Timing of New Black Box Warnings and Withdrawals for Prescription Medications, 287 JAMA 2215, 2218 (2002)(Lasser).

4. Despite limited knowledge about the safety of new drugs, their market uptake and sales volume may be explosive. The pharmaceutical industry promotes the early use of new drugs, and influences physicians' adoption of such drugs. Direct-to-consumer advertising also generates high volume of new drug prescriptions. Drug firms may rush new drugs to market because of concerns about patent life, a desire to mold prescribing habits prior to market entry of competitors, and hopes for a fast "ramp-up" in sales that will encourage investors and increase stock prices. New drug safety may be further compromised by the apparent failure by drug companies to conduct post-marketing (phase 4) studies, which are required by the FDA when a safety question arises during the preapproval period. Id. at 2219 The authors make the following recommendation:

> .... [C]linicians should avoid using new drugs when older, similarly efficacious agents are available. Patients who must use new drugs should be informed of the drug's limited experience and safety record, and be observed for possible hepatic, hematologic, or cardiac toxicity. Clinicians should report ADRS to MEDWATCH, the voluntary reporting system. Lasser at 2219–20.

5. Drugs and devices involved in cases invoking the doctrine to dismiss suits include Viagra (Brumley v. Pfizer, Inc., 149 F.Supp.2d 305 (S.D.Tex.2001) (Viagra manufacturer provided adequate warning of cardiac risk under l.i. doctrine); spinal implants (McCombs v. Synthes, 553 S.E.2d 17 (2001); pedicle screws (Dyer v. Danek Med., Inc., 115 F.Supp.2d 732 (N.D. Tex. 2000)(Pl. failed to demonstrate safer alternative); penile implants (Williams v. American Med. Sys., 248 Ga.App.

682, 548 S.E.2d 371 (2001); breast implants (Miller v. Bristol–Myers Squibb Co., 121 F.Supp.2d 831 (D.Md.2000); surgical lasers (Banker v. Hoehn, 278 A.D.2d 720, 718 N.Y.S.2d 438 (App.Div.2000); and contraceptive implants (Wyeth–Ayerst Labs. v. Medrano, 28 S.W.3d 87 (Tex.App.2000).

6. The doctrine does not govern the adequacy of a drug manufacturer's warnings in a class action involving a nonsteroidal anti-inflammatory drug. Rivera v. Wyeth–Ayerst Labs. Co., 121 F.Supp.2d 614 (S.D.Tex.2000). And where the representations and verbal assurances from a drug manufacturer's sales agent contradict or supersede the manufacturer's product insert, the manufactuer can be liable for failure to warn despite the consumer's awareness of the package inserts. Brown v. Glaxo, Inc., 790 So.2d 35 (La.Ct.App.2000).

7. Critics are concerned about judicial abandonment of the Learned Intermediary Rule. "Shifting some of the tort liability from physicians to drug companies may have unintended effects on physician incentives to discuss risks and on patients' incentives to seek out those discussions, and could well result in drug price increases." Michelle Mello, Meredith Rosenthal, and Peter J. Neumann, Direct–To–Consumer Advertising and Shared Liability for Pharmaceutical Manufacturers, 289 J.A.M.A. 477, 480 (2003). Mello, et al., recommend a case-by-case evaluation of the Learned Intermediary Rule in failure-to-warn cases, with the courts looking at several factors:

> [T]he amount of physician discretion and evaluation involved in the prescribing decision, the need for an individualized patient assessment, and the number of risks involved and the practicability of meaningfully conveying them in a written or verbal warning. Also relevant may be the aggressiveness and truthfulness of the advertising campaign, with extremes cases of abusive marketing presenting a stronger case for heightened liability."

8. Federal Policy. The problem of post-market surveillance and the need to better handle it is finally being taken seriously. See Report of the Quality Interagency Coordination Task Force (QuIC) to the President, Doing What Counts for Patient Safety: Federal Actions to Reduce Medical Errors and Their Impact (February 2000). The Task Force has recommended in Recommendation 7.3 that the Food and Drug Administration (FDA) should increase attention to the safe use of drugs in both pre-and post-marketing processes through the following actions: develop and enforce standards for the design of drug packaging and labeling that will maximize safety in use; require pharmaceutical companies to test (using FDA-approved methods) proposed drug names to identify and remedy potential sound-alike and look-alike confusion with existing drug names; and work with physicians, pharmacists, consumers, and others to establish appropriate responses to problems identified through post-marketing surveillance, especially for concerns that are perceived to require immediate response to protect the safety of patients.

## H. PHYSICIAN OFF–LABEL PRESCRIBING OF FDA–APPROVED DRUGS

Many drugs are approved by the FDA for a narrow clinical purpose, but may have other uses supported by clinical research even though the FDA has not yet approved them for these off-label uses. This is another form of physician experimentation, actively encouraged by the pharmaceutical companies in both direct and subtle ways.

## RICHARDSON v. MILLER

Court of Appeals of Tennessee, 2000.
44 S.W.3d 1.

[A prenatal patient who suffered a heart attack brought action against a physician who ordered use of infusion pump to administer a drug subcutaneously to arrest premature labor, against supplier of pump, and against other parties, alleging medical malpractice and products liability. When the contractions showed no signs of abating, Dr. Miller had opted to affirmatively retard Ms. Richardson's premature labor by tocolysis, *i.e.*, giving her medication to stop her contractions by relaxing her uterine muscles.]

Dr. Miller first prescribed and administered magnesium sulfate with limited success. On June 24, 1993, when the frequency of Ms. Richardson's contractions did not decrease, Dr. Miller ordered a different tocolytic drug–terbutaline sulfate ("terbutaline"). While terbutaline had been approved by the FDA only for treating bronchial asthma, it was also being widely used as a tocolytic agent because it relaxes smooth muscles, including the muscles of the uterus. Her doctor decided to use a terbutaline infusion pump, even though he lacked experience with them. Ciba–Geigy's package insert warned that the drug is dangerous to use for tocolysis, producing severe adverse reactions to women in labor.

\* \* \*

Ms. Richardson received regular subcutaneous doses of terbutaline for approximately the next forty-eight hours. Her labor contractions did not stop immediately; however, they eventually began to decrease. By around noon on June 27, three days after their onset, the contractions stopped. Although Ms. Richardson experienced shakiness and what she characterized as a "rapid heart rate," the nurses' notes stated that Ms. Richardson's vital signs were "stable" around the time her contractions stopped.

Ms. Richardson visited with her sister at approximately 3:00 p.m. on June 27. She became upset when her sister told her that their mother's dog had died. At that time, Ms. Richardson's chest, arm, jaw, and head began hurting. When a nurse arrived, Ms. Richardson exclaimed that she was having a heart attack and insisted that she be removed from the terbutaline pump. After some confusion and hesitation, the nurses disconnected Ms. Richardson from the pump, and she was subsequently transferred to a critical care unit where an electrocardiogram confirmed that she had, in fact, experienced a heart attack.

That night Ms. Richardson gave birth to a healthy, six-pound boy. A few days later, Ms. Richardson underwent open-heart by-pass surgery to repair a tear in her coronary artery associated with her heart attack. After recuperating for several days, Ms. Richardson and her baby were discharged from Memorial Hospital.

[The court gave a superb and lengthy discussion of the FDA's history and approach to off-label uses. It acknowledged that "[o]ff-label prescriptions are now an integral part of the modern practice of medicine."]

\* \* \*

We adopt the majority approach regarding the introduction and evidentiary weight to be given to FDA-approved drug labeling and the parallel PDR reference. Neither of these materials, by themselves, are prima facie evidence of the prescribing physician's standard of care. Thus, proof of a departure from the recommendations in a drug's labeling or PDR reference is not alone sufficient to prove a breach of the standard of care. However, the labeling and the PDR reference can provide significant assistance in identifying the standard of care. Accordingly, we find that a prescription drug's labeling or its PDR reference, when introduced along with other expert evidence on the standard of care, is admissible to assist the trier-of-fact to determine whether the drug presented an unacceptable risk to the patient.

## VI. DAMAGE INNOVATIONS

### B. INCREASED RISKS AND FEAR OF THE FUTURE

**Add, at p. 269, a new note 3:**

3. In Dillon v. Evanston Hospital, 771 N.E.2d 357 (Ill. 2002), a catheter was left in plaintiff's body. Because it migrated in the body it had become too dangerous to try to remove it, though there was some risk that it would migrate to the heart and cause serious trouble. The Court adopted the rationale of Petriello v. Kalman to allow recovery of a percentage of the risk that could now be shown: "We hold simply that a plaintiff must be permitted to recover for all demonstrated injuries. The burden is on the plaintiff to prove that the defendant's negligence increased the plaintiff's risk of future injuries. A plaintiff can obtain compensation for a future injury that is not reasonably certain to occur, but the compensation would reflect the low probability."

# Chapter 5

# THE PROFESSIONAL–PATIENT RELATIONSHIP

## INTRODUCTION

**Add, at p. 272, before Part I, the following:**

Insurance and pre-employment physicals continue to divide the courts. In Reed v. Bojarski, 166 N.J. 89, 764 A.2d 433 (2001), an employer paid the defendant physician to give the plaintiff a pre-employment physical. The defendant discovered a serious medical problem and told the employer but did not tell the plaintiff. The court held that the defendant had a non-delegable duty to tell plaintiff of potentially serious medical problems found. That duty was not met by informing the employer. *Contra*, see Petrosky v. Brasner, 279 A.D.2d 75, 718 N.Y.S.2d 340 (App.Div.2001), where the decedent had a physical exam as part of application for life insurance. He was explicitly advised that the tests were not for the purpose of treatment or evaluation by the medical technician. The EKG results were abnormal but nobody told the decedent, who died two months later of a myocardial infarction. The court, 4–1, held that no duty of disclosure existed, since there were no misleading statements, decedent had been told not to rely on the tests, and there was no showing that he relied in any way.

## I. THE CONTRACT BETWEEN PATIENT AND PHYSICIAN

### A. EXPRESS AND IMPLIED CONTRACT

**Add, at p. 281, before Part B, a new Note, 8:**

8. **Trust in Medical Relationships.** Trust has been revived as a unifying theme in analyzing medical ethics, professionalism, and the doctor-patient relationship generally. In the words of Mark Hall, "[t]rust is the core, defining characteristic of the doctor-patient relationship—the "glue" that holds the relationship together and makes it possible. Preserving, justifying, and enhancing trust is a prominent objective in health care law and public policy and is the fundamental goal of much of medical ethics." Mark Hall, Law, Medicine, and Trust, 55 Stan. L. Rev. 463, 470–71 (2002). Hall concludes as follows:

> This article has sought to establish the following foundational truths about medical care delivery:

(1) Trust is essential and unavoidable in medical relationships. Patients need and want to trust, and without trust medical relationships never form or entirely dysfunctional.

(2) Beyond the mechanics of forming and conducting treatment relationships, trust confers therapeutic benefit by activating non-specific or self-healing mechanisms, or by enhancing the effects of active therapies. Medical trust has this unique instrumental value because of its strong emotional content, which results from the deep vulnerability of illness that gives rise to trust.

(3) Law can (and does) enforce trust-related expectations, punish violations of trust, facilitate the psychology of trust, and undermine trust. These effects occur both through direct regulation and through the law's expressive function and its relationship with social and professional norms.

(4) These legal attitudes toward trust sometimes come into conflict because enforcing trust or punishing its violations can also weaken the psychological foundations of trust.

(5) Striking the best compromise among competing legal stances toward trust often requires subtlety, complexity, and detailed empirical information about the psychology of trust.

(6) Honoring these principles may require that formal legal rights be softened somewhat with the therapeutic reality of trust.

As you examine the problems of quality, access, control, and patient personhood during your examination of health law, consider Hall's unifying theory of trust, and consider whether it helps to explain the law's reaction to physicians, hospitals, and managed care plans. Does it work best as a unifying principle as to the law's treatment of physicians?

## D. EXCULPATORY CLAUSES

**Add, at p. 289, a new section 2:**

2. Binding arbitration, virtually universal in agreements between stock brokers and customers, is being tried by physicians as they seek ways to avoid malpractice exposure. The Florida Medical Association, for example, has a program instructing physicians in their use. The goal is to help physicians reduce their liability risk. California has a binding arbitration provision in MICRA (Medical Injury Compensation Reform Act) and it is estimated that about 10% of medical malpractice disputes go to binding arbitration. The Florida standard provision reads:

> The patient agrees that any controversy, including any malpractice claim, arising out of or in any way relating to the diagnosis, treatment, or care of the patient by the undersigned physician ... shall be submitted to binding arbitration.... The patient further agrees that any controversy arising out of or in any way relating to the past diagnosis, treatment, or care of the patient by a provider of medical services, or the provider's agents or employees, shall likewise be submitted to binding arbitration.

See Tanya Albert, Patients In Liability Hot Spots Asked to Arbitrate, Not Litigate, AMA News 1 (February 10, 2003).

What objections might be raised to such forms of binding arbitration imposed by contract?

## II. CONFIDENTIALITY AND DISCLOSURE IN THE PHYSICIAN–PATIENT RELATIONSHIP

### B. FEDERAL MEDICAL PRIVACY STANDARDS

**Add, at p. 327, the following paragraphs to Note 1, after the first paragraph:**

The original Privacy Rule was published on December 28, 2000, and modifications were adopted on August 14, 2002. The biggest change was the elimination of prior patient consent requirement for uses and disclosures of identifiable health information for treatment, payment, and health care operations. The Office of Civil Rights released guidance as to the Rules and the changes on December 3, 2002 (at *www.hhs.gov/ocr/hipaa.*) OCR noted that "[t]he consent requirement created the unintended effect of preventing health care providers from providing timely, quality health care to patients in a variety of circumstances." The example they give is of a pharmacist being unable to fill a prescription or search for harmful drug interactions before an individual arrives at the pharmacy. Written permission is no longer required before a patient's information can be disclosed. Instead, providers must give patients notice of their new rights and make a "good faith effort" to obtain written acknowledgment from patients saying they had received the information.

Patient advocates are concerned that the changes abolish the traditional control that patients have had over their records, and may discourage them from revealing information to their physicians that is necessary for their treatment. It may also encourage doctors not to record critical but embarrassing information in the medical chart of that patient.

The definition of "minimum necessary" has not changed, and the OCR guidance responds to worries among providers that they could not discuss a patient's treatment among themselves. "Disclosures for treatment purposes (including requests for disclosures) between health care providers are explicitly exempted from the minimum necessary requirements."

Incidental uses and disclosures of individual identifiable health information are generally allowed when the covered entity has in place reasonable safeguards and "minimum necessary" policies and procedures to protect an individual's privacy. OCR confirmed that providers may have confidential conversations with other providers and patients even when there is a chance that they might be overheard. Nurses can speak over the phone with a patient or family member about the patient's condition. Providers may also discuss a patient's condition during training rounds at an academic medical institution.

## III. INFORMED CONSENT: THE PHYSICIAN'S OBLIGATION

### B. THE LEGAL FRAMEWORK OF INFORMED CONSENT

#### 1. *Negligence as a Basis for Recovery*

**Add, at p. 358, a new Note 6:**

6. Some courts are willing to consider a more complex view of informed consent in light of the special needs of the patient. In Jacobo v. Binur, 70 S.W.3d 330 (Tex.App.2002), Donna Jacobo sued Dr. Binur for his failure to obtain her

informed consent to a double mastectomy. The court denied the defense motion for summary judgment. Binur was an assistant surgeon or co-surgeon during mastectomy. Jacobo claimed that her consent was not properly informed, since she was not told that the mastectomy might not have been necessary. Dr. Binur told her when she asked about her risk of developing breast cancer, that "it was not a matter of "if" she would develop it but a matter of "when", that there was no risk that the mastectomy was unnecessary because it was a certainty that she would develop breast cancer.

Jacobo's witness testified that the risk was not 100%, that a biopsy should have been ordered of the lump in her breast to see if cancer was present. The court concurred with the expert that because she was not provided with a more accurate description of her risk for breast cancer, she was not in a position to make a truly informed choice. Her mother had just died from breast cancer, she was distressed, and she needed more consultation, support, and information.

## 2. *Disclosure of Physician–Specific Risk Information*

**Add, at p. 367, to Note 2:**

In Howard v. University Medicine & Dentistry of New Jersey, 172 N.J. 537, 800 A.2d 73 (2002), the plaintiff went to see a surgeon about his back problems. The procedure went badly. The plaintiff suit claimed in part that the defendant had misrepresented both his credentials and his experience in doing procedure he proposed. The court held that the plaintiff may claim lack of informed consent because of the false answers allegedly given by the surgeon. They left open the question as to whether a physician might have an affirmative duty to disclose the information in question.

In Duttry v. Patterson, 565 Pa. 130, 771 A.2d 1255 (2001), a surgeon misrepresented the number of times he had done the procedure in question, saying sixty when he had done it nine times. The Court held that held that surgeon's personal characteristics and experience are not relevant to the issue of informed consent, though the case might be analyzed as one for misrepresentation. The dissent responded: "I fail to see how a patient who specifically asks her physician how many times he has performed a surgical procedure can be said to have given her informed consent to surgery when the physician misleads the patient by grossly exaggerating his experience."

# Chapter 6

# LIABILITY OF HEALTH CARE INSTITUTIONS

## I. FROM IMMUNITY TO VICARIOUS LIABILITY

### B. VICARIOUS LIABILITY DOCTRINE

#### 2. *Stretching Vicarious Liability Doctrine*

**Add, at p. 433, before Problem: Creating a Shield, a new section e:**

e. *The Non–Delegable Duty Doctrine*

### SIMMONS v. TUOMEY REGIONAL MEDICAL CENTER

Supreme Court of South Carolina, 2000.
341 S.C. 32, 533 S.E.2d 312.

WALLER, J.

This case presents the novel issue of whether a hospital owes a common law nondelegable duty to render competent service to its emergency room patients, such that it may not avoid liability for the negligent acts of emergency room physicians hired as independent contractors under a contract between the hospital and a separate corporation.

\* \* \*

### FACTS

P.J. McBride received medical care at Tuomey Regional's emergency room for a head injury he suffered in a moped accident. His daughter, Simmons, signed a form consenting to treatment at the emergency room that contained a provision stating, "THE PHYSICIANS PRACTICING IN THIS EMERGENCY ROOM ARE NOT EMPLOYEES OF TUOMEY REGIONAL MEDICAL CENTER. THEY ARE INDEPENDENT PHYSICIANS, AS ARE ALL PHYSICIANS PRACTICING IN THIS HOSPITAL." Simmons said she did not read the form because she was upset about her father's injuries. She believed the physicians were Tuomey Regional employees.

The emergency room physicians examined McBride, but released him without treating a serious head injury that was visible on the back of his head, Simmons alleged. The physicians apparently believed his confused state was a result of intoxication. McBride was returned to Tuomey Regional's emergency room the next day by ambulance after his condition worsened. This time, physicians diagnosed him as suffering from a subdural hematoma and transferred him to a Columbia hospital. McBride died about six weeks later of complications caused by the head injury, Simmons alleged.

Cooper, who had suffered a previous heart attack, experienced chest pains while driving. A friend drove him to Tuomey Regional's emergency room, where Cooper informed the receptionist he was having a heart attack and asked for immediate help. Cooper alleged he sat on a gurney for at least 1 ½ hours before seeing a doctor, causing him serious injury. Unlike Simmons, he did not sign any form containing the "independent physician" statement. He believed the physicians were Tuomey Regional employees. Both Simmons and Cooper stated in affidavits they saw no signs or other indications that the physicians, working in an area that was an integral part of the hospital campus, were not Tuomey Regional employees.

Tuomey Regional signed a contract with Coastal Physicians Services, Inc. (Coastal), in 1987. The contract describes Coastal as an "independent contractor" that provides "independent-contractor physicians" to work in Tuomey Regional's emergency room on an around-the-clock basis. The contract provides that, "[e]xcept as hereinafter provided and to the extent practice and professional conduct of all Hospital's medical staff members are regulated by the Hospital, the Physicians shall not be under the direction or supervision of the Hospital in performance of their Emergency Department duties."

The contract states the physicians are not Tuomey Regional's employees, and the hospital does not directly pay or provide any benefits to the physicians. Under a 1989 amendment to the original contract, Tuomey Regional bills patients and their insurers for emergency room services provided by both it and Coastal physicians. Tuomey Regional then pays Coastal under a formula based on the "direct cost" plus a specified amount for each hour Coastal physicians work in the emergency room. Coastal physicians must maintain their own liability insurance coverage in minimum amounts.

Coastal physicians must meet many of the same requirements as any physician who seeks staff privileges, i.e., the right to admit patients to Tuomey Regional. Coastal physicians must, for example, apply and qualify for medical staff privileges in accordance with the bylaws and regulations of the medical staff. Their professional conduct is governed by Tuomey Regional and medical staff bylaws and rules, as well as standards set by the Joint Commission on the Accreditation of Hospitals, applicable statutes, and regulations of governmental bodies.

Tuomey Regional, however, maintains much more extensive control over Coastal physicians than physicians who only have staff privileges. For example, Tuomey Regional selects the emergency room medical director from among the physicians, with the consent of Coastal. Coastal physicians must remain on Tuomey Regional's premises during their shift, and must provide services to anyone who desires treatment. Tuomey Regional has the authority to prevent any physician from working in the emergency room when it "deems the clinical performance of any Physician ... to be detrimental to the health or safety of Hospital's patients." Within five days written notice, Coastal "shall reassign that Physician from the Hospital and shall not permit him to provide further services at the Hospital without the Hospital's approval."

Tuomey Regional retains the last word in most disagreements. The contract provides that "[a]ll matters relating to the Hospital's policies, rules, regulations, services, and other items of conduct wherein the Physicians may be involved, shall be determined jointly by [Coastal] and the Hospital's Chief Executive Officer, and in the event of a disagreement ... the decision of the Hospital shall be final."

### ISSUE

Did the Court of Appeals err in holding that hospitals have a nondelegable duty under the common law to render competent service to the patients of their emergency rooms?

\* \* \*

### DISCUSSION

It is uncontroverted that the role that hospitals play in the delivery of health care across America has changed dramatically since the days when the doctrine of charitable immunity shielded hospitals from malpractice liability.

> The hospital of the early to mid-nineteenth century would not be recognizable as such to a modern observer. "Respectable" people who fell sick or who were injured were treated by their doctors at home; only the lowest classes of society sought help in the "hospital," which was most often a separate wing on the almshouse. As late as 1873, there were only 178 hospitals in the United States, with a total of 50,000 beds. These hospitals were private charities, and their trustees were usually unable to raise sufficient funding to provide a pleasant stay. The hospital of the time was dirty, crowded and full of contagious diseases. The "nurses" were usually former patients. Doctors, who were not paid, tended the ill for a few hours per week out of a sense of charity mixed with the knowledge that they could "practice" their cures on the poor and charge young medical students for instruction in the healing arts. These young "house doctors" also worked without pay, practicing cures on the ill.

Steven R. Owens, Note, 1990 Wis. L.Rev. 1129, 1131–32 (description drawn from C. Rosenberg, *The Care of Strangers—The Rise of America's Hospital System* (1987)).

Until the 1940s, hospitals were protected from malpractice liability by the doctrine of charitable immunity. Courts and legislators reasoned that a charitable institution should devote its resources to the endeavor at hand and the greater good, not to reimbursing individuals injured by the institution's negligent acts. [ ]

Hospitals and the medical sciences improved dramatically throughout the twentieth century, and with those improvements came a concomitant increase in the importance of hospitals' role in providing medical care. Today, hospitals compete aggressively in providing the latest medical technology and the best facilities, as well as in attracting patients and physicians who will funnel patients to them. Hospitals not only strive to be a source of pride in the local community, but they also seek to avoid operating at a financial loss. Regardless of whether they are profit-seeking enterprises, they are run much like any large corporation and must operate in a fiscally responsible manner. Like any business dependent upon attracting individual people as customers, hospitals in the aggregate spend billions to advertise their facilities and services in a variety of media, from newspapers and billboards to television and the Internet. Among the many forces that have caused this sea change are the commercialization of the practice of medicine, the public's demand for access to modern medical technology, the prevalence and impact of government-funded programs such as Medicare and Medicaid, and the rise of managed care in the private sector. [ ]

\* \* \*

It is against this backdrop that we are asked to decide whether the Court of Appeals properly imposed a common law nondelegable duty on hospitals with regard to physicians who work in their emergency rooms. Tuomey Regional presents several arguments explaining why it believes the Court of Appeals erred.

\* \* \*

This Court and the Court of Appeals have applied the nondelegable duty doctrine in several situations. An employer has a nondelegable duty to employees to provide a reasonably safe work place and suitable tools, and remains vicariously liable for injuries caused by unsafe activities or tools under the employer's control. A landlord who undertakes repair of his property by use of a contractor has a nondelegable duty to see that the repair is done properly, and remains vicariously liable for injuries caused by improper repairs.

\* \* \*

Tuomey Regional mentions some of the above cases and argues they are distinguishable because in this case it is the independent-contractor physician—not the hospital—who controls a patient's medical treatment. Tuomey Regional also contends regulations promulgated by the state Department of Health and Environmental Control do not impose such a duty.

We find Tuomey Regional's arguments unpersuasive. The cited cases clearly illustrate that a person or entity entrusted with important duties in certain circumstances may not assign those duties to someone else and then expect to walk away unscathed when things go wrong. A principle that applies in cases of poorly repaired brick floors and sloppily loaded cargo certainly applies to situations in which people must entrust that most personal of things, their physical well-being, to physicians at an emergency room intimately connected with and closely controlled by a hospital. However, as explained further below, we do not believe it is necessary, as the Court of Appeals did, to impose an *absolute* nondelegable duty on hospitals.

\* \* \*

Alaska, Florida, and New York courts have applied the nondelegable duty doctrine to care provided by a hospital's emergency room physicians. [ ]

In contrast, Texas and Missouri courts have rejected the nondelegable duty doctrine in connection with care provided by emergency room physicians. [ ]

While few courts have adopted the nondelegable duty doctrine, numerous courts have endorsed the doctrine of apparent authority or apparent agency to hold hospitals liable when an injured patient proves a physician was the hospital's apparent agent. * * * [ ]

Under the apparent agency doctrine, the injured patient must establish that (1) the hospital consciously or impliedly represented the physician to be its agent, (2) the patient relied upon the representation, and (3) the patient changed his position to his detriment in reliance on the representation. [ ] The focus is on the acts and conduct of the principal, not the agent. [ ]

* * *

In sum, our decision is amply supported by law in other jurisdictions. Courts throughout the nation have struggled with this issue, and nearly all have held hospitals liable under one or more theories. The Ohio cases illustrate what we perceive to be the likely trend among the many courts that have adopted an apparent agency theory in these cases. Under that trend, hospitals will not be allowed to escape liability by giving last-minute notice of independent-contractor practitioners through admission forms or emergency room signs. The result is that hospitals may be held liable for the malpractice of their emergency room physicians, regardless of whether it is through a theory of apparent agency or nondelegable duty.

We also conclude it is appropriate to find a nondelegable duty in this case because apparent agency in its traditional form requires a representation by the principal (the hospital) and proof of reliance on that representation by the patient. [ ] Most courts applying the apparent agency doctrine in the emergency room setting have relaxed those requirements substantially in order to hold the hospital liable, a decision criticized by some commentators. [ ]

The point often made in the cases and commentary, either implicitly or explicitly, is that expecting a patient in an emergency situation to debate or comprehend the meaning and extent of any representations by the hospital—which likely would be based on an opinion gradually formed over the years and not on any single representation—imposes an unfair and improper burden on the patient. Consequently, we believe the better solution, grounded primarily in public policy reasons we explain below, is to impose a nondelegable duty on hospitals.

Tuomey Regional asserts that no public policy considerations support the Court of Appeals' conclusion. First, Tuomey Regional argues the duty is unnecessary because physicians must carry professional liability insurance, making judgments collectible. Second, holding hospitals liable will not improve care because hospitals may not practice medicine. Third, patients do not care whether a physician is a hospital employee or independent contractor, and no one in need of medical care decides where to go based upon the relationship of the physicians with the hospital. Finally, Tuomey Regional argues that the adoption of the nondelegable duty doctrine in this setting is a decision for the Legislature to make, not the courts. We disagree.

Commentators have debated whether compensation is a goal of tort law, or simply a means by which other goals are accomplished. [ ] Regardless, Tuomey Regional's focus on the availability of compensation misses another important aspect of tort law: the desire to give parties with crucial duties a keen incentive to do everything possible to avoid violating those duties. [ ] Imposing a nondelegable duty on hospitals in this context fulfills both goals.

We reject Tuomey Regional's insistence that "hospitals may not practice medicine"—a point it has asserted throughout this litigation. It is true that a hospital may not decide that Patient X is to receive a dose of a particular medication twice a day; nor may a hospital order that Patient Y undergo specified tests at 2 p.m. on a particular day. Only licensed physicians may make such decisions. But the "practice of medicine" encompasses a much broader range of actions than those specific directives. It includes innumerable decisions regarding the type and quality of medical equipment, staffing levels, and the renovation or addition of facilities. Hospital and emergency room administrators make countless decisions that intimately affect the "practice of medicine" all day, every day. The contract between Tuomey Regional and Coastal in the present cases illustrates how the hospital, in ways both obvious and subtle, affects and controls the practice of medicine. [ ]

Furthermore, we disagree with Tuomey Regional's assertion that patients do not decide where to seek care based on the relationship between a hospital and its physicians. While an emergency room may be selected because it is the nearest one, patients in urban areas often may choose from several. Patients make those decisions based primarily on the reputation of the hospital, which it often has aggressively promoted, and not on the reputation of individual emergency room physicians. In such situations, patients understandably and correctly expect to be cared for by physicians and other staff members carefully selected and approved by the hospital.

We reject Tuomey Regional's contention that this decision should be left to the Legislature. Courts created, then eliminated, charitable immunity for hospitals. The same policy considerations at work in those cases make it proper for the courts to impose this nondelegable duty on hospitals. [ ]

We conclude the Court of Appeals properly outlined and applied the public policy considerations in question. Our decision, like those made by other courts that have considered this issue and held hospitals liable under one or more theories, is grounded primarily in those considerations. Given the fundamental shift in the role that a hospital plays in our health care system, the commercialization of American medicine, and the public perception of the unity of a hospital and its emergency room, we hold that a hospital owes a nondelegable duty to render competent service to its emergency room patients.

However, we conclude it is not necessary, as the Court of Appeals did in the cases at hand, to impose an *absolute* nondelegable duty on hospitals. Instead, we adopt the approach expressed in Restatement (Second) of Torts: Employers of Contractors § 429 (1965). That section, sometimes described as ostensible agency, provides:

> One who employs an independent contractor to perform services for another which are accepted in the reasonable belief that the services are being rendered by the employer or by his servants, is subject to liability

for physical harm caused by the negligence of the contractor in supplying such services, to the same extent as though the employer were supplying them himself or by his servants.

Section 429 applies not only when the injured person accepts services in the belief they are being rendered by the independent contractor's employer, but also when a third person accepts such services on the injured person's behalf and reasonably believes the services are being rendered to the injured person by the independent contractor's employer. *See* section 429 cmt. a; Restatement (Second) of Torts, Introductory Note to §§ 416–429 at p. 394 (explaining that various nondelegable duties are imposed "in situations in which, for reasons of policy, the employer is not permitted to shift the responsibility for the proper conduct of the work to the contractor").

Under section 429, the plaintiff must show that (1) the hospital held itself out to the public by offering to provide services; (2) the plaintiff looked to the hospital, rather than the individual physician, for care; and (3) a person in similar circumstances reasonably would have believed that the physician who treated him or her was a hospital employee. When the plaintiff does so, the hospital will be held vicariously liable for any negligent or wrongful acts committed by the treating physician. The hospital may attempt to avoid liability for the physician's acts by demonstrating the plaintiff failed to prove these factors.

Numerous courts have relied on section 429 in decisions allowing a plaintiff to attempt to hold a hospital vicariously liable for a purportedly independent physician's negligent acts. [ ]

Although the present cases involve emergency room physicians, our decision is not necessarily limited to such physicians. It is limited, however, to those situations in which a patient seeks services at the hospital as an institution, and is treated by a physician who reasonably appears to be a hospital employee. Our holding does not extend to situations in which the patient is treated in an emergency room by the patient's own physician after arranging to meet the physician there. Nor does our holding encompass situations in which a patient is admitted to a hospital by a private, independent physician whose only connection to a particular hospital is that he or she has staff privileges to admit patients to the hospital. Such patients could not reasonably believe his or her physician is a hospital employee. [ ]

Viewed in the light most favorable to respondents, the record in the present cases shows that they may allege that they or their relative sought care at Tuomey Regional's emergency room based on the hospital's offering of services to the public, that they looked to the hospital to provide the care, not an individual physician, and that they were treated by physicians who reasonably appeared to be hospital employees. Genuine issues of material fact exist; therefore, summary judgment is not appropriate.

* * *

## Notes and Questions

1. The court outlines the substantial policy reasons for imposing a nondelegable duty on hospitals in a variety of treatment situations. Then it falls back on reliance on apparent authority doctrine. Why? What difference will § 429 mean to a plaintiff's proof of her case against a hospital?

2. Other courts are moving toward restrictions on the independent contract defense. In Baragan v. Providence Memorial Hospital, 2000 WL 1731286 (Tex. App.—El Paso) (Nov.22, 2000), a twelve-year old boy was admitted to the ER of Providence Memorial Hospital upon instructions given by Dr. Roberto Canales, who informed Omar's parents that he would meet them there. The boy was in acute pain from the torsion and atrophy of a testicle. The parents had been waiting over an hour for Dr. Canales when the father requested that one of Providence's doctors see his son. Dr. Wade examined Omar without any further discussion as to the doctor's status. There were delays in the diagnosis, treatment, and surgery of the torsion and during surgery, the testicle was found to be nonviable and had to be removed. The "Conditions of Admission" form which Mrs. Barragan was required to sign was a one-page preprinted document written entirely in English and set in eight point type. The form included a provision stating that doctors of medicine, including emergency room physicians, "are independent contractors and are not employees of Providence Memorial Hospital." In January 1992, Providence had entered into a contract with Texas Emergency Room Services ("TERS"), to obtain independent contractor physicians ("physicians"), to treat patients in Providence's emergency department. The contract provided that physicians were required to cooperate with Providence in informing patients of their independent status, and to comply with all of Providence's policies, bylaws, and regulations for the hospital's medical staff. All physicians' fees were to be approved by Providence and the hospital was responsible for their billing and collection. By the terms of an agreement between Dr. Wade and TERS, he was an independent contractor for TERS.

The court ran through the arguments for aborting the independent contractor defense: hospitals are "run much like any large corporation and must operate in a financially responsible manner"; the community sees the hospital as the provider of medical services.... [P]atients come to the hospital to be cured, and the doctors who practice there are perceived to be the hospital's instrumentalities, regardless of the nature of the private arrangements between the hospital and a physician." The result is hospital liability for the malpractice of their ER physicians, whether through ostensible agency or manifestations of control, both of which could be found here.

## II. HOSPITAL DIRECT LIABILITY

### E. THE EMERGENCE OF CORPORATE NEGLIGENCE

Add, at p. 468, before the Problem: Referrals, a new section 3:

#### 3. *The Duty of a Hospital to Obtain Patient Consent*

A hospital normally has no legal duty to obtain a patient's consent, since the treating physician or surgeon is responsible for explaining risks and treatment options to patients. Special situations may exist, however, which impose a direct duty on the hospital, such as a deaf patient. In Alcalde v. Deaton Specialty Hospital Home, Inc., 133 F.Supp.2d 702 (D.C.Md.2001), suit was brought by the mother of a deaf hospital patient who had not received a sign language interpreter during her 89–day hospitalization that preceded her death. The suit claimed violations of Section 504 of the Rehabilitation Act, malpractice, failure to obtain informed consent, and the intentional infliction of emotional distress. The Court dismissed the emotional distress claim but allowed the others to proceed. The court held, considering the plaintiff's allegations in a light favorable to her, that "the Maryland law of professional malpractice recognizes a duty "to provide communication services" and it also recognizes a patient's concomitant right to "communicate ... distress" about an incipient medical condition (the deprivation of which can constitute a "harm" under the general law of negligence) ..."

See generally Chapter 11, pp. 759–770 for a discussion of the Americans With Disabilities Act.

**Add, at p. 469, a new section III:**

## III. REFORMING THE TORT SYSTEM FOR MEDICAL INJURIES

### A. THE SOURCES OF THE MALPRACTICE CRISIS

A new malpractice crisis resurfaced in 2001, triggered by a rapid escalation in malpractice insurance premiums for most physicians and problems of availability of insurance in some states as carriers went bankrupt or left the malpractice line of insurance. A new round of legislative reform efforts, spearheaded by angry physician groups, has emerged from this latest "crisis", as physicians have faced increases in their insurance premiums and pockets of unavailability in some areas and for some specialties.

#### 1. *The Nature of the Insurance Industry*

Any serious analysis of the malpractice "crisis" begins (and some say it ends) with the insurance industry. The most visible manifestation of the malpractice crisis today, as in the 1970s and 1980s, has been rapid increases in premiums for malpractice insurance purchased by health care professionals and institutions. Insurance carriers have gone bankrupt or dropped out of the malpractice market, while others raised their malpractice premiums precipitously to compensate for investment losses. The insurance market has shrunk, rates have risen, and physicians and hospitals have felt the pinch. See Missouri Department of Insurance, Medical Malpractice Insurance In Missouri: The Current Difficulties in Perspective (2003).

Health care providers buy medical malpractice insurance to protect themselves from medical malpractice claims. Under the insurance contract, the insurance company agrees to accept financial responsibility for payment of any claims up to a specific level of coverage during a fixed period in return for a fee. The insurer investigates the claim and defends the health care provider. This insurance is sold by commercial insurance companies, health care provider owned companies, and joint underwriting associations. Some large hospitals also self-insure for medical malpractice losses rather than purchasing insurance, and a few physicians practice without insurance. Joint underwriting associations are nonprofit pooling arrangements created by state legislatures to provide medical malpractice insurance to health care providers in the states in which they are established.

Malpractice insurance is written as either an occurrence or claims-made policy. An occurrence policy makes the insurance company liable for any incidents that occurred during the period the policy is in force, regardless of when the claim may be filed. A claims-made policy provides for coverage for malpractice incidents for which claims are made while the policy is in force. Premiums for claims-made policies are generally lower and increase each year during the initial 5 years of the policy because the risk exposure is lower. However, usually after 5 years, the premiums mature or stabilize. To cover claims filed after a claims-made policy has expired, health care providers can purchase insurance known as "tail" coverage. The claims-made policies are now the typical form of policy written for medical malpractice coverage.

Medical malpractice insurance policies typically have a dollar limit on the amount that the insurance company will pay on each claim (per occurrence) and a dollar limit for all claims (in aggregate) for the policy period, which is usually 1 year. Insurance companies usually have minimum and maximum levels of coverage they will write which may vary depending on the risk or physician's specialty. Malpractice insurance coverage may be purchased in layers because many insurance companies have maximum limits of coverage they will write for individual risks. If the health care provider desires additional coverage above the company's maximum limits, additional coverage may be purchased from one or more other insurance companies. The first layer of coverage is commonly known as basic coverage; the liability coverage above the basic level is known as excess coverage. Umbrella policies usually cover in a single policy professional, personal, and premises liability up to a specified limit. Generally, umbrella policies provide coverage when the aggregate limits of underlying policies have been exhausted.

Insurance rate setting uses actuarial techniques to set rates, to generate funds to cover (1) losses occurring during the period, (2) the administrative costs of running the company, and (3) an amount for unknown contingencies, which may become a profit if not used. The profit may be retained as capital surplus or returned to stockholders as dividends.

Ratemaking is an actuarial exercise in predicting future claims and expenses based on past experience. This ratemaking is very complicated, for at least two reasons. First, circumstances change over time, and many of these changes affect the number (frequency) of claims or the dollar amount (severity) of losses—the two primary factors that affect the cost of insurance. Inflation increases the average severity of claims, and changes in legal theories may increase the frequency and severity of claims. Second, the use of historical statistics to predict future losses is based on the law of large numbers—as the number of insured physicians and hospitals increases, actual losses will approach more closely expected losses. The medical malpractice insurance market is small and the statistical base for making estimates of future losses is relatively small. As a result, it is difficult to set accurate premium prices. And the "long tail" of malpractice insurance (the long length of time that may elapse after an injury occurs before a claim is filed and settled) is a further complicating factor because the data base used for estimating future losses may not reflect current actual losses.

Malpractice insurance rates for physicians vary by specialty and geographic location and generally increase proportionate to the amount and complexity of surgery performed. Rates may vary from state to state and within a state. For rating purposes, insurance companies usually group physician specialties into distinct classes. Each class represents a different level of risk for the company. The number of and composition of rating classes may vary from company to company, with rates typically determined based on the claims experience of the rating class rather than on the experience of the individual physician. Some insurance companies assess a surcharge, in addition to the standard rate, for physicians with an unfavorable malpractice claims experience. Malpractice insurance rates for hospitals are frequently based on the malpractice loss experience (in terms of numbers of claims filed and the amount per paid claim) of the individual hospital.

Insurance companies are required by state law to establish reserves to cover future losses from claims. Reserves are liabilities based on estimates of future amounts needed to satisfy claims. In addition to amounts covering indemnity payments, the reserves may also include amounts to cover the company's administrative and legal expenses in handling the claims. In most states regulation of liability insurance is not considered to be particularly thorough or effective, and even in those states with strong laws, resources to audit insurance companies are usually scarce.

Setting reserve levels for medical malpractice claims is difficult since the claims require years to be resolved. Accurate reserves are difficult to establish because the companies must estimate losses incurred but not reported, losses reported but not paid, and losses partially paid but which continue for several years. Insurance companies derive investment income from those assets encumbered for loss and loss expense reserves, from unearned premium reserves, and from the company's capital and surplus. Insurance companies also buy reinsurance from other insurers to cover potential losses that may be too large for the individual company to absorb. Reinsurance allows companies to share their risks with other companies and to stabilize insurance losses, which may fluctuate considerably.

See generally U.S. GENERAL ACCOUNTING OFFICE, MEDICAL MALPRACTICE: NO AGREEMENT ON THE PROBLEMS OR SOLUTIONS 66–72 (1986), from which the above discussion was taken, describing the crises of the 1970s and mid–1980s.

## *Notes and Questions*

1. **The Flaws in the Malpractice Insurance Market.** The market for malpractice insurance fails to satisfy many of the economist's conditions for an ideal insurance market. The ideal market consists of a pooling by the insurer of a large number of homogeneous but independent random events. The auto accident insurance market is perhaps closest to fulfilling this condition. The large numbers of events involved make outcomes for the insurance pool actuarially predictable. Malpractice lacks these desirable qualities of "... large numbers, independence, and risk beyond the control of the insured." Patricia Danzon, Medical Malpractice: Theory, Evidence, and Public Policy 90 (1985) (hereafter Danzon). The pool of potential policyholders is small, as is the pool of claims, and a few states have most of the claims. The awards vary tremendously, with 50% of the dollars paid out on 3% of the claims. In small insurance programs, a single multimillion dollar claim can have a tremendous effect on total losses and therefore average loss per insured doctor.

Second, losses are not independent, since neither claims against an individual doctor nor against doctors as a group are independent; multiple claims against a doctor relate usually to some characteristic of his practice or his technique, and a lawyer can use knowledge gained in one suit in another. Claims and verdicts against doctors generally reflect social forces—shifts in jury attitudes and legal doctrine. Social and legal attitudes toward medicine recently have been in flux. Given the long tail, or time from medical intervention to the filing of a claim, the impact of these shifts is increased.

Finally, the problems of moral hazard and adverse selection distort the market. Moral hazard characterizes the effect of insurance in reducing an insured's incentives to prevent losses, since he is not financially responsible for losses. Adverse selection occurs when an insurer attracts policy holders of above-average risk, ending up with higher claim costs and lower profits as a result. This may have occurred because a competing insurer has attracted away lower risk policyholders through the use of lower rates and selective underwriting. Danzon at 91.

2. **Premium Increases and the Medical Rate of Inflation.** Causes of premium increases are disputed. Consumer groups such as Americans for Insurance Reform (AIR) contend that there is no malpractice "crisis" driven by rapid increases in frequency or severity of litigation. To the contrary, the AIR contends that malpractice insurer payouts, including all jury awards and settlements, track the rates of medical inflation. The cost of medical goods and services has increased faster than the Consumer Price Index, and this is reflected in malpractice settlements and payouts. There has been no explosion in insurance payouts over the past thirty years; to the contrary, payments (in constant dollars) have been stable and flat since the mid–1980s. Studies in some states have confirmed that all increases in award sizes are accounted for by medical inflation, wage inflation (for lost earnings) and the increase in severity of the injury to the patient. Missouri Department of Insurance, Medical Malpractice Insurance in Missouri: The Current Difficulties in Perspective 6 (February 2003).

3. **The Underwriting Cycle.** The malpractice crisis is more a product of the way the insurance industry does business than of changes in the frequency of medical malpractice litigation or the severity of judgments. The malpractice market is a "lumpy" market, prone to cycles of underpricing and catchup. What doctors and hospitals see as "sudden" price increases are actually deferred costs passed on when premiums no longer cover payments plus profit. Once premiums reach actuarially sound levels, profits rise, new insurers enter the market with lower rates, competitive pressures return, and the cycle starts all over again.

The cyclical nature of interest rates, as a measure of return on investments, plays a central role in insurers' pricing decisions. The insurance industry engages in cash-flow underwriting, in which insurers invest the premiums they collect. When interest rates and investment returns are high, insurance companies accept riskier exposures to acquire more investable premium and loss reserves. The insurance industry managed to be profitable from 1976 to 1984, and again during the 1990s. If underwriting and investment results are combined during these periods, investment gains more than offset losses. Malpractice insurance premiums charged by insurance companies do not relate to payouts, but rather rise and fall in concert with the state of the economy, reflecting gains and losses of invested reserves and the insurance industry's calculation of their rate of return on the investment "float" (the time between collecting premium dollars and paying out losses) provided by the physician premiums.

See AIR, Medical Malpractice Insurance: Stable Losses/Unstable Rates (October 10, 2002), www.insurance-reform.org/StableLosses.pdf.

4. **Price Wars.** Insurance carriers sometimes act like gasoline stations that enter into pricing wars to gain market share, inflicting wounds on themselves in an attempt to grab more of the market. Favorable operating results in the malpractice line of insurance led insurers to compete aggressively. New companies started up to capture some of the profitable malpractice market. The rate of return on investment income, that is, premiums invested in the bond and stock markets, was high in the 1990s as the nation's economy boomed and the stock market increased dramatically in value. The overall performance of the market is thus a major factor in medical malpractice insurance. Companies sacrificed underwriting gains to attract more business and enhance their investment gains. In some cases the prices charged were far below good actuarial levels. If insurance premiums are priced low in competitive markets, carriers expect to generate investment income to offset underwriting losses. When return on investments decreases as a result of economic downturns, as has occurred starting in 2000 with the bursting of the stock market bubble, this underwriting strategy creates instability in the market, since losses have to be paid. If interest rates and investment yields drop, insurance companies must raise their premiums and drop some lines of insurance, in order to compete. See testimony of James Hurley, spokesman for the American Academy of Actuaries, testimony to the House Energy and Commerce Subcommittee on Health, www.actuary.org. See also Charles Kolodkin, Gallagher Healthcare Insurance Services, Medical Malpractice Insurance Trends? Chaos! (September 2001), at www.irmi.com/expert/articles/kolodkin001.asp.

One cause of this latest price war was due to accounting practices of one large carrier, St. Paul Company. An investigative report by the Wall Street Journal found that St. Paul, at that time with 20% of the national malpractice market, pulled out after a series of missteps in handling their reserves. In the 1980s they had set aside too much in reserve for claims. In the 1990s, using a new accounting strategy, they released $1.1 billion in reserves, which appeared in their income statements as profits. New carriers, responding to this perception of high profitability in the malpractice lines of coverage, moved aggressively to compete, forcing existing carriers to slash prices to compete. From 1995 to 2000, rates fell to such a low level that they could not cover claims, and with the drop of the stock market starting in 2000 many companies collapsed. St. Paul then stopped writing malpractice insurance, and that left physicians in many states with both a pricing and an access problem. Christopher Oster and Rachel Zimmerman, Insurers' Missteps Helped Provoke Malpractice 'Crisis,' Wall Street Journal, June 24, 2002.

This has happened before. The Government Accounting Office concluded of the insurance "crisis" of the early 1980s that "[t]he underwriting losses resulted, in part, from the industry's cash flow underwriting pricing strategy in which companies sacrificed underwriting gains in an attempt to attract more business and thereby enhance investment gains." Government Accounting Office, Insurance: Profitability of Medical Malpractice and General Liability Lines (1987). See also Stephen Zukerman, Randall R. Bovbjerg, and Frank Sloan, Effects of Tort Reforms and Other Factors on Medical Malpractice Insurance Premiums, 27 Inquiry 167, 181 (1990); Frank A. Sloan, Randall R. Bovbjerg and Penny B. Githens, Insuring Medical Malpractice 7–10 (1991). Hunter and Borzilleri, The Liability Insurance Crisis, 22 Trial 42, 43 (1986). For other similar critical perspectives, see James R. Posner, Trends in Medical Malpractice Insurance,

1970–1985, 49 Law and Contemp.Problems 37 (1986) (vice-president of Marsh & McLennan, a large professional liability insurer, on the crisis); Jack Olender, The Great Insurance Fraud of the '80s, 8 The National Law Journal 15 (July 21, 1986); Hunter, Taming the Latest Insurance "Crisis", The New York Times, April 13, 1986, at F3.

5. **Premium Escalation.** Post 9/11, critics accuse the insurance industry generally of price gouging in many lines of insurance , taking advantage of a changed political climate to raise premiums in all lines of insurance beyond what is actuarially justified. The malpractice lines may also be part of this pricing. See "Avoid Price Gouging, Consultant Warns," National Underwriter, January 14, 2002.

6. **Limitations on State Insurance Regulation.** Many states grant their insurance regulators limited authority to regulation medical malpractice insurance rates unless they are either excessive and the market is not competitive. States tend to rely on the marketplace to adjust rates instead of granting broader regulatory powers to their insurance commissioners. Some states are considering allowing their insurance departments to reject malpractice rate filings that do not meet acceptable standards. See, e.g., Missouri Department of Insurance, Medical Malpractice Insurance in Missouri: The Current Difficulties in Perspective 4 (February 2003).

7. Given the above materials, how would you approach reform of the insurance industry and its approach to malpractice insurance pricing and competition? Is wholesale reform needed? Or should means be found to assure coverage for physicians temporarily while waiting for the market to stabilize and premiums drop again?

## 2. *Insurance Availability and Cost: Some Evidence*

A Florida study of claims in the 1970s concluded that the primary cause of malpractice premium increases, measured over a nine-year period, was the increase in loss payments to claimants. The frequency of claims payments was not primarily responsible for increased claims costs, since the likelihood that a Florida physician would be sued for malpractice had not changed from 1975 to 1986. See David J. Nye, Donald G. Gifford, Bernard L. Webb, and Marvin A. Dewar, "The Causes of the Medical Malpractice Crisis: An Analysis of Claims Data and Insurance Company Finances," 76 Georgetown L.J. 1495 (1988).

Other variables that affect insurance premiums have been considered by researchers in earlier studies. Zukerman et al, in their study of insurance closed claims, found that:

- premiums are higher when a population's exposure to iatrogenic injuries increases. A 10% increase in surgery rates increases premiums by 3.8%;

- as the number of practicing physicians increases, premiums fall. This may be due to quality competition or increased monitoring within the profession, or a higher volume of services that improve quality;

- higher real income per capita increases premiums, indicating that plaintiffs with higher incomes are better compensated for lost earnings;

- urbanization is unrelated to premiums (contrary to Danzon's findings), and population mobility lowers premiums, perhaps because it is too difficult to follow through on a claim;

- the percentage of the population over 65 is strongly correlated to premiums, for no clear reason;

- more lawyers do not mean higher premiums;

- premium regulation based on prior approval by the state insurance regulator is associated with lower premiums.

See Stephen Zukerman, Randall R. Bovbjerg, and Frank Sloan, Effects of Tort Reforms and Other Factors on Medical Malpractice Insurance Premiums, 27 Inquiry 167, 180 (1990).

## B. RESPONSES TO THE CRISIS

The response to the perceived "crisis" in malpractice litigation and insurance availability over the past thirty years has been twofold. First, the availability of insurance has been enhanced by a variety of changes in the structure of the insurance industry. Second, physicians have lobbied with substantial success at the state level for legislation to impede the ability of plaintiffs to bring tort suits and to restrict the size of awards.

### 1. Benchmarks for Evaluating Reforms

Malpractice reform proposals can be evaluated by three overall standards. First, do the reforms improve the operation of the tort system for compensating victims of medical injuries? Second, will the reforms create incentives for the reduction of medical error and resulting injury to patients? Third, are changes likely to encourage insurers to make malpractice insurance more available and affordable?

Institute of Medicine, Beyond Malpractice: Compensation for Medical Injuries 29–30 (1978). For a federal study that builds upon the Institute of Medicine report, see U.S. General Accounting Office (GAO), Medical Malpractice: No Agreement on the Problems or Solutions (1986). (hereafter GAO Malpractice Report).

Can you think of other goals by which we should test tort reform? Should we rank the goals which the Institute of Medicine proposes in a particular order of priority? If so, what should come first, and how do you decide? As you read through these materials, ask yourself if the various reforms are likely to promote or impede particular goals, and at what cost.

### 2. Improving Insurance Availability for Physicians

#### a. New Sources of Insurance

New sources of insurance were created in response to earlier crises, either by the states or by providers. Joint underwriting associations, reinsurance exchanges, hospital self-insurance programs, state funds, and provider owned insurance companies have sprung into being. Physician-owned companies now write as much as 60% of malpractice coverage nationally. Hospitals have begun to self-insure. Some states have adopted state programs, such as patient compensation funds, to limit doctor liability to individual patients.

### b. Claims-Made Policies

Medical malpractice insurers changed in the late seventies to writing policies on a claims-made rather than an occurrence basis. Before 1975, most policies had been occurrence policies, covering claims made at any time as long as the insured doctor was covered during the time the medical accident giving rise to the claim occurred. The increase in the frequency and severity of claims in the mid–70s revealed the long tail problem of this kind of insurance. Insurers struggled to reliably predict their future losses and set premium prices, and often failed. Most insurers therefore have shifted to a claims-made policy, allowing them to use more recent claims experience to set premium prices and reserve requirements. The claims-made policy covers claims made during the year of the policy coverage, avoiding the predictability problem of the occurrence policy. Such policies arguably have allowed companies to continue to carry malpractice insurance lines, serving the goal of availability by keeping premium costs lower than they would otherwise have been.

### c. Stop-Gap State Coverage

Self-insurance pools are also being considered by several states to provide a temporary fix for coverage until carriers reenter a state to offer coverage. See State Actions on Liability Crisis: From Self–Insurance to Damage Caps, 12 Health Law Reporter 247 (February 13, 2003).

### d. Hospital Provision of Coverage for Staff Physicians

Some hospitals in states facing the highest premium escalation or coverage gaps in the insurance market in 2003 proposed to provide temporary assistance to staff physicians in obtain insurance. This could operate theoretically as an incentive for hospitals to better monitor their staff physicians to keep risks low. The problem is that such assistance runs afoul of the anti-kickback or Stark II statutes (see Chapter 14). The Office of the Inspector General, in a Letter dated January 15, 2003, in response to a hospital inquiry, noted that safeguards were present in the arrangement discussed, including the temporary nature of the assistance; its availability only to current medical staff; the divorce of assistance from volume or referrals; the maintenance of physician payment at the level he or she currently pays; the relinquishment of some litigation rights; and assistance will be available regardless of where physicians practice. However, the Department of Justice has independent jurisdiction over the anti-kickback statute and CMS over Stark II, requiring further advisory opinions before a hospital could safely offer such assistance.

### e. Selective Insurance Marketing

Physician mutual companies, with physician-investors, have often ridden out the underwriting cycle with less distress than the commercial carriers. One new entrant in this market is Pennsylvania Healthcare Providers Insurance Exchange (PAHPIX), formed in 2002. It promises an intensive commitment to risk management, "looking for physicians who want to control their premium costs through a 'best practices' approach to clinical care." They promise not to seek temporary market share gains through lower prices. And they market to physicians who will remain loyal through up and down markets: "We believe that the current crisis of availability is a result of under pricing the market. Our structure enables our members to benefit in the event our pricing exceeds what is needed to cover claims and expenses." The company wants to make the control of claims a daily task for covered physicians. The theory is that a malpractice carrier must manage risks as well as underwriting them, in order to control exposure.

### f. Hospital Complaint Profiling

For hospitals, complaint profiling has been proposed, spotting litigation-prone staff physicians and intervening to retrain them to avoid risks. The Hickson study took six years worth of hospital patient advocacy files and concluded that unsolicited patient complaints about physicians are a highly reliable predictor of litigation-prone physicians. The study found that 9% of the physicians produced 50% of the complaints, and the study showed an 86% success rate in predicting physicians with multiple claims. The various explanations given for higher physician loss ratios, such as serving a litigation-prone population, treating higher-risk patients, technical incompetence were not statistically significant. Only "connecting" to patients was significant. See Gerald B. Hickson et al., Patient Complaints and Malpractice Risk, 287 J.A.M.A. 2951 (2002). See also Nalini Ambady et al, Surgeons' Tone of Voice: A Clue To Malpractice History, 132 Surgery 5 (2002).

## 3. Altering the Litigation Process

Starting in the 1970s, states enacted tort reform legislation. The preamble to the California Medical Injury Compensation Reform Act, the current Holy Grail for tort reformers of the malpractice system, is typical of the legislative perceptions of the malpractice crisis:

> The Legislature finds and declares that there is a major health care crisis in the State of California attributable to skyrocketing malpractice premium costs and resulting in a potential breakdown of the health delivery system, severe hardships for the medically indigent, a denial of access for the economically marginal, and depletion of physicians such as to substantially worsen the quality of health care available to citizens of this state.

Tort reform measures were intended by their proponents to reduce either the frequency of malpractice litigation or the size of the settlement or judgment. The goal was not to improve the lot of the injured patient, but instead to satisfy both the medical profession and the insurance industry.

These measures can be subdivided into four groups:

- those affecting the filing of malpractice claims;
- those limiting the award recoverable by the plaintiff;
- those altering the plaintiff's burden of proof through changes in evidence rules and legal doctrine;
- those changing the role of the courts, substituting an alternative forum.

These are characterized by Eleanor Kinney as 'first generation' reforms. See generally Eleanor D. Kinney, Learning from Experience, Malpractice Reforms in the 1990s: Past Disappointments, Future Success?, 20 J. Health Pol. Pol'y & L. 99 (1995).

*Common Tort Reforms*

  *a. Reducing the Filing of Claims.* If the frequency of litigation is lowered, it is reasonable to assume that insurance companies will have to pay out less money, which in turn should lower premiums. Several reforms are intended to either bar certain claims that could previously have been brought, or create disincentives for the bringing of suits.

  *(1) Shortened statutes of limitations.* Shortening statutes of limitations simplifies insurance prediction of claims and improves certainty in portfolio management. Historically, the time period for a medical injury was tolled, or began to run, when the injury was discovered. This created the "long tail" problem. States have reduced the time period, typically by requiring that claims be brought within a short time, for example within two years of the injury or one year of the time that the injury should have been discovered with due diligence.

  *(2) Controlling legal fees.* More than twenty states have regulated attorney fees in a variety of ways, including establishing rigid contingency fee structures or requiring judicial review of the "reasonableness" of the fees. The intended effect of these statutes was to make lawyers more selective in screening out nonmeritorious claims, thus eliminating excessive litigation. Danzon found that contingent fees tend to result in equalizing plaintiff attorney compensation to that of the defense bar (whose income is not controlled), and that controls reduce not only lawyers' income, but also plaintiff compensation. Danzon, supra at 63.

  *(3) Payment of costs for frivolous claims.* Under such a statute or court rule, a malpractice claimant found to have acted frivolously in suing must reimburse the provider for reasonable legal fees, witness fees, and court costs.

  *b. Limiting the Plaintiff's Award.* If the previous reforms aim to cut down on the number of cases in court, the next category of reforms is designed to reduce the overall size of the award.

  *(1) Elimination of the ad damnum clause.* This clause, as part of the initial pleading, states the total monetary claim requested by the plaintiff, an amount presumably inflated beyond the level of actual damages suffered. It is feared that such claims expose the defendant to harmful pretrial publicity, damage his reputation, and induce juries to make larger awards than the evidence supports. Thirty-two states have legislated to eliminate the ad damnum clause.

  *(2) Periodic Payments.* Provisions allow or require a court to convert awards for future losses from a single lump sum payment into periodic payments over the period of the patient's disability or life. Such a mode of payment is intended to eliminate a windfall payment to heirs if the injured party dies.

  *(3) Collateral source rule modifications.* The collateral source rule has operated to prevent the trier of fact from learning about other sources of compensation (such as medical insurance) which the plaintiff might possess. The rule arguably permits double recovery. The modifications have either required the court to inform juries about payments from other sources to the patient, or to offset against the award some or all of the amount of payment from other sources.

*(4) Limits on liability.* The most powerful reform in actually reducing the size of malpractice awards has been a dollar limit, or cap, on awards. Caps may take the form of a limit on the amount of recovery of general damages, typically pain and suffering; or a maximum recoverable per case, including all damages. Indiana has a $500,000 limit per claim; Nebraska $1 million; South Dakota a limit of $500,000 for general damages; and California $250,000 on recovery for noneconomic damages, including pain and suffering.

One reform proposal that has resurfaced in legislative discussions in some states has been to "schedule" pain and suffering awards, rather than capping them, to narrow the range of variability in jury awards. See Randall R. Bovbjerg, Frank Sloan, and James Blumstein, Valuing Life and Limb in Tort: Scheduling "Pain and Suffering," 83 Nw.Univ.L.Rev. 908 (1989).

*c. Altering the Plaintiff's Burden of Proof.* Several reforms have altered evidentiary rules or legal doctrine to increase the plaintiff's burden of proof.

*(1) Res ipsa loquitur.* Res ipsa loquitur was judicially expanded during the 1970's by a number of state courts, creating an inference of negligence (or in three states, a presumption) even where expert testimony was needed to establish the "obviousness" of the defendant's negligence. Doctors objected that they were forced to shoulder a defense burden for some patient harms that were not the result of their negligence.

*(2) Expert witness rules.* As Chapter 4 demonstrates, the plaintiff is normally required to present expert medical testimony as to the standard of care, the defendant's deviation from it, causation, and damages. Some states have now adopted specific requirements that plaintiff experts be qualified in the particular specialty at issue or devote a large percent of their practice to the specialty. The intent of these reforms is to reduce the ability of the plaintiff to use a so-called "hired gun," a forensic doctor who has never practiced, or no longer practices, in the area of the defendant physician.

*(3) Standards of care.* The standard of care has evolved from a locality rule to a national standard in most states, not only as to specialists, but also as to general practitioners. Some states have redefined the standard by statute to specify the particular locality (local, similar, state) that governs the litigation. The purpose of these changes has been fairness to rural practitioners, and again to limit the use of forensic experts from other states.

*d. Changing the Judicial Role.* The role of the jury as trier of fact has been perceived by critics of the tort system as introducing bias against defendants and causing delay in compensating plaintiffs. Some argue that development of either screening or alternative dispute resolution devices (ADRs) will speed resolution of cases and screen out frivolous claims more effectively than common law litigation. These reforms are important, because they set up a complicated parallel track for disputes which reduces the judicial role.

*(1) Pretrial screening devices.* Screening panels are intended to rule on the merits of the case before it can proceed to trial and to speed settlement of cases by pricing them in advance of trial. Screening panel laws vary significantly from state to state, but usually require that all cases be heard by the panel before the plaintiff is entitled to trial. A plaintiff is not prevented from filing suit after a panel's negative finding, but the panel's decision is admissi-

ble as evidence at trial. The panels range in size from three to seven members, and often include a judge or a lay person, at least one lawyer, and one or more health care providers from the defendant's specialty or type of institution. The panel conducts an informal hearing in which it hears testimony and reviews evidence. The finding of the panel may cover both liability and the size of the award. For a detailed discussion of such panels, see Jean A. Macchiaroli, Medical Malpractice Screening Panels: Proposed Model Legislation to Cure Judicial Ills, 58 Geo.Wash.L.Rev. 181 (1990).

Proponents have contended that such panels are less formal and less time consuming, and therefore less expensive as a way of resolving claims. Better informed panel members, including health care professionals, may also reach more accurate decisions than a lay jury could. See generally Institute of Medicine, Beyond Malpractice: Compensation for Medical Injuries, National Academy of Sciences, 33 (1978); GAO Report at 133; Peter E. Carlin, Medical Malpractice Pre-trial Screening Panels: A Review of the Evidence, Intergovernment Health Policy Project 15 (1980).

The concerns as to the panels are that they will delay dispute resolution, will favor the provider, and will be ignored unless their use is mandatory.

*(2) Arbitration.* While screening panels supplement jury trials, arbitration is intended to replace them. The expected advantages of arbitration include diminished complexity in fact-finding, lower cost, fairer results, greater access for smaller claims, and a reduced burden on the courts. See GAO Report at 139–40; American Arbitration Association, Arbitration—Alternative to Malpractice Suits, 5 (1975); Irving Ladimer, Joel Solomon, and Michael Mulvihill, Experience in Medical Malpractice Arbitration, 2 J.Legal Med. 443 (1981). No state requires compulsory arbitration. Like screening panels, the arbitration process uses a panel to resolve the dispute after an informal presentation of evidence. The panel typically consists of a doctor, a lawyer and a layperson or retired judge. The arbitration panel, however, uses members trained in dispute resolution and has the authority to make a final ruling as to both provider liability and damages. The process is initiated only when there is an agreement between the patient and the health care provider to arbitrate any claims.

Arbitration has many advocates, particularly in the managed care setting. They argue that an express contract to arbitrate all disputes allows the parties to adjust their preferences to their needs, to have a quicker resolution of issues, and to receive compensation more swiftly. Arbitration through contract becomes an extension of the express contracts that already define the provider-HMO-subscriber relationship. See, e.g., Carl M. Stevens, The Benefits of ADR for Medical Malpractice: Adopting Contract Rather Than Tort Law, 50 Disp. Resol. J. 65 (June 1995); Armand Leone, Jr., Is ADR the Rx for Malpractice?, Dispute Resolution Journal 7 (September 1994); Carl M. Stevens, Medical Malpractice: Some Implications of Contract and Arbitration in HMOs, 59 Milbank Memorial Fund Quarterly/Health and Society 1 (1981).

Arbitration also has distinct limitations from a consumer perspective. Lawyers can drive up the costs and length of arbitration to match litigation. Evidence is also emerging that the "repeat player" phenomenon means a much higher victory rate for employers and other institutional players who regularly engage in arbitration in contrast to one-shot players such as employees or consumers. In employment arbitration cases, one study found that the odds are 5-to-1 against the employee in a repeat-player case. Much of this imbalance may be due to the ability and incentive of repeat players to track the predisposition of arbitrators and bias the selection process in their favor. See Richard C. Reuben, The Lawyer Turns Peacemaker, 82 ABA Journ. 55, 61 (1996).

To understand the effect of tort reform, you have to look at an actual case before and after reform provisions are enacted. The following problem, an amalgam of California, New York and Michigan provisions, provides such an opportunity.

### *Problem: Coping With Reform*

You represent Marcia Schotz, the mother of Christopher Schotz, a child with severe brain damage and retardation. Marcia has just approached you as to the merits of a lawsuit against the Verdain Hospital, several nurses, Dr. Fred Mulch, her obstetrician at the time of the birth of Christopher, and Dr. Ed James, a pediatrician. The facts are as follows:

Marcia's pregnancy with Chris, her first, had been uneventful. She went into labor on December 18, 1984, and arrived at the hospital at around 11:30 p.m. In the labor room she was attached to a fetal monitor with external electrodes and then examined by nurse Joyce Huzinga. An hour later, Dr. Mulch examined her. He was unable to tell if the baby was presenting headfirst or breech. He therefore ordered an x-ray to resolve his uncertainty. Marcia was then detached from the monitor; while waiting for an orderly to take her for x-rays, her membranes burst. Twenty minutes later she was taken to x-ray, and brought back after an hour. She was then left unsupervised until 2:30. Another nurse, Sally Fields, then came in and discovered that the membranes had ruptured. She attempted to hook up the external monitor again, but her efforts were inept. The monitor therefore failed to register any intelligible information. Dr. Mulch came back at 2:45, confirmed that the membranes had ruptured, but made no attempt to get the fetal heart rate either by monitor or fetoscope until 3:15. At 3:15, an internal monitor was properly connected and fetal distress noted on the printouts. Despite the distress, normal delivery procedures were commenced, including an intravenous anesthetic for Marcia, delaying the birth of Christopher by another 20 minutes, during which time he was being asphyxiated in the uterus. After delivery, Dr. Mulch failed to clear the trachea of meconium (fecal matter) which was then ingested into the lungs. Dr. James, a resident pediatrician, summoned to help in the resuscitation, handled an endotracheal tube in such a way as to cause a hole in one of the baby's lungs and a resulting pneumothorax.

Marcia was unconscious during delivery and had been heavily sedated from about 1:00 on. She was not aware of the errors during delivery since Dr. Mulch said nothing to her afterwards and had altered the medical records and deleted incident reports that would have suggested malpractice. It was only now that Marcia has learned of the possibility of malpractice during the delivery.

This is a complicated case requiring extensive discovery, and expert testimony will be required on a number of issues of nursing, obstetric, and pediatric negligence. Your jurisdiction, Columbia, has just enacted the Medical Malpractice Justice Act and you have not yet had experience with its provisions. Work up the file, considering the theories of recovery, defenses, and potential damages for a brain-damaged infant. Then evaluate the effects of the various reform provisions on the resolution of the case, the possible outcomes, and your fee.

## THE COLUMBIA MEDICAL MALPRACTICE JUSTICE ACT

Section 1.

No health care liability claim may be commenced unless the action is filed within two years from the occurrence of the breach or tort or from the date the health care treatment that is the subject of the claim is completed; provided that minors under the age of 12 shall have until their 14th birthday in which to file or have filed on their behalf, the claim.

Section 2.

(1) In an action for damages alleging medical malpractice against a person or party, damages for noneconomic loss which exceeds $500,000 shall not be awarded.

(2) In awarding damages in an action alleging medical malpractice, the trier of the fact shall itemize damages into economic and noneconomic damages.

(3) "Noneconomic loss" means damages or loss due to pain, suffering, inconvenience, physical impairment, physical disfigurement, or other noneconomic loss.

(4) Subsection (1) of this section does not apply to the amount of damages awarded on a health care liability claim for the expenses of necessary medical, hospital, and custodial care received before judgment or required in the future for treatment of the injury.

(5) In any action on a health care liability claim that is tried by a jury in any court in this state, the following shall be included in the court's written instructions to the jurors: Do not consider, discuss, nor speculate whether or not liability, if any, on the part of any party is or is not subject to any limit under applicable law.

Section 3.

In any malpractice action in which the plaintiff seeks to recover for the cost of medical care, custodial care or rehabilitation services, loss of earnings or other economic loss, evidence shall be admissible for consideration by the court to establish that any such past or future cost or expense was or will, with reasonable certainty, be replaced or indemnified, in whole or in part, from any collateral source such as insurance, social security, workers' compensation or employee benefit programs. If the court finds that any such cost or expense was or will, with reasonable certainty, be replaced or indemnified from any collateral source, it shall reduce the amount of the award by such finding, minus an amount equal to the premiums paid by the plaintiff for such benefits for the two-year period immediately preceding the accrual of such action and minus an amount equal to the projected future cost to the plaintiff of maintaining such benefits.

Section 4.

(1) An action alleging medical malpractice shall be mediated pursuant to subsection (4).

(2) The judge to whom an action alleging medical malpractice is assigned or the chief judge shall refer the action to mediation by written order not less than 91 days after the filing of the answer or answers.

(3) An action referred to mediation pursuant to subsection (1) shall be heard by a mediation panel selected pursuant to subsection (4).

(4) A mediation panel shall be composed of 5 voting members, 3 of whom shall be licensed attorneys, one of whom shall be a licensed or registered health care provider selected by the defendant or defendants and one of whom shall be a licensed or registered health care provider selected by the plaintiff or plaintiffs. If a defendant is a specialist, the health care provider members of the panel shall specialize in the same or a related, relevant area of health care as the defendant.

(5) Except as otherwise provided in subsection (1), the procedure for selecting mediation panel members and their qualifications shall be as prescribed by the court rules or local court rules.

(6) A judge may be selected as a member of a mediation panel, but may not preside at the trial of any action in which he or she served as a mediator.

(7) In the case of multiple injuries to members of a single family, the plaintiffs may elect to treat the action as involving one claim, with the payment of one fee and rendering of one lump sum award to be accepted or rejected. If such an election is not made, a separate fee shall be paid for each plaintiff, and the mediation panel shall then make separate awards for each claim, which may be individually accepted or rejected.

(8) At least 7 days before the mediation hearing date, each party shall submit to the mediation clerk five copies of the documents pertaining to the issues to be mediated and five copies of a concise brief or summary setting forth that party's factual or legal position on issues presented by the action. In addition, one copy of each shall be served on each attorney of record.

(9) A party has the right, but is not required, to attend a mediation hearing. If scars, disfigurement, or other unusual conditions exist, they may be demonstrated to the mediation panel by a personal appearance; however, testimony shall not be taken or permitted of any party.

(10) The rules of evidence shall not apply before the mediation panel. Factual information having a bearing on damages or liability shall be supported by documentary evidence, if possible.

(11) Oral presentation shall be limited to 15 minutes per side unless multiple parties or unusual circumstances warrant additional time. The mediation panel may request information on applicable insurance policy limits and may inquire about settlement negotiations, unless a party objects. Following deliberation, the mediation panel shall render an evaluation, to which a majority of the panel must agree.

(12) Statements by the attorneys and the briefs or summaries are not admissible in any subsequent court or evidentiary proceeding.

(13) If a party has rejected an evaluation and the action proceeds to trial, that party shall pay the opposing party's actual costs unless the verdict is more favorable to the rejecting party than the mediation evaluation. However, if the opposing party has also rejected the evaluation, that party is entitled to costs only if the verdict is more favorable to that party than the mediation evaluation.

(14) For the purpose of subsection (13), a verdict shall be adjusted by adding to it assessable costs and interest on the amount of the verdict from the filing of the complaint to the date of the mediation evaluation. After this adjustment, the verdict is considered more favorable to a defendant if it is more than 10% below the evaluation, and is considered more favorable to the plaintiff if it is more than 10% above the evaluation.

(15) For the purpose of this section, actual costs include those costs taxable in any civil action and a reasonable attorney fee as determined by the trial judge for services necessitated by the rejection of the mediation evaluation.

(16) Costs shall not be awarded if the mediation award was not unanimous.

Section 5.

In an action alleging medical malpractice, if the defendant is a specialist, a person shall not give expert testimony on the appropriate standard of care unless the person is or was a physician licensed to practice medicine or osteopathic medicine and surgery or a dentist licensed to practice dentistry in this or another state and meets both of the following criteria:

(1) Specializes, or specialized at the time of the occurrence which is the basis for the action, in the same specialty or a related, relevant area of medicine or osteopathic medicine and surgery or dentistry as the specialist who is the defendant in the medical malpractice action.

(2) Devotes, or devoted at the time of the occurrence which is the basis for the action, a substantial portion of his or her professional time to the active clinical practice of medicine or osteopathic medicine and surgery or the active clinical practice of dentistry, or to the instruction of students in an accredited medical school, osteopathic medical school, or dental school in the same specialty or a related, relevant area of health care as the specialist who is the defendant in the medical malpractice action.

Section 6.

In order to determine what judgment is to be entered on a verdict in an action to recover damages for dental or medical malpractice under this article, the court shall proceed as follows:

(1) The court shall apply to the findings of past and future damages any applicable rules of law, including set-offs, credits, comparative negligence, additurs, and remittiturs, in calculating the respective amounts of past and future damages claimants are entitled to recover and defendants are obligated to pay.

(2) The court shall enter judgment in lump sum for past damages, for future damages not in excess of two hundred fifty thousand dollars, and for any damages, fees or costs payable in lump sum or otherwise under subsection (3). For the purposes of this section, any lump sum payment of a portion of future damages shall be deemed to include the elements of future damages in the same proportion as such elements comprise of the total award for future damages as determined by the trier of fact.

(3) With respect to awards of future damages in excess of two hundred fifty thousand dollars in an action to recover damages for dental or medical malpractice, the court shall enter judgment as follows:

After making any adjustments prescribed by this subsection and subsection (2), the court shall enter a judgment for the amount of the present value of an annuity contract that will provide for the payment of the remaining amounts of future damages in periodic installments.

Section 7.

(1) Notwithstanding any inconsistent judicial rule, a contingent fee in a medical malpractice action shall not exceed the amount of compensation provided for in the following schedule:

30 percent of the first $250,000 of the sum recovered;

25 percent of the next $250,000 of the sum recovered;

20 percent of the next $500,000 of the sum recovered;

15 percent of the next $250,000 of the sum recovered;

10 percent of any amount over $1,250,000 of the sum recovered.

(2) In the event that claimant's or plaintiff's attorney believes in good faith that the fee schedule set forth in subsection (1) of this section, because of extraordinary circumstances, will not give him adequate compensation, application for greater compensation may be made upon affidavit with written notice and an opportunity to be heard to the claimant or plaintiff and other persons holding liens or assignments on the recovery.

### *Problem: Designing State Law Reforms*

You represent the Columbia Medical Association, which is drafting model legislation for consideration in the state legislature. The Association membership is interested in three proposals. First, they would like to take advantage of the national trend toward the development of medical practice guidelines or practice protocols. They want you to draft a proposal that allows such protocols to be used as an affirmative defense by a physician in a malpractice suit or by an institutional provider when corporate negligence is alleged, to show compliance with accepted practice.

Second, the Association has concluded that pain and suffering is a source of inflation in malpractice awards. It is also aware that the state trial association is likely to successfully resist any attempt at a flat cap on pain and suffering awards. Try to develop a conceptual approach to pain and suffering that provides a schedule for such damage awards for the jury to evaluate. You have three choices. One approach might create a matrix of values that would award fixed damage amounts according to severity of injury and age of the injured party. A second approach would give juries systematic information on awards based on past experience, providing a small set of paradigmatic injury scenarios with associated dollar values. These would be nonbinding, but would guide the jury's award. A third approach would mandate fixed limits on awards of non-economic damages, but instead of a fixed cap, a system of flexible floors and ceilings would be used, varying with injury severity and victim age. See generally James Blumstein, Randall R. Bovbjerg, and Frank Sloan, Beyond Tort Reform: Developing Better Tools for Assessing Damages for Personal Injury. 8 Yale Journal of Regulation 171 (1991); Randall R. Bovbjerg, Frank Sloan, and James Blumstein, Valuing Life and Limb in Tort: Scheduling "Pain and Suffering," 83 Nw. Univ. L. R. 908 (1989).

Third, the Association is interested in alternative dispute resolution techniques such as mediation or arbitration, but is uncertain whether to mandate such approaches by statute, or allow for contractual arbitration with certain mandated safeguards.

Elaborate on each of the three areas as part of a proposal for a Model Act. Consider any constitutional problems that might be presented by your proposals.

## C. THE EFFECTS OF REFORM: A PRELIMINARY ASSESSMENT

The Robert Wood Johnson Foundation, the federal government, and others have funded several major studies to determine the effects of reform. The results of these studies are solidifying our understanding of the benefits and the limits of reform.

### 1. *Caps on Awards and Statutes of Limitations*

Caps on damage awards and reductions in the amount of time the plaintiff has to file suit have proved effective in lowering the amount paid to plaintiffs, by almost 40% according to one study of closed insurance company claims. See Frank Sloan, Paula M. Mergenhagen & Randall R. Bovbjerg, Effects of Tort Reforms on the Value of Closed Medical Malpractice Claims: A Microanalysis, 14 J.Health Pol., Pol'y., & Law 663 (1989). See also Stephen Zukerman, Randall R. Bovbjerg, and Frank Sloan, Effects of Tort Reforms and Other Factors on Medical Malpractice Insurance Premiums, 27 Inquiry 167, 180 (1990).

### 2. *Pretrial Screening Panels*

The use of screening panels reduced obstetrics/gynecology premiums by about 7% the year after they were introduced and about 20% in the long run. The study by Zukerman et al. followed up on an earlier study by Sloan, which had evaluated the effect of several reforms on the levels and rates of change in insurance premiums paid from 1974 through 1978 by general practitioners, ophthalmologists, and orthopedic surgeons. Frank Sloan, State Responses to the Malpractice Insurance "Crisis" of the 1970's: An Empirical Assessment, 9 J.Health Pol., Pol'y., & Law 629 (1985). Sloan concluded that only screening panels displayed a statistically significant connection to lower malpractice insurance premiums.

A 1988 study of Maryland arbitration panels concluded that the panel system had reduced the number of claims requiring formal adjudication in the courts and decreased the average length of time for resolution. They also were more likely to find in favor of claimants. See Laura L. Morlock and Faye E. Malitz, Nonbinding Arbitration of Medical Malpractice Claims: A Decade of Experience with Pretrial Screening Panels in Maryland (1988); Thurston, Medical Malpractice Dispute Resolution in Maryland, 1 Courts, Health Science & The Law 81 (1990).

Several earlier studies had looked at panels or arbitration. A 1980 study of screening panels concluded that the panels were effective in disposing of claims before trial, resulting in a significant percentage of claims being dropped or settled after a panel hearing, from a high of 88% of claims disposed of after a panel decision in New Jersey to a low of 38% disposed of in Virginia. Carlin, Medical Malpractice Pre-Trial Screening Panels: A Review of the Evidence, 29, 31 (1980). The very threat of a panel hearing seemed to promote early disposition of claims in some states. The panels in some states also processed claims more quickly than conventional litigation. However, some states were having problems that impaired panel operation. In particular, panels were rarely used where their use was voluntary. Carlin at 32, 37, 39.

A study by the Florida Medical Association in 1985 found that the results of panels were mixed, with some states using panels effectively and others experiencing case backlogs and administrative problems. The authors concluded that panel effectiveness was unproven, and that other court efforts such as a special malpractice court, or other procedural reforms, might be more effective. Florida Medical Association, Medical Malpractice Policy Guidebook 188 (1985). Studies by several states of the performance of their panels have not been encouraging. New Jersey and New York both recommended that a mandatory screening approach be dropped in favor of some form of voluntary system, such as optional mediation. See Perna v. Pirozzi, 92 N.J. 446, 457–59, 457 A.2d 431, 437 (1983) (presenting findings of a committee appointed by the New Jersey Supreme Court to evaluate New Jersey's panel system); see also Ad Hoc Committee on Medical Malpractice Panels, described in Bower, Malpractice Panels and Questions of Fact, 14 Trial L.Q. 4 (1982). An Arizona study found several problems with the Arizona panels, concluding that (1) settlements increased and claims filed decreased between 1976 and 1978 (the good news); but (the bad news) (2) neither the frequency or level of recovery by claimants was affected; (3) the time to process the malpractice case was lengthened by the panel system; (4) the panel system aggravated problems of difficulty and expense in handling cases, from the lawyers' and panel members' perspectives; (5) the panel hearings took longer than expected. See National Center for State Courts, Medical Liability Review Panels in Arizona: An Evaluation (1980); Roy G. Spece, The Case Against (Arizona) Medical Malpractice Panels, 63 U.Det.L.Rev. 7 (1985).

### 3. *Other Reform Measures*

Earlier studies had evaluated the effects of the reforms of the mid–1970's and 80's. One study looked at the effect of post–1975 reforms on the frequency of claims per capita, the amount per claim paid, and the claim cost per capita, using data from closed claims from 1975 to 1978 by all insurers writing malpractice premiums of a million dollars or more in any year since 1970. Patricia Danzon, The Frequency and Severity of Medical Malpractice Claims (1982). Its conclusions were:

—states with caps on awards had awards 19% lower two years after the effective date of the statutes;

—states with contingency fee limits had a somewhat lower amount paid per claim and total claim cost;

—states eliminating the ad damnum had lower total claim costs; there was otherwise no effect on the frequency or amount paid per claim;

—states requiring collateral source offset had 50% lower awards two years after the statute's effective date, but states admitting evidence of collateral sources without required offset displayed no significant effect;

—several reforms displayed no significant effects, including pretrial screening panels, arbitration, res ipsa loquitur or informed consent limitations, and periodic payments.

Another study by Patricia Danzon updated her earlier studies, based upon analysis of claims nationally over the decade 1975 to 1984, for 49 states in some years, based on data from insurance companies that insured approximately 100,000 physicians. Patricia Danzon, The Frequency and Severity of Medical Malpractice Claims: New Evidence, 49 Law & Contemp.Probs. 57 (1986). Her conclusions are:

—the severity of claims rose twice as fast as the Consumer Price Index, a fact related to the fact that health care prices rose faster than consumer prices generally;

—claim severity continues to be higher in urbanized states, consistent with earlier studies, and is also higher in states "with a high ratio of surgical specialists relative to medical specialists";

—severity is less in states with larger elderly populations, a fact related to the low wage loss of the elderly and the low potential for damages in a tort suit;

—no correlation was found between the number of lawyers per capita and claim severity;

—the newer data was consistent with earlier findings as to the impact of tort reforms. Statutory caps reduced average severity by 23%. Collateral source offsets appeared to reduce awards by a range of 11 to 18%. Arbitration reduced claim severity by 20%, compared to states without such statutory arbitration. Screening panels did not have a consistent effect in reducing claims severity.

What do these widely varying, and often conflicting, results mean for the future of reform of the tort system? The results reflect to some extent the limits of the studies and the relative novelty of the reforms such as panels or arbitration at the time studied. Time will tell whether procedural reforms, requiring an elaborate administrative structure, will mature and prove effective. But any ultimate conclusions as to the merits and nature of reform still depend upon the goals sought for the system. Some of the reforms, such as caps and collateral source offset, appear to have slowed the growth of awards in some states. Some reforms, such as statutes of repose, reduce claims filings over the longer term. The claims-made insurance policy and mutual insurance companies may also be a more efficient way of allocating risk and protecting insurance availability.

## D. ALTERNATIVE APPROACHES TO COMPENSATION OF PATIENT INJURY

### 1. *The Rationale for an Alternative System*

The American Medical Association and other groups argue that the existing tort system is flawed and an alternative approach would better serve both patients and physicians. Their criticisms are as follows.

**Criticism 1. The Tort System Fails to Compensate Injured Patients.**

The critics observe that too few malpractice suits are brought, for reasons that include the costs of bringing lower dollar amount claims, the lack of return for the plaintiff lawyer on small cases, and a lack of awareness on the part of many injured patients that they even had a potential claim for malpractice. Patients with small claims rarely sue, so that a substantial number of potential claims are never brought into the civil justice system. The current system therefore compensates far fewer patients than actually suffer injury, at least in the hospital setting. The Harvard Medical Practice Study concluded as follows:

> We estimated that the incidence of malpractice claims filed by patients for the study year was between 2,967 and 3,888. Using these figures, together with the projected statewide number of injuries from medical negligence during the same period, we estimated that eight times as many patients suffered an injury from negligence as filed a malpractice claim in New York State. About 16 times as many patients suffered an injury from negligence as received compensation from the tort liability system.

Report of the Harvard Medical Practice Study to the State of New York (1990), Patients, Doctors, and Lawyers: Medical Injury, Malpractice Litigation, and Patient Compensation in New York. One investigator concluded, based on a match between hospital files and litigated actions, that fewer than 2% of negligent adverse events, or less than 1 in fifty, resulted in claims, since many claims filed reflect cases where researchers found no negligent adverse event. See Troyen A. Brennan, An Empirical Analysis of Accidents and Accident Law: The Case of Medical Malpractice Law, 36 St. Louis U.L.J. 823, 847 (1992).

An alternative compensation system might well improve the ability of plaintiffs to sue, and thereby extend compensation to more injured patients. The problem is the current lack of political will to enact such complex reforms. The current system at least functions adequately for larger claims, and any alternative system promising expanded compensation is going to be resisted by both the insurance industry and health care providers.

**Criticism 2. The Tort System Sends an Inaccurate Deterrence Signal.**

Critics argue that physicians are haphazardly exposed to litigation, regardless of their practice or skill. Physicians believe that claim filings and jury awards bear little relationship to physician negligence. Since jury awards cast a long shadow over the settlement process, irrational jury awards dilute or cancel any deterrent effect of successful plaintiff suits. If jury awards are largely random, then why should providers reform their practices?

This criticism is overstated. Malpractice suits are not simply random events that unfairly single out physicians. The authors of a study of closed claims for anesthesia-related injuries concluded that payment was made in more than 80% of the claims in which patients were judged to have received substandard anesthetic care. But payment was also made in more than 40% of the claims when the anesthesia care was judged to be appropriate.

The authors concluded that the tort system has a high probability of awarding injuries caused by substandard care (true positives), but also compensates claims that physician reviewers would describe as undeserving (false positives). See Frederick Cheney, Karen Posner, Robert A. Caplan, and Richard J. Ward, Standard of Care and Anesthesia Liability, 261 JAMA 1599 (1989). This false positive rate may well be a cost of a functioning compensation system, however. The burden of persuasion in a jury trial is not the same as the burden imposed by a physician reviewer examining insurance closed claims. It is arguable that the tort system intentionally tolerates a higher level of false positives than would physician reviewers, in order to insure that the true positives are more often awarded. See Frank Sloan and Hsieh, Variability in Medical Malpractice Payments: Is the Compensation Fair?, 24 Law & Soc'y Rev. 997 (1990).

The AMA and other critics also attack the jury system as irrational and biased, the primary source of whatever irrationality and randomness the system produces in its verdict distribution. The evidence is to the contrary. Most scholars of the jury system have concluded that it is reasonably competent at assessing liability.

> ... juries do not favor claimants over doctors and do not make negligence judgments based on the depth of defendants' pockets or the severity of patients' injuries. In fact, their verdicts are remarkably consistent with doctors' ratings of negligence. There is even some evidence to suggest that far from holding prejudice against doctors and health care providers juries display a tilt slightly in favor of them.

Neil Vidmar, Medical Malpractice and the American Jury: Confronting the Myths about Jury Incompetence, Deep Pockets, and Outrageous Damage Awards 265 (1995).

Obstetrics has been one of the hardest hit medical specialties, experiencing a high level of claims and high severity of awards. Obstetrics practice is thus a good test of the hypothesis that juries give large awards based primarily on the sympathy they feel for brain-damaged babies and their families. One study of jury decisions in obstetric/gynecological cases concluded that (1) juries can distinguish clear violations of a standard of care, (2) they will find for the defendant readily in the absence of such a clear violation, and (3) they will find for the plaintiffs in cases where an older technology, such as the use of oxytocin to speed delivery, is abused in the face of clear limitations and contraindications. Stephen Daniels and Lori Andrews, The Shadow of the Law: Jury Decisions in Obstetrics and Gynecology Cases, in Institute of Medicine, Medical Professional Liability and the Delivery of Obstetrical Care: An Interdisciplinary Review (Vol. II) 161, 191 (1989). The evidence therefore suggests that the jury based fact finding process, while not optimal, is neither arbitrary nor unfair. See also Frank Sloan, et al., Medical Malpractice Experience of Physicians: Predictable or Haphazard? 262 J.A.M.A. 3291 (1989).

Tort litigation clearly has a substantial psychological impact on physicians in excess of the diluted financial incentives created. See generally Peter A. Bell, Legislative Intrusions into the Common Law of Medical Malpractice: Thoughts About the Deterrent Effect of Tort Liability, 35 Syracuse L.Rev. 939 (1984), for a general discussion of the deterrent value of malpractice suits.

The standard critique also points to defensive medical practices as an overreaction to the fear of liability, and as an inflationary force in health care. The evidence for a high degree of defensive medical practices is equivocal at best. The strongest influence on physician use of medical resources is clinical information and how it is processed. While physicians express concern about liability, they choose treatments and tests based on other factors than fear of suit. See generally David Klingman et al., Measuring Defensive Medicine Using Clinical Scenario Surveys, 21 J.Health Pol.,Pol'cy & Law 185 (1996); Peter A. Glassman et al., Physicians' Personal Malpractice Experiences Are Not Related to Defensive Clinical Practices, 21 J.Health Pol.,Pol'cy & Law 219 (1996).

Is the deterrent value of the tort system worth its costs? Consider the comments of Patricia Danzon.

Patricia Danzon, Medical Malpractice: Theory, Practice, and Public Policy 225–227 (1985):

> \* \* \* [T]he fault-based system is worth retaining if the benefits, in terms of injuries deterred, exceed the costs of litigating over fault and other associated costs, such as defensive medicine. \* \* \* [W]e can make a very rough calculation of the benefits, in terms of injury reduction, that would be required to offset the additional costs of operating the tort system, rather than simply compensating victims through first-party insurance and forgoing all aim at deterrence. \* \* \* If the tort system deters at least one injury of comparable severity for every injury currently compensated, the deterrence benefits outweigh the additional costs of the liability system.
>
> We do not know how many injuries are actually deterred, but we can estimate the percentage reduction in the rate of negligent injury that is required. Using the 1974 estimate that 1 in 10 incidents of negligence leads to a claim and 1 in 25 receives compensation, only a 4 percent reduction in the rate of negligent injury is required to justify the costs of the tort system. If the rate of compensation per negligent injury is currently, say, twice as high as it was in 1974, then an 8 percent reduction in the rate of negligent injury would be required. Similarly, if the tort system entails significant costs other than the litigation costs considered so far—such as defensive medicine, public costs of operating the courts, time and psychic costs of litigation to patients and providers—then the deterrence benefits would have to be higher. On the other hand, to the extent that the compensation received by victims through tort understates their willingness to pay for injury prevention, the deterrence necessary to justify the system is less.
>
> This rough calculation suggests that if the number of negligent injuries is, generously, 20 percent lower than it otherwise would be because of the incentives for care created by the malpractice system, the system is worth retaining, despite its costs. Danzon at 225–227.

In other words, despite its flaws, the current tort system may well serve its deterrent function well. However, a system designed to properly address systemic medical error in advance of their occurrence would be far preferable to the diluted and indirect deterrence effect of tort judgments and settlements.

## Criticism 3. The Administrative and Social Costs of the Malpractice System are too High

Another common criticism is that the tort system imposes excessive costs on physicians and their insurance companies, with too little of the malpractice premium dollar going to the plaintiff in a malpractice suit. The critics correctly observe that the portion of the health insurance premium dollar that goes to a claimant is much higher that the amount returned by the tort system. A study of medical accidents in the United States and Canada offered a ringing critique of the current system:

\* \* \* tort compensation for medical injuries is doctrinally inappropriate, procedurally inefficient, and distributively unjust. Available benefits are often excessive, but very few victims are eligible to recover at all. When it is paid, malpractice compensation is slow, insufficient, and costly to administer. Finally, the manner in which malpractice insurance is generally financed achieves a regressive transfer of resources.

Optimal compensation should reflect a patient's hypothetical decision about the purchase of insurance. But when one considers its regressivity, overhead costs, benefit structure, individualized method of claims assessment, delays in payment, settlement incentives, maldistribution, and highly restricted criteria of eligibility, it is evident that no rational consumer would voluntarily purchase the insurance that is implicitly offered through the civil liability system.

Don Dewees, David Duff, and Michael Trebilcock, Exploring the Domain of Accident Law: Taking the Facts Seriously 117 (1996).

Frank Sloan et al. respond to this criticism:

An insured seeks out a high-return policy for first-party coverage; the insured's own money is returned to him under circumstances specified by contract. The insured's "entitlement" to payment and the aggregate amounts of payment are relatively clear cut. In contrast, liability insurance defends the insured against claims of negligence (mainly) and also pays compensation to third parties not involved in the insurance contract. Major inquiry by claims adjustors and possibly also by courts and lawyers must individually determine whether payment is due, and, if so, how much. Damages are multifaceted, often with uncertain prospects of future loss. A tort law and insurance system may cost "too much" for the benefits achieved, but they are very different benefits from those of health insurance, so simple comparisons do not advance thoughtful policy. Perhaps provider negligence is dealt with more efficiently and more fairly under a third-party system.

See Frank Sloan, Paula M. Mergenhagen & Randall R. Bovbjerg, Effects of Tort Reforms on the Value of Closed Medical Malpractice Claims: A Microanalysis, 14 J.Health Pol., Pol'y., & Law 663, 680 (1989). For an argument that the tort system works well as an insurance mechanism, giving people what they want, see Steven P. Croley and Jon D. Hanson, The Nonpecuniary Costs of Accidents: Pain-and-Suffering Damages in Tort Law, 108 Harvard L. Rev. 1785, 1897 (1995).

Various reforms of the tort system might well improve the payout to a claimant and reduce administrative costs. An administrative system modelled on workers compensation would be more efficient. The tradeoff with such systems is the loss of deterrence effect as the system moves toward compensation and downplays the search for medical error. See generally Paul Weiler et al., A Measure of Malpractice: Medical Injury, Malpractice Litigation, and Patient Compensation 149–51 (1993).

### Criticism 4. Patient Access to Health Care has been Impaired by Rising Malpractice Insurance Costs and by Physicians' Fears of Suits

Rising malpractice premiums, particularly in obstetrics, has allegedly driven physicians from practice, leaving many rural areas in particular without obstetricians. Rising premium costs have cut deeply into obstetric income, causing physicians to alter their practice patterns. It is claimed that access to care has suffered, with the malpractice system the culprit. Some states, such as Virginia, have enacted special legislation just to "solve" the "obstetrics" problem, primarily created by a threat by insurers to leave the state and thereby leave obstetricians without any coverage for malpractice.

Rural areas have been unattractive locations for physicians for a long time, for reasons related more to the amenities of daily life and the need for professional colleagues than malpractice insurance cost and availability. However, the insurance premium costs for family physicians and nurse-midwives have been excessive in relation to their income, and disproportionate to their actual likelihood of being sued. Both availability of coverage and high cost has limited the availability of obstetrical care by nurse-midwives. See IOM Study I at 51. A survey of maternity care centers concluded that the access problem for low-income women is created by unconscionable practices by malpractice insurers. Insurers have imposed "astronomical rates" on physicians and midwives, rates that bear no relation to claims profiles. Dana Hughes et al., Obstetrical Care for Low–Income Women: The Effects of Medical Malpractice on Community Health Centers 59, 74 in Institute of Medicine, Medical Professional Liability and the Delivery of Obstetrical Care: An Interdisciplinary Review (Vol. II) 74 (1989).

In summary, the tort system for medical accidents is surprisingly accurate in ascertaining negligent physician conduct; provides compensation for more serious injuries but not for smaller ones; and makes a delicate tradeoff between an effective level of deterrence of future provider error and levels of compensation. While the system is far from perfect, the issue is always whether an alternative system will function any better, or instead trade off too much deterrence for more compensation, administrative savings for accurate factfinding.

### 2. *No–Fault Reforms*

Second-generation reform proposals aim to eliminate or reduce some of these perceived flaws of the current system, without impairing consumer access to compensation. Such proposals can be categorized in light of several central attributes. The following article offers a framework for thinking about such reforms.

## ABRAHAM, MEDICAL LIABILITY REFORM: A CONCEPTUAL FRAMEWORK

260 Journal of the American Medical Association 68–72 (1988).

\* \* \*

Medical liability reform is essentially an exercise in choosing variables from a series of categories representing the different components of the system. The variables chosen then can be assembled into a single package that modifies existing law. There are five categories from which these variables must be selected: (1) the compensable event, (2) the measure of compensation, (3) the payment mechanism, (4) the forum used to resolve disputes, and (5) the method of implementing the new rights and responsibilities. Traditional medical malpractice law is just one of many possible combinations of variables from each category. Virtually every proposed and adopted reform of medical liability is simply a different combination of these variables. Because each of the five categories contains several variables, the range of reform alternatives is considerable.

## THE COMPENSABLE EVENT

The compensable event is the combination of medical treatment and resulting injury or disease that triggers a patient's right to compensation. The event may be based on malpractice, on the occurrence of a treatment-related injury even in the absence of malpractice, or on the occurrence of a defined loss regardless of whether it is related to malpractice or treatment. For convenience, I refer to these three different triggers as fault, cause, and loss.

### *Fault*

A medical injury caused by malpractice is the compensable event embodied in traditional medical liability law. * * * [I]n theory, malpractice is defined as the failure to conform to an accepted medical standard of performance, although in practice there is often doubt that the jury is capable of understanding and applying such standards. * * *

### *Cause*

Instead of basing the right to compensation on the occurrence of a malpractice-related injury or disease, that right could be triggered whenever the patient suffers an iatrogenic injury or disease or some defined subset of these adverse outcomes. * * * By encompassing a range of compensable injuries far broader than those caused only by malpractice, this approach removes any fault inquiry from the compensation decision.

There are two other important implications, however, entailed in the cause-based approach to compensation. First, because iatrogenic injury is a far more inclusive notion than malpractice-related injury, cause-based compensation may radically expand the number of persons entitled to compensation. For example, one study estimated that only 17% of the potentially compensable events that occur in hospitals result in tort compensation. A system that compensated close to 100% of these injuries would either raise the overall cost of providing compensation or require a reduction in the amount of compensation payable to any given patient.

Also, it is by no means clear that a cause-based standard can be easily applied in practice. Determining what "caused" a patient's injury or disease accounts for a considerable portion of the litigation costs of the current system. * * *

### *Loss*

An even more broadly applicable set of compensable events can be defined by reference to specified losses without regard to cause. This is the method adopted by health and disability insurance whether it is publicly or privately financed. * * *

At present, a loss-based system of compensation composed of health and disability insurance operates parallel to malpractice liability. * * * The loss-based system could be relied on more heavily or exclusively, however, if liability for malpractice were limited or abolished. This could be accomplished either by requiring the universal purchase or provision of private health and disability insurance or through expansion of the governmentally provided forms of social insurance for medical expenses. * * *

### THE MEASURE OF COMPENSATION

The second important feature of any approach to medical liability is the measure of compensation available to those who suffer compensable events. * * *

#### *Full Tort Damages*

A successful plaintiff in any tort liability suit, including those for medical malpractice, is entitled to recover compensation for all losses proximately caused by the defendant's actions. These losses normally include medical expenses and lost wages together with a sum that may vary a great deal from case to case to compensate for the conscious pain and suffering associated with these other losses. * * *

#### *Full Out-of-pocket Losses*

An alternative measure of compensation would award no sum for pain and suffering but full compensation for actual expenses incurred in connection with the compensable event. * * *

#### *Partial Out-of-pocket Losses*

Most non-tort systems of compensation do not award even full out-of-pocket losses. Rather, they tend to contain copayment provisions—floors in the form of deductibles, ceilings on amounts payable, and coinsurance requirements. * * *

#### *"Scheduled" Damages for Specified Losses*

The administrative expense of making individualized loss determinations is a cost of any of the measures of compensation discussed so far. In cause-and loss-based systems this expense is likely to be small, because payments normally are limited to objectively determinable expenses. When the losses in question are subjective, however—damages for pain and suffering payable in the tort system, for example—the cost of determining the extent of a plaintiff's loss can be high. Moreover, jury awards for similar losses are likely to vary considerably precisely because of the subjectivity of both the suffering and each jury's valuation of it.

An alternative to complete denial of compensation for such subjective losses—whether in tort suits or under other approaches—would be to award payments in a way that makes no effort to individualize. This is the compromise struck in workers' compensation, in which there is no explicit award for pain and suffering, but scheduled sums above out-of-pocket losses often are awarded. * * *

In a sense, the legislative ceilings on pain and suffering damages adopted in a number of states in the past several years are a crude example of this approach. * * *

### Periodic Payment of Losses

Cutting across the preceding variables is the distinction between lump-sum and periodic payment of losses. Medical liability awards generally are paid in a lump sum to compensate for actual past and estimated future losses. * * * Such awards might of course be calculated only at the time of the trial and then be paid periodically as annuities, but they might also be recalculated periodically to avoid overpayment or underpayment. Many cause-and loss-based systems adopt this latter approach, incurring extra administrative costs to achieve greater accuracy and avoid making windfall payments. * * *

### Limits on Counsel Fees

The typical medical malpractice plaintiff pays his or her attorney a percentage of any amount recovered. Since recoveries for pain and suffering are generally understood to help finance such payment, placing limits on counsel fees that can be charged plaintiffs is an indirect method of reducing the measure of compensation. * * *

## THE PAYMENT MECHANISM

There are three basic approaches to the payment of compensation for injury and disease and a fourth variation that is largely a hybrid. The payment mechanism adopted depends on the party or parties selected to bear "liability" under the system in force—health care providers, patients, the government, or some combination of the three.

### Third–Party Insurance

Third-party insurance is an appropriate financing mechanism when a party other than the patient is responsible for paying compensation. Thus, third-party insurance is the payment mechanism used preponderantly to pay medical malpractice judgments. Third-party insurance could also be used to finance payment under cause-based systems such as medical no-fault. * * *

### First–Party and Social Insurance

In contrast, first-party and social insurance are used to finance the payment of compensation under loss-based approaches. Both these forms of insurance, however, could also be used to finance payment under cause-based systems of compensation. Under first-party insurance, patients would purchase coverage before treatment, with premiums roughly calibrated to the probability that the patient (or patients in the same risk class) would suffer a compensable iatrogenic injury. * * *

### The Patient Compensation Fund

In some states, ceilings on the amounts for which health care providers are liable in malpractice suits have been adopted, but without restricting the amounts that can be paid to the successful plaintiff. This apparent anomaly is resolved by the creation of a state-operated "Patient Compensation Fund" that is responsible for the portion of any award above the ceiling. Such funds need not be limited to awards above the ceiling, however; they can be employed to finance sums awarded under any of the systems explored so far. Moreover, the method of creating and replenishing the fund might also vary, including assessments against health care providers alone, assessments against patients alone, general revenue, or some combination of these sources. * * *

### The Forum for Resolution of Disputes

The next feature of any approach to liability/compensation issues is the forum that resolves disputes over the rights of patients and providers. This is an important issue, for the identity and qualifications of the decision maker can dramatically influence both the outcome of the dispute and the parties' attitude toward the decision.

#### *Trial by Jury*

The chief characteristic of the American jury system that impinges on the medical liability problem is the use of lay jurors. Several consequences follow from this practice. One is potential inconsistency. * * * Moreover, partly because jurors are lay people and partly for reasons of history, trials by jury are highly formal. Rules of evidence apply, information is produced mainly through questions by counsel, and jurors may not question the parties or witnesses. * * * Finally, because of the medical complexity of the issues, because of the need to educate the jury from scratch about both the facts and these medical issues, and because of the formal procedure of the trial itself, the typical medical malpractice case is preceded by years of pretrial information gathering or "discovery". * * *

The great advantage of this approach is its political legitimacy. For the most part, trial by jury in civil cases is constitutionally required at both the state and federal levels. Jury trials are accepted by the public as an important protection for the powerless as well as a means by which decisions about legal rights may be made without relying on an entrenched bureaucracy or on rule by a class of experts. In addition, the right to bring a lawsuit before a lay jury may satisfy the primitive impulse for vindication in a way that should not be overlooked. * * *

#### *Expert Review Panels*

One variation on pure trial by jury that would retain the jury is to provide an impartial expert assessment of the technical issues to the parties before the trial and to the jury during the trial. Such an assessment might encourage settlement or guide the jury if a settlement does not occur. The panel may consist exclusively of medical experts (a medical review board) or include legal or lay members as well (a screening panel). Unfortunately, experience in many states over the past decade with different versions of the expert review panel suggests that this device has minimal if any impact on rates of settlement or results at trial.

#### *Bench Trial*

This is simply a trial without a jury—that is, a trial before a judge alone. The principal difference between this approach and the use of a jury is that bench trials provide less opportunity for emotionalism and can proceed with somewhat less formality. * * *

### Binding Arbitration

Under binding arbitration, an arbitrator or arbitrators chosen by the parties hear a presentation of the claim and the provider's response to it and decide the case. The recent proposal of the American Medical Association Specialty Society Medical Liability Project for fault-based arbitration is a version of this approach. Normally, the arbitrator has some expertise in the subject area of the case, and his or her decision can be appealed to a court only if there is a failure to follow the terms of the arbitration agreement. Because of the arbitrator's expertise, the proceeding can be streamlined and can be shorter than a trial by jury or a bench trial, and it is much less likely to involve emotionalism than trial by jury. * * *

### Administrative Panels

Once the requirement of malpractice is eliminated as a feature of the compensable event, there is little need to use any of the above devices to determine whether that event has occurred. Typically, a cause-based system financed by health care providers would use an administrative system of compensation under which a board either in permanent existence or specially convened would determine whether the patient had suffered a compensable event and the amount of the losses suffered. * * *

### Insurance Company Determination

In contrast, a cause-or loss-based system based on first-party insurance would not even require administrative panels. Health, life, or disability insurers would simply determine whether the insured compensable event had occurred and award the compensation required by the insurance policy embodying its contract with the claimant. * * *

## THE METHOD OF IMPLEMENTATION

The last determination that must be made in fashioning medical liability reform is how to implement the reformed system. There are two basic approaches: legislation and contract.

### Legislation

One legislative alternative would be simply to prescribe a new mandatory system that would replace the current malpractice liability approach. By statute, a new set of variables would be adopted, and patients and health care providers would be required to act accordingly. On the other hand, legislation implementing the new system need not be mandatory; instead, it might be "elective" in one or more ways, specifically authorizing patients and health care providers to fashion their own legal relationship. Such an approach would of course require detailed description of the contract options available and the options (if any) foreclosed.

* * *

## Categories and Choices of Reform Alternatives

| Compensable Event | Measure of Compensation | Payment Mechanism | Forum for Resolution of Disputes | Method of Implementation |
|---|---|---|---|---|
| Fault<br>Cause<br>Loss | Full tort damages<br>Full out-of-pocket losses<br>Partial out-of-pocket losses<br>Scheduled damages<br>Lump-sum payment<br>Periodic payment | First-party insurance<br>Third-party insurance<br>Taxation<br>Hybrid Funding | Jury trial<br>Expert review panels<br>Bench trial<br>Binding arbitration<br>Administrative boards<br>Insurance company decision | Legislation<br>  Mandatory reform<br>  Elective options<br>Private contract |

*Private Contract*

The nonlegislative method of implementing reform is for patients and health care providers to fashion their own legal relationship by contract. Under this approach, they might adopt any combination of variables that would constitute their legal rights and responsibilities. The great advantage of this approach, of course, is that it would allow the parties freedom of choice. There are two disadvantages, however, that might be difficult to overcome: (1) It is doubtful that the courts would approve such a contractual approach in the absence of prior legislative authorization, at least in cases in which a patient's legal rights seemed to be limited rather than expanded. (2) The pure contract approach requires the agreement of both parties; in contrast, a legislatively authorized optional system could permit the replacement of malpractice liability at the election of only one of the parties in cases in which this seems desirable. * * *

THE VARIABLES COMBINED: A FULL RANGE OF REFORMS

A full range of reform alternatives can be created by combining the variables chosen from all five of the categories discussed into systems that could replace current medical liability law. The choices available are reflected in the Table. * * *

\* \* \*

In sum, the possibilities for medical liability reform are no longer limited to tinkering with tort law by altering a few technical legal doctrines governing litigation. There is more to potential reform than merely making lawsuits more accurate, predictable, or cost efficient. Retaining the basic model of adversarial litigation is by no means the only available approach. A whole range of alternatives has developed, providing the reformer with a series of choices that must be made on the way to reform. No combination of reforms is without its problems, but no effort to adopt the most appropriate system of liability and compensation should ignore the variety of options that are available to deal with the concerns raised by the critics of reform.

### 3. *Current Federal Proposals*

H.R. 4600 is the latest Congressional foray into malpractice reform. It has the following key features:

1. The statute of limitations is 3 years from the injury or 1 year from the patient's discovery of injury, or should have discovered it in the exercise of due diligence. Section 3.

2. Noneconomic loss is capped at $250,000. Section 4 (b).

3. Joint and several liability is eliminated. Section 4 (d).

4. The court can supervise contingency fees, which are subject in any event to the following limits:

40 percent of the first $50,000 recovered by the claimant(s).

33 1/3 percent of the next $50,000 recovered by the claimant(s).

25 percent of the next $500,000 recovered by the claimant(s).

15 percent of any amount by which the recovery by the claimant(s) is in excess of $600,000. Section 5 (a)

5. Evidence of collateral source payments may be introduced, along with premiums paid for such benefits.

6. Punitive damages are capped at a maximum of $250,000, and subject to a requirement of proof by clear and convincing evidence that the defendant acted with malicious intent to injure. Absent compensatory damages, punitive damages may not be rewarded. Such damages can only be demanded after an amended pleading in which the trial court determines upon affidavits or a hearing that the claimant has shown by a substantial probability that the claim will prevail on the claim. Specific tests for evaluating such a claim are provided in the statute.

7. Periodic payment of damages is required.

8. The definitions section, section 9, provides an expansion set of definitions of whom the statute protects:

(9) HEALTH CARE LIABILITY CLAIM—The term 'health care liability claim' means a demand by any person, whether or not pursuant to ADR, against a health care provider, health care organization, or the manufacturer, distributor, supplier, marketer, promoter, or seller of a medical product, including, but not limited to, third-party claims, cross-claims, counter-claims, or contribution claims, which are based upon the provision of, use of, or payment for (or the failure to provide, use, or pay for) health care services or medical products, regardless of the theory of liability on which the claim is based, or the number of plaintiffs, defendants, or other parties, or the number of causes of action.

(10) HEALTH CARE ORGANIZATION—The term 'health care organization' means any person or entity which is obligated to provide or pay for health benefits under any health plan, including any person or entity acting under a contract or arrangement with a health care organization to provide or administer any health benefit.

(11) HEALTH CARE PROVIDER—The term 'health care provider' means any person or entity required by State or Federal laws or regulations to be licensed, registered, or certified to provide health care services, and being either so licensed, registered, or certified, or exempted from such requirement by other statute or regulation.

(12) HEALTH CARE GOODS OR SERVICES—The term 'health care goods or services' means any goods or services provided by a health care organization, provider, or by any individual working under the supervision of a health care provider, that relates to the diagnosis, prevention, or

treatment of any human disease or impairment, or the assessment of the health of human beings.

9. State law is preempted to the extent it is less protective of providers than the provisions of H.R. 4600.

This bill typifies the current legislative mood in Congress. It attempts to enact the provisions of California's MICRA, imposing a harsh cap that is not adjusted for inflation. It also provides a blanket application of the provisions to all health care providers, including managed care plans. The shape of legislation if any, is likely to be determined by the Senate, which wants a more generous set of provisions.

### 4. Second-Generation Reforms

Second-generation reforms are designed to alter central attributes of the tort system to improve both accuracy in factfinding and compensation of malpractice claims, without reducing either the severity or the frequency of claims filed. The two most popular proposals, as measured by Congressional bills and academic writing, are mandated alternative dispute resolution (ADR) and mandated medical practice guidelines. No-fault systems have been tried for certain classes of injuries in two states and enterprise liability has been proposed by the American Law Institute.

#### a. Medical Practice Guidelines as the Standard of Care

Medical practice guidelines can be treated as the standard of care. The guidelines could be given a negligence per se effect, or at least treated as a rebuttable presumption that could then be countered with evidence. The American Medical Association (AMA) has opposed direct adoption of practice guidelines as a legal standard, urging instead that they be offered only as evidence of the customarily observed professional standard of practice and that their degree of authority depend on the degree of their acceptance among medical practitioners. Why would the AMA object to the use of guidelines as a presumptive standard of care?

Such guidelines provide a particularized source of standards against which to judge the conduct of the defendant physician. A widely accepted clinical standard may be presumptive evidence of due care, but expert testimony will still be required to introduce the standard and establish its sources and its relevancy. See generally Arnold J. Rosoff, The Role of Clinical Practice Guidelines in Health Care Reform, 5 Health Matrix 369 (1995); Institute of Medicine, Clinical Practice Guidelines: Directions For A New Program 8 (Marilyn J. Field & Kathleen N. Lohr eds., 1990).

Michelle Mello argues that use of such guidelines are problematic. Michelle M. Mello, Of Swords and Shields: The Role of Clinical Practice Guidelines in Medical Malpractice Litigation, 149 U.Pa. L. Rev. 645 (2001). She finds that physician compliance with guidelines is low, so they cannot be said to reflect customary practice; and departing from custom in favor of such guidelines could weaken the deterrent effect of tort law by increasing physician uncertainty about the law's requirements. Her conclusion is that "... increased reliance on clinical practice guidelines to establish the standard of care in medical malpractice cases would be undesirable whether the guidelines are used in an inculpatory or an exculpatory way."

### b. *Alternative Dispute Resolution (ADR)*

Mandatory alternative dispute resolution has been proposed as an alternative to the tort system. The ADR decision is comparable to a jury verdict and could be overturned only if corruption, fraud, or undue influence is shown or new evidence unavailable at the ADR proceeding is presented. Judicial review of ADR decisions would be similar to review of adjudications by administrative agencies, limited to questions of whether the decision is sufficiently supported by the evidence or otherwise is in accord with the law. See Thomas Metzloff, Alternative Dispute Resolution Strategies in Medical Malpractice. 9 Alaska Law Review 429 (1992); Simpson, D., Compulsory Arbitration: An Instrument of Medical Malpractice Reform and a Step towards Reduced Health Care Costs? 17 Seton Hall Legislative Journal 457 (1993); U.S. Congress, Office of Technology Assessment, Impact of Medical Malpractice Tort Reform on Malpractice Costs (1993).

Mediation has also been proposed as an attractive alternative to litigation. See Edward A. Dauer, Leonard J. Marcus, and Susan M. C. Payne, Prometheus and the Litigators: A Mediation Odyssey, 21 J. Leg. Med. 159 (2000).

### c. *No–Fault Systems*

#### (1) Medical Adversity Insurance

Medical adversity insurance, first proposed by Clark Havighurst and Lawrence Tancredi, is a system whereby a patient experiencing a medical outcome which is on a list of avoidable outcomes would be automatically compensated for certain expenses and losses, and foreclosed from any other recovery for those outcomes. Litigation or arbitration could be pursued for outcomes not covered by the policy.

The lists of adverse outcomes would be developed by panels of doctors, lawyers, and consumers. These outcomes would be clearly described to reduce the potential for claims disputes. The panels would also establish the amounts of compensation for lost wages. Pain and suffering awards could vary based on the temporary or permanent nature of the injury. Panels would periodically review covered outcomes and compensation in order to make adjustments reflecting changes in medical practice and costs.

When the adverse outcome first occurred, the patient or provider would file the claim with the insurer, who would decide whether the injury was covered. If so, it would make prompt payment. Disputes would be resolved through the courts or arbitration.

The plan as proposed would experience rate insurance premiums paid by providers, in order to create incentives for the providers to improve the quality of care, thereby reducing their exposure for the adverse outcomes listed. Provider experience under the plan would also be used to strengthen peer review within hospitals.

The original Havighurst–Tancredi proposal assumed that legislation would be needed to effectuate the plan. More recently, Havighurst has suggested that private contracts rather than legislation should be used. Under the contractual approach, providers would voluntarily contract with insurers to cover certain outcomes, which would then be paid on a no-fault basis.

Patients would also contract with the providers to accept those amounts listed in the policy. This would allow more flexibility, with variations possible in both covered events and compensation amounts among providers. Noncovered injuries could be handled through the courts or arbitration.

See Clark Havighurst and Laurence Tancredi, "Medical Adversity Insurance"—A No-Fault Approach to Medical Malpractice and Quality Assurance, 51 Milbank Memorial Fund Quarterly 125 (1973); Clark Havighurst, "Medical Adversity Insurance—Has Its Time Come?", 1975 Duke L.J. 1254; Laurence Tancredi, Designing a No–Fault Alternative, 49 Law & Contemp. Probs. 277 (1986).

Another version of the Tancredi concept is called "accelerated-compensation events" (ACEs). The central idea, as with medical adversity insurance, is that lists of medically caused injuries should be drawn up, covering those injuries that should not normally occur and are avoidable if good care is given. These lists are based on professionally selected classes of bad outcomes that medical professionals consider avoidable on a probabilistic basis. See Lawrence Tancredi and Randall R. Bovbjerg, Creating a Selective No–Fault System to Replace Malpractice: Methodology of Accelerated–Compensation Events (ACEs), University of Texas Health Science Center Paper (Houston Texas, 1990).

A variation on the Tancredi proposals is provided by Professor O'Connell, who has proposed a variety of elective no-fault options using a list of covered injuries and contract agreements between providers and patients. See Jeffrey O'Connell, No–Fault Insurance for Injuries Arising from Medical Treatment: A Proposal for Elective Coverage, 24 Emory L.J. 35 (1975); Jeffrey O'Connell, Neo–No–Fault Remedies for Medical Injuries: Coordinated Statutory and Contractual Alternatives, 49 Law & Contemp.Probs. 125 (1986); O'Connell, Offers That Can't Be Refused: Foreclosure of Personal Injury Claims by Defendants' Prompt Tender of Claimants' Net Economic Losses, 77 Nw. U.L.Rev. 589 (1982); Institute of Medicine Report at 43.

### *Notes and Questions*

1. What is gained by the Tancredi proposal? It takes certain adverse outcomes out of a fault-based system, and places them in a loss-based system, most likely in the hospital setting. What are the advantages of this approach from the physician's perspective? The hospital's? The patient's?

2. How should the panels set the level below which an adverse event is judged to be avoidable if good care is given? Should national data be used, with this approach implemented on a national basis, perhaps through the Medicare program? Or should this be left state-by-state, or hospital-by-hospital? What approach do you prefer? Why?

### (2) Offers to Pay Patient Losses

A medical offer proposal has circulated in Congress since the early 1970s, resurfacing in a variety of legislative proposals. The federal government is now supporting demonstration projects that explore such a offer system.

Some states are now expressing interest in this idea of medical offers by institutions. The GAO Malpractice Report summarized the content of the legislation as follows:

The proposal is considered a quasi-no-fault plan because, under the plan, health care providers can selectively decide to foreclose a patient's right to sue the provider for damages from medical malpractice. Under the proposal, health care providers within a designated period of time (180 days from an occurrence) can offer to pay a patient's net economic losses arising from medical injuries and, by tendering the offer, foreclose the patient's right to sue the provider for medical malpractice *except* for cases in which the provider intentionally caused the injury or a wrongful death occurred. Under the proposal, the health care provider and his or her insurer could choose which cases would be in the provider's interest to tender an offer.

Only the patient's economic losses, above amounts paid by other sources such as private health insurance, from the injury would be paid under the proposal. Economic losses include medical expenses, rehabilitation and training expenses, work losses, and replacement services losses. Reasonable attorney's fees to collect benefits would also be allowed. No compensation would be available for any noneconomic losses from the injury, such as pain, suffering, mental anguish, or loss of consortium.

* * * [T]he vast majority of payments would be made to patients as the losses are incurred rather than in lump sum. Patients would submit reasonable proof of net economic losses incurred to the health care provider's insurer, which would be required to make payments within 30 days. Payments would be available as long as the patient's injury continues. However, future payments for the injury would not be available if no payments have been made within the last 5 years. Provisions also allow the health care provider or his insurer to require the injured party to submit to a mental or physical examination if the injured party's mental or physical condition is material and relevant to compensation benefits.

The proposal requires that any lump-sum settlement over $5,000 be reviewed by the court to ensure that it is fair to the injured party.

In cases where the health care provider does not make an offer, the patient can request within 90 days that the claim be resolved by binding arbitration. Recovery from arbitration would be limited to the patient's net economic losses and reasonable attorney fees.

To participate in the program, health care providers would be required to carry sufficient malpractice insurance or post sufficient bond. This provision is designed to protect patients from providers unable to pay compensation.

The concept of the offer of compromise has also shown up in more recent legislative proposals as an option on a menu of choices to be offered the states for adoption.

### 4. *Administrative Systems*

Another proposal has been to legislate a state system loosely based on the Workers' Compensation model. The AMA developed an elaborate proposal in the late 1980s, but to date such state-administered systems have been limited to special categories of injuries, such as brain-damaged infants. The State of Virginia has led the states in implementing a no-fault system for obstetric mishaps. The state enacted the "Birth–Related Neurological Injury Compensation Act", creating a compensation fund for neurologically damaged newborns. Virginia Code Ann. §§ 38.2–5000 to–5021; King v. Virginia Birth–Related Neurological Injury Compensation Program, 242 Virginia 404, 410 S.E.2d 656 (1991).

The critical definition for compensation purposes in the Virginia statute is "[b]irth-related neurological injury". This is defined as "injury to the brain or spinal cord of an infant caused by the deprivation of oxygen or mechanical injury occurring in the course of labor, delivery or resuscitation in the immediate post-delivery period in a hospital which renders the infant permanently nonambulatory, aphasic, incontinent, and in need of assistance in all phases of daily living. This definition shall apply to live births only."

A claim under this Act excludes all other tort remedies, with the exception of a suit "against a physician or a hospital where there is clear and convincing evidence that such physician or hospital intentionally or willfully caused or intended to cause a birth-related neurological injury, provided that such suit is filed prior to and in lieu of payment of an award under this chapter."

Compensation under the statute is for "net economic loss" only, including medical expenses, rehabilitation expenses, residential and custodial care and service, special equipment or facilities, and related travel. Loss of wages from age eighteen (50% of the average weekly wage in Virginia), and reasonable expenses and attorneys' fees incurred are also included. Compensation for non-economic loss, "pain and suffering", is disallowed, as are expenses covered by insurance.

The Industrial Commission of Virginia, the state's worker's compensation commission, handles the claims filed. The Commission will decide whether the claimed injury falls within the definition of a birth-related neurological injury, aided by an expert panel of three impartial physicians. This panel will operate according to guidelines developed by the deans of the state's medical schools. A hearing must be held within 120 days of the date of filing. One member of the expert physician panel must be available to testify at this hearing.

Each claim filed under this program will also be referred automatically to the state Board of Medicine for evaluation to decide whether the injury resulted from substandard care.

Physicians licensed to practice medicine in Virginia who practice obstetrics or perform obstetrics either full-or part-time, including family physicians, may, but are not required to, participate in the program. Participating physicians must agree in advance with the state Board of Medicine to submit to a review of their obstetric practice in the case of a finding of substandard care. They must also certify to the Commissioner of Health that they will participate in the development of a program to provide maternity care to Medicaid and other low-income patients.

Participating obstetrician-gynecologists and family physicians are required to pay $5,000 into the fund annually, while all other physicians in the state will be required to pay $250 per year into the fund. Hospital participation is also voluntary. Participating hospitals will be required to pay $50 per delivery per year into the fund, with an absolute cap of $150,000 per hospital per year. Participating hospitals are also to assist in the development of a state-sponsored maternity care program for low-income women.

Only a handful of claims have qualified each year under the statute, and no claim has been filed. The definition is so narrow that only the most severe injuries are covered, and most of those eligible die as infants. Are the pressures toward participation by physician strong enough? If it is true that very few claims are being filed, what incentives exist for physicians to elect to participate? Can you suggest a redrafting of the eligibility provision to provide for better coverage?

See generally James Henderson, The Virginia Birth–Related Injury Compensation Act: Limited No–Fault Statutes as Solutions to the "Medical Malpractice Crisis", Institute of Medicine, Medical Professional Liability and the Delivery of Obstetrical Care: An Interdisciplinary Review (Vol. II) (1989); David G. Duff, Compensation for Neurologically Impaired Infants: Medical No–Fault In Virginia, 27 Harv.J.Legis. 391 (1990). For criticisms of the Virginia system, see Richard A. Epstein, Market and Regulatory Approaches to Medical Malpractice: The Virginia Obstetrical No–Fault Statute, in Institute of Medicine, Medical Professional Liability and the Delivery of Obstetrical Care: An Interdisciplinary Review (Vol. II), 115 (1989). Florida also adopted a no-fault system. See Florida State. Ann. § 408.02.

## *Notes and Questions*

1. If you represent a hospital, what problems would you see in the Medical Offer and Recovery Act? Why should a provider come forward to inform a patient that he has suffered a compensable injury? What is in it for the provider in an uncertain case? Is the doctor in charge of the case likely to admit error, so that the hospital can present its offer to the patient? How can the hospital encourage staff doctors to come forward? How might legal rules improve the possibilities of disclosure of errors?

2. One of the primary goals in a no-fault system is to reduce the cost of insurance to providers. Measured by this goal, a proposal like the Medical Offer and Recovery Act may fail. The California study in the 1970s estimated that a no-fault system in California could increase malpractice premiums 300% higher than the tort system's insurance costs. California Medical and Hospital Associations, Report on the Medical Insurance Feasibility Study (1977). A critique of the Harvard New York study likewise concluded that the costs of a no-fault system could be greater than the present tort system, when the costs of many more claims and system administrative costs are combined. See Mehlman, Saying "No" to No–Fault: What the Harvard Malpractice Study Means for Medical Malpractice Reform (New York State Bar Association 1990).

From the insurance industry perspective, these proposals are worrisome, since there seems to be far more malpractice in the world than is ever detected or litigated. A no-fault system may set off an avalanche of litigation. For an account of such fears, see the comments of the Jerry Engelelter, government affairs officer for St. Paul's insurance, in Kleinfield, The Malpractice Crunch at St. Paul, The New York Times, Sunday, February 24, 1985 at p. 4F.

If a compensation system rewards many more claimants, particularly small ones, in an evenhanded and more rapid fashion than does the current tort system, it may well be an improvement. But it is unlikely to be a cheaper system. This suggests that we move directly to a social insurance scheme that moves financing out of the private insurance market and into the taxation structure of the government.

3. For the academic origins of many of these proposals, see generally Jeffrey O'Connell, Offers that Can't Be Refused: Foreclosure of Personal Injury Claims by Defendants' Prompt Tender of Claimants' Net Economic Losses, 77 Nw. Univ. L. R. 589(1982); Neo–No–Fault Remedies for Medical Injuries: Coordinated Statutory and Contractual Alternatives, 49 Law and Contemporary Problems 125 (1986).

### 5. *Enterprise Liability*

President Clinton's original health reform proposal in 1993 made enterprise liability the cornerstone of malpractice reform. See Health Security Act, s. 1775, 103rd Cong., 1st Sess., Nov. 22, 1993, § 1400 (hereafter "Health Security Act"). The original proposal called for the Health Plans to bear all liability for medical malpractice. After opposition arose from organized medicine, however, the proposal was downgraded to a demonstration project in the Act. Enterprise liability continues, however, to be a favorite of tort reformers. Current tort reform efforts in Congress have focused on product liability rules, especially punitive damage awards, while malpractice reform has slipped out of the spotlight. At the moment, it is unclear that any major legislation will emerge from Congress addressing professional liability issues.

Enterprise liability, also referred to as "organizational liability" by the American Law Institute, changes the locus of liability for patient injuries without other significant alterations to the rules of proof and damages. The idea is not new; developments in vicarious liability and corporate negligence have moved the locus of much medical liability from independent contractor physicians to the hospital. See generally George Priest, The Invention of Enterprise Liability: A Critical History of the Intellectual Foundations of Modern Tort Law, 14 J.Leg.Stud. 461 (1985). This proposal, as articulated by the American Law Institute, would make a hospital liable for physician negligence that injures patients within the hospital:

> ... we would exculpate doctors from personal liability for negligence (and thus eliminate their need to purchase insurance against such liability), on the condition that the hospital assume such liability and provide the insurance, a change that would leave untouched the patient's present entitlement to recover for injuries caused by the doctor's negligence.

The American Law Institute, Reporters' Study, Enterprise Responsibility for Personal Injury, Vol.II: Approaches to Legal and Institutional Change (April 15, 1991) 115 (hereafter ALI Study).

Such channeling of liability to the hospital is justified by several arguments. First, insurers would have an improved ability to price insurance, since difficulties in pricing for individual physicians in high-risk specialties will be eliminated; in most other areas of tort law, from environmental to products risks, business enterprises bear the cost of insuring against liability. Second, by eliminating the insurance problems inherent in the fragmented malpractice market, specialties such as obstetrics would no longer face onerous burdens, nor will physicians have to face premiums that fluctuate excessively from year to year. Third, physicians would be freed from the psychological stress inflicted by being named defendants in malpractice suits. Fourth, administrative and litigation costs would be reduced by having only one defendant, rather than the multiplicity of providers named in the typical malpractice suit. Fifth, and most important, patterns of poor medical practice would be deterred by placing liability on institutions rather than individuals, since organizations have superior data collecting abilities and management tools for managing risks. See William M. Sage and James M. Jorling, A World that Won't Stand Still: Enterprise Liability By Private Contract, 43 DePaul L. Rev. 1007 (1994); Lewis A. Kornhauser, An Economic Analysis of the Choice Between Enterprise and Personal Liability for Accidents, 70 Cal.L.Rev. 1345 (1982).

The critique of such enterprise liability begins with its impact on the autonomy of physicians. Physicians fear that such liability will force them from the status of autonomous practitioners into the status of employees for large health care institutions, with attendant loss of power. The ALI proposal acknowledges that enterprise liability will treat physicians as staff physicians in managed care settings. But such forces are already in operation, as evidenced by the rapid growth of managed care organizations, the purchase of group medical practices by hospitals, and other forces that have reduced the autonomy of physicians.

The issue for health care reform in the next decade will be how to implement such a liability approach in a changing health care environment where care is as likely to be delivered through loose networks of providers as through hospitals. The benefits of deterrence and risk management may be elusive if enterprise liability is applied to broad regional health authorities or other networks that lack the centralizing powers of individual hospitals. Enterprise liability may also increase compensation costs due to the increased volume of claims filed. The California study in the 1970s estimated that a no-fault system in California could increase malpractice premiums 300% higher than the tort system's insurance costs. California Medical and Hospital Associations, Report on the Medical Insurance Feasibility Study (1977). A critique of the Harvard New York study likewise concluded that the costs of a no-fault system could be greater than the present tort system, when the costs of many more claims and system administrative costs are combined. See Maxwell Mehlman, Saying "No" to No–Fault: What the Harvard Malpractice Study Means for Medical Malpractice Reform (New York State Bar Association 1990).

From the insurance industry perspective, these proposals are worrisome, since there seems to be far more malpractice in the world than is ever detected or litigated. A no-fault system may set off an avalanche of litigation, depending upon the design of the system, methods of discussing misadventures to the injured patient, and other structural issues, as yet unresolved. Patients are also more likely to sue their HMO or Health Alliance than their personal physician.

If a compensation system rewards many more claimants, particularly small ones, in a more evenhanded and rapid fashion than does the current tort system, it will be an improvement even if it is not cheaper. See generally Paul C. Weiler et al., A Measure of Malpractice: Medical Injury, Malpractice Litigation, and Patient Compensation (1993) for an excellent economic discussion of the costs of a no-fault system to replace medical malpractice litigation. Weiler et al estimate that a no-fault scheme would cost somewhat more than liability under the current system, but argue that "... a reasonably comprehensive patient compensation scheme—which would fully reimburse all actual longer-term financial losses that patients suffer as a result of iatrogenic injury—would be a small and readily affordable item in the budget of the health care system that generates these injuries ..." Id. at 109.

See Kenneth S. Abraham and Paul C. Weiler, Enterprise Liability and the Evolution of the American Health–Care System, 108 Harv. L.Rev. 381(1994); Barry R. Furrow, Enterprise Liability, 39 St. Louis L. Rev. 79(1995); Paul C. Weiler, The Case for No–Fault Medical Liability, 52 Md.L.Rev 908 (1993); Paul C. Weiler, Medical Malpractice on Trial (1991).

Newer proposals for variations on no-fault proposals include David M. Studdert & Troyen A. Brennan, Toward a Workable Model of "No–Fault" Compensation for Medical Injury in the United States, 27 Am. J.L. & Med. 225 (2001); David M. Studdert, Troyen A. Brennan & Eric J. Thomas, Beyond Dead Reckoning: Measures of Medical Injury Burden, Malpractice Litigation, and Alternative Compensation Models from Utah and Colorado, 33 Ind. L. Rev. 1643 (2000); David M. Studdert et al., Negligent Care and Malpractice Claiming Behavior in Utah and Colorado, 38 Med. Care 250 (2000); Eric J. Thomas et al., Incidence and Types of Adverse Events and Negligent Care in Utah and Colorado, 38 Med. Care 261 (2000); Eric J. Thomas et al., Costs of Medical Injuries in Utah and Colorado, 36 Inquiry 255 (1999).

The only Federal no-fault program now in operation covering a health care related injury is the National Childhood Vaccine Injury Act of 1986, effective in 1988. It covers solely those individuals injured or killed by vaccines. The program requires a petition to the U.S. Claims Court and an adjudication by that court. The petitioner must elect to accept or reject the judgment of the court. Acceptance bars any tort suit against the manufacturer. The federal government will pay compensation to those who develop specified symptoms or reactions to a vaccine within specified periods of time and suffer a vaccine-related injury that lasts for at least six months. See 42 U.S.C.A. § 300aa–1 et seq., Pub.L. 99–660, tit. III, § 311(a), 100 Stat. 3756 (Nov. 14, 1986).

### 6. *Conclusion*

First-generation reforms are now in place in most states. Second-generation reforms, ranging from enterprise liability to contractual arbitration models, are far less likely to be adopted by either Congress or the states. The current push is to enact statutory caps on pain and suffering awards, using the California model as the solution to the problem. It remains to be seen whether broader innovations in malpractice compensation systems will be tried at either the federal or state levels. The vested interests are entrenched at this point, and serious system reform seems unlikely.

*

# Part II

# ACCESS AND COST CONTROL

# Chapter 7

# HEALTH CARE COST AND ACCESS: THE POLICY CONTEXT

## I. THE PROBLEMS

### A. THE PROBLEM OF ACCESS

**Add, at p. 473:**

According to U.S. Census figures, the number of uninsured, after declining in the late 1990s, grew in 2000, declined slightly in 2001, and started growing again in 2002. The relative lack of growth in the uninsured population during the early years of the 2000s, however, is entirely due to growth in public programs. The percentage of the population under 65 privately insured dropped from a high of 73.1% in 1999 to 72% in 2000, 71.9% in 2001, and 70.1% in the first quarter of 2002. This decline undoubtedly reflects both growing unemployment and employed persons declining health insurance as employee premium costs continue to rise. At the same time, the percentage of the population publicly insured grew from 12.4% in 1999 to 15.6% in the first quarter of 2002. The most dramatic growth in public insurance coverage was for children under the age of 18, where the percentage who are publicly insured grew from 20.5% in 1999 to 27.7% in the first quarter of 2002. This reflects both the growth in the SCHIP program and a rebound in Medicaid coverage as states have reached out more effectively to those who lost coverage under welfare reform in the late 1990s. See CDC, National Center for Health Statistics, National Health Interview Survey, Sept. 20,. 2002.

The Institute of Medicine is publishing a very helpful series of monographs on the problems of the uninsured. Volumes released to date include Health Insurance is a Family Matter (2002); Care Without Coverage: Too Little, Too Late (2002) and Coverage Matters: Insurance and Health Care (2001).

### B. THE PROBLEM OF COST

#### 1. *Recent Developments in Health Care Cost Inflation*

**Add, at p. 475:**

After the relative calm of the 1990s, health care cost inflation has returned with a vengeance at the beginning of the 2000s. In 2001, the most recent year for which data are available, national health expenditures grew by

8.7% from 1.31 to 1.42 trillion dollars. Health care spending now equals 14.1% of gross domestic product (GDP), up from 13.3% in 2000. The dramatic growth in health spending as a percentage of GDP is due both to the rapid rise in health care costs and the overall slow growth in the GDP.

The fastest growing expenditure category during 2001 was prescription drugs, which grew by 15.7%. Growth in prescription drug spending was down, however, from growth rates of 16.4% in 2000 and 19.7% in 1999, when a wave of new blockbuster drugs were entering the market and dramatically driving up costs. Declining growth in the cost of drugs may also be attributable to higher copayments and increasing use of multitier copayment plans to control drug utilization. Hospital expenditures grew at a rate of 8.3%, the fastest growth since 1991, driven by a 4.2% increase in the use of hospital services per capita. Spending on physician services grew by 8.6%, reflecting a weakening of managed care constraints on the use of physician services.

Public sector spending increased by 9.4%, led by Medicaid and SCHIP expansions. Medicare spending increased by 7.8%, driven by increased payments to providers under post-Balanced Budget Act legislation which has eased up on constraints imposed by the BBA. Medicaid spending increased by 10.8%, reflecting a 8.5% rise in enrollment, driven by the recession and by state eligibility expansions. Private insurance premiums increased by 10.5% in 2001, as insurers tried to recap revenue shortfalls from previous years. All the signs point to continued growth of health care costs in 2002 and 2003. See Katharine Levit, et al, Trends in U.S. Health Care Spending, 2001, 22 Health Affairs, Jan./Feb. 2003 at 154.

Current projections are that health care spending will continue to increase over the next decade, but at a decreasing rate. By 2012, health care spending may equal 17.7% of GDP, and exceed three trillion dollars. See Stephen Heffler, et al., Health Care Spending Projections for 2002–2012, Health Affairs Web Exclusive, available at http://www.healthaffairs.org/WebExclusives/Heffler_Web_Excl_020703.htm.

## II. APPROACHES TO HEALTH CARE REFORM

### A. OPTIONS FOR EXPANDING ACCESS TO CARE

**2. *Approaches to Insuring the Uninsured based on Private Insurance***

**Add, at p. 491:**

Though the use of tax credits to expand health insurance coverage among the uninsured continued to be politically popular during 2001 and 2002, little concrete progress was made toward adopting legislation to create such credits at the federal level. The one exception was the Trade Act of 2002 (H.R. 3009). This legislation gives the President fast-track trade authority to negotiate trade agreements. The law includes a ten-year, $12 billion, plan to give workers displaced from their jobs through fast-track trade agreements health insurance coverage and other benefits. It provides displaced workers with a refundable tax credit to cover 65% of the cost of health insurance premiums to purchase insurance from specified sources, including continuation coverage

## B. COST CONTROL

### 2. *Consumer Choice in Purchasing Health Care Services: The Medical Savings Account*

**Add, at p. 495:**

In June of 2002 the Internal Revenue Service issued IRS Notice 2002–45 and Revenue Ruling 2002–41 approving employer-funded health reimbursement arrangements (HRAs). HRAs resemble FLEX accounts under section 125 of the IRC, but are different in several important respects, including 1) a requirement that HRAs be funded solely by the employer, without any contributions from the employee, and 2) a provision that any unused money in the HRA account may be carried over at the end of the year, and may be maintained by the employee upon termination or retirement. HRA funds may only be used for substantiated medical expenses of the employee or dependents.

Commentators see the new HRA as an attempt to encourage consumer-driven health care plans, also known as defined contribution health plans. Under these arrangements, employers establish accounts for their employees, who can use the funds to purchase routine health care services and a high deductible health plan. The carry-over feature of the HRAs gives employees covered by such arrangements more flexibility in covering expenses from year to year.

Though consumer-driven health plans are being much discussed, they are still relatively uncommon. Whether they will increase employee choice and bring down health care costs through competition, or drive up costs through loss of bargaining power and higher administrative costs, and encourage cherry picking and adverse selection, remains to be seen. See Jon Gabel, Anthony T. Lo Sasso and Thomas Rice, Consumer–Driven Health Plans: Are They More Than Talk Now? Available at http://www.healthaffairs.org/WebExclusives/Gabel_Web_Excl_112002.htm.

**Add, at p. 498:**

The federal HIPAA MSA experiment was also extended for another year until December 31, 2003, by Pub. L. No. 107–147, enacted in the spring of 2002.

# Chapter 8

# PRIVATE HEALTH INSURANCE AND MANAGED CARE: STATE REGULATION AND LIABILITY

## III. TORT LIABILITY OF MANAGED CARE

### D. REPAIR TEAM LITIGATION AND RICO

At p. 567, substitute a new Note 2:

2. **The REPAIR Team Class Actions.** A series of Multi–District Litigation class action lawsuits was filed in 1999 by a group of lawyers known as the REPAIR Team, short for **RICO and ERISA Prosecutors Advocating for Insurance Industry Reform**. The cases are in two tracks: Provider and Subscriber lawsuits. The REPAIR Team, which had litigated state lawsuits against the tobacco industry, filed class actions lawsuits against several large HMOs—Aetna, Cigna, Foundation, Humana, PacifiCare, Prudential, and United—accusing them of depriving enrollees of adequate treatment and engaging in a fraudulent scheme of misrepresenting coverage and treatment decisions. These class actions suits were allowed to proceed by a Florida court. The two classes of suits were consolidated in 2000 by the Judicial Panel on Multi–District Litigation before Judge Federico A. Moreno in the U.S. District Court for the Southern District of Florida. In re Managed Care Litigation, 150 F.Supp.2d 1330 (S.D.Fla.2001), Judge Moreno had granted the plaintiffs standing to sue under RICO, and had dismissed without prejudice the RICO claims for failure to plead predicate acts of mail and wire fraud with particularity, and failing to state a RICO conspiracy. He also dismissed, without prejudice, all of the ERISA claims due to the failure of plaintiffs to comply with ERISA's requirement for exhaustion of available plan review remedies.

On September 26, 2002, Judge Moreno rejected class standing for the subscriber track, in In re Managed Care Litigation, 209 F.R.D. 678 (S.D.Fla.2002). He found in part that plaintiffs could not support their allegation that "[d]efendants engaged in a "common scheme" or "pattern or practice" of uniform activity.

> "The "scheme," however, if there is one at all, is not promulgated by centralized authority, or uniform in all respects, but rather controlled on an individual level through subsidiaries and employers, thus differing amongst them. The Defendants have demonstrated the material differences in the documents upon which Plaintiffs rely to support their claim of uniformity. Because this Court can find no uniform scheme, the merits of the Plaintiffs

claims turn on the Defendants individualized dealings with each Plaintiff. This renders the ERISA class unsuitable for class treatment under Rule 23(b)(2)." Judge Moreno also rejected subscriber standing on the RICO count:

> Litigating the Plaintiffs' claims as a class action comprising *145 million members*, no matter what the cost in terms of judicial economy, efficiency and fairness, runs counter to the policies underlying *Rule 23(b)(3). See Fed. R.Civ.P. 23* advisory committee's note (1966 amendment) (stating that subdivision (b)(3) encompasses those cases "in which a class action would achieve economies of time, effort, and expense"). While this Court recognizes *Rule 23* is to be applied flexibly, the manageability problems discussed above defeat the Rule's underlying purposes and render these claims inappropriate for class treatment. Finally, the Court notes that Plaintiffs' assertion that the small size of each member's claims makes class treatment appear to be the only feasible method of adjudication, does not hold true. Even small individual claims under RICO can be feasible given the possibility of the award of treble damages and attorneys' fees to successful plaintiffs. Id. at 692–693.

His bottom line: "To the extent that there are common issues of law and fact present in this case, they do not predominate, and this case, if treated as a class action, would not be manageable, as it includes 145 million members. It is neither convenient nor desirable to accord class status to this case given its factual and legal complexities. Thus, class certification is DENIED."

The REPAIR Team is led by a group of plaintiffs lawyers who were successful in suits against the tobacco companies, and saw managed care as the next vulnerable and destructive institution in our culture. REPAIR's strategy, in the words of one commentator, is to "(r)aise the stakes so high that neither side can afford to lose...." Adam Bryant, Who's Afraid of Dickie Scruggs?, Newsweek, Dec. 6, 1999, at 46. In their complaints, MCO plaintiffs alleged that the managed care organizations have operated the affairs of an enterprise in interstate commerce through a pattern of racketeering activity and have injured the business or property of the plaintiffs as a result, in violation of sections 18 U.S.C. 1964 and 1962(c) of RICO. The racketeering activity is the use of the U.S. mails and wire services to defraud consumers—both by misrepresenting coverage and operations of the health plans, so as to fraudulently induce them to enroll, and by fraudulently misrepresenting the reasons why their claims were denied. See generally Margaret G. Farrell, Consumer Class Actions Challenging Managed Care Practices, SG013 ALI–ABA 517(ALI–ABA Course of Study, October 18–19, 2001).

MCO class actions assert traditional tort and trust obligations embodied in RICO and ERISA to curb managed care abuses and correct the market for managed care. The REPAIR suits do not challenge the divided loyalties of HMOs under fiduciary law; instead these suits look at particular abuses of managed care, alleging that they have fraudulently conducted their businesses in violation of RICO and failed to meet their obligation to disclose essential benefit information and to carry out the terms of their policies in violation of ERISA. The suits are not brought because MCOs have denied plaintiffs treatment or provided poor quality of care, but because MCOs have deprived plaintiffs of the promised coverage they paid for, which is claimed by the plaintiffs to constitute deception and unjust enrichment.

The REPAIR team alleged that the managed care organization have operated the affairs of an enterprise in interstate commerce through a pattern of racketeering activity and have injured the business or property of the plaintiffs as a result, in violation of sections 18 U.S.C. 1964 and 1962(c) of RICO. The alleged racketeering activity (defined in 18 U.S.C. 1961), is the use of the U.S. mails and wire services to defraud consumers—both by misrepresenting coverage and operations of the health plans, in the nature of fraudulent inducement, and by fraudulently breaching insurance contracts by misrepresenting the reasons why claims were denied. Existing precedent is not favorable to such a claim. The pattern of such racketeering activity is allegedly the health plans' repeated acts of mail and wire fraud over a period of at least four years and the prospect of its continuing.

The enterprise under RICO is an association-in-fact enterprise consisting of the national MCO and its subsidiaries, on the one hand, and its network of providers, on the other. The on-going association of these entities "for a common purpose of engaging in a course of conduct" is sufficient under RICO to allege the existence of an enterprise within the meaning of the statute. United States v. Turkette, 452 U.S. 576, 583, 101 S.Ct. 2524, 69 L.Ed.2d 246 (1981). National MCOs centralized national structure and their mechanisms for controlling and directing the affairs of the group support the concept that MCOs and their networks share a common purpose of providing health insurance coverage and medical services to customers and earning profits from providing those services. Metrahealth Insurance Co., 1997 WL 728084 (M.D.Fla. Oct. 23, 1997).

RICO provides for the recovery of three times the injury to property interests of plaintiffs proximately caused by defendant's racketeering activity. In the case of MCOs, the injury to policyholders' property interest that is proximately caused to policyholders is the loss in the value of coverage resulting from MCO's misrepresentations. The value of the lost coverage can be quantified as the difference between the value coverage as represented and the value of coverage actually provided to policyholder, an amount to be established at trial.

The alleged abusive practices challenged in the MCO suits stem largely from their failure to truthfully represent the coverage they sell and their failure to fairly administer health plans in the interest of subscribers. They include the following allegations:

1. Failure to disclose physician incentives. Although many people are aware that HMOs assemble providers in networks and offer coordinated care, often they are not aware of how those providers are paid and how it makes a difference to them as subscribers and patients.

2. Affirmative misrepresentation of coverage and failure to disclose coverage determination criteria. The litigation alleges that subscribers are deceived about covered, believing that plans will cover all "medically necessary services" of the type included in the plan. The term "medically necessary" is often specifically defined as services prescribed for diagnosis or treatment of a condition, not for convenience, in keeping with good medical practice and of an appropriate level of supply. There would be no misrepresentation if these were the services for which the plan actually provided coverage. The problem is that plans often use more specific criteria to make coverage determinations on individual claims, and the REPAIR suits claim that these criteria add more restrictive requirements of coverage which have never been disclosed to subscribers.

3. Failure to disclose that third party contractors and untrained reviewers are used to make coverage determinations. The plan does not make coverage

decisions, but instead third parties using their own criteria, and consumers are not fully informed of this.

4. Failure to apply policies' medical necessity definition in making benefit determinations. Use of such criteria as the Milliman & Robertson guidelines to deny claims breaches plan insurance contract with insureds. When MCOs use the mails to notify insured's that their claims are not medically necessary, knowing that the medical necessity definition in the policies has not been applied to the claims, MCOs engage in a fraudulent pattern of activity to operate their enterprises.

In Maio, the plaintiffs asserted similar claims against Aetna, Inc., Aetna–U.S. Healthcare, Inc., and Aetna U.S. Healthcare, Inc.'s 24 regional subsidiary health plans for violations of the Racketeer Influenced and Corrupt Organizations Act ("RICO") and state law. The case attacked "Aetna's failure to disclose its restrictive and coercive internal policies and practices, which render its advertising, marketing and membership materials false and misleading in violation of RICO." Plaintiffs claimed that "Aetna has engaged in a massive nationwide fraudulent advertising campaign designed to induce people to enroll in its HMO by representing that Aetna affirmatively manages its members' health care so as to, inter alia, raise the quality of care to a 'level of health care never available under the old fee-for-service system,' "when in fact, Aetna designed undisclosed internal policies to "improve defendants' profitability at the expense of quality of care." The relief sought was compensatory damages and an injunction enjoining appellees from pursuing the "policies, acts and practices" alleged in the complaint, together with punitive damages, treble damages, and attorney's fees under RICO.

The court rejected the RICO claims based on the financial losses plaintiff claimed to suffer by enrolling in Aetna's "inferior" HMO plan in the absence of allegations to the effect that each appellant suffered negative medical consequences resulting from Aetna's enactment of the policies and practices at issue.

> ... [W]e hold that appellants cannot establish that they suffered a tangible economic harm compensable under RICO unless they allege that health care they received under Aetna's plan actually was compromised or diminished as a result of Aetna's management decisions challenged in the complaint. It seems clear to us that unless appellants claim that Aetna failed to provide sufficient health insurance coverage to the members of their HMO plan in the sense that such individuals were denied medically necessary benefits, received inadequate, inferior or delayed medical treatment, or even worse, suffered personal injuries as a result of Aetna's systemic policies and practices, there is no factual basis for appellants' conclusory allegation that they have been injured in their "property" because the health insurance they actually received was inferior and therefore "worth less" than what they paid for it.

The court noted that the plaintiffs' RICO claims are essentially attacking the fundamental characteristics of a managed care plan, which does attempt to influence physician judgment about what is "cost-effective" care: "Thus, we think it fair to characterize appellants' injury theory as bottomed on the notion that Aetna's policies challenged in the complaint render its HMO structure "bad" in comparison to the other types of health care insurance available in the marketplace." They then observed that Pegram undercut this argument, given the Supreme Court's acknowledgment that managed care may appropriately use incentive designs to reduce costs.

The heart of the Maio claim against managed care is that any attempt by an MCO to restrict a physician's decisionmaking is presumptively undesirable. The RICO statute has been used primarily against organized crime, and RICO claims have not been successful against managed care plans historically. See Teti v. U.S. Healthcare, Inc., 1989 WL 143274 (E.D.Pa.1989)(RICO claim against HMO for failing to disclose physician incentives to withhold medical care dismissed).

The REPAIR TEAM litigation also pleaded a breach of ERISA. In Varity v. Howe, 516 U.S. 489, 116 S.Ct. 1065, 134 L.Ed.2d 130 (1996) the Supreme Court held that ERISA participants may sue on their own behalf for breach of fiduciary duty under section 502(a)(3). Varity allows individual employees under ERISA to sue on their own behalf to enforce the fiduciary obligations that the Act imposes on plan administrators. The TEAM litigation therefore has also pleaded ERISA violations.

Plaintiffs in the MCO suits maintain that the health plans are fiduciaries under ERISA and have breached their duty of loyalty to plaintiffs. ERISA imposes general fiduciary duties of loyalty and prudence, derived from the common law of trusts, on plan administrators, officers, trustees, and custodians and other persons who exercise discretionary authority over plan management and administration. These require fiduciaries to discharge their duties with respect to the plan solely in the interest of the participants and beneficiaries, and to discharge their duties in accordance with the terms of the plan.

The REPAIR Team litigation alleges that the health plans act as fiduciaries because they have de facto or express authority to exercise their discretion to determine eligibility for and the scope of benefits due participants in the plans. The defendants have not contested their status as fiduciaries. The specific violations alleged include misrepresentation and the failure to disclose essential benefit information section 404(a)(1), 29 U.S.C. § 1104(a)(1). ERISA's embodiment of common law trust principles requires an MCO, as a fiduciary managing Plaintiffs' benefit plans, to disclose critical benefit information to beneficiaries. See e.g. Eddy v. Colonial Life Ins. Co., 919 F.2d 747, 750 (D.C.Cir.1990)(plan administrator had affirmative fiduciary duty to disclose to participant suffering from AIDS information about his conversion rights). Thus, an ERISA fiduciary has "not only a negative duty not to misinform, but also an affirmative duty to inform when the trustee knows that the silence might be harmful." Bixler v. Central Pa. Teamsters Health & Welfare Fund, 12 F.3d 1292, 1300 (3d Cir.1993).

The plaintiffs also claim that MCOs violated their fiduciary obligations under ERISA section 404(a)(1) by not disclosing such specifically enumerated information—its restrictive coverage criteria—because such information is specifically required by sections 102(b) and 104 of ERISA 29 U.S.C. § 1022(b) and § 1024. ERISA itself expressly requires certain fundamentally important information be included in Summary Plan Descriptions (SPDs) provided to plan participants. This includes "the plan's requirements respecting eligibility for ... benefits; ... [and] circumstances which may result in ... denial or loss of benefits." 29 U.S.C. § 1022(b). When MCOs exercise discretion in denying claim, they arguably breach their fiduciary obligation if they fail to disclose the restrictive criteria as "requirements" and "circumstances" limiting benefits within the meaning of sections 102(b), 29 U.S.C. § 1022(b).

A second charge is that the plans failed failed to carry out the terms of ERISA governed health benefit plans, section 404(a)(b)(D), 29 U.S.C. § 1104(a)(1)(D). An MCO breaches a separate fiduciary obligation to carry out the terms of the benefit plans when it applies more restrictive criteria to limit the medical necessity coverage described in plaintiffs policies. MCOs have an obligation to apply that definition of coverage—the medically necessary services as defined in certificates of coverage—when exercising their fiduciary authority. It could not impose different, conflicting restrictions. Schoonmaker v. Employee Sav. Plan of Amoco Corp., 987 F.2d 410, 413–14 (7th Cir.1993) (plan administrator's informal practice of freezing investment accounts held an unreasonable interpretation of the plan's written procedures and thus an unauthorized modification and a violation of section 404(a)(1)(D) of the Act). However, that is just what the restrictive criteria were. An MCO's use of these undisclosed criteria violated ERISA. Thus, either the restrictive criteria are part of the plan and must be disclosed or they are not part of the plan and cannot be applied to limit the coverage described there.

Third, the plaintiffs allege a denial of coverage as a denial of benefits under ERISA plans.

The TEAM litigation is a clever attempt to attack managed care disclosure and decisionmaking about medical necessity. The difficulties in defining "damage", as the Maio court indicated, make the prospects for the success of such litigation unlikely.

## V. STATE REGULATION OF MANAGED CARE

### A. INTRODUCTION

**Add, at p. 576:**

The wave of managed care legislation that swept through the states in the late 1990s seemed largely spent by 2002. For the first time since 1997, no new states adopted legislation subjecting managed care organizations to liability in 2002. (Legislation adopted by West Virginia, Oregon, North Carolina and New Jersey had brought to ten the total number of states that have statutes providing for managed care liability). Only 46 new insurance mandates were adopted by the states in 2002, down from 82 in 2001, 68 in 2000 and 103 in 1999. Only four states each adopted new external review and utilization review legislation during 2002. New legislation continued to emerge on one front—prompt payment laws, which require that insurers pay providers within specified time limits or face sanctions (10 new laws in 2002)—but even these laws were somewhat less demanding than those that had been adopted in the preceding years. See Jeffrey L. Gabardi, State Issue Tracking Report: Year in Review, 2002, http://membership.hiaa.org/pdfs/state/charts/YearInReview-02.pdf. (Prompt payment law enforcement, also, incidentally seems to be the area of greatest activity in terms of state fines or penalties imposed on insurers, and to account for some of the largest fines imposed by the states, including a $4 million fine against 22 health insurers levied by New York in April of 2002.)

What accounts for this decline in state legislation? Effective lobbying by managed care organizations and insurers? Rapid increases in health care premiums, giving credence to the claims of insurer lobbyists that managed care regulation drives up costs? Lack of interest by voters, distracted by threats of terrorism and the state of the economy? Saturation? (By 2001, 42 states had adopted external review laws.) An alternative explanation is that the need for regulation has become less pressing as managed care entities adapted to market forces (and to legal forces) and produced more consumer friendly products. See M. Gregg Bloche, One Step Ahead of the Law: Market Pressures and the Evolution of Managed Care, in M. Gregg Bloche, ed. The Privatization of Health Care Reform: Legal and Regulatory Perspectives (2003).

On the other hand, was managed care regulation ever justified in the first place? See, Frank A. Sloan and Mark A. Hall, Market Failures and the Evolution of State Managed Care Regulation, 65 Law & Contemp. Prob. 169 (2002), carefully weighing the market failure arguments for and against managed care regulation. And has it helped consumers, or simply made it more difficult for those who cannot afford the most generous forms of insurance to get coverage? See Clark C. Havighurst, The Backlash Against Managed Health Care: Hard Politics Make Bad Policy, 34 Ind. L. Rev. 395 (2001). See also, describing the development of managed care regulation, Alice A. Noble and Troyen A. Brennan, The Stages of Managed–Care Regulation: Developing Better Rules, in John E. Billi and Gail B. Agrawal, The Challenge of Regulating Managed Care, 29 (2001).

Finally, see discussing comprehensively the range of consumer concerns about health care, and appropriate regulatory responses, Eleanor DeArman Kinney, Protecting American Health Care Consumers (2002).

# Chapter 9

# REGULATION OF INSURANCE AND MANAGED CARE: THE FEDERAL ROLE

## II. THE EMPLOYEE RETIREMENT INCOME SECURITY ACT OF 1974 (ERISA)

### A. ERISA PREEMPTION OF STATE HEALTH INSURANCE REGULATION

At p. 602, Delete Corporate Health Insurance, Inc. v. Texas Department of Insurance, and substitute:

#### RUSH PRUDENTIAL HMO, INC. v. MORAN, ET AL.

Supreme Court of the United States, 2002.
536 U.S. 355, 122 S.Ct. 2151, 153 L.Ed.2d 375.

Justice SOUTER delivered the opinion of the Court.

\* \* \*

Petitioner, Rush Prudential HMO, Inc., is a health maintenance organization (HMO) that contracts to provide medical services for employee welfare benefit plans covered by ERISA. Respondent Debra Moran is a beneficiary under one such plan, sponsored by her husband's employer. Rush's "Certificate of Group Coverage," issued to employees who participate in employer-sponsored plans, promises that Rush will provide them with "medically necessary" services. The terms of the certificate give Rush the "broadest possible discretion" to determine whether a medical service claimed by a beneficiary is covered under the certificate. The certificate specifies that a service is covered as "medically necessary" if Rush finds:

"(a) [The service] is furnished or authorized by a Participating Doctor for the diagnosis and treatment of a Sickness or Injury or for the maintenance of a person's good health."

"(b) The prevailing opinion within the appropriate specialty of the United States medical profession is that [the service] is safe and effective for its intended use, and that its omission would adversely affect the person's medical condition."

"(c) It is furnished by a provider with appropriate training, experience, staff and facilities to furnish that particular service or supply." [ ]

As the certificate explains, Rush contracts with physicians "to arrange for or provide services and supplies for medical care and treatment" of covered persons. Each covered person selects a primary care physician from those under contract to Rush, while Rush will pay for medical services by an unaffiliated physician only if the services have been "authorized" both by the primary care physician and Rush's medical director. [ ]

In 1996, when Moran began to have pain and numbness in her right shoulder, Dr. Arthur LaMarre, her primary care physician, unsuccessfully administered "conservative" treatments such as physiotherapy. In October 1997, Dr. LaMarre recommended that Rush approve surgery by an unaffiliated specialist, Dr. Julia Terzis, who had developed an unconventional treatment for Moran's condition. Although Dr. LaMarre said that Moran would be "best served" by that procedure, Rush denied the request and, after Moran's internal appeals, affirmed the denial on the ground that the procedure was not "medically necessary." [ ] Rush instead proposed that Moran undergo standard surgery, performed by a physician affiliated with Rush.

In January 1998, Moran made a written demand for an independent medical review of her claim, as guaranteed by § 410 of Illinois's HMO Act, [ ] which provides:

"Each Health Maintenance Organization shall provide a mechanism for the timely review by a physician * * * who is unaffiliated with the Health Maintenance Organization, jointly selected by the patient ..., primary care physician and the Health Maintenance Organization in the event of a dispute between the primary care physician and the Health Maintenance Organization regarding the medical necessity of a covered service proposed by a primary care physician. In the event that the reviewing physician determines the covered service to be medically necessary, the Health Maintenance Organization shall provide the covered service."
* * *

When Rush failed to provide the independent review, Moran sued in an Illinois state court to compel compliance with the state Act. Rush removed the suit to Federal District Court, arguing that the cause of action was "completely preempted" under ERISA. [ ]

While the suit was pending, Moran had surgery by Dr. Terzis at her own expense and submitted a $94,841.27 reimbursement claim to Rush. Rush treated the claim as a renewed request for benefits and began a new inquiry to determine coverage. The three doctors consulted by Rush said the surgery had been medically unnecessary.

Meanwhile, the federal court remanded the case back to state court on Moran's motion, concluding that because Moran's request for independent review under § 410 would not require interpretation of the terms of an ERISA plan, the claim was not "completely preempted" so as to permit removal * * * The state court enforced the state statute and ordered Rush to submit to review by an independent physician. * * * [The reviewer] decided that Dr. Terzis's treatment had been medically necessary, based on the definition of medical necessity in Rush's Certificate of Group Coverage, as well as his own medical judgment. Rush's medical director, however, refused to concede that the surgery had been medically necessary, and denied Moran's claim in January 1999.

Moran amended her complaint in state court to seek reimbursement for the surgery as "medically necessary" under Illinois's HMO Act, and Rush again removed to federal court, arguing that Moran's amended complaint stated a claim for ERISA benefits and was thus completely preempted by ERISA's civil enforcement provisions, 29 U.S.C. § 1132(a), * * * The District Court treated Moran's claim as a suit under ERISA, and denied the claim on the ground that ERISA preempted Illinois's independent review statute. The Court of Appeals for the Seventh Circuit reversed. * * *

To "safeguar[d] . . . the establishment, operation, and administration" of employee benefit plans, ERISA sets "minimum standards . . . assuring the equitable character of such plans and their financial soundness," [ ] and contains an express preemption provision that ERISA "shall supersede any and all State laws insofar as they may now or hereafter relate to any employee benefit plan. . . ." § 1144(a). A saving clause then reclaims a substantial amount of ground with its provision that "nothing in this subchapter shall be construed to exempt or relieve any person from any law of any State which regulates insurance, banking, or securities." § 1144(b)(2)(A). The "unhelpful" drafting of these antiphonal clauses * * * occupies a substantial share of this Court's time.

In trying to extrapolate congressional intent in a case like this, when congressional language seems simultaneously to preempt everything and hardly anything, we "have no choice" but to temper the assumption that" 'the ordinary meaning . . . accurately expresses the legislative purpose,' [ ] with the qualification " 'that the historic police powers of the States were not [meant] to be superseded by the Federal Act unless that was the clear and manifest purpose of Congress.' " [ ]

It is beyond serious dispute that under existing precedent § 410 of the Illinois HMO Act "relates to" employee benefit plans within the meaning of § 1144(a). * * * As a law that "relates to" ERISA plans under § 1144(a), § 410 is saved from preemption only if it also "regulates insurance" under § 1144(b)(2)(A). * * *

In *Metropolitan Life,* we said that in deciding whether a law "regulates insurance" under ERISA's saving clause, we start with a "commonsense view of the matter,"[ ] under which "a law must not just have an impact on the insurance industry, but must be specifically directed toward that industry." [ ] We then test the results of the commonsense enquiry by employing the three factors used to point to insurance laws spared from federal preemption under the McCarran–Ferguson Act, 15 U.S.C. § 1011 *et seq.* * * *

The common-sense enquiry focuses on "primary elements of an insurance contract[, which] are the spreading and underwriting of a policyholder's risk." [ ] The Illinois statute addresses these elements by defining "health maintenance organization" by reference to the risk that it bears. [ ]

Rush contends that seeing an HMO as an insurer distorts the nature of an HMO, which is, after all, a health care provider, too. This, Rush argues, should determine its characterization, with the consequence that regulation of an HMO is not insurance regulation within the meaning of ERISA.

The answer to Rush is, of course, that an HMO is both: it provides health care, and it does so as an insurer. Nothing in the saving clause requires an either-or choice between health care and insurance in deciding a preemption question, and as long as providing insurance fairly accounts for the application of state law, the saving clause may apply. * * *

"The defining feature of an HMO is receipt of a fixed fee for each patient enrolled under the terms of a contract to provide specified health care if needed." *Pegram v. Herdrich,* [ ] "The HMO thus assumes the financial risk of providing the benefits promised: if a participant never gets sick, the HMO keeps the money regardless, and if a participant becomes expensively ill, the HMO is responsible for the treatment...." *Id.,* * * *.

* * *

On a second tack, Rush and its *amici* dispute that § 410 is aimed specifically at the insurance industry. They say the law sweeps too broadly with definitions capturing organizations that provide no insurance, and by regulating noninsurance activities of HMOs that do. Rush points out that Illinois law defines HMOs to include organizations that cause the risk of health care delivery to be borne by the organization itself, or by "its providers." [ ] In Rush's view, the reference to "its providers" suggests that an organization may be an HMO under state law (and subject to § 410) even if it does not bear risk itself, either because it has "devolve[d]" the risk of health care delivery onto others, or because it has contracted only to provide "administrative" or other services for self-funded plans. []

These arguments, however, are built on unsound assumptions. Rush's first contention assumes that an HMO is no longer an insurer when it arranges to limit its exposure, as when an HMO arranges for capitated contracts to compensate its affiliated physicians with a set fee for each HMO patient regardless of the treatment provided. Under such an arrangement, Rush claims, the risk is not borne by the HMO at all. In a similar vein, Rush points out that HMOs may contract with third-party insurers to protect themselves against large claims.

The problem with Rush's argument is simply that a reinsurance contract does not take the primary insurer out of the insurance business [ ], and capitation contracts do not relieve the HMO of its obligations to the beneficiary. The HMO is still bound to provide medical care to its members, and this is so regardless of the ability of physicians or third-party insurers to honor their contracts with the HMO.

Nor do we see anything standing in the way of applying the saving clause if we assume that the general state definition of HMO would include a contractor that provides only administrative services for a self-funded plan.[6] * * * Rush points out that the general definition of HMO under Illinois law includes not only organizations that "provide" health care plans, but those that "arrange for" them to be provided, so long as "any part of the risk of

---

**6.** ERISA's "deemer" clause provides an exception to its saving clause that forbids States from regulating self-funded plans as insurers. [ ] Therefore, Illinois's Act would not be "saved" as an insurance law to the extent it applied to self-funded plans. * * *

health care delivery" rests upon "the organization or its providers." * * * Rush hypothesizes a sort of medical matchmaker, bringing together ERISA plans and medical care providers; even if the latter bear all the risks, the matchmaker would be an HMO under the Illinois definition. Rush could conclude from this that § 410 covers noninsurers, and so is not directed specifically to the insurance industry. Ergo, ERISA's saving clause would not apply.

It is far from clear, though, that the terms of § 410 would even theoretically apply to the matchmaker, for the requirement that the HMO "provide" the covered service if the independent reviewer finds it medically necessary seems to assume that the HMO in question is a provider, not the mere arranger mentioned in the general definition of an HMO. * * *

* * * Thus, the Illinois HMO Act is a law "directed toward" the insurance industry, and an "insurance regulation" under a "commonsense" view.

The McCarran–Ferguson factors confirm our conclusion. A law regulating insurance for McCarran–Ferguson purposes targets practices or provisions that "ha[ve] the effect of transferring or spreading a policyholder's risk; ... [that are] an integral part of the policy relationship between the insurer and the insured; and [are] limited to entities within the insurance industry." [ ] Because the factors are guideposts, a state law is not required to satisfy all three McCarran–Ferguson criteria to survive preemption, * * * [I]n any event, the second and third factors are clearly satisfied by § 410.

It is obvious enough that the independent review requirement regulates "an integral part of the policy relationship between the insurer and the insured." Illinois adds an extra layer of review when there is internal disagreement about an HMO's denial of coverage. The reviewer applies both a standard of medical care (medical necessity) and characteristically, as in this case, construes policy terms. [ ] The review affects the "policy relationship" between HMO and covered persons by translating the relationship under the HMO agreement into concrete terms of specific obligation or freedom from duty. * * *

The final factor, that the law be aimed at a "practice ... limited to entities within the insurance industry,"[ ] is satisfied for many of the same reasons that the law passes the commonsense test. * * *

* * *

Given that § 410 regulates insurance, ERISA's mandate that "nothing in this subchapter shall be construed to exempt or relieve any person from any law of any State which regulates insurance," 29 U.S.C. § 1144(b)(2)(A), ostensibly forecloses preemption. [ ] Rush, however, does not give up. It argues for preemption anyway, emphasizing that the question is ultimately one of congressional intent, which sometimes is so clear that it overrides a statutory provision designed to save state law from being preempted. * * *

In ERISA law, we have recognized one example of this sort of overpowering federal policy in the civil enforcement provisions, 29 U.S.C. § 1132(a), * * * In *Massachusetts Mut. Life Ins. Co. v. Russell*, [ ] we said those provisions amounted to an "interlocking, interrelated, and interdependent remedial scheme,"[ ] which *Pilot Life* described as "represent[ing] a careful balancing of the need for prompt and fair claims settlement procedures against the public interest in encouraging the formation of employee benefit plans," [ ] So, we have held, the civil enforcement provisions are of such extraordinarily preemptive power that they override even the "well-pleaded complaint" rule for establishing the conditions under which a cause of action may be removed to a federal forum. *Metropolitan Life Ins. Co. v. Taylor*, [ ]

Although we have yet to encounter a forced choice between the congressional policies of exclusively federal remedies and the "reservation of the business of insurance to the States,"[ ] we have anticipated such a conflict, with the state insurance regulation losing out if it allows plan participants "to obtain remedies . . . that Congress rejected in ERISA."

In *Pilot Life*, an ERISA plan participant who had been denied benefits sued in a state court on state tort and contract claims. He sought not merely damages for breach of contract, but also damages for emotional distress and punitive damages, both of which we had held unavailable under relevant ERISA provisions. [ ] We not only rejected the notion that these commonlaw contract claims "regulat[ed] insurance," [ ] but went on to say that, regardless, Congress intended a "federal common law of rights and obligations" to develop under ERISA, [ ] without embellishment by independent state remedies.

Rush says that the day has come to turn dictum into holding by declaring that the state insurance regulation, § 410, is preempted for creating just the kind of "alternative remedy" we disparaged in *Pilot Life*. As Rush sees it, the independent review procedure is a form of binding arbitration that allows an ERISA beneficiary to submit claims to a new decisionmaker to examine Rush's determination *de novo*, supplanting judicial review under the "arbitrary and capricious" standard ordinarily applied when discretionary plan interpretations are challenged [ ]. * * *

We think, however, that Rush overstates the rule expressed in *Pilot Life*.
* * *

* * *

[T]his case addresses a state regulatory scheme that provides no new cause of action under state law and authorizes no new form of ultimate relief. While independent review under § 410 may well settle the fate of a benefit claim under a particular contract, the state statute does not enlarge the claim beyond the benefits available in any action brought under § 1132(a). And although the reviewer's determination would presumably replace that of the HMO as to what is "medically necessary" under this contract, the relief ultimately available would still be what ERISA authorizes in a suit for benefits under § 1132(a). * * *

Rush still argues for going beyond *Pilot Life,* making the preemption issue here one of degree, whether the state procedural imposition interferes unreasonably with Congress's intention to provide a uniform federal regime of "rights and obligations" under ERISA. However, "[s]uch disuniformities . . . are the inevitable result of the congressional decision to 'save' local insurance regulation."[ ].[11]

11. Thus, we do not believe that the mere fact that state independent review laws are likely to entail different procedures will impose burdens on plan administration that would

Although we have recognized a limited exception from the saving clause for alternative causes of action and alternative remedies in the sense described above, we have never indicated that there might be additional justifications for qualifying the clause's application. * * *

To be sure, a State might provide for a type of "review" that would so resemble an adjudication as to fall within *Pilot Life's* categorical bar. Rush, and the dissent,[ ] contend that § 410 fills that bill by imposing an alternative scheme of arbitral adjudication at odds with the manifest congressional purpose to confine adjudication of disputes to the courts. It does not turn out to be this simple, however, and a closer look at the state law reveals a scheme significantly different from common arbitration as a way of construing and applying contract terms.

In the classic sense, arbitration occurs when "parties in dispute choose a judge to render a final and binding decision on the merits of the controversy and on the basis of proofs presented by the parties." [ ] Arbitrators typically hold hearings at which parties may submit evidence and conduct cross-examinations. [ ]

Section 4–10 does resemble an arbitration provision, then, to the extent that the independent reviewer considers disputes about the meaning of the HMO contract and receives "evidence" in the form of medical records, statements from physicians, and the like. But this is as far as the resemblance to arbitration goes, for the other features of review under § 4–10 give the proceeding a different character, one not at all at odds with the policy behind § 1132(a). The Act does not give the independent reviewer a free-ranging power to construe contract terms, but instead, confines review to a single term: the phrase "medical necessity," used to define the services covered under the contract. [ ] This limitation, in turn, implicates a feature of HMO benefit determinations that we described in *Pegram v. Herdrich,* [ ] We explained that when an HMO guarantees medically necessary care, determinations of coverage "cannot be untangled from physicians' judgments about reasonable medical treatment." [ ] This is just how the Illinois Act operates; the independent examiner must be a physician with credentials similar to those of the primary care physician, [ ] and is expected to exercise independent medical judgment in deciding what medical necessity requires. * * *

Once this process is set in motion, it does not resemble either contract interpretation or evidentiary litigation before a neutral arbiter, as much as it looks like a practice (having nothing to do with arbitration) of obtaining another medical opinion. * * *

The practice of obtaining a second opinion, however, is far removed from any notion of an enforcement scheme, and once § 410 is seen as something akin to a mandate for second-opinion practice in order to ensure sound

threaten the object of 29 U.S.C. § 1132(a); it is the HMO contracting with a plan, and not the plan itself, that will be subject to these regulations, and every HMO will have to establish procedures for conforming with the local laws, regardless of what this Court may think ERISA forbids. This means that there will be no special burden of compliance upon an ERISA plan beyond what the HMO has already provided for. And although the added compliance cost to the HMO may ultimately be passed on to the ERISA plan, we have said that such "indirect economic effect[s]," [ ], are not enough to preempt state regulation even outside of the insurance context. We recognize, of course, that a State might enact an independent review requirement with procedures so elaborate, and burdens so onerous, that they might undermine § 1132(a). No such system is before us.

medical judgments, the preemption argument that arbitration under § 410 supplants judicial enforcement runs out of steam.

Next, Rush argues that § 4–10 clashes with a substantive rule intended to be preserved by the system of uniform enforcement, stressing a feature of judicial review highly prized by benefit plans: a deferential standard for reviewing benefit denials. Whereas *Firestone Tire & Rubber Co. v. Bruch,* [ ] recognized that an ERISA plan could be designed to grant "discretion" to a plan fiduciary, deserving deference from a court reviewing a discretionary judgment, § 4–10 provides that when a plan purchases medical services and insurance from an HMO, benefit denials are subject to apparently *de novo* review. If a plan should continue to balk at providing a service the reviewer has found medically necessary, the reviewer's determination could carry great weight in a subsequent suit for benefits under § 1132(a), depriving the plan of the judicial deference a fiduciary's medical judgment might have obtained if judicial review of the plan's decision had been immediate.[15]

Again, however, the significance of § 410 is not wholly captured by Rush's argument, which requires some perspective for evaluation. First, in determining whether state procedural requirements deprive plan administrators of any right to a uniform standard of review, it is worth recalling that ERISA itself provides nothing about the standard. It simply requires plans to afford a beneficiary some mechanism for internal review of a benefit denial, * * *.

Not only is there no ERISA provision directly providing a lenient standard for judicial review of benefit denials, but there is no requirement necessarily entailing such an effect even indirectly. When this Court dealt with the review standards on which the statute was silent, we held that a general or default rule of *de novo* review could be replaced by deferential review if the ERISA plan itself provided that the plan's benefit determinations were matters of high or unfettered discretion, [ ]. Nothing in ERISA, however, requires that these kinds of decisions be so "discretionary" in the first place; whether they are is simply a matter of plan design or the drafting of an HMO contract.

In this respect, then, § 410 prohibits designing an insurance contract so as to accord unfettered discretion to the insurer to interpret the contract's terms. As such, it does not implicate ERISA's enforcement scheme at all, and is no different from the types of substantive state regulation of insurance contracts we have in the past permitted to survive preemption, such as mandated-benefit statutes and statutes prohibiting the denial of claims solely on the ground of untimeliness. [ ] * * *

* * *

**15.** An issue implicated by this case but requiring no resolution is the degree to which a plan provision for unfettered discretion in benefit determinations guarantees truly deferential review. In *Firestone Tire* itself, we noted that review for abuse of discretion would home in on any conflict of interest on the plan fiduciary's part, if a conflict was plausibly raised. That last observation was underscored only two Terms ago in *Pegram v. Herdrich,* [ ] when we again noted the potential for conflict when an HMO makes decisions about appropriate treatment [ ]. It is a fair question just how deferential the review can be when the judicial eye is peeled for conflict of interest. Moreover, as we explained in *Pegram,* "it is at least questionable whether Congress would have had mixed eligibility decisions in mind when it provided that decisions administering a plan were fiduciary in nature." [ ] Our decision today does not require us to resolve these questions.

In deciding what to make of these facts and conclusions, it helps to go back to where we started and recall the ways States regulate insurance in looking out for the welfare of their citizens. Illinois has chosen to regulate insurance as one way to regulate the practice of medicine, which we have previously held to be permissible under ERISA [ ]. While the statute designed to do this undeniably eliminates whatever may have remained of a plan sponsor's option to minimize scrutiny of benefit denials, this effect of eliminating an insurer's autonomy to guarantee terms congenial to its own interests is the stuff of garden variety insurance regulation through the imposition of standard policy terms. * * * And any lingering doubt about the reasonableness of § 410 in affecting the application of § 1132(a) may be put to rest by recalling that regulating insurance tied to what is medically necessary is probably inseparable from enforcing the quintessentially state-law standards of reasonable medical care. See *Pegram v. Herdrich,* [ ] To the extent that benefits litigation in some federal courts may have to account for the effects of § 410, it would be an exaggeration to hold that the objectives of § 1132(a) are undermined. The saving clause is entitled to prevail here, and we affirm the judgment.

Justice THOMAS, with whom THE CHIEF JUSTICE, Justice SCALIA, and Justice KENNEDY join, dissenting.

This Court has repeatedly recognized that ERISA's civil enforcement provision, § 502 of the Employee Retirement Income Security Act of 1974 (ERISA), 29 U.S.C. § 1132, provides the exclusive vehicle for actions asserting a claim for benefits under health plans governed by ERISA, and therefore that state laws that create additional remedies are preempted. [ ] Such exclusivity of remedies is necessary to further Congress' interest in establishing a uniform federal law of employee benefits so that employers are encouraged to provide benefits to their employees. [ ]

* * * Therefore, as the Court concedes, [ ] even a state law that "regulates insurance" may be preempted if it supplements the remedies provided by ERISA, despite ERISA's saving clause, [ ] Today, however, the Court takes the unprecedented step of allowing respondent Debra Moran to short circuit ERISA's remedial scheme by allowing her claim for benefits to be determined in the first instance through an arbitral-like procedure provided under Illinois law, and by a decisionmaker other than a court. [ ] This decision not only conflicts with our precedents, it also eviscerates the uniformity of ERISA remedies Congress deemed integral to the "careful balancing of the need for prompt and fair claims settlement procedures against the public interest in encouraging the formation of employee benefit plans." * * *

From the facts of this case one can readily understand why Moran sought recourse under § 410. * * *

In the course of its review, petitioner informed Moran that "there is no prevailing opinion within the appropriate specialty of the United States medical profession that the procedure proposed [by Moran] is safe and effective for its intended use and that the omission of the procedure would adversely affect [her] medical condition." [ ]. Petitioner did agree to cover the standard treatment for Moran's ailment, [ ] concluding that peer-reviewed literature "demonstrates that [the standard surgery] is effective therapy in the treatment of [Moran's condition]." [ ]

Moran, however, was not satisfied with this option. * * * She invoked § 410 of the Illinois HMO Act, which requires HMOs to provide a mechanism for review by an independent physician when the patient's primary care physician and HMO disagree about the medical necessity of a treatment proposed by the primary care physician. * * *

Dr. A. Lee Dellon, an unaffiliated physician who served as the independent medical reviewer, concluded that the surgery for which petitioner denied coverage "was appropriate," that it was "the same type of surgery" he would have done, and that Moran "had all of the indications and therefore the medical necessity to carry out" the nonstandard surgery. * * * Under § 410, Dr. Dellon's determination conclusively established Moran's right to benefits under Illinois law.

* * *

Section 514(a)'s broad language provides that ERISA "shall supersede any and all State laws insofar as they ... relate to any employee benefit plan," except as provided in § 514(b). 29 U.S.C. § 1144(a). This language demonstrates "Congress's intent to establish the regulation of employee welfare benefit plans 'as exclusively a federal concern.' "[ ] It was intended to "ensure that plans and plan sponsors would be subject to a uniform body of benefits law" so as to "minimize the administrative and financial burden of complying with conflicting directives among States or between States and the Federal Government" and to prevent "the potential for conflict in substantive law ... requiring the tailoring of plans and employer conduct to the peculiarities of the law of each jurisdiction." [ ]

* * * [T]he Court until today had consistently held that state laws that seek to supplant or add to the exclusive remedies in § 502(a) of ERISA, 29 U.S.C. § 1132(a), are preempted because they conflict with Congress' objective that rights under ERISA plans are to be enforced under a uniform national system. [ ] The Court has explained that § 502(a) creates an "interlocking, interrelated, and interdependent remedial scheme," and that a beneficiary who claims that he was wrongfully denied benefits has "a panoply of remedial devices" at his disposal." * * *

In addressing the relationship between ERISA's remedies under § 502(a) and a state law regulating insurance, the Court has observed that "[t]he policy choices reflected in the inclusion of certain remedies and the exclusion of others under the federal scheme would be completely undermined if ERISA-plan participants and beneficiaries were free to obtain remedies under state law that Congress rejected in ERISA." [ ] Thus, while the preeminent federal interest in the uniform administration of employee benefit plans yields in some instances to varying state regulation of the business of insurance, the exclusivity and uniformity of ERISA's enforcement scheme remains paramount. "Congress intended § 502(a) to be the exclusive remedy for rights guaranteed under ERISA." * * *

* * *

Section 4–10 cannot be characterized as anything other than an alternative state-law remedy or vehicle for seeking benefits. In the first place, § 4 10 comes into play only if the HMO and the claimant dispute the claimant's entitlement to benefits; the purpose of the review is to determine whether a claimant is entitled to benefits. * * *

There is no question that arbitration constitutes an alternative remedy to litigation. [ ] Consequently, although a contractual agreement to arbitrate—which does not constitute a "State law" relating to "any employee benefit plan"—is outside § 514(a) of ERISA's preemptive scope, States may not circumvent ERISA preemption by mandating an alternative arbitral-like remedy as a plan term enforceable through an ERISA action.

To be sure, the majority is correct that § 4–10 does not mirror all procedural and evidentiary aspects of "common arbitration." [ ] But as a binding decision on the merits of the controversy the § 410 review resembles nothing so closely as arbitration. * * *

* * *

[I]t is troubling that the Court views the review under § 4–10 as nothing more than a practice "of obtaining a second [medical] opinion." * * * [W]hile a second medical opinion is nothing more than that—an opinion—a determination under § 4–10 is a conclusive determination with respect to the award of benefits. And the Court's reference to *Pegram v. Herdrich,* [ ] as support for its Alice in Wonderland-like claim that the § 4 10 proceeding is "far removed from any notion of an enforcement scheme," *ante,* at 2169, is equally perplexing, given that the treatment is long over and the issue presented is purely an eligibility decision with respect to reimbursement.

Section 4–10 constitutes an arbitral-like state remedy through which plan members may seek to resolve conclusively a disputed right to benefits. Some 40 other States have similar laws, though these vary as to applicability, procedures, standards, deadlines, and consequences of independent review. * * * Allowing disparate state laws that provide inconsistent external review requirements to govern a participant's or beneficiary's claim to benefits under an employee benefit plan is wholly destructive of Congress' expressly stated goal of uniformity in this area. Moreover, it is inimical to a scheme for furthering and protecting the "careful balancing of the need for prompt and fair claims settlement procedures against the public interest in encouraging the formation of employee benefit plans," given that the development of a federal common law under ERISA-regulated plans has consistently been deemed central to that balance. * * *

For the reasons noted by the Court, independent review provisions may sound very appealing. Efforts to expand the variety of remedies available to aggrieved beneficiaries beyond those set forth in ERISA are obviously designed to increase the chances that patients will be able to receive treatments they desire, and most of us are naturally sympathetic to those suffering from illness who seek further options. Nevertheless, the Court would do well to remember that no employer is required to provide any health benefit plan under ERISA and that the entire advent of managed care, and the genesis of HMOs, stemmed from spiraling health costs. To the extent that independent review provisions such as § 410 make it more likely that HMOs will have to subsidize beneficiaries' treatments of choice, they undermine the ability of HMOs to control costs, which, in turn, undermines the ability of employers to provide health care coverage for employees.

As a consequence, independent review provisions could create a disincentive to the formation of employee health benefit plans, a problem that Congress addressed by making ERISA's remedial scheme exclusive and uniform. While it may well be the case that the advantages of allowing States to implement independent review requirements as a supplement to the remedies currently provided under ERISA outweigh this drawback, this is a judgment that, pursuant to ERISA, must be made by Congress. I respectfully dissent.

**Add, at p. 608, note 2 and 610, n. 4:**

What is left of Section 502 field preemption after *Moran*? Several district court cases subsequent to *Moran* have held that ERISA still preempts laws ostensibly intended to regulate insurance, including a Pennsylvania statute providing for punitive damages for "bad faith" denials of benefits, *Bell v. UNUM–Provident Corp.*, 222 F.Supp.2d 692 (E.D.Pa.2002); *Kirkhuff v. Lincoln Technical Inst.*, 221 F.Supp.2d 572 (E.D.Pa.2002); *Sprecher v. Aetna U.S. Healthcare*, 2002 WL 1917711 (E.D.Pa.2002), *but see Rosenbaum v. Unum Life Ins. Co.*, 2002 WL 1769899 (E.D.Pa.2002); and an Illinois statutory cause of action for "unreasonable and vexatious delay in paying benefits," *O'Neil v. Unum Life Ins. Co.*, 2002 WL 31356453 (N.D.Ill.2002). These cases have in general held that *Pilot Life* is still good law after *Moran*, that the statutory causes of action at issue were not saved from preemption as state laws regulating the insurance industry, and that they were in any event preempted as inconsistent with ERISA's remedial scheme.

The Supreme Court examined further the scope of ERISA's savings clause in *Kentucky Association of Health Plans v. Miller*, ___ U.S. ___, 123 S.Ct. 1471, ___ L.Ed.2d ___ (2003). This case involved the claim of an association of managed care plans that Kentucky's "any willing provider" law was preempted by ERISA. The Sixth Circuit had held that the regulatory provision was saved from preemption under ERISA's savings clause.

In a brief and unanimous opinion written by Justice Scalia (who had dissented in *Moran*), the Court affirmed the Sixth Circuit, holding that the Kentucky law is saved from preemption because it is a state law regulating insurance. In reaching this result, the Court abandoned twenty years of trying to interpret ERISA's savings clause in light of the tests the Court had articulated for applying the McCarran–Ferguson Act. The Court acknowledged that use of the McCarran–Ferguson test had "misdirected attention, failed to provide clear guidance to lower federal courts, and * * * added little to relevant analysis." It also admitted that the McCarran–Ferguson tests had been developed for different purposes and interpreted different statutory language, and acknowledged that it had been backing away from the McCarran–Ferguson test since the *Unum* case.

The Court concluded:

Today we make a clean break from the McCarran–Ferguson factors and hold that for a state law to be deemed a 'law ... which regulates insurance' under § 1144(b)(2)(A), it must satisfy two requirements. First, the state law must be specifically directed toward entities engaged in insurance. [ ] Second, * * * the state law must substantially affect the risk pooling arrangement between the insurer and the insured. Kentucky's law satisfies each of these requirements.

Earlier in the opinion it had interpreted the "risk pooling" requirement as follows:

> We have never held that state laws must alter or control the actual terms of insurance policies to be deemed 'laws ... which regulate[e] insurance' under § 1144(b)(2)(A); it suffices that they substantially affect the risk pooling arrangement between insurer and insured. By expanding the number of providers from whom an insured may receive health services, AWP laws alter the scope of permissible bargains between insurers and insureds * * *. No longer may Kentucky insureds seek insurance from a closed network of health-care providers in exchange for a lower premium. The AWP prohibition substantially affects the type of risk pooling arrangements that insurers may offer.

*Kentucky Association* significantly clarifies, and expands, the coverage of ERISA's savings clause. Ironically, however, this clarification comes at a time when many states have lost interest in more aggressive regulation of managed care in the face of sharply escalating health care costs.

**Add, at p. 611, Note 8:**

*Moran* seems to settle definitively that HMOs are in fact insurers and thus subject to state insurance regulation under the savings clause.

## B. ERISA PREEMPTION OF STATE TORT LITIGATION

**Add, at p. 612:**

### CICIO v. DOES 1–8 ET AL.
United States Court of Appeals, Second Circuit, 2003.
321 F.3d 83.

SACK, Circuit J.

Plaintiff Bonnie Cicio appeals from an October 4, 2001 judgment of the United States District Court for the Eastern District of New York (Joanna Seybert, *Judge* ) denying her motion to remand her action to New York Supreme Court, and granting the Fed.R.Civ.P. 12(b)(6) motion of the defendants Vytra Healthcare ("Vytra") and Dr. Brent Spears to dismiss the complaint for failure to state a claim upon which relief can be granted. *Cicio v. Vytra Healthcare,* 208 F.Supp.2d 288, 293 (E.D.N.Y.2001). The district court, adopting the March 13, 2001 report and recommendation of Magistrate Judge E. Thomas Boyle, *id.* at 293, held that all of the plaintiff's claims, which derive from the defendants-appellees' decision to deny the plaintiff's deceased spouse, Carmine Cicio, preauthorization for a requested medical procedure, were preempted by the Employee Retirement Income Security Act of 1974, 88 Stat. 832, as amended, 29 U.S.C. § 1001 *et seq.* ("ERISA"). *Cicio,* 208 F.Supp.2d at 293. The plaintiff now appeals on the sole ground that her claims are not preempted by ERISA.

We agree with the plaintiff that the district court erred in dismissing the medical malpractice claims at this stage of the proceedings. We conclude, however, that the district court correctly dismissed the plaintiff's claims that are based on the defendants' alleged misrepresentations or alleged negligence in delaying a coverage decision with respect to Mr. Cicio's medical care. Accordingly, we affirm in part and remand in part.

## BACKGROUND

*Carmine Cicio's Illness and Treatment*

Because this case comes to us on appeal from the grant of a motion to discuss under Fed.R.Civ.P. 12(b)(6), we review the facts as they have been alleged by the plaintiff.[ ] In March 1997, the plaintiff's spouse, Carmine Cicio, was diagnosed with multiple myeloma.[1] He began chemotherapy the following month. At that time, both he and the plaintiff received health care benefits pursuant to an "Agreement for Comprehensive Health Services" (the "Plan") administered by Vytra, an "Individual Practice Association–Health Maintenance Organization."[2] The plaintiff's employer, North Fork Bank, had purchased the Plan from Vytra. The Plan, it is now undisputed, is an "employee benefit plan," as defined in 29 U.S.C. § 1002(3) of ERISA. [ ]

The Plan's subscriber agreement explains that Vytra provides Plan enrollees with, *inter alia*, "[d]iagnosis and treatment of disease, injury or other conditions." Agreement for Comprehensive Health Servs. Art. III, § 3.1(b). The Plan cautions, however, that "Vytra shall provide only Medically Necessary Vytra Services...." *Id.* Art. III, § 3.5(a). Vytra also disclaims the obligation to provide "[a]ny procedure or service which, in the judgment of Vytra's Medical Director, is experimental or is not generally recognized to be effective for a particular condition, diagnosis, or body area...." *Id.* Art. IX, § 9.3(f).

On January 28, 1998, some ten months after Carmine Cicio's disease was first diagnosed, his treating oncologist, Dr. Edward Samuel, wrote a detailed letter to Vytra "request[ing] insurance approval for treatment of Mr. Cicio with high dose chemotherapy supported with peripheral blood stem cell transplantation, in a tandem double transplant, for a diagnosis of multiple myeloma."[4] Letter from Edward T. Samuel to Vytra dated January 28, 1998, at 1. Dr. Samuel set forth Carmine Cicio's clinical history and prior treatments, including one type of chemotherapy that had failed, before explaining why "a change in strategy of treatment ... had to be made." *Id.* And Dr.

---

1. "Multiple myeloma is the second most prevalent blood cancer and represents approximately 1% of all cancers and 2% of all cancer deaths." Multiple Myeloma Research Foundation, *The Statistics*, at http://www.multiplemyeloma.org/aboutmyeloma/statistics.html

2. An independent practice association is a "local physician group ... comprised of physicians who are active on [a] hospital's medical staff" and contract with a health maintenance organization to provide medical services. [ ] Health Maintenance Organizations ("HMOs") are entities that "offer a form of health insurance [that differs from traditional medical insurance].... HMOs are not guaranteeing to *reimburse* the insured for medical expenses; rather, their obligation to the insured is more direct to actually *provide* medical services to them." [ ]

In an "Individual Practice Association—Health Maintenance Organization," "physicians' services are established with a relatively large number of generally small or medium-sized group practices, with physicians receiving some type of discounted fee-for-service payment from the HMO, rather than ... salaried reimbursement...."[ ]

4. A peripheral blood stem cell transplantation is "[a] procedure in which blood containing mobilized stem cells is collected by apheresis [a procedure in which blood is removed from a donor, a blood component, e.g., white blood cells, is separated out, and the remaining blood is reinfused back into the donor], stored, and infused following high-dose chemotherapy or radiation therapy." Multiple Myeloma Research Foundation, *Myeloma Dictionary*, at http://www.multiplemyeloma.org/aboutmyeloma/defs.html.

Samuel explained why he thought that Mr. Cicio was a good "candidate" for the transplant. *Id.* at 2.

Almost a month later, in a letter dated February 23, 1998, Vytra's medical director, the defendant Dr. Spears, denied Dr. Samuel's request, stating only that the procedure sought was "not a covered benefit according to this member's plan which states [that] experimental/investigational procedures are not covered." Letter from Brent W. Spears to Edward T. Samuel dated February 23, 1998, at 1. On March 4, after unsuccessful attempts to contact Dr. Spears by telephone, Dr. Samuel wrote Dr. Spears "appealing to [him] to reconsider [his] decision." Letter from Edward T. Samuel to Brent W. Spears dated March 4, 1998, at 12. Dr. Samuel argued that

> The treatment of multiple myeloma by high-dose chemotherapy/autologous stem cell transplantation is a well-established method of treatment with a superior response rate, complete response rate, post therapy disease-free interval, and possibly even a long-term cure in some patients, as compared to standard therapies. These facts are true for single transplant methodologies, and the statistical response rate and CR rates are improved even further with double transplants.

*Id.* He further argued, based on medical literature listed in his letter, that "treatment NOW with high-dose chemotherapy and autologous stem transplant . . . offers [Mr. Cicio] better chances of survival than any other available method of treatment." *Id.* at 2 (emphasis in original). While this letter made the one reference to "single transplant methodologies" quoted above, it made clear that Dr. Samuel viewed that procedure as a less appropriate treatment for Mr. Cicio than a double stem cell transplant and was not requesting approval for it. *Id.* at 1.

Three weeks later, in a letter dated March 25, 1998, Dr. Spears tersely replied that "[b]ased on the clinical peer review of the additional material, [presumably the studies referenced by Dr. Samuel in his March 4 letter,] a single stem cell transplant has been approved" but "the original request for [a] tandem stem cell transplant remains denied." Letter from Brent W. Spears to Edward T. Samuel dated March 25, 1998, at 1. Mr. Cicio, who, according to the complaint, was by March 25 no longer a candidate for a stem cell transplant, died less than two months later, on May 11, 1998.[ ]

*The Complaint*

Bonnie Cicio filed a complaint, on behalf of herself and the estate of her late husband, in New York Supreme Court, Suffolk County, naming Vytra, Dr. Spears, and eight unknown physicians employed by Vytra ("John Does 1–8") as defendants. The complaint contains eighteen counts alleging "medical malpractice, negligence, gross negligence, intentional infliction of emotional distress, negligent infliction of emotional distress, misrepresentation, breach of contract, bad faith breach of insurance contract and violation of New York State law" based on Dr. Spears's denial of treatment to Mr. Cicio.

On May 30, 2000, the defendants removed the proceedings from New York state court to the United States District Court for the Eastern District of New York pursuant to 28 U.S.C. § 1441. On June 21, 2000, they filed a Rule 12(b)(6) motion to dismiss the complaint for failure to state a claim.

*The Magistrate Judge's Report and Recommendation and the District Court's Decision*

The case was referred by the district court to Magistrate Judge E. Thomas Boyle, who (1) found that removal jurisdiction obtained, and (2) recommended that the defendants' Rule 12(b)(6) motion be granted. *Cicio*, 208 F.Supp.2d at 294–302. Magistrate Judge Boyle reasoned that the plaintiff's state law claims were preempted under §§ 502(a) and 514(a) of ERISA, 29 U.S.C. §§ 1132(a)(1)(B) & 1144(a), because the plaintiff sought "to enforce the terms of [an employee welfare benefit] plan" and that her claims were "within the scope of" § 502(a). *Cicio*, 208 F.Supp.2d at 296–301. He concluded that both removal and dismissal were therefore required. *Id.* at 302. He also recommended that the plaintiff's state law deceptive business practices claim be dismissed because it was "exceedingly vague." *Id.* at 301–02.

In so concluding, the magistrate judge rejected several counter-arguments proffered by Ms. Cicio. First, he rejected her argument that Vytra's Agreement for Comprehensive Health Services was not a "plan" governed by ERISA. *Id.* at 297. Then he declined to endorse the plaintiff's argument that her medical malpractice claims were not preempted because they concerned "mixed eligibility and treatment decisions," as described in *Pegram v. Herdrich*, 530 U.S. 211, 229, 120 S.Ct. 2143, 147 L.Ed.2d 164 (2000). *Cicio*, 208 F.Supp.2d at 300–01. While many decisions by health insurance providers "involve[ ] some medical judgment," Magistrate Judge Boyle said, "[t]here is no evidence that Congress intended that these quasi-medical/administrative decisions made by a plan administrator survive ERISA preemption." *Id.* Even if such malpractice claims were not preempted, Magistrate Judge Boyle continued, Ms. Cicio had not challenged "the quality of the care but rather ... the benefits decision that was made," and hence had alleged the kind of claim that ERISA preempted. *Id.* at 301.

The plaintiff formally objected to the magistrate judge's report and recommendation. The district court nonetheless adopted it in full. *Id.* at 291. The court agreed that Vytra's health plan was a "benefit plan" as defined by ERISA. *Id.* at 292. The court also disagreed with the renewed contention that under *Pegram*, claims for improper medical care are not preempted by ERISA. It concluded instead that because all of the plaintiff's malpractice claims "involve[d] eligibility for coverage," such that the "[d]efendants' roles, including that of Dr. Spears, were administrative," these claims concerned benefits decisions and thus were also preempted. *Id.* at 293.

The plaintiff appeals.

## DISCUSSION

\* \* \*

II. The Nature of the Plaintiff's Claims

Because the plaintiff asserts a variety of claims, we must first determine which of them remain on appeal. \* \* \*

The claims thus remaining on appeal pertain in substance to (1) the timeliness of Dr. Spears's decisions relating to Mr. Cicio's treatment [ ]; (2) the allegedly misleading nature of Vytra's representations about the Plan, *see* Compl [ ]; and, (3) the quality of the medical decision, if any, made by the defendants with respect to Mr. Cicio's treatment [ ]. Both the magistrate judge, *Cicio*, 208 F.Supp.2d at 301, and the district court, *id.*, determined that the complaint did not challenge the quality of the medical decision because "all of the Plaintiff's state law claims center on Vytra's refusal to approve coverage and thus stem from an adverse benefits determination," *id.* We disagree.

A Rule 12(b)(6) dismissal "is inappropriate unless it appears beyond doubt, even when the complaint is liberally construed, that the plaintiff can prove no set of facts which would entitle [her] to relief." [ ]Under this broad standard, Ms. Cicio's complaint identifies a medical decision that may be the predicate for a state law medical malpractice claim.

The complaint alleges that Dr. Spears and other physicians employed by Vytra "failed to exercise the degree of care required of them and were negligent in the provision and delivery of medically necessary care." [ ]. It is possible that in attacking Dr. Spears's determination that a "tandem double stem cell transplant" was an "experimental/investigational procedure[ ]," Ms. Cicio is questioning only Dr. Spears's assessment of the then-current state of medical science without regard to Mr. Cicio's particular medical affliction. This kind of decision about the scope of generally available benefits lacks a significant application of medical judgment to Mr. Cicio's case and, as the district court correctly noted, would be treated as a decision simply about the scope of benefits. But correspondence between Drs. Samuel and Spears attached to the complaint [ ], and incorporated therein by reference, [FN6] described above, strongly suggests that Ms. Cicio is contending additionally or in the alternative that Dr. Spears, in making negligent medical decisions about Mr. Cicio's condition, was engaged in medical malpractice. The liberal construction we are required to give the complaint requires us to consider this understanding of the allegations it contains.

In his request for approval for treatment dated January 28, 1998, Dr. Samuel provided Vytra's Medical Director, Dr. Spears, with a thorough description of the case history of Mr. Cicio's illness. Letter from Edward T. Samuel to Vytra dated January 28, 1998, at 13. This information at least permitted Dr. Spears to make a medical determination regarding Mr. Cicio's treatment on the basis of his aggregate symptoms. And while Dr. Spears stated in reply only that the requested "procedure is not a covered benefit according to this member's plan," Letter from Brent W. Spears to Edward T. Samuel dated February 23, 1998, at 1, his decision could have rested *either* on an analysis of the appropriate treatment for Mr. Cicio's specific condition, *or* on whether in the abstract a double stem cell transplant to treat multiple myeloma was experimental given the current state of the medical art. Therefore, there is at least a possibility that the February 23rd letter reflected a medical decision.

The impression that the February 23rd letter may have embodied a medical decision is strengthened by the subsequent correspondence. Dr. Samuel's response stressed the appropriateness of double stem cell transplants in light of Mr. Cicio's particular symptoms. Dr. Spears's answer, that "[b]ased on the clinical peer review of the additional information, a single stem cell transplant has been approved [but] the original request for tandem stem cell transplant remains denied," Letter from Brent W. Spears to Edward

T. Samuel dated March 25, 1998, at 1, appears to reflect a decision about an appropriate level of care. By denying one treatment and authorizing another that Dr. Samuel had not specifically requested, Dr. Spears at least seems to have been engaged in a patientspecific prescription of an appropriate treatment, and, ultimately, a medical decision that a single stem cell transplant was the appropriate treatment for Mr. Cicio.

At this stage of the litigation, reading the plaintiff's complaint and the attachments thereto together, then, we conclude that the plaintiff has alleged that the defendants made a decision that could implicate a state law duty concerning the quality of medical decisionmaking, in addition to and independent of her claims concerning the administration of benefits with respect to her late husband's course of care.

We do not, however, draw any conclusion about the availability of a malpractice claim in these circumstances under New York law, or whether any of the elements of such a claim, if it exists, would be satisfied by the facts as alleged in this case. We conclude only that, for the purposes of this Rule 12(b)(6) motion, the plaintiff has alleged more than an adverse benefits decision. She has also alleged that the defendants made a negligent medical determination with respect to the treatment of her late husband.

III. Subject Matter Jurisdiction

The district court concluded that defendants' removal of the complaint to federal court was proper. We agree.

\* \* \*

### B. Complete Preemption and ERISA

[The court here discusses "conflict" preemption, and the "Within the scope of" the civil enforcement provisions of ERISA, noting that conflict preemption "alone is insufficient to support removal jurisdiction."[ ]

\* \* \*

With these two prerequisites of complete preemption in mind, we turn to consider whether there is complete preemption of the plaintiff's timeliness and misrepresentation claims so as to permit their removal.

### C. Removal Jurisdiction over the Timeliness and Misrepresentation Claims

*1. The Timeliness Claims.* [The court concludes that the timeliness claims are conflict preempted by § 514, and are "within the scope of" § 502(a), such that removal jurisdiction therefore properly obtains over them.]

\* \* \*

*2. The Misrepresentation Claims.* [The court here finds that these claims are subject to complete preemption.]

D. Supplemental Jurisdiction [The court here findes that all of Ms. Cicio's claims "derive from a common nucleus of operative fact,"[ ] to wit, the denial by Dr. Spears of authorization for a double stem cell transplant. All relevant events allegedly transpired between January 28, 1998, when Dr.

Samuel first requested the double stem cell transplant, and May 11, 1998, when Mr. Cicio died. The plaintiff "would ordinarily be expected to try [ ] all [of her claims] in one judicial proceeding." *Id.* Subject matter jurisdiction thus exists over Ms. Cicio's malpractice claims under 28 U.S.C. § 1367(a), irrespective of whether, standing alone, they are removable.

IV. Dismissal of the Timeliness and Misrepresentation Claims

[These claims are held to be properly dismissed, leaving only the medical malpractice claims to be considered in light of ERISA preemption.]

V. Preemption of Medical Malpractice Claims

The question whether a state law medical malpractice claim brought with respect to a medical decision made in the course of prospective utilization review by a managed care organization or health insurer is preempted under ERISA § 514, and therefore beyond the reach of state tort law, is one of first impression in this Circuit. We conclude, largely on the basis of recent Supreme Court decisions, that such a state law claim is not preempted.

A. *The Practice of Utilization Review*

The plaintiff's medical malpractice claims are based on Dr. Spears's denial of coverage for a double stem cell transplant for Mr. Cicio. Letter from Brent W. Spears to Edward T. Samuel dated February 23, 1998, at 1. Dr. Spears's decision occurred in the course of Dr. Samuel's attempt to obtain authorization for the double stem cell transplant from Vytra. [ ] The complaint then details a process of utilization review, and it is the nature of this procedure, and its relation to ERISA, upon which we now focus.

Utilization review usually involves "prospective review by a third party of the necessity of medical care." [ ] such as Vytra's Medical Director, Dr. Spears. "Although prospective utilization review involves no traditional face-to-face clinical encounter, it is still quasi-medical in nature. It necessarily involves evaluation of data collected in such an encounter." [ ] Prospective utilization review blurs boundaries between the traditionally "distinct sphere of professional dominance and autonomy" of the medical profession on the one hand, [ ] and the managerial domain on the other. As such, it represents a development apparently unforeseen at the time of ERISA's enactment. [ ]

Moreover, as other courts have noted, "a system of prospective decisionmaking influences the beneficiary's choice among treatment options to a far greater degree than does the theoretical risk of disallowance of a claim facing a beneficiary in a retrospective system."[ ] And, "[i]n many instances, a denial of coverage results in the patient forgoing the procedure altogether." [ ] Thus, decisions with a medical component—i.e., involving the exercise of medical judgment in relation to a particular patient's symptoms—are made in the course of utilization review by staff who are independent of and separate from the locus of traditional medical decisionmaking authority. These medical decisions have possibly dispositive consequences for the course of treatment that a patient ultimately follows.

B. *ERISA's Preemptive Scope*

The Supreme Court, in its early pronouncements on ERISA preemption, suggested that the sweeping reference to "any and all State laws [that] . . .

relate" to benefits plans in ERISA's preemption provision, 29 U.S.C. § 1144(a), entailed an expansive preemptive effect that corresponded to the provision's broad wording.[ ] Since then, however, the Court has "temper [ed] the assumption that the ordinary meaning [of § 514] ... accurately expresses the legislative purpose ... with the qualification that the historic police powers of the States were not meant to be superseded by the Federal Act unless that was the clear and manifest purpose of Congress." *Rush Prudential HMO, Inc. v. Moran,* 536 U.S. 355, 122 S.Ct. 2151, 2159, 153 L.Ed.2d 375 (2002). In recent discussions of ERISA preemption, it has even been hinted that "the criteria set forth in [early cases like *Shaw* and its progeny] have in effect been abandoned." *Dillingham Constr.,* 519 U.S. at 335 (Scalia, J., concurring).

Specifically, the Supreme Court has rejected the notion that any finely filigreed connection between ERISA and a state law establish ERISA preemption, and, instead, has held that a court must begin with the presumption that "in the field of health care, a subject of traditional state regulation, there is no ERISA preemption without clear manifestations of congressional purpose." [ ]. Moving beyond presumptions, the Supreme Court has also, in its own words, thrown "cold water" on the idea that state regulation of health and safety is necessarily preempted even when it overlaps with rights protected by ERISA. *Pegram,* 530 U.S. at 237 (citing *Travelers,* 514 U.S. at 654–55).

In deciding the preemption question, it is also noteworthy that ERISA's "repeatedly emphasized purpose [is] to protect *contractually* defined benefits."[ ] Indeed, one of ERISA's stated goals involves increasing "the likelihood that full benefits will be paid to participants and beneficiaries of [covered] plans." 29 U.S.C. § 1001b(b)(1). State medical malpractice law, by contrast, even if implicated by the execution of a benefits decision, involves the application of duties of conduct that are defined independent of ERISA plans.[11] As such, it is not among the "rights and expectations brought into being by [ERISA],"[ ] that § 502(a) is designed to protect.

We must therefore ask whether the plaintiff's medical malpractice causes of action "relate to" the benefits plan administered by Vytra, keeping in mind both the Supreme Court's warning that state law regulation of medical practice is not to be lightly disturbed, and the observation that ERISA's primary focus is the protection of contractual rights defined by benefits plans.

*C. The Preemption of Medical Malpractice Claims Against Utilization Review Decisions*

*1. Pegram v. Herdrich.* At first blush, the defendants' contention that Dr. Spears's decision concerned a benefits determination about what medical treatments Mr. Cicio could receive pursuant to the plan, a decision that can only be challenged in a § 502(a)(1)(B) action, has considerable force. Other courts addressing similar facts have concluded that malpractice claims based on utilization review decisions are indeed preempted by § 514. They have reasoned, first, that utilization review involves "medical decisions as part and parcel of [a plan's] mandate to decide what benefits are available," and then

---

11. Even if, absent a benefits contract, no medical care would in fact have been furnished, so that the medical judgment in one sense is a "benefit" and a direct consequence of the exercise of a contractual right, the state law obligation to provide care of a given level of quality when providing care is nonetheless distinct from the contract.

held that, as benefits decisions, utilization review decisions can be challenged only in a § 502(a)(1)(B) action. [ ] These cases rest on the proposition that a decision cannot be the basis of a malpractice claim even if it involves the exercise of medical judgment if at the same time it has a benefits determination component. According to these cases, the performance of contractual interpretation in order to determine benefits triggers preemption without regard to the medical content of a decision.

But *Corcoran, Jass,* and *Tolton* were decided before the Supreme Court's recent retrenchment of ERISA preemption's margins, and before the Court, in its unanimous decision in *Pegram v. Herdrich,* addressed (albeit in dicta) medical malpractice actions against those engaged in medical decision making.

*Pegram* concerned a defendant physician who "decided (wrongly, as it turned out) that [the plaintiff's] condition did not warrant immediate action; the consequence of that medical determination was that [the defendant HMO] would not cover immediate care, whereas it would have done so if [the defendant physician] had made the proper diagnosis and judgment to treat."[ ] *Pegram* addressed only whether an HMO had, by its method of sharing profits with doctors, breached its fiduciary duty to members, disclaiming any suggestion that it was addressing the interaction between § 502 and state law claims.[ ] *Pegram* is nonetheless relevant to the case at hand because of the reasoning upon which the Court's conclusion was based. The Court decided that no fiduciary breach action could be brought under ERISA because, in part, such an action would be a "mere replication of state malpractice actions with HMO defendants,"[ ]. The creation of a fiduciary breach action through "the formulaic addition of an allegation of financial incentive [to a malpractice claim] would do nothing but bring the same claim into a federal court under federal-question jurisdiction." [ ]. We thus infer that the continued availability of some state law malpractice actions based on at least some varieties of utilization review decisions was a predicate of the Court's holding.

But the *Pegram* opinion has further ramifications for our analysis because of its detailed description and analysis of decisionmaking in the context of health care provision. The Court categorized the defendant Dr. Pegram's act as a "mixed eligibility and treatment" decision, i.e., an "eligibility decision [that] cannot be untangled from physicians' judgments about reasonable medical treatment." *Id.* at 229. The *Pegram* Court then explained:

> What we will call pure "eligibility decisions" turn on the plan's coverage of a particular condition or medical procedure for its treatment. "Treatment decisions," by contrast, are choices about how to go about diagnosing and treating a patient's condition: *given a patient's constellation of symptoms, what is the appropriate medical response?*
>
> These decisions are often practically inextricable from one another.... This is so *not merely because,* under a scheme like [the benefits plan in *Pegram* ], *treatment and eligibility decisions are made by the same person, the treating physician. It is so because a great many and possibly most coverage questions are not simple yes-or-no questions,* like whether appendicitis is a covered condition (when there is no dispute that a patient has appendicitis), or whether acupuncture is a covered procedure for pain relief (when the claim of pain is unchallenged). The more common

coverage question is a when-and-how question. Although coverage for many conditions will be clear and various treatment options will be indisputably compensable, physicians still must decide what to do in particular cases. The issue may be, say, whether one treatment option is so superior to another under the circumstances, and needed so promptly, that a decision to proceed with it would meet the medical necessity requirement that conditions the HMO's obligation to provide *or pay for* that particular procedure at that time in that case. [ ].

*Pegram* thus suggests that some decisions involve interpretation of a benefits contract, eligibility decisions, and some involve application of medical judgment to a particular patient's condition, treatment decisions. And these two categories overlap. The resulting third category, described in *Pegram,* of "mixed eligibility and treatment decisions," *id.* at 229, is not limited to decisions made by treating physicians, such as Dr. Pegram, who both assess which benefits a plan provides and make treatment decisions. A decision about who will "pay for" a procedure, even when this decision is not made by a "treating physician," is also a "mixed eligibility and treatment decision" if it involves answering the question: "given a patient's constellation of symptoms, what is the [most] appropriate medical response?" *Id.* at 228–29. In other words, even if a physician does not directly control, direct, or influence a plaintiff's treatment, and even if the sole consequence of a physician's decision is reimbursement or its denial, that decision may nonetheless be a mixed eligibility and treatment decision like Dr. Pegram's. *Id.*

*Pegram* thus alters the framework used in *Corcoran, Jess,* and *Tolton,* in which a decision must be about either "treatment" or "eligibility," and in which any element of benefits determination suffices to make a decision an "eligibility" decision that may only be challenged in a § 502(a) action. The *Pegram* court's analysis suggests instead that courts should recognize that "[i]n recent years, the medical profession's monopoly on the authority to define appropriate health care outcomes for society has been severely eroded." [ ]. The "separation between professional providers and lay financiers," which *Corcoran, Jess,* and *Tolton* presumed, "no longer exists." [ ] Frankel, *supra,* at 1320; *cf.* Starr, *supra,* at 447 (observing "increasing corporate [as opposed to professional] influence over the rules and standards of medical care"); Shuren, *supra,* at 748 (noting that utilization review agents "interpos[e] themselves into medical decisionmaking"). Decisions now regularly made by third-party payers, such as "whether one treatment option is so superior to another under the circumstances, and needed so promptly, that a decision to proceed with it would meet the medical necessity requirement" in a health benefits contract, "cannot be untangled from physicians' judgments about reasonable medical treatment," *Pegram,* 530 U.S. at 229. And such coverage decisions based on medical determinations often have an outcome-determinative effect.[ ] Among such decisions, noted the *Pegram* Court, are ones concerning "the experimental character of a proposed course of treatment." [ ].

The defendants' decision in this case, in the current procedural posture of this appeal, must be treated as a mixed decision because it allegedly involved both an exercise of medical judgment and an element of contract interpretation.

2. *Applying Pegram's Tripartite Analysis to ERISA Preemption.* We conclude that a state law malpractice action, if based on a "mixed eligibility

and treatment decision," is not subject to ERISA preemption when that state law cause of action challenges an allegedly flawed medical judgment as applied to a particular patient's symptoms. We reach this conclusion by applying the presumptions previously discussed, our understanding of congressional intent in enacting ERISA, and the analytic framework established in *Pegram*.

At the threshold, we decline to adopt the categorical distinction between "quality of care" decisions and "benefits administration" questions applied by other courts in the ERISA preemption context,[ ] and by the district court in the case at bar [ ]. To frame the issue in that fashion is to ignore the nature of "countless medical administrative decisions every day" in which "the eligibility decision and the treatment decision [are] inextricably mixed." [ ] *Pegram* teaches that this dichotomy is no longer tenable.

Further, *Pegram* demonstrates that the mere presence of an administrative component in a health care decision no longer has determinative significance for purposes of preemption analysis when the decision also has a medical component. In its brief discussion of the "puzzling issue of preemption," the *Pegram* Court rejected one of the plaintiff's arguments as "a prescription for preemption of state malpractice law."[ ] The Court said, as we have noted, that previous cases had already thrown "cold water on the preemption theory [with regard to state law malpractice claims]."[ ] The Court's analysis strongly suggests, without holding, that the plaintiff's malpractice action against Dr. Pegram would not be preempted even though Dr. Pegram simultaneously made a contractual interpretation concerning Herdrich's eligibility for given benefits, and that a defendant can no longer simply point to the overlay of medical decisionmaking on contractual claims and ask the court to conclude that, because ERISA preempts the contract claims, it also preempts all state tort-law claims based on the same decision.

As we have explained, nothing in ERISA suggests that Congress intended any displacement of "the quintessentially state-law standards of reasonable medical care" as applied to the medical component of a mixed decision.[ ] And ERISA requires that we distinguish between "contractually defined benefits,"[ ] and those rights that state law delimits independent of benefits plans, such as medical quality standards, which hinge instead on statutory and common law development of malpractice law unique to each state.

Finally, we note our skepticism of a line of reasoning that would draw from "a comprehensive statute designed to promote the interests of employees and their beneficiaries in employee benefit plans,"[ ] the elimination of protective standards of professional conduct. We see no reason then to bar as preempted state law malpractice actions that rest on the application of standards for medical decision-making—which are established by states independent of and prior to health benefits contracts—to "a patient's constellation of symptoms"[ ].

Focusing on mixed eligibility and treatment decisions, then, we conclude that § 514 preemption does not obtain with regard to those claims predicated on the violation of a state tort law by a failure to meet a state law defined standard of care in diagnosing or recommending treatment of a plaintiff "patient's constellation of symptoms"[ ].

3. *The Distinction Between Treating Physicians and Utilization Review Agents.* The district court appeared to distinguish between a tort action based

on a precertification decision, such as Dr. Spears's decision here, and one based on a contemporaneous treatment decision, such as Dr. Pegram's.[ ] In support of this distinction, it might be argued that, in the precertification context, the treatment analysis precedes the contract interpretation question such that adjudication of a tort action *necessarily* involves an interpretation of the ERISA contract, which in turn triggers preemption. And it might be further argued that in contemporaneous treatment questions, the contract interpretation question does not play the same intervening role.

But we are not convinced such a distinction can in fact be drawn. *Pegram,* as noted, did not distinguish between the decisions of a treating physician empowered to interpret a benefits contract, and medical administrative decisions executed prior to the delivery of care. Its category of mixed eligibility and treatment decisions consisted of "when-and-how question[s]," including, critically, the question whether "a decision to proceed with [a procedure] would meet the medical necessity requirement that conditions the HMO's obligation to provide *or pay for* that particular procedure." [ ]. Even when making decisions about whether to pay for particular procedures, "physicians still must decide what to do in particular cases" on the basis of medical assessments.[ ]

And, "[i]n practical terms, . . . eligibility decisions cannot be untangled from physicians' judgments about reasonable medical treatment," or, at least, the untangling will in many instances be no easy task. *Id.* For instance, some managed care organizations require that utilization review agents "negotiate with the treating physician to achieve conformity" in levels of care provided.[ ] That sort of negotiation is reflected in the correspondence between Drs. Spears and Samuel. While Dr. Samuel initiated negotiations with a detailed description of Mr. Cicio's status, Dr. Spears parried with an assertion of the requested treatment's experimental nature. Dr. Samuel then supplemented his argument with support from the medical literature. In response, Dr. Spears apparently made a patient-specific prescription of appropriate treatment by denying one treatment and authorizing another that Dr. Samuel had not requested. At least on the basis of the material on which we review the grant of the Rule 12(b)(6) motion by the district court, we cannot identify distinct moments at which treatment decisions as distinct from eligibility decisions were made in the course of this negotiation, let alone the sequence of such decisions.

In the *Pegram* context of contemporaneous treatment decisions, too, how to distill the moment of the eligibility determination from the facts is far from obvious. Examining the Supreme Court's description of Dr. Pegram's behavior, we cannot determine whether she (1) thought first about how soon Herdrich needed an ultrasound and then considered whether the plan comprised ultrasound tests in a given medical facility, or (2) considered first which benefits were available, and only then analyzed which one was medically warranted within that constrained range.[ ]. In other words, it is difficult, at best, to determine whether her violation of the standard of medical care was apart from and independent of a determination of benefits, or whether the benefits determination preceded and controlled the medical determination.

In sum, it would likely often be difficult to delve into physicians' minds to examine their decisions, which are frequently executed in very brief time periods and under tremendous pressures, to determine what part of them is medical and what part is administrative. Nor do we think it likely that significant contract interpretation issues will arise in an ensuing tort action. Assuming *arguendo* that Ms. Cicio were to establish that Dr. Spears's decision violated a state law duty of professional care, we are hard pressed to see how the defendants could successfully contend—as a defense to the *tort* action—that the *contract* permitted them to violate a state law duty standard of care.[13]

### D. Caveats

We underscore the fact that this case comes before us on appeal from the grant of a Rule 12(b)(6) motion to dismiss. We therefore hold only that a set of facts consistent with the allegations contained in the complaint would permit the granting of relief—oddly, in this case, remand to state court for a determination, *inter alia,* of whether the complaint states a cause of action under the law of New York. If Dr. Spears's actions that are the subject of the complaint indeed constituted a medical decision or a mixed medical and eligibility decision, then Ms. Cicio's remaining medical malpractice claims should not be dismissed, but remanded to state court for resolution.[ ]. It may nonetheless be that, as a matter of fact, Dr. Spears's decision was purely one concerning eligibility, i.e., a determination that, without regard to Mr. Cicio's "constellation of symptoms" but in the abstract, double cell stem transplants were experimental as treatment for multiple myeloma. In that case, the claims would be completely preempted by ERISA and therefore subject to dismissal. We therefore do not rule out the possibility that the defendants can demonstrate, *as a matter of fact,* that dismissal of the complaint is warranted. We leave it to the district court to determine what proceedings, if any, would be appropriate to that end.

Finally, we reiterate that we do not decide under what circumstances, if any, the decisions made by Vytra or Dr. Spears, or utilization review decisions generally, may when negligently made be actionable under New York law. Perhaps they never are. Unless the district court determines that Dr. Spears was in fact making pure eligibility decisions with respect to Mr. Cicio's health care and dismisses the claim on that ground, that will be a question for the New York courts to decide upon remand.

### CONCLUSION

We affirm the district court's disposition of the timeliness and misrepresentation claims, but vacate its resolution of the medical malpractice claims and remand for further proceedings consistent with this opinion.

## C. BENEFICIARY REMEDIES PROVIDED BY ERISA

### 2. *Administrative Claims and Appeals Procedures under ERISA*

**Add, at p. 635:**

After delaying the effective date of these rules for a year, the Bush administration finally allowed them to go fully into effect on January 1, 2003.

---

**13.** Certainly, it would be a different matter if the complaint alleged only that the health benefits plan did not cover a given procedure without regard to what symptoms a patient presented. In that case, the defendants would in fact be contending that they made no medical decision that could be subject to state law standards for medical care, but rather only interpreted the contract. In such cases, a court would have to make a threshold determination, as we have done in the case at bar, as to whether a medical decision made by the defendants has been alleged.

## D. PROVIDER FIDUCIARY OBLIGATIONS UNDER ERISA

**Add, at p. 654, Notes:**

See, among the many insightful analyses of *Pegram,* E. Haavi Morreim, Another ERISA Twist: The Mysterious Case of *Pegram* and the Missing Fiduciary, 63 U.Pitt.L.Rev. 235 (2002); Peter J. Hammer, *Pegram v. Herdrich*: Of Peritonitis, Preemption, and the Elusive Goal of Managed Care Accountability, 26 J. Health Pol., Pol'y & L. 767 (2001); Michael T. Cahill and Peter D. Jacobson, *Pegram's* Regress: A Missed Chance for Sensible Judicial Review of Managed Care Decisions, 27 Am.J.L. & Med. 421 (2001); Thomas R. McLean & Edward P. Richards, Managed Care Liability for Breach of Fiduciary Duty after *Pegram v. Herdrich*: The End of ERISA Preemption for State Law Liability for Medical Care Decision Making, 53 Fla. L. Rev. 1 (2001); and Arnold J. Rosoff, Breach of Fiduciary Duty Lawsuits Against MCOs: What's Left After *Pegram v. Herdrich*, 22 J. Legal Med. 55 (2001). See also, Peter Jacobson, Strangers in the Night: Law and Medicine in the Managed Care Era (2002), examining the idea of fiduciary obligation as a principle for governing the relationship between managed care organizations and their members.

## E. PROVIDER DISCLOSURE REQUIREMENTS

**Add, at p. 659, before Section III., the following:**

For a good discussion of approaches to disclosure, with some sample language, see Mark Hall, The Theory and Practice of Disclosing HMO Physician Incentives, 65 Law & Contemp. Prob. 207 (2002).

## III. FEDERAL INITIATIVES TO EXPAND PRIVATE INSURANCE COVERAGE: THE HEALTH INSURANCE PORTABILITY AND ACCOUNTABILITY ACT OF 1996, THE CONSOLIDATED OMNIBUS RECONCILIATION ACT OF 1995 AND THE AMERICANS WITH DISABILITIES ACT

### A. THE HEALTH INSURANCE PORTABILITY AND ACCOUNTABILITY ACT OF 1996 AND COBRA COVERAGE REQUIREMENTS

**Add, at p. 666:**

Legislation signed by the President in the spring of 2002 extended until December 21, 2003, the mental health parity legislation, which would otherwise have expired in 2002.

# Chapter 10

# PUBLIC HEALTH CARE PROGRAMS: MEDICARE AND MEDICAID

## I. INTRODUCTION

**Add, at p. 680:**

For a comprehensive discussion of our nation's health care entitlements and the problems they currently face, see Timothy Stoltzfus Jost, Distentitlement: The Threats Facing our Health Care Entitlements and a Rights–Based Response (2003).

## II. MEDICARE

**Add, at p. 683:**

While Medicare remained very much in the public eye during 2001 and 2002, no consensus emerged as to how the program should be changed. Medicare spending growth accelerated to 7.8% in 2001, up over 50% from the rate of spending growth the year before, but still well below the 10.5% increase that private health insurance premiums experienced in 2001. Expenditure growth was driven by legislation that added $7.5 billion to total Medicare spending, but was sector specific, with the rate of inpatient hospital spending growth increasing, for example, while physician spending did not increase as much as it had in 2000. See Katharine Levit, et al., Trends in U.S. Health Care Spending, 2001, 22 Health Affairs Jan./Feb. 2003 at 154, 161.

### B. BENEFITS

#### *1. Coverage*

**Add, at p. 684:**

The Medicare, Medicaid and SCHIP Program Benefits Improvement and Protection Act of 2000 (BIPA) makes further changes in the process of making national and local coverage determinations. (NCDs and LCDs) Under BIPA amendments to 42 U.S.C.A. § 1395ff(f)(4) & (5), a beneficiary in need of a noncovered item or service may request a NCD. The Secretary must act on the request within ninety days (though one of the actions the Secretary may take is to state that the review will take longer than ninety days, and explain why). A person adversely affected by a NCD may seek review by the Departmental Appeals Board (DAB), subject to judicial review. 42 U.S.C.A. § 1395ff(f)(1). LCDs may be appealed to administrative law judges, and then further to the DAB. 42 U.S.C. § 1395ff(f)(2).

BIPA does not grant standing to providers or to drug or device manufacturers whose products or procedures are affected by coverage determinations to appeal LCDs or NCDs. Proposed DHHS rules also prohibit the assignment of appeal rights to providers or manufacturers. See Proposed Rule 42 C.F.R. § 426.330. 67 Fed. Reg. 54354, 54550 (2002). The proposed rules do not even recognize standing in beneficiaries who have already received noncovered services and are seeking payment for them, as DHHS considers such beneficiaries to not be "in need of the items or services," the statutory standard. See 67 Fed. Reg. 54534, 54538 (2002). What are the reasons for circumscribing standing to this extent? What will be its effect?

The proposed rules also tightly circumscribe the authority of ALJs in reviewing LCDs or the DAB in reviewing NCDs. The DAB, for example, may not order CMS to modify a NCD, order CMS to pay a specific claim, set a time limit for CMS to establish or modify an NCD, or order or address how CMS implements an NCD. All an ALJ or the DAB may do is to hold the coverage determination in the particular case to be invalid, at which point CMS will ask its contractors to readjudicate the claim without consideration of the LCD or NCD, and to review the LCD or NCD, either revoking, modifying, or supplementing it. Proposed 42 C.F.R. §§ 426.450, 426.460, 426.555, 426.560, 56 Fed. Reg., 54534, 54555, 54562–63. See Eleanor D. Kinney, Guide to Medicare Coverage Decision–Making and Appeals (2002).

**Add, at p. 684:**

Though the House of Representatives adopted a plan for providing prescription drug coverage to Medicare beneficiaries in 2002 (H.R. 9454), support in the Senate was split between a Republican plan (S. 2736) sponsored by Senators Hagel and Ensign, a Democratic plan sponsored by Senators Graham, Miller and Kennedy (S. 2625), and a "tri-partisan" plan (S. 2729), sponsored by a group of Republicans and Democrats and the Senate's lone independent (Senators Grassley, Breaux, Hatch, Jeffords, and Snowe). The Senate failed to pass any legislation. President Bush attempted again to implement his prescription drug discount card program during 2002, this time through formal rulemaking, but program implementation was again enjoined, National Association of Chain Drug Stores v. Thompson, 241 F.Supp.2d 29 (D.D.C.2003).

Everyone seems to agree that prescription drug costs are becoming an increasingly unbearable burden for elderly and disabled Medicare beneficiaries. Nearly 40% of Medicare beneficiaries lack drug coverage, including 50% of those living in rural areas, and 44% of those with incomes between $10,000 and $20,000. Average out of pocket drug expenditures for Medicare beneficiaries topped $1000 in 2002, and 22% of seniors (35% of those without coverage) in a recent survey reported either skipping doses to make drugs last longer or not filling needed prescriptions. See Kaiser Family Foundation, Medicare and Prescription Drugs, Dana Gelb Safran, et al., Prescription Drug Coverage and Seniors: How Well Are States Closing the Gap?

There is no consensus, however, as to how to solve the problem. The 2002 House legislation would have created a program with a $250 annual deductible and $33 a month premium, offering 80% of coverage for the first $1000 of drug costs, 50% for the next $2000, and 100% coverage for all costs above an out of pocket maximum $4800. It would have been administered by private insurance companies, and would have cost $320 billion over 10 years. The Graham, Miller, Kennedy bill, by contrast, would have imposed a $25 premium, no deductible, and $10 copayments for generics and $40 for brand drugs to an out-of-pocket maximum of $4000. It would have been administered by the Center for Medicare and Medicaid Services through contractors (like traditional Medicare) and cost about $594 billion over 10 years. Finally, the Tripartisan plan would have cost about $24 a month in premiums, imposed at $250 deductible, and required cost-sharing of 50% to $3450 with an out-of-pocket maximum of $3700. It would have been administered by private plans and cost about $370 billion over 10 years. All plans would have provided subsidies for low income recipients. See Kaiser Family Foundation, Prescription Drug Coverage for Medicare Beneficiaries: A Side-by-Side Comparison of Selected Proposals,

## C. PAYMENT FOR SERVICES

### 5. *Medicare Managed Care*

**Add, at p. 707:**

The Medicare+Choice program continued to collapse in 2001 and 2002. After 95 plans withdrew or reduced their service areas, affecting 407,000 enrollees, in 1999; and an additional 99 plans withdrew in 2000 affecting 327,000 enrollees; plan withdrawals and reductions affected another 934,000 enrollees in 2001 and 500,000 in 2002. In many instances, moreover, plans that remained with the program reduced their service areas, eliminated optional benefits, or raised their premiums. The percentage of plans providing a zero premium option dropped from 80% in 1999 to 46% in 2001, while the percentage of plans offering prescription drug coverage dropped from 84% to 70%. The mean premium for plans rose from $6 a month to $23, while the percentage of plans that only offered drug coverage subject to a coverage cap of $500 or less rose from 11% to 28%.

Many beneficiaries, faced with reduced MSO benefits or increased premiums, returned to the traditional fee-for-service program, where at least they had free choice of physician. The number of Medicare beneficiaries in Medicare Risk or M+C plans peaked in 1999 at 6.3 million, had dropped by February 2002 to about 5 million, and will probably decline to 4.1 million by 2005 if the current law is not changed. Attempts by Congress to bail out the Medicare+Choice program in the 1999 Medicare, Medicaid, and SCHIP Balanced Budget Refinement Act (BBRA) and the Benefit Improvement and Protection Act (BIPA), of 2000, had little effect. Of the 118 M+C plans that had planned withdrawals or service area reductions in 2001, only four decided to return because of BIPA.

While plan withdrawals were to a considerable extent due to the failure of Medicare managed care rates to keep up with premium increases demanded by managed care firms, plan withdrawals and cutbacks do not seem to have simply been a matter of payment limits. Many plan withdrawals took place in areas where rates had increased sharply under the BBA, and Medicare+Choice rates continued to exceed payments for Medicare fee-for-service beneficiaries at least through 2001. Unless Congress is willing to spend substantially more per beneficiary for Medicare managed care than it does in the fee-for-service program, it seems unlikely that managed care plans will return to the program. The 2004 budget presented by President Bush called for such increases. Can they be justified?

See Marsha Gold, Can Managed Care and Competition Cure Medicare Costs? Health Affairs Web Exclusive, available at http:/www.healthaffairs.org/WebExclusive/2203Gold.pdf (2002). Robert A. Berenson, Medicare+Choice: Doubling or Disappearing? Health Affairs Web Exclusive available at http://www.healthaffairs.org/WebExclusives/Berenson_Web_Excl–112801.htm; Kenneth Thorpe and Adam Atherly, "Medicare+Choice: Current Role and Near–Term Prospects," Health Affairs Web Exclusive, http://www.healthaffairs.org/Web–Exclusives/Thorpe_Web_Excl_071702.htm; Lori Achman and Marsha Gold, Medicare + Choice 1999–2001: An Analysis of Managed Care Plan Withdrawals and Trends in Benefits and Premiums (New York: Commonwealth Fund, 2002).

## D. ADMINISTRATION AND APPEALS

**Add, at p. 711:**

The Medicare appeals process was dramatically changed by sections 521 and 522 of the Medicare, Medicaid and State Children's Health Insurance Program Benefits Improvement and Protection Act of 2000, or BIPA (which amended 42 U.S.C.A. § 1395ff). These provisions of BIPA, which took effect on October 1, 2002, establish a uniform appeals process for Part A and Part B. BIPA creates a four step administrative appeal process, which begins with the initial carrier or intermediary determination. A beneficiary aggrieved by such a decision must request a redetermination by the carrier or intermediary within 120 days. 42 U.S.C.A. § 1395ff(a)(3). A beneficiary dissatisfied with this redetermination may then request a reconsideration. 42 U.S.C.A. § 1395ff(b)(1)(A). This reconsideration—which on the Part B side replaces the former carrier hearing–will be handled by a new group of twelve "qualified independent contractors" (QICs), private entities with which Medicare will contract to make these decisions. 42 U.S.C.A. § 1395ff(b)(2) & (c). A beneficiary who remains dissatisfied may appeal to an Administrative Law Judge (ALJ), then to the Departmental Appeals Board (DAB), and finally to the federal district court. 42 U.S.C.A. § 1395ff (d).

BIPA contains a number of provisions that are supposed to aid beneficiaries (and providers, who in fact bring 90% of appeals). First, it lowers the jurisdictional amount to $100 for ALJ appeals. 42 U.S.C.A. § 1395ff(b)(1)(E)(I). Second, it imposes time limits at every step of the way, 30 days at the carrier or intermediary and QIC level, 90 days at the ALJ and DAB level. 42 U.S.C.A. §§ 1395ff(a)(3)(C)(ii); (c)(3)(C); (d). Third, BIPA provides for expedited (within 72 hours) reconsideration where a beneficiary is threatened with a service termination and the failure to provide the services is likely to put the beneficiary's health at significant risk or with discharge from a provider. 42 U.S.C.A. § 1395ff(b)(1)(F). Finally, BIPA provides for de novo, rather than appellate review at the DAB and federal court level. 42 U.S.C.A. § 1395ff(d)(2)(B).

Even before BIPA went into effect, however, Medicare was overwhelmed with appeals. During the second quarter of 2001, for example, Medicare received almost a million requests for Part B reviews, 24,507 requests for carrier hearings, 12,257 requests for ALJ hearings, and 2289 new requests for DAB hearings. At the end of that quarter, 31,223 ALJ hearings and 10,333 DAB hearings were pending. Medicare has no ALJs of its own, but rather uses Social Security Administration ALJs. The DAB has only two senior judges. DHHS does not have the resources to establish the QIC. Moreover, even were resources available, the time frames provided by BIPA do not allow sufficient time to work up complex Medicare appeals. See DHHS Office of Inspector General, Medicare Administrative Appeals: The Potential Impact of BIPA, OEI–04–01–00290 (January 2002). On October 7, 2002, the Centers for Medicare and Medicaid Services (CMS) confessed its inability to implement most of BIPA (other than a few largely self-enforcing provisions like cutting the time allowed for appeal or lowering the jurisdictional amount), and announced its intention to delay BIPA implementation. Proposed rules to implement the BIPA appeals requirement were published at 67 Fed. Reg. 69312 (Nov. 15, 2002).

One of the key changes that BIPA makes in the previous law is that it sets definite deadlines for making decisions at various appellate levels, and specifies the consequences of the failure of DHHS and its contractors to meet appellate deadlines. The provisions dealing with ALJ and DAB decisions, for example, follow:

42 U.S.C. § 1395ff (d)

(3) Consequences of failure to meet deadlines

(A) Hearing by administrative law judge—In the case of a failure by an administrative law judge to render a decision by the end of the period described in paragraph (1) [90 days], the party requesting the hearing may request a review by the Departmental Appeals Board of the Department of Health and Human Services, notwithstanding any requirements for a hearing for purposes of the party's right to such a review.

(B) Departmental Appeals Board review—In the case of a failure by the Departmental Appeals Board to render a decision by the end of the period described in paragraph (2), [90 days] the party requesting the hearing may seek judicial review, notwithstanding any requirements for a hearing for purposes of the party's right to such judicial review.

How should the courts treat the appeals of appellants who have skipped appellate steps because of these provisions? If no record has been developed below because the case has moved up at each level for failure to meet time deadlines, what should be the basis of judicial review? (The statute also provides for automatic advancement to the next level for failure to meet deadlines at the redetermination level.) Should the court remand for failure to exhaust administrative remedies? Should it try the case itself? What opportunities does the new system offer to appellants who detect that one level of the review process is friendlier than others? What temptations does it create for reviewers under great time pressure (as it takes less time to rule for an appellant than to justify a decision against an appellant). If the courts remand to DHHS for the development of a record, what happens next? How should Congress have dealt with speeding up appeals? See OIG, Medicare Administrative Appeals, supra. See also, Eleanor D. Kinney, Medicare Beneficiary Appeals Processes, in Eleanor D. Kinney, ed., Guide to Medicare Coverage Decision–Making and Appeals, 65 (2002).

## E. MEDICARE REFORM

**Add, at p. 720:**

New ideas for Medicare reform are not much in abundance in early 2003. For the most part, proposals for reform still focus on the managed competition, managed care models mooted by the Bipartisan Commission.

Medicare reform was prominently featured in President Bush's 2003 State of the Union address. In early March, 2003, the Bush Administration also released an outline of a Medicare reform plan. Under this plan, traditional Medicare would be maintained, and beneficiaries who wished to stay with it would be given a drug discount card and some, as yet unspecified, coverage against catastrophic drug costs. Beneficiaries could also, however, elect to enroll in "enhanced Medicare," a managed competition program involving regional point-of-service plans or PPOs, which would offer prescription drug coverage, full coverage of preventive services, a cap on hospital cost-sharing, and a single deductible for all services. Medicare would contribute to premium costs for these plans, but those who elected more generous plans would have to pay extra premiums. Finally, beneficiaries could elect lower cost "Medicare advantage" HMOs, some of which would not offer drug coverage. Low income beneficiaries would receive additional help with prescription drug costs.

The plan was greeted with a great deal of skepticism, even among congressional Republicans. First, it would do very little for beneficiaries who would remain in traditional Medicare, undoubtedly the majority of beneficiaries. Second, the plan was essentially unfunded. To accomplish all of these goals, the Administration's budget proposed spending $400 billion over 10 years, however, most was budgeted for after 2008. Only $6 billion additional was budgeted for FY 2004. By contrast, the cheapest of the prescription drug plans considered by Congress in 2002 were estimated by the Congressional Budget Office to cost over $300 billion alone over 10 years. Third, the Administration relied mainly on the magic of the market to make the whole plan affordable, but the magic of the market failed dramatically in the Medicare+Choice program, and there is no reason to believe that it will succeed now.

## III. MEDICAID

**Add, at p. 727:**

Following a period of enrollment decline during 1995–1998 in response to welfare reform and the booming economy, the number of Medicaid recipients began growing again at the beginning of the 2000s. Some of the growth was due to eligibility expansions. As of September 30, 2002, the phase-in of the

1989 law requiring coverage of all children under the age of 19 was completed, while a new program was added in 2000 that gave states the option of covering treatment for breast and cervical cancers discovered through the Centers for Disease Control breast and cervical cancer screening program.(42 U.S.C. § 1396a(aa).) Enrollment also grew because of the souring economy and growing unemployment. The combined effect of enrollment growth and health care cost inflation generally was to drive Medicaid expenditures up dramatically. State Medicaid expenditures rose 11% in FY 2000 and 2001, and were expected to be up over 13% in FY 2002. By contrast, Medicaid spending between 1995 and 1998 had grown at a rate of less than 4% per year.

As Medicaid expenditures were shooting up in the early 2000s, however, state tax revenues plummeted. State sales and income tax collections had increased significantly in the late 1990s as the economy boomed, even as the states enacted repeated tax cuts. Revenue growth came to a halt in 2001, however, and declined dramatically during 2002. Forty-three states opened budget gaps of at least $36 billion in 2002. In response, 45 states implemented Medicaid cost containment measures attempting to plug the gaps. Once again it became obvious that there are problems with funding our nation's primary health care program for the poor—which inevitably costs more during economic recessions—though the states, which inexorably lose tax revenues when the economy goes bad, and which are not allowed to run budget deficits like the federal government. For an excellent overview of these issues see Alan Weil, There's Something About Medicaid, Health Affairs, Jan/Feb. 2003 at 13; Lawrence D. Brown and Michael S. Sparer, Poor Program's Progress: The Unanticipated Politics of Medicaid Policy, Health Affairs, Jan/Feb. 2003 at 31; Donald J. Boyd, The Bursting State Bubble an State Medicaid Budgets, Jan./Feb. 2003 at 46.

## D. PROGRAM ADMINISTRATION: FEDERAL/STATE RELATIONSHIPS

**Add, at p. 747:**

The lower court decision in Westside Mothers v. Haveman, 133 F.Supp.2d 549 (E.D.Mich.2001), sent shockwaves through the Medicaid advocacy community. It effectively held that Medicaid was no longer a federal entitlement, i.e. the rights of Medicaid recipients (and, by extension providers) were no longer enforceable in federal court. Though state attorneys general quickly filed "Westside Mothers" motions to dismiss in Medicaid cases across the country, they were uniformly rejected by the district courts, and then by the courts of appeal, led by the Fourth Circuit in Antrican v. Odom, 290 F.3d 178 (4th Cir.2002). Finally, *Westside Mothers* itself was reversed:

### WESTSIDE MOTHERS v. HAVEMAN
United States Court of Appeals, Sixth Circuit, 2002.
289 F.3d 852.

MERRITT, Circuit Judge.

This suit filed under 42 U.S.C. § 1983 alleges that the state of Michigan has failed to provide services required by the Medicaid program. Plaintiffs, Westside Mothers, * * * allege that defendants James Haveman, director of the Michigan Department of Community Health,* * * did not provide the early and periodic screening, diagnosis, and treatment services mandated by the Medicaid Act and related laws.

The Medicaid program, created in 1965 when Congress added Title XIX to the Social Security Act, provides a federal subsidy to states that choose to reimburse poor individuals for certain medical care.[ ] "Although participation in the program is voluntary, participating states must comply with certain requirements imposed by the Act and regulations promulgated by the Secretary of Health and Human Services." *Wilder v. Virginia Hosp. Assoc.*, [ ]. Like all other states, Michigan participates in the Medicaid program. Since 1997, operating under a waiver from the Health Care Finance Administration, Michigan has provided eligible residents Medicaid services by requiring them to enroll in Health Maintenance Organizations, which provide medical care in exchange for a flat monthly fee per participant [ ].

The Medicaid Act and related regulations set out a detailed list of services every state program must provide. *See* 42 U.S.C. § 1396 *et seq.*; 41 C.F.R. §§ 430 *et seq.* (2000). The Act allows the Secretary of Health and Human Services to limit or end payments to a state whose Medicaid program does not provide these services. *See* 42 U.S.C. § 1396c.

At issue here is the federal requirement that participating states provide "early and periodic screening, diagnostic, and treatment services ... for individuals who are eligible under the plan and are under the age of 21." *Id.* § 1396d(a)(4)(B)[ ]. The required services include periodic physical examinations, immunizations, laboratory tests, health education, *see* 42 U.S.C. § 1396d(r)(1), eye examinations, eyeglasses, *see id.* § 1396d(r)(2), teeth maintenance, *see id.* § 1396d(r)(3), diagnosis and treatment of hearing disorders, and hearing aids, *see id.* § 1396d(r)(4).

In 1999, plaintiffs sued the named defendants under § 1983, which creates a cause of action against any person who under color of state law deprives an individual of "any right, privileges, or immunities secured by the Constitution and laws" of the United States. 42 U.S.C. § 1983. They alleged that the defendants had refused or failed to implement the Medicaid Act, its enabling regulations and its policy requirements, by (1) refusing to provide, and not requiring participating HMOs to provide, the comprehensive examinations required by §§ 1396a(a)(43) and 1396d(r)(1) and 42 C.F.R. § 441.57; (2) not requiring participating HMOs to provide the necessary health care, diagnostic services, and treatment required by § 1396d(r)(5); (3) not effectively informing plaintiffs of the existence of the screening and treatment services, as required by § 1396a(a)(43); (4) failing to provide plaintiffs the transportation and scheduling help needed to take advantage of the screening and treatment services, as required by § 1396a(a)(43)(B) and 42 C.F.R. § 441.62; and (5) developing a Medicaid program which lacks the capacity to deliver to eligible children the care required by §§ 1396(a)(8), 1396a(a)(30)(A), and 1396u2(b)(5).[ ]

Defendants moved to dismiss the plaintiffs and for dismissal of the suit. * * *

In March 2001 the district court granted defendants' motion to dismiss all remaining claims. *See Westside Mothers v. Haveman*, 133 F.Supp.2d 549, 553 (E.D.Mich.2001). In a detailed and far-reaching opinion, the district court held that Medicaid was only a contract between a state and the federal government, that spending-power programs such as Medicaid were not supreme law of the land, that the court lacked jurisdiction over the case because Michigan was the "real defendant and therefore possess[ed] sovereign immunity against suit," id., that in this case *Ex parte Young* was unavailable to circumvent the state's sovereign immunity, and that even if it were available § 1983 does not create a cause of action available to plaintiffs to enforce the provisions in question.

This appeal followed. We reverse on all issues presented.

*Analysis*

A. *Medicaid Contracts and the Spending Power*

Much of the district court's decision rests on its initial determinations that the Medicaid program is only a contract between the state and federal government and that laws passed by Congress pursuant to its power under the Spending Clause are not "supreme law of the land." We address these in turn.

1. *Whether Medicaid is only a contract.* The district court held that "the Medicaid program is a contract between Michigan and the Federal government." [ ] The program, it points out, is not mandatory; states choose whether to participate. [ ] If a state does choose to participate, Congress may then "condition receipt of federal moneys upon compliance by the recipient with federal statutory and administrative directives." [ ]

To characterize precisely the legal relationship formed between a state and the federal government when such a program is implemented, the district court turned to two Supreme Court opinions on related subjects. In *Pennhurst State School and Hosp. v. Halderman* ("*Pennhurst I*"), the Court described the Medicaid program as "much in the nature of a contract," and spoke of the " 'contract' " formed between the state and the federal government. [ ] * * *

Justice Scalia expanded on this contract analogy in his concurrence in *Blessing v. Freestone*. He maintained that the relationship was "in the nature of a contract" because:

> The state promises to provide certain services to private individuals, in exchange for which the Federal government promises to give the State funds. In contract law, when such an arrangement is made (A promises to pay B money, in exchange for which B promises to provide services to C), the person who receives the benefit of the exchange of promises between two others (C) is called a third-party beneficiary.

520 U.S. 329, 349, 117 S.Ct. 1353, 137 L.Ed.2d 569 (1997) (Scalia, J., concurring).

Drawing on above language, the district judge then concluded that the "Medicaid program is a contract between Michigan and the Federal government," [ ] further describing it as a "contract ... between sovereigns," and "the Medicaid contract," [ ] The only significant difference between Medicaid and an ordinary contract, he asserted, is "the sovereign status of the parties," which limits the available remedies each can seek against the other. [ ]

Contrary to this narrow characterization, the Court in *Pennhurst I* makes clear that it is using the term "contract" metaphorically, to illuminate certain aspects of the relationship formed between a state and the federal government in a program such as Medicaid. It does not say that Medicaid is *only* a contract. It describes the program as "much in the nature of" a contract, and places the term "contract" in quotation marks when using it alone. [ ] It did not limit the remedies to common law contract remedies or suggested that normal federal question doctrines do not apply. Justice Scalia's concurrence in *Blessing* does not alter this.

Binding precedent has put the issue to rest. The Supreme Court has held that the conditions imposed by the federal government pursuant to statute upon states participating in Medicaid and similar programs are not merely contract provisions; they are federal laws. In *Bennett v. Kentucky Department of Education,* Kentucky argued that a federal-state grant agreement "should be viewed in the same manner as a bilateral contract." [ ] The Court rejected this approach, holding that, "[u]nlike normal contractual undertakings, federal grant programs originate in and remain governed by statutory provisions expressing the judgment of Congress concerning desirable public policy." [ ]

2. *Whether acts passed under the Spending Power are Supreme Law of the Land.*After holding that Medicaid is only a contract to pay money enacted under the spending power, the district court then held that programs enacted pursuant to the Constitution's spending power are not the "supreme law of the land" and do not give rise to remedies invoked for the violation of federal statutes.[ ] Relying on its determination that Medicaid and similar programs are "contracts consensually entered into by the States with the Federal Government . . .," the district court then reasons that they are "not statutory enactments by which States must automatically submit to federal prerogatives." [ ] There are two ways to understand this passage. One is that the district court is merely following the logic of its previous finding, and holding that federal state programs are not supreme law because they are only contracts. We have already rejected the line of reasoning that begins with the assumption that Medicaid is only a contract.

The district court may also be claiming that acts passed under the spending power are not supreme law because the spending power only gives Congress the power to set up these programs, not to force states to participate in them.\* \* \* "Because congressional enactments pursuant to the Spending Power that set forth the terms of federal-state cooperative agreements depend on the voluntary agreement of participating States . . .," the district court concludes, they are "not within the ambit of the Supremacy Clause [and so] are not the supreme law of the land." [ ] \* \* \* *South Dakota* upholds the power of Congress to place conditions on a state's receipt of federal funds. 483 U.S. at 21112, 107 S.Ct. 2793. *Pennhurst I* holds that if Congress wishes to impose obligations on states that choose to participate in volitional spending power programs, it must make the obligations explicit. 451 U.S. at 25, 101 S.Ct. 1531.

\* \* \*

The district court acknowledges that "the Supreme Court has in the past held that federal-state cooperative programs enacted under the Spending Power fall within the ambit of the Supremacy Clause." [ ] It then states that in "recent years ... the Supreme Court has conducted a more searching analysis of the nature and extent of the Supremacy Clause," suggesting erroneously that its departure from precedent is dictated by recent Supreme Court jurisprudence. [ ] * * * The well-established principle that acts passed under Congress's spending power are supreme law has not been abandoned in recent decisions.

* * *

B. *Whether the suit is barred under sovereign immunity*

The district court next held that the plaintiffs' suit is foreclosed by doctrines of sovereign immunity because Michigan is the "real party at interest" in the suit and plaintiffs cannot invoke any of the exceptions to sovereign immunity that would allow their suit. [ ]

As explained by the Supreme Court in many cases, sovereign immunity, though partially codified in the Eleventh Amendment, is a basic feature of our federal system. [ ] * * *

Under the doctrine developed in *Ex parte Young* and its progeny, a suit that claims that a state official's actions violate the constitution or federal law is not deemed a suit against the state, and so barred by sovereign immunity, so long as the state official is the named defendant and the relief sought is only equitable and prospective. [ ]

Of course, *Ex parte Young* is a "fiction" to the extent it sharply distinguishes between a state and an officer acting on behalf of the state, but it is a necessary fiction, required to maintain the balance of power between state and federal governments. "The availability of prospective relief of the sort awarded in *Ex parte Young* gives life to the Supremacy Clause."[ ] * * * On its surface this case fits squarely within *Ex parte Young*. Plaintiffs allege an ongoing violation of federal law, the Medicaid Act, and seek prospective equitable relief, an injunction ordering the named state officials henceforth to comply with the law.

The district court nonetheless held that *Ex parte Young* was inapplicable for four separate reasons. Two can be quickly dismissed. First, it held that plaintiffs could not invoke *Ex parte Young* because that doctrine can only be invoked to enforce federal laws that are supreme law of the land. [ ] Since we held above that spending clause enactments are supreme law of the land, they may be the basis for an *Ex parte Young* action. Second, the district court held *Ex parte Young* is unavailable because under this doctrine a court lacks "authority to compel state officers performing discretionary functions." [ ] This correctly states the holding in *Young*, but misunderstands what it means by "discretion." "An injunction to prevent [a state official] from doing that which he has no legal right to do is not an interference with the discretion of an officer." *Ex parte Young*, 209 U.S. at 159, 28 S.Ct. 441. Since the plaintiffs here claim that the defendants are acting unlawfully in refusing to implement mandatory elements of Medicaid's screening and treatment program, they seek only to prevent the defendants from doing "what [they] have no legal right to do," and their suit is permitted under *Ex parte Young*.

Third, the district court asserts that *Ex parte Young* is unavailable because the state "is the real party in interest when its officers act within their lawful authority." [ ] It has two reasons for finding Michigan the real party in interest. Its first reason follows from its finding that Medicaid is a contract. If Medicaid were only a contract, then this would be a suit seeking to compel a state to specific performance of a contract. Such suits are barred under a nineteenth century Supreme Court case, *In re Ayers*, 123 U.S. 443, 8 S.Ct. 164, 31 L.Ed. 216 (1887), which held that a "claim for injunctive relief against state officials under the Contracts Clause is barred by state sovereign immunity because the state [is] the real party at interest." [ ] We have already held that Medicaid is not merely a contract, but a federal statute. This suit seeks only to compel state officials to follow federal law, and thus is not barred by *Ayers*.

The district court also says erroneously that Michigan is the real party in interest because "[t]here is no personal, unlawful behavior attributed" to the defendants that plaintiffs seek to enjoin [ ] In their initial complaint, plaintiffs make clear that they are suing the named defendants because of "their failure to provide children in Michigan ... with essential medical, dental, and mental health services *as required by federal law*." [ ]

Finally, the district court refused to allow plaintiffs to proceed under *Young* because of the Supreme Court's holding in *Seminole Tribe* that "[w]here Congress has prescribed a detailed remedial scheme for the enforcement against a State of a statutorily created right, a court should hesitate before casting aside those limitations and permitting an action against a state officer based upon *Ex parte Young*." [ ] The Medicaid Act allows the Secretary of Health and Human Services to reduce or cut off funding to states that do not comply with the program's requirements.[ ] This one provision, the district court held, was a detailed remedial scheme sufficient to make *Ex parte Young* unavailable. [ ]

We disagree. In *Seminole Tribe*, the Supreme Court found *Ex parte Young* was unavailable because Congress had established a *"carefully crafted and intricate* remedial scheme.... for the enforcement of a *particular* federal right." [ ] The scheme here, in contrast, simply allows the Secretary to reduce or cut off funds if a state's program does not meet federal requirements. See 42 U.S.C. § 1396c. This is not a detailed "remedial" scheme sufficient to show Congress's intent to preempt an action under *Ex parte Young*. [ ]

Plaintiffs seek only prospective injunctive relief from a federal court against state officials for those officials' alleged violations of federal law, and they may proceed under *Ex parte Young*.

C. *Whether there is a private right of action under § 1983*

Section 1983 imposes liability on anyone who under color of state law deprives a person of "rights, privileges, or immunities" secured by the laws or the constitution of the United States. 42 U.S.C. § 1983. The Supreme Court and this court have held that in some circumstances a provision of the Medicaid scheme can create a right privately enforceable against state officers through § 1983. *See Wilder*, [ ].

In *Blessing*, the Supreme Court set down the framework for evaluating a claim that a statute creates a right privately enforceable against state officers through § 1983. [ ] A statute will be found to create an enforceable right if, after a particularized inquiry, the court concludes (1) the statutory section was intended to benefit the putative plaintiff, (2) it sets a binding obligation on a government unit, rather than merely expressing a congressional preference, and (3) the interests the plaintiff asserts are not so "'vague and amorphous' that [their] enforcement would strain judicial competence." [ ] If these conditions are met, we presume the statute creates an enforceable right unless Congress has explicitly or implicitly foreclosed this.[ ] The district court erred when it did not apply this test to evaluate plaintiffs' claims.

We now apply this test. First, the provisions were clearly intended to benefit the putative plaintiffs, children who are eligible for the screening and treatment services. [ ] We have found no federal appellate cases to the contrary. Second, the provisions set a binding obligation on Michigan. They are couched in mandatory rather than precatory language, stating that Medicaid services "*shall* be furnished" to eligible children, 42 U.S.C. § 1396a(a)(8) (emphasis added), and that the screening and treatment provisions "*must* be provided," *id.* § 1396a(a)(10)(A). Third, the provisions are not so vague and amorphous as to defeat judicial enforcement, as the statute and regulations carefully detail the specific services to be provided. *See* 42 U.S.C. § 1396d(r). Finally, Congress did not explicitly foreclose recourse to § 1983 in this instance, nor has it established any remedial scheme sufficiently comprehensive to supplant § 1983. [ ]

Plaintiffs have a cause of action under § 1983 for alleged noncompliance with the screening and treatment provisions of the Medicaid Act.

\* \* \*

## *Notes*

1. Though court of appeals decisions reaffirming the applicability of the *Ex parte Young* doctrine and 42 U.S.C. § 1983 in Medicaid cases seemed to preserve the Medicaid entitlement for the time being, two Supreme Court cases decided in 2002 left its long term vitality in doubt. First, in Barnes v. Gorman, 536 U.S. 181, 122 S.Ct. 2097, 153 L.Ed.2d 230 (2002), a case rejecting the availability of punitive damages against a municipality under federal disability discrimination statutes, Justice Scalia again opined that spending clause programs operate "much in the nature of a contract," and held that punitive damages were not available because they were not unambiguously provided under the "contract" with the state in the case at bar. More significantly, the Court again tightened the screws on § 1983 claims in Gonzaga University v. Doe, 536 U.S. 273, 122 S.Ct. 2268, 153 L.Ed.2d 309 (2002), holding that a federal cause of action was not available to enforce the Family Educational Rights and Privacy Act. Writing for the Court, Justice Rehnquist concluded "[I]f Congress wishes to create new rights enforceable under § 1983, it must do so in clear and unambiguous terms–no less and no more than what is required for Congress to create new rights enforceable under an implied private right of action." The Court distinguished *Wilder* as a case in which Congress had provided a clear and enforceable right, but it seems obvious that the expansion of federal rights which the Court led in the 1970s continues to be in hot retreat.

Though continuing to recognize the possibility of federal actions to enforce Medicaid obligations, the lower courts seem increasingly reluctant to recognize federal claims in actual cases. In Frazar v. Gilbert, 300 F.3d 530 (5th Cir.2002), for example, the court of appeals held that the provisions of a consent decree that the state of Texas had entered into with respect to alleged EPSTD program violations were not enforceable under § 1983 (though the Court also took pains to reject the lower court's decision in *Westside Mothers*). The Supreme Court has taken certiorari on *Frazar,* and might use it as a platform for revisiting more broadly the rights of Medicaid recipients in federal court, though it might limit its consideration to the enforceability of consent decrees. The decision will be posted on our TWEN site when it appears. In Burlington United Methodist Family Services v. Atkins, 227 F.Supp.2d 593 (S.D.W.Va.2002), the court, explicitly relying on *Gonzaga,* held that 42 U.S.C.A. § 1396a(a)(30)(a) (which requires that state Medicaid plans "assure payments that are consistent with efficiency, economy, and quality of care and are sufficient to enlist enough providers so that care and services are available under the plan at least to the extent that such care and services are available to the general population in the geographic area") did not afford providers a cause of action under § 1983. It is possible, therefore, that the courts may continue to give lip service to a federal Medicaid entitlement while being increasingly restrictive in recognizing such an entitlement in actual cases. See Timothy Stoltzfus Jost, The Tenuous Nature of the Medicaid Entitlement, Health Affairs, Jan./Feb. 2003 at 145.

2. The Supreme Court's only Medicaid case in the 2001–2002 term addressed a rather technical question of calculation of the community spouse resource allowance in situations in which one spouse in a couple is institutionalized and applying for Medicaid and the other spouse remains in the community. Wisconsin Department of Health and Family Services v. Blumer, 534 U.S. 473, 122 S.Ct. 962, 151 L.Ed.2d 935 (2002). The plaintiff had challenged Wisconsin's "income-first" approach to the problem as inconsistent with federal law, but the Court upheld Wisconsin's approach. The Court observed:

> The Medicaid statute, in which the MCCA is implanted, is designed to advance cooperative federalism. [ ] When interpreting other statutes so structured, we have not been reluctant to leave a range of permissible choices to the States, at least where the superintending federal agency has concluded that such latitude is consistent wit the statute's aims.\* \* \*
>
> The Secretary's position [permitting the "income first" approach] warrants respectful consideration. \* \* \*
>
> Eliminating the discretion to choose income-first would hinder a State's efforts to "strik[e] its own balance" in the implementation of the Act.\* \* \* We perceive nothing in the Act contradicting the Secretary's conclusion that such a result is unnecessary and unwarranted.

This case, therefore, like *Gonzaga* and *Barnes,* is in line with a trend toward deference to the states in Supreme Court federalism jurisprudence, though it also defers to the federal executive in the management of the Medicaid program.

3. The Department of Health and Human Services has been at least as active as the Supreme Court in shifting the balance of power to the states in the Medicaid program. On August 4, 2001, the Bush administration announced its Health Insurance Flexibility and Accountability Initiative (HIFA). The primary focus of HIFA is to encourage comprehensive waiver programs to increase the number of insured individuals by using current Medicaid and SCHIP resources. Program expansions are to focus on individuals with incomes below 200% of the federal poverty level. In particular, the initiative contemplates cutting back on services or imposing additional cost-sharing obligations on optional Medicaid groups (who make up about 29% of current Medicaid recipients, including 56% of seniors and 43% of low income parents). The only limitations as to services that must be provided to optional populations under HIFA are that the benefit package

must be equivalent to those permissible under SCHIP, and that cost-sharing obligations for children should not exceed 5% of family income. Benefits for the expanded populations need only cover "basic primary care," i.e. non-specialist physician services. The states are strongly encouraged under the HIFA program, moreover, to subsidize the purchase of private insurance. The waiver program also does not impose any floor on benefits or ceiling on cost-sharing for private plans, unlike current federal law. HIFA programs are supposed to be budget neutral with respect to federal funding. This neutrality is enforced through a per person federal budget cap. CMS has issued an application template to facilitate applications for HIFA waivers.

Medicaid advocates have been sharply critical of the HIFA program. They point out that HIFA is likely to cut Medicaid benefits for some of its most needy recipients, while providing inadequate benefits for expansion populations and inefficient subsidies for private insurance. They note that the HIFA waiver template apparently contemplates enrollment caps, currently not permitted for Medicaid recipients. The HIFA guidelines also do not, they argue, require the states to reinvest their Medicaid and SCHIP savings in coverage expansions, as long as they do not impose additional costs on the federal government. Perhaps the most serious complaint about the new guidelines, however, is that they make radical changes in the nature of the Medicaid program without Congressional oversight. Indeed, the waiver process does not seem to contemplate any public input at the federal level, and CMS has refused to permit stakeholders to review waiver applications prior to approval.

The Bush administration's Medicaid reform proposal released in the spring of 2003 would give the states far more discretion to deal with optional populations and services, but would also give the state's capped block grants to cover their costs. It promised slightly more financial support up front to states that accepted block grants, but would require the states eventually to pay back the increased funds.

**Add, at p. 750:**

## V. STATE PHARMACEUTICAL BENEFIT PROGRAMS

As this book goes to press, the Supreme Court is still considering the legality of the Maine Act to Establish Fairer Pricing for Prescription Drugs. As soon as the Court decides *Pharmaceutical Research and Manufacturers of America v. Concannon* we will post an edited version of it on our TWEN site.

The problem addressed by the Maine program is a familiar one. In the recent past the cost of pharmaceuticals has risen dramatically. Expenditures for retail prescription drugs increased at a rate of 17.3% in the year 2000 and 16.4% in the year 2001, and are expected to increase at double digit rates through the rest of this decade. While drugs still represent a relatively small part of national health care expenditures (a little over 10%), the burden of drug costs falls disproportionately on a small number of individuals with chronic diseases. For these persons, the high cost of drugs often means going without. A recent 8–state study of Medicare beneficiaries, found that 25% of uninsured beneficiaries failed to fill at least one prescription during 2001 due to cost, 27% skipped doses to make their medications last longer, and 20% spent less on other basic needs to afford prescription drugs. Dana Safran, et al, Prescription Drugs and Seniors, How Well are the States Closing the Gaps, Health Affairs Web Exclusive, available at http://www.healthaffairs.org/WebExclusive/2105Safran.pdf. The incidence of insurance coverage of drugs, moreover, though greatly expanded from two decades ago, is still less than for other health care goods and services. Seventy million Americans have no insurance for prescription drugs.

Although a Medicare drug benefit has been on the Congressional agenda for several years, it has stalled because of its high cost and because of ideological disagreement as to how to structure the program. At least in the short run, therefore, any progress in expanding public programs for helping out those with high drug costs and without drug coverage is likely to come at the state level. The states have in fact been very active in recent years in attempting to address this problem.

The most straightforward solution is simply to offer assistance to those most in need of drug coverage, usually through subsidized insurance plans. As of November, 2002, 31 states had adopted laws to authorize pharmaceutical assistance programs, and 27 were operational. All of these programs covered senior citizens, but many covered disabled persons as well, and a few covered the uninsured generally. Most impose income eligibility limits, which varied from $7,974 (Arkansas) to $44,300 (Massachusetts), for a single individual in 2002. National Conference of State Legislatures, State Pharmaceutical Assistance Programs, Available at http://www.ncsl.org/programs/health/drugaid.htm. The greatest drawback of these programs, however, is that they must be paid for by the states, virtually all of which are under a state constitutional obligation to balance their budget every year and most of which are facing very tight budgets during the current economic downturn. Most of these programs, therefore are still small (only 6 had more than 100,000 members in 2002), and under threat.

A more attractive strategy to the states for expanding drug coverage is to force down prices charged by drug manufacturers. The most obvious way to do this is for states to use the approach already taken to drug pricing under the Medicaid program. Though outpatient prescription drugs are an optional service under the federal/state Medicaid program, all states in fact cover prescription drugs. The basic structure through which Medicaid programs pay for prescription drugs was worked out in the Omnibus Budget Reconciliation act of 1990. Pub. L. No. 101–508, § 4401, 104 Stat. 1388, 13880 143–159 (1990), codified as amended at 42 U.S.C. § 1396r–8. Under this legislation, drug manufacturers must provide state Medicaid programs with "rebates" for drugs sold to Medicaid beneficiaries. The rebates equal the difference between the drug manufacturers' average wholesale price and the "best price" that they offer to other buyers (other than the federal government) or at least 15.1%, essentially giving the states the price discrimination benefit enjoyed by other large purchasers like hospitals or HMOs. 42 U.S.C. § 1396r–8(c). The federal government tracks pricing information provided by drug manufacturers for the states, and determines the size of the rebate that the states can demand for any particular drug based on these figures, though in fact the 15.1% minimum often constitutes the amount of the rebate. The 1990 legislation, on the other hand, also provided an important benefit for the drug manufacturers—a provision prohibiting the states from excluding from a state drug formulary any of the products of a manufacturer that agrees to a rebate program. See David Chavkin, Medicaid and Viagra: Restoring Potency to an Old Program? Health Matrix 11(2001): 190–262, 204, describing the compromise that birthed this legislation.

Though states are not generally permitted to exclude the products of manufacturers with drug rebate agreements through formularies, they are allowed to impose prior authorization requirements on some drugs, subject to several protections for beneficiaries. 42 U.S.C. § 1396r–8(d). The effects of a Medicaid prior authorization program is often to deny access to a drug, particularly as Medicaid recipients often do not learn of the program until a pharmacy refuses to fill a prescription presented by the recipient whose doctor did not obtain a prior authorization.

States have used their Medicaid programs in several different ways to make drugs more available to the poor and uninsured. First, several states have simply expanded their Medicaid programs, thus giving their indigent residents the full benefit of Medicaid coverage, including prescription drug coverage. See Families USA, Expanding Medicaid: State Options, Could Your State do More to Expand Medicaid for Seniors and Adults with Disabilities? Available at http://www.familiesusa.org/media/pdf/ExpandingMedicaid.pdf. This option is very costly to the states, however, as they must pay the state share of the Medicaid match, and must also cover all mandatory services (including hospital and nursing home care) for the populations covered by these programs—not just drugs.

Several states, therefore, including as of late 2002, Illinois, Wisconsin, South Carolina, Florida, Maine and Maryland, have received federal Medicaid waivers to create a new Medicaid expansion that covers drugs only to optional Medicaid populations, usually senior citizens and disabled persons with incomes under 200% of the poverty level. Drug-only Medicaid coverage is not an alternative explicitly contemplated by the Medicaid statute, but the Department of Health and Human Services has indicated its willingness to offer such waivers and has made them available to states that have pursued this option. See Center for Medicare and Medicaid Services, Pharmacy Plus Section 1115 Waiver Research and Demonstration Projects, Technical Guidance and Fact Sheet, Available at http://www.cms.gov/Medicaid/1115/factsheet41202.pdf.

Drug-only Medicaid programs could be funded just like other Medicaid programs, but as the drug-only program was implemented in Vermont (and initially Maine), pharmacies would sell drugs to persons enrolled in the program for the Medicaid price, including a discount for the drug rebate. The state would then collect the rebate from the manufacturer, and pass it on to the pharmacy, covering the discount. No state money was otherwise be involved in the program, and no additional benefits would be offered the recipient. The Vermont program was struck down because the court viewed it basically as a sham Medicaid program since no state funding was involved. PhaRMA v. Thompson, 251 F.3d 219 (D.C.Cir.2001). The Maine program, which involved minimal state payments in addition to the rebates, has also been struck down by the federal court of appeals, though on the grounds that the current program was not approved by DHHS, and that the only approved program involved no state contributions, like the Vermont program. PhaRMA v. Thompson, 313 F.3d 600 (D.C.Cir.2002).

The Supreme Court's case in *Concannon* addresses a more expansive Maine drug program, the Maine Rx Program, covering all residents of the state of Maine, regardless of income. 22 Me. Rev.Stat.Ann. 2681(2)(F), (5). Through this program, Maine attempted to extract from drug manufacturers "voluntary" agreements to extend to the general population rebates on their drugs equal to those extended to the state under the Medicaid program. §§ 2681(3) & (4). Again, these rebates would be passed back to pharmacies that sold drugs to eligible Maine residents at discounts reflecting the rebates. Drug manufacturers who refused to extend voluntary rebates would be sanctioned by having their identities released to the public and their products covered under the Medicaid program only on a "prior authorization" basis. § 2681(7).

PhaRMA, the drug manufacturers trade association, challenged the Maine program, arguing that the Maine statute creating the program violated Medicaid program requirements by imposing an impermissible prior authorization program, as well as the Dormant Commerce Clause because it 1) set prices for drugs sold by manufacturers and thus regulated transactions between manufacturers and wholesalers, which in most instances take place outside of Maine, which only has a very small drug manufacturing industry, and 2) favored Maine consumers at the expense of drug manufacturers located in other states. The federal district court accepted both of these arguments. The Court of Appeals reversed. PhaRMA v. Concannon, 249 F.3d 66 (1st Cir.2001). We await the Supreme Court decision.

# Chapter 11

# ACCESS TO HEALTH CARE: THE OBLIGATION TO PROVIDE CARE

## I. PHYSICIANS' DUTY TO TREAT

### B. THE AMERICANS WITH DISABILITIES ACT

**Add, at p. 770, at the end of Note 2:**

*Bragdon* was eagerly awaited to resolve the question of whether asymptomatic HIV constituted a disability under the ADA. As you read, the Supreme Court, by a bare majority, concluded that asymptomatic HIV worked a substantial impairment in the major life activity of reproduction. The four dissenters disagreed, in part because the respondent had not proven that she had intended to bear children prior to the infection. In a case subsequent to *Bragdon*, the Fifth Circuit affirmed a district court ruling that a plaintiff was not disabled because the record showed that his wife had undergone a surgical sterilization procedure prior to his infection with HIV. Blanks v. Southwestern Bell Communications, 310 F.3d 398 (5th Cir.2002)

The Supreme Court has continued to narrow the interpretation of disability under the ADA. The Court has reinforced the need for a fact-intensive, individualized analysis of the impact of the impairment in substantially limiting a major life activity. In Toyota Motor Manufacturing v. Williams, 534 U.S. 184, 122 S.Ct. 681, 151 L.Ed.2d 615 (2002), the inability of an employee suffering from carpal tunnel syndrome to perform manual work-related tasks did not qualify her as disabled because it did not restrict any major life activities; and, therefore, her employer was not required to provide accommodations.

In Barnes v. Gorman, 536 U.S. 181, 122 S.Ct. 2097, 153 L.Ed.2d 230 (2002), the Supreme Court held that punitive damages were not allowed for claims under the provisions of the ADA relating to actions against state and local governments.

## II. HOSPITALS' DUTY TO PROVIDE TREATMENT

**Add, at the end of p. 771:**

The Office of the Inspector General (OIG) in the Department of Health and Human Services is the administrative agency charged with the sanction process under EMTALA. Although cases involving a private claim against facilities provide a comprehensive overview of the statutory requirements, a significant enforcement effort under EMTALA is administrative. Sanctions that may be imposed by HHS include monetary penalties against the hospital and the examining, treating and transferring physician as well as termination of the hospital's provider agreement. Gross, flagrant or repeated violations by a particular physician may result in exclusion of the physician from the Medicare program.

Between April and September of 2002, OIG collected approximately $501,000 from hospitals and physicians for violations of EMTALA. In its annual report to Congress, OIG briefly described the cases in which providers were sanctioned, from OIG's viewpoint. For example, a $64,000 penalty was imposed on a Nevada hospital that denied screening and treatment to a 10-month-old child because the parents were uninsured and could not afford a cash deposit. An Arizona hospital paid a $34,000 fine after discharging a patient from the emergency room with severe symptoms and without a diagnosis. That patient died the next morning at another facility. A tertiary care center in Florida was fined $20,000 for improper screening and transfer when a patient involved in a motor vehicle accident was transferred after only seven minutes of assessment when she had actually sustained a serious injury to her liver. Dept. of HHS, OIG, Semi ann. report to Congress, April–September 2002, available at http://oig.hhs.gov/publications/docs/semiannual/2002/SemiannualFall02.pdf.

**Add, at p. 777, after Note 1:**

The subsequent GAO report to Congress concluded that administrative enforcement actions under EMTALA were few; that monetary penalties were small; that termination was very rare; and that there were regional differences in the number of complaints of EMTALA violations as well as the number of investigations and violations. GAO reported that about 400 hospitals each year were investigated for EMTALA violations and that half of these were found to be in violation, although over the six-year period examined (1995 to 2001), the OIG processed only 605 hospital violations and declined to move forward to penalty on 368 of those.

The report details provider concerns including the fact that a termination notice would be issued prior to any procedure allowing the hospital to contest the finding of violation, even though the opportunity exists for 23 to 90 days after that. Both providers and CMS said that they wanted intermediate sanctions short of termination. The report states that OIG exercises discretion in the decision whether to sanction when a violation is found. Some of the factors used to guide that decision are the seriousness of the patient's condition, the nature of the violation, the culpability of the provider, and the effect a fine would have on the hospital's ability to provide care. Correction of violations is the first priority.

The GAO also heard from hospitals and physicians that EMTALA had resulted in more patients coming to the emergency department for nonurgent care, but the GAO notes that this phenomenon may be attributable to the increase in the number of uninsured individuals. GAO, Emergency Care: EMTALA Implementation and Enforcement Issues, GAO 01–747 (June 2001)

**Add, at p. 779, at the end of Note 4:**

The issue of whether the patient has "come to" the emergency department has many permutations. In Arrington v. Wong, 237 F.3d 1066 (9th Cir.2001), a patient suffering a heart attack was denied access to the initial hospital despite being in severe respiratory distress. The patient's symptoms were communicated by radio to the emergency room physician who nonetheless instructed the ambulance personnel to take the patient to a more distant hospital. The emergency room physician issued that directive even though the hospital was not on formal diversionary status. The court reversed the district court's finding that the patient had not "come to the hospital," and instead held that a hospital may only divert an ambulance that has contacted the emergency room and is in route if the hospital is on formal diversion.

For a more in-depth discussion of the *Arrington* case, see Tricia J. Middendorf, Note, Ambulances: Hospital Property or Not? Interpreting the Expanding Boundaries of EMTALA Through Arrington v. Wong, 46 St. Louis L. J. 1035, 1035–1058 (2002). (This article also discusses the issues under EMTALA relating to hospital-owned ambulances.) See also, Caroline J. Stalker, Comment: How Far is Too Far?: EMTALA Moves from the Emergency Room to Off–Campus Entities, 36 Wake Forest L. Rev. 823 (Fall 2001). Proposed regulations attempt to rectify a reported difficulty with hospital-owned ambulances that operate in a local EMS system. A hospital-owned ambulance acting in such a capacity, that has been directed to take a patient to a different hospital by the EMS protocol, triggers no EMTALA obligation to the owning hospital. Instead, the individual is deemed to have "come" to the hospital to which the individual is transported. 67 Fed. Reg. 31479 (May 9, 2002).

Proposed regulations also attempt to clarify that individuals presenting to the dedicated emergency department of a hospital must receive at least a screening exam. For example, a patient that presents to the emergency department for the specific purpose of having sutures removed from a wound must receive an appropriate screening from a qualified medical person, in this case a nurse. Upon determination by the nurse that the wound is healing and the patient does not have an emergency medical condition, the hospital does not have to provide treatment and may direct the patient elsewhere to have the sutures removed. The hospital is bound under the Act to provide the screening in order to determine with reasonable clinical confidence if the patient has an emergency medical condition. 67 Fed. Reg. 31473.

Individuals who present to other areas of hospital property must receive a screening exam only when the individual requests examination or treatment or has such a request made on his behalf. An individual who, for example, enters a hospital through the visitor entrance but is bleeding from a severe head laceration will trigger the hospital's obligations under the Act. A receptionist, as a prudent layperson observing the individual's condition would believe the patient is seeking emergency treatment and thereby triggers the hospital's EMTALA obligations. 67 Fed. Reg. 31474.

These obligations do not include patients who come to the hospital for non-emergency reasons such as to keep outpatient appointments with a physician or therapist. 67 Fed. Reg. 31472–77. The hospital may have obligations under other Medicare standards, however.

**Add, at p. 780, after Note 7:**

Although the GAO stated in the report discussed earlier that health care providers supported the goals of EMTALA, the Act is widely criticized by emergency medicine physicians as overly burdensome and ineffective in achieving its purported goal. Among the evils attributed to compliance with EMTALA are soaring costs and emergency department overcrowding. James S. Cohen, MD, FAAEM, advocated a "major overhaul" including "an appropriate financing mechanism, a better understanding of ED operations, and the elimination of the punitive attitude toward well-trained staff who routinely treat patients rejected by the rest of the health care system." James S. Cohen, EMTALA, Is the Cure Worse Than the Disease?, 21 The Journal of Emergency Medicine 439 (2001). See also Press Release, American College of Emergency Physicians, Proposed Revisions to EMTALA Address Critical Issues; Won't Solve Fundamental Problems in the Health Care System (May 14, 2000) (available at http://www.acep.org/1,5203,0.html).

**Add, at p. 788, after Note 3:**

Health care providers who refuse to provide services on the basis of the patient's HIV status may be doing so because of the fear of transmission of the virus from the patient to the health care worker or because the HIV-positive patient requires care that the health care provider cannot provide. Of course, it may be difficult in any particular case to prove the basis for the refusal of treatment. In Lesley v. Chie, 81 F. Supp. 2d 217 (D.Mass.2000), the District Court adopted the following standard for reviewing such cases:

> The case requires us to determine how far courts should defer to a doctor's judgment as to the best course of treatment for a disabled patient in the context of discriminatory denial of treatment claims. We hold that the doctor's judgment is to be given deference absent a showing by the plaintiff that the judgment lacked any reasonable medical basis.

Does this mean that physicians who do not want to treat patients with HIV can escape liability by hiding behind "medical judgment?" How would you go about proving or defending against a claim that the medical judgment is a subterfuge? The *Lesley* court suggested a fact-intensive inquiry in each case rather than a blanket rule.

Dr. Chie had been Lesley's OB/GYN for thirteen years when he discovered her HIV-positive status after testing her as part of her prenatal care. Lesley's pregnancy was indeed high-risk before the diagnosis of HIV with a history of manic-depression for which she took multiple medications, diabetes insipidus, and a recent late-term abortion that created a risk of early labor. After making the diagnosis, Dr. Chie consulted with Lesley's psychiatrist and numerous community resources on the treatment of HIV and transmission reduction to the child. He also contacted the hospital where he was on staff and attempted to order a supply of AZT to administer to Lesley during labor and delivery. Given his inexperience in the area and the limited experience of the other staff physicians at the hospital, Dr. Chie recommended to Lesley that she obtain treatment at a nearby hospital that had participated in NIH studies of treatment for HIV-positive women and infants. He had arranged with that hospital for Lesley's enrollment in the program should she consent. For an overview of the psychological variables surrounding a physician's refusal to treat, see Dana Richter, Not in My Office: Medical Professionals and Their Refusal to Treat HIV/AIDS Patients, 23 Law & Psychology Review 179, Spring 1999.

## Problem: Delayed Treatment

You are general counsel for hospital Y. You have been asked by hospital administration to review a recent situation in which a patient's admission from the emergency room and treatment were delayed by a variety of factors. The medical records, interviews and in-house reports revealed the following.

Lisa Carty, the patient, called the local emergency service just after midnight for trouble breathing and a fever of 102.6 degrees. An ambulance owned by hospital X responded and transported Ms. Carty to Hospital Y, the closest hospital with a dedicated emergency room, shortly before 1:00 a.m. Dr. March, the emergency room physician at Hospital Y, evaluated Ms. Carty within minutes, suspected pneumonia and recorded her diagnosis as pneumonia and possible sepsis (a toxic systemic infection following a localized infection that can lead to organ failure). As an independent contractor for emergency medicine only, Dr. March did not have admitting privileges. He, therefore, contacted Ms. Carty's primary care provider to have her admitted. While attempting to contact her physician, Dr. March ordered blood work, x-rays, Tylenol and oxygen therapy to be administered. He did not order antibiotics at that time.

Dr. No, the physician on call for Ms. Carty's primary care physicians' group, refused Dr. March's request that she be admitted to the intensive care unit for further treatment. Dr. No, who was not familiar with Ms. Carty, suspected a possible blood clot in her lung and directed March to order a ventilation and perfusion scan (VQ scan) to rule it out. Dr. March thought the test was not necessary but agreed to order it in an attempt to get Lisa's admission rolling. Dr. No and Dr. March also have a history of a prior quarrel over a patient admission, and Dr. March explained that he was trying to cooperate with Dr. No's requests in the interest of communication. However, the VQ scanner was unavailable because of a shortage of isotopes required to perform the scan. Isotopes used in a VQ scan can run low as they must be specially prepared by the hospital pharmacy (usually in the morning), expire readily, and must be ordered conservatively and often in estimated amounts based on the scheduled number of tests for a day. It is often cost prohibitive to restock the isotopes in the evening. Additionally, Xenon gas is used for part of the exam and there is occasionally a shortage of Xenon in the country.

Dr. No was told of these problems concerning his request for a VQ scan. Still, he continued to refuse Ms. Carty's admission until the testing was available and complete.

In the meantime, Lisa was sleeping but continued to have labored breathing. Her oxygen saturation levels were slightly lower than when she arrived, and her fever was up to 103 degrees. Dr. March, becoming increasingly alarmed, called Lisa's actual primary care physician, Dr. Maybe, at home. Dr. Maybe wanted to examine Ms. Carty personally and told Dr. March that she would come in, see her, and admit her from there.

Five hours after Dr. March's phone call, Dr. Maybe admitted Lisa to the ICU for treatment of her pneumonia. He wrote admitting orders including antibiotics, oxygen, and constant monitoring. Her antibiotic order was incorrectly transmitted to the pharmacy by the division secretary; and Ms. Carty's nurse, Ms. Polly, in her haste to care for multiple patients, did not track it down. Ms. Carty's did not receive her antibiotics. Two hours after her admission to the ICU, she suffered respiratory and cardiac arrest and died despite resuscitation efforts.

Which hospital is under an EMTALA obligation here, if either? Did the hospital fail to provide the appropriate screening? Is there a violation of EMTALA's stabilization requirement? What about the issue of medical resources and the potential unavailability of technology? Should it affect EMTALA liability if the facility does not have equipment or materials readily at its disposal? Should all emergency room physicians have admitting privileges to avoid this kind of situation? What additional problems could that create? How likely is it that Ms. Carty's family would prevail in an EMTALA action? In a malpractice action?

Facts loosely based on Harry v. Marchant, 291 F.3d 767 (11th Cir.2002).

**Add, at p. 790, after first paragraph:**

The concern about racial inequality in health care continues. For an insightful analysis of the potential of using systems design and the patient safety movement as a mechanism for assuring equal access to health care, see Sidney D. Watson, Race, Ethnicity and Quality of Care: Inequalities and Incentives, 27 Am.J.L.M. 203 (2001). For a creative analysis of legal claims related to racial bias in medical decisionmaking, see Mary Crossley, Infected Judgment: Legal Responses to Physician Bias, 48 Vill.L.Rev. 195 (2003), which includes a detailed analysis of the research in the area of racial disparities. See also, Charles Sullivan, Racial Distinctions in Medicine, 5 DePaul Journal of Health Care Law 249 (2002) (examining the racial differences in drug efficacy and the role race must play in medical decision making); Michael S. Shin, Redressing Wounds: Finding a Legal Framework to Remedy Racial Disparities in Medical Care, 90 California Law Review 2047 (2002) (exploring the caregiver's cognitive bias as the basis for unequal treatment); Rene Bowser, Racial Profiling in Health Care: An Institutional Analysis of Medical Treatment Disparities, 7 Mich. J. Race & L. 79 (2001); Symposium on Current Racial and Ethnic Disparities in Health, 1 Yale J. Health Policy, Law & Ethics (2001).

The Institute of Medicine issued a report on racial disparities in health care in 2002. This study was commissioned by the Agency on Healthcare Research and Quality, which had been charged by Congress to prepare annual reports on health disparities beginning in fiscal year 2003, to assist the Agency in designing those mandated reports. IOM, Guidance for the National Health Care Disparities Report (2002), available through the IOM website at www.iom.edu. The IOM report recommends that the AHRQ studies follow the following design:

> Present analyses of disparities in ways that account for the effects of socioeconomic status;
>
> Develop methods to more accurately and meaningfully measure the effects of socioeconomic status on access, utilization, and quality;
>
> Give priority to access issues as they are significant contributors to quality of health care;
>
> Include measures both of high utilization and low utilization of health care services as either can indicate poor quality health care in particular circumstances;

Focus on the state level, and present data using a continuum of urban-rural settings;

Consult with current collectors of data to assure high quality of data collection in subnational databases through standardization of core elements; and

Secure adequate resources to accomplish an accurate and meaningful study of health disparities.

In 2001, the Institute of Medicine released a report detailing the fundamental biological differences between men and women and encouraging more gender specific medical research. Exploring the Biological Contributions to Human Health, Does Sex Matter? available at http://www.nap.edu/books/0309072816/html.

**Add, at p. 790:**

The United States Supreme Court decided a landmark Title VI case in 2001. In a five-to-four decision in Alexander v. Sandoval, 532 U.S. 275, 121 S.Ct. 1511, 149 L.Ed.2d 517 (2001), the Court held that only intentional discrimination is actionable through private suit under Title VI of the Civil Rights Act. There is no private right of action for disparate impact cases under the statute, according to Justice Scalia joined by Chief Justice Rehnquist, Justices O'Connor, Kennedy, and Thomas.

In *Alexander*, a class of non-English speaking persons challenged an Alabama policy of administering driver's license exams in English only as a policy in violation of § 601 of the Civil Rights Act, having a discriminatory impact based on national origin. The majority strictly construed the text of Title VI, and in the absence of an express provision for private enforcement, held that no private right of action had been created. According to Justice Scalia, the elaborate regulatory enforcement method providing for termination of federal funding reinforces that § 601 focuses on regulatory agencies rather than classes of persons protected.

The case would seem to be the death knell for litigation like that in *Linton*. Justice Stevens, joined by Justices Souter, Ginsburg and Breyer issued a strongly worded dissent.

> Today, in a decision unfounded in our precedent and hostile to decades of settled expectations, a majority of this Court carves out an important exception to the right of private action long recognized under Title VI. In so doing, the Court makes three distinct, albeit interrelated, errors. First, the Court provides a muddled account of both the reasoning and the breadth of our prior decisions endorsing a private right of action under Title VI, thereby obscuring the conflict between those opinions and today's decision. Second, the Court offers a flawed and unconvincing analysis of the relationship between §§ 601 and 602 of the Civil Rights Act of 1964, ignoring more plausible and persuasive explanations detailed in our prior opinions. *Alexander*, 532 U.S. 275 at 294–95.

Stevens ended his dissent by saying that "the Court should have declined to take this case. Having granted certiorari, the Court should have answered the question differently by simply according respect to our prior decisions. But most importantly, even if it were to ignore all of our post–1964 writing, the

Court should have answered the question differently on the merits." *Id.* at 317.

In anticipation of the *Alexander* decision, President Clinton issued an Executive Order directing all Federal agencies to develop individually tailored plans to ensure compliance with Title VI in providing assistance to persons with limited English proficiency. Executive Order No., 13166, 65 Fed.Reg. 50121 (Aug. 11, 2000).

In response to the *Alexander* decision, the Department of Justice issued a memorandum reaffirming the validity of the need under Title VI for special policies for non-English speaking persons. Memorandum from Ralph C. Boyd, Assistant Attorney General, Civil Rights Division for Heads of Departments and Agencies, General Counsel and Civil Rights Directors (Oct. 26, 2001). HHS reissued a statement of policy guidance. The Prohibition against National Origin Discrimination as it Affects Persons with Limited English Proficiency, 67 Fed.Reg. 4968, 4970–4977 (Feb. 2002). The policy clarified existing provider responsibilities in securing meaningful access to services through the use of oral and written aids; through the use trained interpreters rather than family or friends; provision of educational materials in the person's native language; and other recommendations applying to all recipients of federal funds. *Id.*

For more on the issues raised by the *Alexander* decision, see Barbara Plantiko, Not So Equal Protection: Securing Individuals of Limited English Proficiency with Meaningful Access to Medical Services, 32 Golden Gate U.L. Review 239 (2002).

*

# Part III

# ORGANIZING THE HEALTH CARE ENTERPRISE

# Chapter 12

# PROFESSIONAL RELATIONSHIPS IN HEALTH CARE ENTERPRISES

## I. STAFF PRIVILEGES AND HOSPITAL–PHYSICIAN CONTRACTS

**Add, at p. 800, at note 3:**

The context of the question of whether medical staff by-laws create an enforceable contract remains important (see discussion in note 3 at page 807 of the casebook and in this supplement); but even as to the question of whether the procedures for adverse privileges actions specified in the by-laws are binding on the hospital, courts appear to be less likely to find a contractual obligation. See, for example, Madsen v. Audrain, 297 F.3d 694 (8th Cir.2002), relying on an earlier Missouri case and concluding that "[t]he expressed policy in Missouri is the assurance of quality health care, which is unduly impinged by allowing a physician to seek damages for an alleged failure of a hospital to follow the procedures established by its bylaws." The court does allow the physician's claim for slander to survive the hospital's motion to dismiss based on immunity under the Health Care Quality Improvement Act, holding that HCQIA immunity requires that more of a record be developed than is available at the point of a motion to dismiss. (It is most common that HCQIA immunity supports the grant of summary judgment in such cases. See discussion below.)

In O'Byrne v. Santa Monica–UCLA Medical Center, 94 Cal.App.4th 797, 114 Cal.Rptr.2d 575 (2001), the California Court of Appeals held that hospital by-laws created an enforceable contract that would support an action for injunctive relief when the hospital violated its by-laws but not an action for damages for breach of contract action. This holding mirrors the distinction made under the HCQIA where hospitals in compliance with the procedural requirements of the Act receive limited immunity from damages claims but not from actions for injunctive relief.

**Add, at p. 801, at note 5:**

### *Note on HCQIA Litigation*

The HCQIA has withstood constitutional challenge in several courts. See, e.g., Freilich v. Upper Chesapeake Health, Inc., 313 F.3d 205 (4th Cir.2002), holding that the Act did not violate Equal Protection, the Tenth Amendment (limiting federal power in areas of state authority), nor exceeded the scope of Congressional authority under the Commerce Clause; Singh v. Blue Cross/Blue Shield of Massachusetts, Inc., 308 F.3d 25 (1st Cir.2002), holding that the Act did not violate the doctor's Seventh Amendment right to jury trial.

A plaintiff physician does not have a private right of action and cannot make a claim under the HCQIA. Rather, the HCQIA provides the health care entity with a defense of immunity to damage claims filed by the physician, with the exception of civil rights claims. HCQIA immunity claims are most often resolved through summary judgment. See, for example, Ching v. Methodist Children's Hosp., ___ S.W.3d ___, 2003 WL 943740 (Tex.App.2003). Although the defendant health care entity moves for dismissal or summary judgment of the plaintiff's claim, the plaintiff bears the burden of proving that the hospital did not meet the standards of the Act and so does not have immunity. In order to succeed in rebutting the Act's statutory presumption that the credentialing decision ("professional review action") complied with the standards of the Act, the plaintiff must prove by a preponderance of the evidence that the health care entity (1) did not act in the reasonable belief that the action was in furtherance of quality health care; (2) did not make a reasonable effort to obtain the facts of the matter; (3) did not afford the physician adequate notice and hearing procedures and such other procedures required by fairness under the circumstances; and (4) did not act in the reasonable belief that the action was warranted by the facts known after such reasonable effort to obtain facts and after meeting the procedural requirements.

In considering physicians' efforts to rebut immunity, the courts have been supportive of hospital adverse credentialing decisions. They emphasize the "reasonableness" of the basis for the hospital's action, not its ultimate accuracy. For a case that clearly and simply lays out the plaintiff's burden in "disproving" HCQIA immunity, see Van v. Anderson, 199 F.Supp.2d 550 (N.D.Tex.2002). A review of published opinions indicates that physicians do not frequently succeed in overturning the rebuttable presumption of validity. (But see, Clark v. Columbia/HCA Information Services, Inc., 117 Nev. 468, 25 P.3d 215 (2001).)

In fact, the HCQIA provides that physicians who bring frivolous or bad faith suits may be ordered to pay attorney's fees and costs to the defendant. See, e.g., Sithian v. Staten Island University Hosp., 189 Misc.2d 410, 734 N.Y.S.2d 812 (Sup.Ct.2001), aff'd sub nom. Sithian v. Spence, 300 A.D.2d 387, 750 N.Y.S.2d 783 (App.Div. 2002). The Act provides that the court shall award fees and costs to the defendant if the "claim, or the claimant's conduct during the litigation of the claim, was frivolous, unreasonable, without foundation, or in bad faith." The trial court found it particularly "retaliatory" that the plaintiff filed suit before the Board of Trustees made their final decision and that the defendant external peer reviewer had had no prior contact with the plaintiff, making it difficult to believe that the plaintiff had any actual indication of malice on the defendant physician's part. The trial court awarded the defendants almost $250,000 in fees and costs. In contrast, see Berg v. Shapiro, 36 P.3d 109 (Colo.App.2001), reversing the trial court's award of attorney's fees in part because application of the HCQIA was relatively unsettled during the first five years following its enactment. See also, Dallas County Medical Society v. Ubinas Brache, 68 S.W.3d 31 (Tex.App.2001), remanding to the trial court the question of whether fees should be awarded. Awards of attorney's fees under the Act do not appear to be very common; *Sithian* was the first case in New York to have done so as of that date.

The hospital's obligation to report adverse actions against physicians to the National Practitioner Data Bank extends to situations where the physician has resigned once an investigation into quality of care issues has begun. This has created a small window where a physician may resign prior to the beginning of an "investigation." It has been thought by some that this affords physicians and hospitals too great an opportunity to bypass reporting. In any case, it is not entirely clear when the opportunity to resign without report has passed. In Wheeler v. Methodist Hospital, 95 S.W.3d 628 (Tex.App.2002), in which the court held that the resignation triggered a duty to report, the following occurred:

> In March 1995, [Dr.] Wheeler performed a successful outpatient procedure, after which the patient requested to go home. When Wheeler attempted to contact certain physicians for consultation [in compliance with a practice proctoring system which the hospital required of Dr. Wheeler], his calls were not returned. Rather than wait for a returned phone call from one of these physicians while the patient remained in the hospital, Wheeler allowed the patient to go home as requested. Shortly thereafter, on March 17, 1995, Wheeler was contacted by telephone by Drs. David Zepeda and Terry Simon. (Dr. Zepeda was the acting chief of staff because the chief of staff, Dr. Joe Leigh Simpson, was out of town.) Later that same day, Wheeler voluntarily resigned from Methodist. The substance of the telephone conversation between Wheeler, Zepeda, and Simon is disputed—Wheeler said they informed him that he *would be suspended* when Dr. Simpson returned from out of town because, by discharging his patient before obtaining a consultation, he did not comply with the [the proctoring requirement]; Drs. Zepeda and Simon said they informed Wheeler that he *was suspended.*

> On March 24, 1995, Methodist notified Wheeler by letter that his voluntary resignation had been received. The letter stated:

> "This will serve as official notification of the acceptance of your voluntary resignation from the Medical Staff of The Methodist Hospital, notice of which was received in the Hospital's Medical Staff Services Department at 3:30 p.m., on Friday March 17, 1995. Please be advised that as your Medical Staff membership and clinical privileges *were suspended at the time of your resignation, the Hospital will list your status as suspended,* until final approval of your deletion from the Medical Staff by the Board of Directors, whose next meeting is scheduled for Wednesday, July 26, 1995. *As you voluntarily resigned while under investigation,* the Hospital, as required, will report this action to the National Practitioner Data Bank through the Texas State Board of Medical Examiners." (Emphasis in original.)

Hospital reports to the Data Bank made once an investigation has begun often describe the issues that were being investigated. For example, in Ulrich v. City and County of San Francisco, 308 F.3d 968 (9th Cir.2002), a physician had voiced within the hospital his opposition to physician layoffs, which did not directly affect his own position. Shortly after Dr. Ulrich signed a letter of protest sent to the San Francisco Department of Health concerning the impact of the layoffs on patient safety, the hospital notified Ulrich that its credentials committee had opened an investigation of allegations of professional incompetence against him. A month after the notice and a month before the scheduled meeting with the committee, Ulrich posted a notice of his resignation at the hospital's nurses' station. The resignation was accepted in writing by the hospital; but when Dr. Ulrich was informed by his attorney that the resignation could trigger the hospital's obligation to report to the NPDB, Ulrich tried to rescind the resignation. The hospital refused, and filed a report with the Data Bank.

The hospital's report stated that Ulrich had resigned after an investigation was begun "prompted as a result of concerns regarding apparent deficiencies in his practice and conduct spanning the full range of Hospital care, including incomplete diagnoses, inappropriate diagnostic and therapeutic orders, failures to accept appropriate responsibility for the course of patient treatment, and an overall absence of clear, effective management of hospitalizations." The California medical board reviewed the merits of the allegations reported by the hospital and found that there was "no departure in the standard of care" in Dr. Ulrich's practice. The hospital refused to void the report.

The HCQIA provides hospitals limited immunity for their reports to the Data Bank. Again, the plaintiff bears the burden of proving that the hospital did not meet the standards of the Act and so does not have immunity.

Dr. Ulrich filed for damages and injunctive relief against the public hospital for violation of his First Amendment rights, claiming that the investigation, the report to the NPDB, and the hospital's refusal to void the report were all retaliatory for his exercise of protected speech in opposing the layoffs. The Court of Appeals allowed the plaintiff to pursue his claim under the First and Fourteenth Amendments.

HCQIA extends immunity to health care entities beyond the hospital setting. See, e.g., Singh v. Blue Cross/Blue Shield of Massachusetts, Inc., 308 F.3d 25 (1st Cir.2002), considering the Act's application to a health care plan. Such an entity must qualify as a "professional review body" engaged in a "professional review action" as described in the statute in order to qualify for immunity. The Court held that the plan could so qualify. In Lipson v. Anesthesia Services, P.A., 790 A.2d 1261 (Del.Super.2001), the court refused to extend the Act to a private medical group practice finding that although the hospital for which the group provided anesthesiology services said that the group should consider taking action against the physician, the group did not act "on behalf of the hospital" and so could not qualify for immunity under that argument. Further, "in the absence of any internal 'formal peer review' process to guide their investigation, [the group's] conduct—at least in the eyes of the HCQIA—was nothing more than employee discipline, cloaked with no more protection or immunity from suit than any other personnel decision it may have made." Should a medical group practice establish formal procedures like those used in hospitals in order to try to gain HCQIA immunity? What considerations would be at play in deciding this question? How would you advise them?

**Add, at p. 807, at the end of note 3:**

In the area of restructuring and exclusive contracting for physicians, the issue of the legal status of the relationship between the medical staff and the hospital is usually presented as a question of whether the hospital board has authority to restructure the medical staff, which the courts resolve by examining the scope of authority delineated within the hospital's governing by-laws and the by-laws of the medical staff, with the result that is described in this note in the text. A permutation of this issue occurred in New Hampshire where a medical staff sued the hospital challenging a "gag order" that was imposed on the president of the medical staff when the hospital board removed him from his *ex officio* position on the hospital board of trustees. Under the gag order, which the board of trustees viewed as implementing the confidentiality agreement that each board member signed when joining the board, the physician was prohibited from discussing the reasons for his removal with other members of the medical staff. The New Hampshire Supreme Court held in Exeter Hosp. Medical Staff v. Board of Trustees of Exeter Health Resources, Inc., 148 N.H. 492, 810 A.2d 53 (2002) that the medical staff could not sue the hospital:

> We conclude that the medical staff in this case is not a legal entity separate and apart from the hospital, but rather is a subordinate administrative unit dependent upon and accountable to the hospital. Hospital licensure regulations, promulgated by the New Hampshire Department of Health and Human Services, the Exeter Hospital (hospital) bylaws and the medical staff bylaws reflect that the medical staff serves under the authority of the hospital board of trustees....
>
> ... As the governing body, the board of trustees appoints the medical staff, delegates responsibility to it, and "oversee[s] its organization into a responsible administrative unit." The board retains ultimate authority to approve or deny requests for clinical privileges and recommendations to revoke, suspend or condition clinical privileges already granted. Although the medical staff develops and adopts bylaws, rules and regulations, it is required to submit them to the governing body for approval, and the governing body reserves the right to unilaterally adopt or amend them as necessary....
>
> Despite the mechanisms for limited self-governance built into the regulations and bylaws, the medical staff lacks independence and autonomy and is ultimately accountable to the hospital board of trustees. We therefore conclude that [t]he medical staff has no legal life of its own and is merely one component of the hospital corporation. This in no way denigrates the role which the staff plays in the modern hospital. It is, in fact, the single most important department in the hospital. But the fact that it is a "department" means that the staff cannot sue or be sued as a body. Accordingly, we affirm the trial court's ruling that the medical staff lacks status under the law to sue as a separate entity.
>
> The petitioners further argue that the medical staff should be accorded standing because recognition and protection of its existence, functions and self-governance are required by New Hampshire public policy and because the boards' actions have directly and adversely affected the medical staff, which has a direct and substantial interest in the outcome of the litigation. Whether the medical staff can maintain an action against the boards turns upon its status under the law. Having concluded that the medical staff is not a legal entity, we need not address these policy arguments.

**Add, at p. 807, at the end of note 4:**

In cases of disputes between individual physicians and health care entities, the courts remain supportive of decisions based on practice patterns relating to utilization of resources. For example, in Singh v. Blue Cross/Blue Shield of Massachusetts, 182 F. Supp.2d 164 (2001), aff'd. 308 F.3d 25 (1st Cir.2002), in which the District Court rejected the doctor's claims regarding his termination from a health plan, the court stated:

> As to the issue of whether Blue Cross was acting to further the quality of health care, it is clear that the [credentialing committee] believed that it was acting to protect patients. While concerns about "over-utilization" have an economic component, they also have a direct connection to patient care. Too much testing or medicine is not in the best interests of a patient's health.

"Economic credentialing" has been used primarily to describe privileges decisions based on the individual doctor's practice patterns with regard to utilization intensity, or on the financial advantage to the hospital in restructuring its medical staff from an open staff to an exclusive contract with a particular group practice, or the selection of one group over another based on financial concerns.

A more recent development in economic credentialing is occurring with some hospitals refusing privileges to physicians who compete directly with hospitals in service areas the hospital offers. For example, a not-for-profit hospital system in Ohio has declared that it will not grant privileges to physicians who invest in for-profit specialty hospitals that treat only a defined set of cases, such as neurosurgery or orthopedic surgery, which are profitable. The chairman of the board of the non-profit system said that these specialty hospitals "cherry pick" the profitable services, making it impossible for the nonprofit hospital to provide charity care, and that the nonprofit hospital has "the fiduciary duty to protect and preserve the charitable mission" of the hospital. Hospital System Pulls Staff Privileges for Doctors Who Invest in Competitors, 11 Health Law Reporter 1451.

Does this decision fall within the category of "restructuring" the medical staff? If so, how would the court in *Mateo-Woodburn* address the decision if the action were challenged? Does the decision to exclude physician competitors fall within the authority of the hospital's governing board as do other restructuring decisions? Is this the same situation as when a hospital decides to revoke privileges for "overutilization?" (Refer also to antitrust implications in Chapter 15 and fraud and abuse in Chapter 14.) Consider the following case.

## MAHAN v. AVERA ST. LUKE'S

Supreme Court of South Dakota, 2001.
621 N.W.2d 150.

Gilbertson, Justice.

Orthopedic Surgery Specialists (OSS), a South Dakota corporation, and its individual physicians, commenced this action against Avera St. Lukes (ASL) alleging breach of contract. The trial court granted OSS' motion for summary judgment and entered a mandatory permanent injunction against ASL. ASL then filed this appeal. We reverse.

### FACTS AND PROCEDURE

ASL is a private, nonprofit, general acute care hospital located in Aberdeen, South Dakota, organized under the nonprofit corporation laws of South Dakota.

ASL is part of Avera Health, a regional health care system sponsored by the Sisters of the Presentation of the Blessed Virgin Mary of Aberdeen, South Dakota. Since 1901, the Presentation Sisters have been fulfilling their mission statement "to respond to God's calling for a healing ministry ... by providing quality health services" to the Aberdeen community. ASL has expanded its mission beyond the Aberdeen community to become the only full-service hospital within a 90–mile radius of Aberdeen.

\* \* \*

In mid–1996, ASL's neurosurgeon left Aberdeen. After his departure, the Board passed a resolution to recruit two neurosurgeons or two spine-trained orthopedic surgeons to fill the void. During the recruitment process, ASL learned that most neurosurgeon applicants would not be interested in coming to Aberdeen if there was already an orthopedic spine surgeon practicing in the area. This was due to the small size of the community and the probable need for the neurosurgeon to supplement his or her practice by performing back and spine surgeries. Back and spine surgeries are also performed by orthopedic spine surgeons and the applicants were doubtful whether Aberdeen could support the practice of both a neurosurgeon and an orthopedic spine surgeon.

ASL was successful in recruiting a neurosurgeon who arrived in December, 1996. Around this time, ASL learned that OSS, a group of Aberdeen orthopedic surgeons, had decided to build a day surgery center that would directly compete with ASL. During the first seven months that OSS' surgery center was open, ASL suffered a 1000 hour loss of operating room usage. In response to the loss of operating room income, ASL's Board passed two motions on June 26, 1997. The first motion closed ASL's medical staff with respect to physicians requesting privileges for three spinal procedures: (1) spinal fusions, (2) closed fractures of the spine and (3) laminectomies. The second motion closed ASL's medical staff to applicants for orthopedic surgery privileges except for two general orthopedic surgeons being recruited by ASL. The effect of "closing" the staff was to preclude any new physicians from applying for privileges to use hospital facilities for the named procedures. The Board's decision did not affect those physicians that had already been granted hospital privileges, including the physician-members of OSS. In making its decision, the Board specifically determined that the staff closures were in the best interests of the Aberdeen community and the surrounding area.

In the summer of 1998, OSS recruited Dr. Mahan (Mahan), a spine-fellowship trained orthopedic surgeon engaged in the practice of orthopedic surgery. While OSS was recruiting Mahan, one of the OSS physicians advised Mahan that the staff at ASL had been closed to orthopedic surgery privileges. Despite this warning, Mahan began practicing with OSS. On at least two occasions, Mahan officially requested an application for staff privileges with ASL. These requests were denied due to the Board's decision on July 26, 1997.

In September of 1998, Mahan and OSS (Plaintiffs) commenced this action against ASL, challenging the Board's decision to close the staff. Plaintiffs claimed that the action was a breach of the medical/dental staff bylaws (Staff Bylaws) and sought a writ of mandamus and permanent injunction ordering ASL to consider Mahan's application for hospital privileges. Both parties submitted cross motions for summary judgment. After a hearing, the circuit court determined that ASL had breached the Staff Bylaws by closing the staff. In making its decision, the circuit court relied exclusively on the Staff Bylaws. The circuit court determined that the Board had delegated a significant amount of its power and authority concerning staff privileges to the medical staff. The circuit court reasoned that because of this delegation, the Board no longer had the power to initiate actions that affected the privileges of the medical staff. The circuit court concluded the Board had breached its contract with the medical staff when it closed the staff to the named procedures without first consulting the staff. Plaintiffs' request for a permanent injunction was granted, requiring ASL to consider Mahan's application for privileges. ASL appeals raising the following issues:

1. Whether the individual OSS physicians have standing to challenge the Board's decision.

2. Whether the Board's decision breached its contract with the Staff.

ANALYSIS

1. Whether the individual OSS physicians have standing to challenge the Board's decision.

It is well settled in South Dakota that "a hospital's bylaws constitute a binding contract between the hospital and the hospital staff members." [ ] It is also well settled that when such bylaws are approved and accepted by the governing board they become an enforceable contract between the hospital and its physicians. [ ]

\* \* \*

In regard to whether the OSS staff doctors suffered an injury, the circuit court found:

"It is undisputed that the Board's decision resulted in an economic benefit for ASL and an economic hardship for these doctors in their private medical practice, OSS. It is also undisputed that the OSS staff doctors, through their medical corporation OSS, spent time and money to recruit Mahan, only to end up with him unable to perform certain procedures because of his inability to obtain staff privileges at ASL. As a result, the OSS staff doctors have had to support Mahan while being unable to build their practice or increase their patient base as expected. Clearly [the OSS] [d]octors ... have standing."

The circuit court properly found that the OSS staff doctors have standing to bring a cause of action for breach of contract.

2. Whether the Board's decision breached its contract with the Staff.

A. The relationship and specific terms of the Bylaws.

\* \* \*

Pursuant to its authority, the Board of ASL has delegated certain powers associated with the appointment and review of medical personnel to its medical staff. These designated powers are manifested in the Staff Bylaws. Plaintiffs now claim that the Staff Bylaws trump the decision-making ability of the Board as to all decisions relating in any way to, or incidentally affecting, medical personnel issues. We do not agree.

The circuit court failed to give sufficient weight to the fact that the Staff Bylaws are derived from the Corporate Bylaws. Under Article XIV, section 14(u) of the Corporate Bylaws, any powers supposedly granted under the Staff Bylaws must originate from, and be authorized by, the Board pursuant to the Corporate Bylaws. Their legal relationship is similar to that between statutes and a constitution. They are not separate and equal sovereigns....

Therefore, the medical staff has no authority over any corporate decisions unless specifically granted that power in the Corporate Bylaws or under the laws of the State of South Dakota. Plaintiffs have not alluded to any powers that arise under the statutory or common-law of South Dakota.

* * *

Under section 14(u), all that is designated to the medical staff is the responsibility to make recommendations to the Board regarding the professional competence of staff members and applicants. Article XVI, section 1(a) directs the Board to organize the staff under medical-dental bylaws, which must be approved by the Board before they become effective. Finally, article XVI, section 2(a) commands the Board to "assign to the medical-dental staff reasonable authority for ensuring appropriate professional care to the hospital's patients."

Clearly, under these explicit powers, the Board has the authority to make business decisions without first consulting the medical staff. Nowhere in the Corporate Bylaws is the staff explicitly authorized to make business decisions on behalf of the corporation. Plaintiffs instead rely on the Staff Bylaws as their source of authority to assume the Board's power. Yet, even within the Staff Bylaws, there is no explicit provision granting the medical staff control over personnel issues. Instead, the circuit court found that the actions of the Board violated "the spirit of the bylaws taken as a whole." Such reliance on the "spirit of the [Staff] bylaws" turns the corporate structure of ASL upside down, granting control over day to day hospital administration to a medical staff that is not legally accountable for the hospital's decisions, has no obligation to further the mission of the Presentation Sisters, and has unknown experience in running a hospital or meeting the medical needs of the community....

When the Board made its decision to close the medical staff to the three procedures on June 26, 1997, it was acting within the powers granted it in the Corporate Bylaws. When making these decisions, the Board specifically determined that the staff closures were in the Aberdeen community's best interests, and were necessary to insure 24-hour neurosurgical coverage for the Aberdeen area. By preserving the profitable neurosurgical services at ASL, the Board also insured that other unprofitable services would continue to be offered in the Aberdeen area. When, as here, it is clear from the Corporate Bylaws that the Board has the authority to manage the corporation, that authority "would necessarily include decisions on how to operate individual departments in order to best serve the corporation's purposes.... The cost of such care and promotion of community health is vitally important to the community and a legitimate concern for the board." Bartley v. Eastern Maine Medical Center, 617 A.2d 1020, 1022 (Me 1992). ASL cannot continue to offer unprofitable, yet essential services including the maternity ward, emergency room, pediatrics and critical care units, without the offsetting financial benefit of more profitable areas such as neurosurgery. The Board responded to the effect the OSS hospital would have on the economic viability of ASL's hospital and the health care needs of the entire Aberdeen community. These actions were within the power of the Board. It surely has the power to attempt to insure ASL's economic survival. As such, the courts should not interfere in the internal politics and decision making of a private, nonprofit hospital corporation when those decisions are made pursuant to its Corporate Bylaws.

* * *

Under the Corporate Bylaws, the Board has the authority to analyze and evaluate data reflecting the present and projected health care needs of the Aberdeen community. In light of that data, the Board must develop a "plan for the hospital's growth and development; to provide appropriate physical and financial resources and personnel required to meet the needs of the community and the patients." Corporate Bylaws, art V, § 14(r). The Board determined that it was in the best interests of the community to provide 24 hour access to neurosurgical services. To provide this coverage, ASL needed to recruit two neurosurgeons or two orthopedic spine surgeons. To recruit the required personnel, the Board determined that it was necessary to close the staff of ASL as to the three procedures and orthopedic surgery privileges. Under the Corporate Bylaws, this decision was reasonable and this Court has no legal basis to second-guess its decision.

Within its broad powers of management, some of the business decisions made by the Board will undoubtedly impinge upon matters that relate to or affect the medical staff of the hospital. This fact is unavoidable. However, merely because a decision of the Board affects the staff does not give the staff authority to overrule a valid business decision made by the Board. Allowing the staff this amount of administrative authority would effectively cripple the governing Board of ASL. ASL would cease to function in its current corporate form if its staff were given such power.

In its decision, the circuit court attempted to distinguish between this present situation and the situation wherein a hospital enters into an exclusive contract. We find this attempt to be unpersuasive. An exclusive contract arises when the hospital contracts with an outside physician or group of physicians, whereby the hospital agrees that the physician or group of physicians shall be the only personnel allowed to use certain facilities in the hospital, such as radiology units or emergency room units. Such exclusive contracts are common practice for most hospitals today, and have been almost universally found valid and enforceable, even if not explicitly provided for in corporate bylaws. [ ] In the past, ASL has closed several areas of its facility to physicians not part of an exclusive contract. Such areas include anesthesiology, radiology, emergency room care, pathology, EKG interpretation, pulmonary function interpretation and cardiac catheterization.

Plaintiffs do not allege that the prior exclusive contracts entered into by ASL are invalid. Neither is it alleged that the Board does not have the authority to enter into such exclusive contracts. Yet, they claim that the action of the Board they now challenge is somehow invalid. There is no logical reason why ASL could close certain areas of its facility to all but a few physicians (via an exclusive contract), yet not be allowed to close its facilities to any new orthopedic surgeons performing certain, named procedures. In a sense, ASL has entered into an implied exclusive contract with all current orthopedic spine surgeons. The same implicit authority that allows the Board to enter into exclusive contracts allows it to close ASL's staff as was done here.

* * *

B.  Contractual Element of Good Faith.

* * *

The Board's decision to close the hospital's facility for certain, named procedures was a reasonable administrative decision. It had determined that the closures were necessary to insure the continued viability of the hospital. The Board must be allowed to make such reasonable, independent decisions if it is to continue to provide comprehensive medical services to the Aberdeen community. It should also be noted that the Board did not abrogate any right for which the staff had previously negotiated. Nor was the medical staff denied the benefit of its bargain. The rights and benefits that the staff is now claiming are not mentioned in the Staff Bylaws, nor are they delegated to the staff in the Corporate Bylaws. It is clear from the record that the Board did not interfere with the staff's performance of the Staff Bylaws. It simply made an economically reasonable decision not to allow any additional physicians to perform the three named procedures and orthopedic surgeries. Therefore, any allegations that ASL breached its implied duty of good faith must fail.

* * *

How can a doctor who is a part owner of the for-profit OSS be expected to fulfill his or her duties towards his or her co-owners and in the same instance fulfill the duties towards the principal, ASL, who is a not-for-profit hospital? This does not imply ill-will on the part of the doctor, it simply faces fundamental medical issues such as at which institution does the doctor place his or her patients, OSS or ASL? We have often stated that an agent cannot serve two masters.

This rule applies to medical professionals as well.

### Conclusion

Because the actions of ASL's Board were permissible under the Corporate Bylaws and done in good faith, there has been no breach of the contract between the Board and the staff. Therefore, the circuit court's judgment is reversed. The circuit court's imposition of a permanent injunction is likewise reversed.

JOHNSON, Circuit Judge (concurring in part, and dissenting in part)

I concur with the majority on Issue I, but dissent on Issue II.

* * *

The trial court found:

> [i]n reading the bylaws, as a whole, the Court concluded that the bylaws contemplate taking applications from any doctor who wishes to have staff privileges at ASL. The bylaws do not contain any restrictions as to who may apply, they only put professional and logistical qualifications on who can be accepted to the staff. These qualifications center on a physician's competence to practice medicine and his or her availability to be at the hospital. The bylaws do not provide for restrictions of staff for any other reason. Any other interpretation would lead to a result contrary to the spirit of the bylaws taken as a whole. (emphasis in original).

There is no flaw in this conclusion. The staff bylaws did not contain restrictions on who may apply for staff privileges, but did place restrictions on who may be accepted to the staff. This was a benefit to the staff members, as it allowed them to recruit physicians to their clinics with the exception that the new doctors would receive staff privileges (to the only full service hospital within 90 miles of Aberdeen) if they met the professional and geographic requirements of the staff bylaws.

ASL unilaterally denied this benefit to staff members by blatantly ignoring the amendment provisions of the staff bylaws. "Every contract contains an implied covenant of good faith and fair dealing which prohibits either contracting party from preventing or injuring the other party's right to receive the agreed benefits of the contract." [ ] ASL's partial closure of the orthopedic staff, for strictly economic reasons, was not reasonable, not in good faith, and was a breach of contract. Either party may sue for breach of contract "even though the conduct failed to violate any of the express terms of the contract agreed to by the parties." Id. at 841. The trial court was correct in issuing a permanent injunction requiring ASL to provide Dr. Mahan with an application for staff privileges.

Accordingly, I would affirm the circuit court on Issue II.

**Add, at p. 807, at note 5:**

The courts have had little difficulty in enforcing "clean sweep" provisions in physician-hospital contracts. See, for example, Madsen v. Audrain, 297 F.3d 694 (8th Cir.2002), deferring to hospital's discretion on the decision to terminate privileges and enforcing a specific contractual provision for automatic termination of physician recruitment agreement once the hospital terminated physician's privileges. The court also held that the medical staff by-laws, which were referenced in the contract as binding on the physician but with no mention of the hospital's reciprocal duty of complying with the by-laws, were not incorporated into the contract with the result that the physician had no contractual claim under the by-laws.

**Add, at p. 807, after note 5:**

6. Exclusive contracting has been most frequent in the hospital-based practices of radiology, pathology, and anesthesiology. It has extended further in some instances, where the hospital might require coverage in emergency situations or in the intensive care units. Physicians employed by or contracted with the hospital to provide monitoring of patient care or direct patient care in ICUs are called "hospitalists," and are becoming more common.

7. The state of California has been participating in an interesting "experiment" in relation to exclusive contracting of non-hospital-based specialties. In early 2000, the state's Medicaid (Medi–Cal) agency announced that exclusive contracting was prohibited, except in the hospital-based practices of radiology, pathology, and anesthesiology, by the state's Medi–Cal statute:

California Welfare and Institutions Code

§ 14087.28 Denial of medical staff membership or clinical privileges; grounds

A hospital contracting with the Medi–Cal program pursuant to this chapter, shall not deny medical staff membership or clinical privileges for reasons other than a physician's individual qualifications as determined by professional and ethical criteria, uniformly applied to all medical staff applicants and members. Determination of medical staff membership or clinical privileges shall not be made upon the basis of:

(a) The existence of a contract with the hospital or with others.

(b) Membership in or affiliation with any society, medical group or teaching facility or upon the basis of any criteria lacking professional justification, such as sex, race, creed or national origin.

The special negotiator may authorize a contracting hospital to impose reasonable limitations on the granting of medical staff membership or clinical privileges in the following instances:

(a) To permit an exclusive contract for the provision of pathology, radiology, and anesthesiology services, except consulting services requested by the admitting physician. [Ed. Note: There is no section (b),]

The statute had been enacted in 1982, but was not enforced until a pediatrician contacted the agency in 1998 about St. Joseph Medical Center's exclusive contract for neonatal care under which the hospital had precluded his pediatric medical group from treating patients in the neonatal intensive care unit. The state agency first issued a letter to hospitals stating that the statute required them to allow physicians to treat their Medi–Cal patients even where there was an exclusive contract. A year later, the agency issued a letter stating that exclusive contracts (except in the hospital-based practices listed in the statute) were prohibited entirely in hospitals that accepted any Medi–Cal patients.

At the time, the California Medical Association hailed the decision, but the California Hospital Association (CHA) predicted that the prohibition would make it difficult to provide on-call coverage in specialty areas such as neurosurgery and would damage outcomes in procedures where practice makes perfect, such as cardiac surgery. A report in the BNA Health Law Reporter in late 2000 quoted a CHA spokesperson as saying that "[This] went off our radar screens months ago; it's a non-issue." California hospitals still use exclusive contracts for certain clinical specialty services, but a hospital attorney attributed the lack of impact to the fact that there were not many physicians applying for privileges in those areas. When a physician in a specialty for which the hospital has an "exclusive contract" applies for privileges, the hospital grants privileges under its usual medical staff by-laws provisions. In a compliment to ingenuity, the Medi–Cal agency said that the statute had lain dormant for 18 years because no one had ever raised the issue. See 9 Health Law Reporter 245 and 9 Health Law Reporter 1901.

## II. MANAGED CARE CONTRACTS FOR PROFESSIONAL SERVICES

**Add, at p. 815, at note 4:**

In Equality Emergency Medical Group v. Valley Presbyterian Hospital, 2002 WL 1293011 (Cal.App.2002), an unpublished opinion that by California procedure is not citable in litigation, the court considered a case in which the exclusive contract held by EEMG was allowed to expire. EEMG contended that the hospital allowed the contract to expire because EEMG had complained about inadequacies in the hospital emergency facilities and had refused to "lie" to JCAHO about conditions. The plaintiff claimed that the California statute, included in this note in the casebook, prohibited adverse actions based on their advocacy for patients. The court held that the statute did not apply in this case because the plaintiff was a medical corporation and not a "physician."

The Fourth Circuit dismissed the claim of a physician against a hospital where the doctor argued that her privileges were revoked because she opposed actions taken by the hospital that she believed would place dialysis patients at risk. Freilich v. Upper Chesapeake Health, Inc., 313 F.3d 205 (4th Cir.2002):

> ... Dr. Freilich asserts a claim of associational discrimination under the ADA. [ ] Dr. Freilich alleges that HMH denied her reappointment because of her "patient advocacy." Under Title III of the ADA, 42 U.S.C. § 12182(b)(1)(E), it is discriminatory to "exclude or otherwise deny equal goods, services, facilities, privileges, advantages, accommodations, or other opportunities to an individual or entity because of the known disability of an individual with whom the individual or entity is known to have a relationship or association." There is little case law applying this provision. We therefore look for guidance from a similar provision in Title I of the ADA which governs associational discrimination in employment. See 42 U.S.C. § 12112(b)(4).
>
> The associational discrimination provision in Title I "was intended to protect qualified individuals from adverse job actions based on 'unfounded stereotypes and assumptions' arising from the employees' relationships with particular disabled persons." Oliveras-Sifre v. Puerto Rico Dept. of Health, 214 F.3d 23, 26 (1st Cir.2000) (citing Barker v. Int'l Paper Co., 993 F.Supp. 10, 15 (D.Me.1998)). In Oliveras-Sifre, the plaintiffs alleged that they were punished for their advocacy on behalf of AIDS patients. However, the First Circuit rejected the plaintiffs' contention that the defendants' actions violated the associational discrimination provision of the ADA. The plaintiffs did not allege "a specific association with a disabled individual." Instead, they "contend[ed], in essence, that they were punished for their advocacy on behalf of individuals with AIDS." Id. In Barker, the court granted summary judgment in favor of the defendants along the same lines: the plaintiff alleged that he was terminated because of his advocacy on behalf of the plaintiff's disabled wife, which was held insufficient to support an associational discrimination claim.
>
> Dr. Freilich's allegations suffer from similar defects as the allegations in Oliveras-Sifre and Barker. Dr. Freilich alleges that HMH "coerced, intimidated, threatened, or interfered ... with [her] because she exercised rights protected by the ADA," and that HMH discriminated against her because she refused "to end her advocacy of the dialysis patients' rights that were being violated under [the] ADA." She further alleges that she was "denied equal use of facilities, privileges, advantages or other opportunities because of her association with and her relationship to patients with disabilities." But such generalized references to association with disabled persons or to advocacy for a group of disabled persons are not sufficient to state a claim for associational discrimination under the ADA. Every hospital employee can allege at least a loose association with disabled patients. To allow Dr. Freilich to proceed on such a basis would arm every hospital employee with a potential ADA complaint. A step of that magnitude is for Congress, not this court, to take.

In *Oliveras–Sifre*, the District Court had raised the ADA associational claim *sua sponte*; plaintiffs had not made a claim under that portion of the statute. In *Barker*, the court found against the plaintiff on a motion for summary judgment, not a motion to dismiss, finding that the discharge actually was not based on the situation with the employee's spouse.

Should the Fourth Circuit have resolved Freilich's claim on a motion to dismiss? How different, in risk of creating a flood of litigation, is the ADA claim from the California statute included in this note in the casebook? See discussion of ADA claims by patients in Chapters 10 and 11 of the casebook.

**Add, at p. 815, after note 5:**

6. The HCQIA, described in note 5 at page 801 of the casebook and *supra* in these materials, applies to adverse decisions against physicians by HMOs that have a formal review process. Health care plans can enjoy the immunity provided under the Act if they comply with the Act's procedural standards in making their decision. See, for example, Singh v. Blue Cross/Blue Shield of Massachusetts, Inc., 308 F.3d 25 (1st Cir.2002).

7. The California Court of Appeals, in an unpublished decision, declined to extend *Potvin* in Siegel v. CHW West Bay, 2002 WL 31599012 (Cal.App.2002). The Court held that even if *Potvin* were extended to hospitals, the facts did not meet the *Potvin* requirement that the decisionmaker hold economic power substantial enough to impair the physician's ability to practice. See also, Edson v. Valleycare Health System, 21 Fed.Appx. 721 (9th Cir.2001), relying on the absence of economic power to hold that *Potvin* did not apply to the hospital defendant.

**Add, at p. 815:**

## *Note on In re Managed Care Litigation*

As this supplement went to press, the Supreme Court had just decided PacifiCare Health Systems, Inc. v. Book, ___ U.S. ___, 123 S.Ct. 1531, ___ L.Ed.2d ___ (2003) reviewing the enforceability of arbitration clauses in managed care contracts. Such arbitration clauses can cover a range of issues in the physician-plan relationship, including payment issues as well as termination of contract. The issue before the Court was whether arbitration clauses prohibiting the award of "punitive or exemplary damages" would apply to the physicians' claims that the plans' refusal to pay for certain services violated the Racketeering Influenced Corruption Act (RICO), which provides for treble damages. The Court decided that the issue was whether the treble damages under RICO were punitive or remedial, citing cases in which the Court had held that treble damages under the False Claims Act were "essentially punitive" but that treble damages under the Clayton Act were "in essence a remedial provision." The court held that that issue should be considered first in the arbitration process and refused to decide whether an arbitration clause that is interpreted to prohibit treble damages for RICO claims is enforceable. The Eleventh Circuit had held that the prohibition against punitive damages in the contracts frustrated the application of RICO and that the doctors should be free to sue under RICO outside of the arbitration clause. In it Humana Inc. Managed Care Litigation, 285 F.3d 971 (11th Cir.2002), *cert.* granted *sub nom.* PacifiCare Health Systems, Inc. v. Book, ___ U.S. ___, 123 S.Ct. 409, 154 L.Ed.2d 289 (2002).

Federal law under the Federal Arbitration Act (FAA) and the courts' interpretation of that statute are highly committed to the enforcement of arbitration clauses, especially those in which the signatories are relatively sophisticated. The issue of the arbitrability of federal statutory claims arose in the last term as well. In E.E.O.C. v. Waffle House Inc., 534 U.S. 279, 122 S.Ct. 754, 151 L.Ed.2d 755(2002), the Supreme Court held that the Equal Employment Opportunity Commission could itself enforce Title VII against an employer and obtain monetary relief for the individual employee. The Supreme Court had earlier held that the FAA applied to claims by employees that they had been discriminated against in violation of Title VII. Circuit City Stores, Inc. v. Adams, 532 U.S. 105, 121 S.Ct. 1302, 149 L.Ed.2d 234 (2001). Although not specifically decided by the Supreme Court in *Circuit City,* all of the federal circuit courts of appeals, with the exception of one panel in the Ninth Circuit, have held that a mandatory arbitration clause is enforceable (provided the clause meets standards that have been established in the courts) and blocks employees from bringing suit themselves.

*PacifiCare* is part of a nationwide class action lawsuit involving ever 600,000 physicians. The RICO claims are only one route they have take to challenge managed care payment policies and other contractual issues. 12 Health Law Reporter 295 (February 27, 2003), reporting on oral arguments and background of the litigation. The lawsuits are now under the management of the federal Judicial Panel on Multidistrict Litigation, which manages litigation that develops across the country but that revolves around common facts such as major products liability litigation. The cases are now consolidated in Florida district court. Expect a constant flow of developments in this litigation over the next several months under the title of *In re Managed Care Litigation*. See In re Humana Inc. Managed Care Litigation, 2000 WL 1925080 (Jud.Pan.Mult.Lit.2000), for a listing of the lawsuits included in the consolidation as of that date.

## III. LABOR AND EMPLOYMENT

### A. EMPLOYMENT–AT–WILL

**Add, at p. 819, at note 1:**

New York's highest court has held that the public policy exception to employment–at-will does not apply to physicians "employed by a non-medical employer." Horn v. New York Times, ___ N.E.2d ___, 2003 WL 443259 (N.Y. 2003). In *Horn*, the physician was employed by the New York Times as a company doctor to evaluate employees for return to work and for workers' compensation claims as well as providing them some health care services. According to Dr. Horn, the Times human resources department asked her to give them employees' confidential medical records several times, and she refused. When the Times restructured its on-site medical department and eliminated Horn's position as well as two others, Horn sued for wrongful discharge under the public policy exception to the employment-at-will doctrine.

The court rejected the plaintiff physician's claim. The court distinguished an earlier case in which it held that attorneys were protected from discharge when the employer asked the attorney to violate professional ethics. The court distinguished the two cases on several points. The court believed that the attorney's legal representation of clients was the core of his work at his law firm, while Horn's medical treatment of employees was only incidental to her responsibilities to her employer in providing health assessments. The court also reiterated that the earlier case involved discharge of an attorney after he asked the firm to report a law firm colleague to the professional disciplinary agency, a duty that the court found to be essential to self-policing of the profession. In contrast, the physician's duty of confidentiality did not, in the court's view, hold the same position.

**Add, at p. 820, in note 4:**

In Equality Emergency Medical Group v. Valley Presbyterian Hospital, 2002 WL 1293011 (Cal.App.2002), discussed *supra*, the court held that EEMG was not protected by state whistleblower statutes because it was not an "employee."

**Add, at p. 820, in note 5:**

In Ulrich v. City and County of San Francisco, 308 F.3d 968 (9th Cir.2002), discussed *supra*, the Ninth Circuit Court of Appeals reversed the district court's granting of summary judgment to the defendant public hospital in plaintiff's claim that the hospital violated his First Amendment rights in initiating an investigation of his treatment of patients, in refusing to allow him to rescind his resignation, and in refusing to void a report the hospital made to the National Practitioner Data Bank.

The plaintiff physician had been critical of layoffs of physicians. He had spoken out at a hospital meeting on August 17 and had signed a letter of protest with other hospital personnel that was sent to the department of health the following week. On August 28, the hospital informed him that the credentials committee would begin a formal investigation into allegations of professional incompetence. On September 30 prior to any hearing or meeting on the investigation, Dr. Ulrich posted his notice of resignation at the nurses' station. The hospital accepted the resignation and refused his later request to rescind the resignation. Ulrich asked to rescind his resignation when he discovered that it might trigger a report to the NPDB. A later investigation of his practice, by the California medical board, triggered by the hospital's report to the Board of the investigation and resignation as required by the HCQIA, resulted in a finding that there was no evidence that he had departed from the standard of care in treating patients.

Citing *Waters v. Churchill*, the Court of Appeals found that Ulrich had First Amendment rights in the context of his employment. In order to succeed in his First Amendment claim, Ulrich had to prove that he suffered an adverse employment action; that his speech related to a matter of public concern; that the "form and context" of his speech was appropriate; and that his protected speech was a "substantial motivating factor" for the adverse employment action. The Court reversed the District Court's order and held that the plaintiff's claim should be tried.

## B. NATIONAL LABOR RELATIONS ACT

### 2. *Supervisor?*

**Substitute for Kentucky River on page 825:**

## NLRB v. KENTUCKY RIVER COMMUNITY CARE

Supreme Court of the United States, 2001.
532 U.S. 706, 121 S.Ct. 1861, 149 L.Ed.2d 939.

SCALIA, J., delivered the opinion for a unanimous Court with respect to Part II, and the opinion of the Court with respect to Parts I and III, in which REHNQUIST, C.J., and O'CONNOR, KENNEDY, and THOMAS, JJ., joined. STEVENS, J., filed an opinion concurring in part and dissenting in part, in which SOUTER, GINSBURG, and BREYER, JJ., joined.

Justice *SCALIA* delivered the opinion of the Court.

Under the National Labor Relations Act, employees are deemed to be "supervisors" and thereby excluded from the protections of the Act if, *inter alia*, they exercise "independent judgment" in "responsibly ... direct[ing]" other employees "in the interest of the employer." 29 U.S.C. § 152(11). This case presents two questions: which party...bears the burden of proving or disproving an employee's supervisory status; and whether judgment is not "independent judgment" to the extent that it is informed by professional or technical training or experience.

I

In Pippa Passes, Kentucky, respondent Kentucky River Community Care, Inc., operates a care facility for residents who suffer from mental retardation and mental illness. The facility, named the Caney Creek Developmental Complex (Caney Creek), employs approximately 110 professional and nonprofessional employees in addition to roughly a dozen concededly managerial or supervisory employees. In 1997, the Kentucky State District Council of Carpenters (a labor union that is co-respondent here, supporting petitioner) petitioned the National Labor Relations Board to represent a single unit of all 110 potentially eligible employees at Caney Creek. []

At the ensuing representation hearing, respondent objected to the inclusion of Caney Creek's six registered nurses in the bargaining unit, arguing that they were "supervisors" under § 2(11) of the Act and therefore excluded from the class of "employees" subject to the Act's protection and includable in the bargaining unit. [ ] The Board's Regional Director, to whom the Board has delegated its initial authority to determine an appropriate bargaining unit, [ ], placed the burden of proving supervisory status on respondent, found that respondent had not carried its burden, and therefore included the nurses in the bargaining unit. The Regional Director accordingly directed an election to determine whether the union would represent the unit. [ ]. The Board denied respondent's request for review of the Regional Director's decision and direction of election, and the union won the election and was certified as the representative of the Caney Creek employees.

\* \* \*

II

The Act expressly defines the term "supervisor" in § 2(11), which provides:

> "The term 'supervisor' means any individual having authority, in the interest of the employer, to hire, transfer, suspend, lay off, recall, promote, discharge, assign, reward, or discipline other employees, or responsibly to direct them, or to adjust their grievances, or effectively to recommend such action, if in connection with the foregoing the exercise of such authority is not of a merely routine or clerical nature, but requires the use of independent judgment." 29 U.S.C. § 152(11).

The Act does not, however, expressly allocate the burden of proving or disproving a challenged employee's supervisory status. The Board therefore has filled the statutory gap with the consistent rule that the burden is borne by the party claiming that the employee is a supervisor. For example, when the General Counsel seeks to attribute the conduct of certain employees to the employer by virtue of their supervisory status, this rule dictates that he bear the burden of proving supervisory status. [] Or, when a union challenges certain ballots cast in a representation election on the basis that they were cast by supervisors, the union bears the burden. []

... The Board's rule is supported by "the general rule of statutory construction that the burden of proving justification or exemption under a special exception to the prohibitions of a statute generally rests on one who claims its benefits." [] ... Supervisors would fall within the class of employees, were they not expressly excepted from it. [] The burden of proving the applicability of the supervisory exception, [] should thus fall on the party asserting it. In addition, it is easier to prove an employee's authority to exercise 1 of the 12 listed supervisory functions than to disprove an employee's authority to exercise any of those functions, and practicality therefore favors placing the burden on the party asserting supervisory status. We find that the Board's rule for allocating the burden of proof is reasonable and consistent with the Act, and we therefore defer to it.

\* \* \*

### III

The text of § 2(11) of the Act that we quoted above, [] sets forth a three-part test for determining supervisory status. Employees are statutory supervisors if (1) they hold the authority to engage in any 1 of the 12 listed supervisory functions, (2) their "exercise of such authority is not of a merely routine or clerical nature, but requires the use of independent judgment," and (3) their authority is held "in the interest of the employer." *NLRB v. Health Care & Retirement Corp. of America*, 511 U.S. 571, 573–574, 114 S.Ct. 1778, 128 L.Ed.2d 586 (1994). The only basis asserted by the Board, before the Court of Appeals and here, for rejecting respondent's proof of supervisory status with respect to directing patient care was the Board's interpretation of the second part of the test—to wit, that employees do not use "independent judgment" when they exercise "ordinary professional or technical judgment in directing less-skilled employees to deliver services in accordance with employer-specified standards." ... The Court of Appeals rejected that interpretation, and so do we.

Two aspects of the Board's interpretation are reasonable, and hence controlling on this Court. [] First, it is certainly true that the statutory term "independent judgment" is ambiguous with respect to the *degree* of discretion required for supervisory status. [] Many nominally supervisory functions may be performed without the "exercis[e of] such a degree of ... judgment or discretion ... as would warrant a finding" of supervisory status under the Act. [] It falls clearly within the Board's discretion to determine, within reason, what scope of discretion qualifies. Second, as reflected in the Board's phrase "in accordance with employer-specified standards," it is also undoubtedly true that the degree of judgment that might ordinarily be required to conduct a particular task may be reduced below the statutory threshold by detailed orders and regulations issued by the employer....

The Board, however, argues further that the judgment even of employees who are permitted by their employer to exercise a sufficient *degree* of discretion is not "independent judgment" if it is a particular *kind* of judgment, namely, "ordinary professional or technical judgment in directing less-skilled employees to deliver services." The first five words of this interpretation insert a startling categorical exclusion into statutory text that does not suggest its existence. The text, by focusing on the "clerical" or "routine" (as opposed to "independent") nature of the judgment, introduces the question of degree of judgment that we have agreed falls within the reasonable discretion of the

Board to resolve. But the Board's categorical exclusion turns on factors that have nothing to do with the degree of discretion an employee exercises. [] Let the judgment be significant and only loosely constrained by the employer; if it is "professional or technical" it will nonetheless not be independent.[1] The breadth of this exclusion is made all the more startling by virtue of the Board's extension of it to judgment based on greater "experience" as well as formal training. What supervisory judgment worth exercising, one must wonder, does not rest on "professional or technical skill or experience"? If the Board applied this aspect of its test to every exercise of a supervisory function, it would virtually eliminate "supervisors" from the Act.

As it happens, though, only one class of supervisors would be eliminated in practice, because the Board limits its categorical exclusion with a qualifier: Only professional judgment that is applied "in directing less-skilled employees to deliver services" is excluded from the statutory category of "independent judgment." This second rule is no less striking than the first, and is directly contrary to the text of the statute. *Every* supervisory function listed by the Act is accompanied by the statutory requirement that its exercise "requir[e] the use of independent judgment" before supervisory status will obtain, [] but the Board would apply its restriction upon "independent judgment" to just 1 of the 12 listed functions: "responsibly to direct." There is no apparent textual justification for this asymmetrical limitation, and the Board has offered none. Surely no conceptual justification can be found in the proposition that supervisors exercise professional, technical, or experienced judgment only when they direct other employees. Decisions "to hire, ... suspend, lay off, recall, promote, discharge, ... or discipline" other employees, must often depend upon that same judgment, which enables assessment of the employee's proficiency in performing his job. Yet in no opinion that we were able to discover has the Board held that a supervisor's judgment in hiring, disciplining, or promoting another employee ceased to be "independent judgment" because it depended upon the supervisor's professional or technical training or experience. When an employee exercises one of these functions with judgment that possesses a sufficient degree of independence, the Board invariably finds supervisory status. []

The Board's refusal to apply its limiting interpretation of "independent judgment" to any supervisory function other than responsibly directing other employees is particularly troubling because just seven years ago we rejected the Board's interpretation of part three of the supervisory test that similarly was applied only to the same supervisory function. See *NLRB v. Health Care & Retirement Corp. of America,* 511 U.S. 571, 114 S.Ct. 1778, 128 L.Ed.2d 586 (1994). In *Health Care,* the Board argued that nurses did not exercise their authority "in the interest of the employer," as *§ 152(11)* requires, when their "independent judgment [was] exercised incidental to professional or technical

---

1. The Board in its reply brief in this Court steps back from this interpretation and argues that it has only drawn distinctions between degrees of authority. But the opinions of the Board that developed its current interpretation of "independent judgment" clearly draw a categorical distinction. See, *e.g., Providence Hospital, 320 N.L.R.B. 717, 729 (1996)* ("Section 2(11) supervisory authority does not include the authority of an employee to direct another to perform discrete tasks stemming from the directing employee's experience, skills, training, or position"). It is those opinions that were cited in the Regional Director's opinion resolving the representation dispute, which was accepted without further review by the Board....

judgment" instead of for "disciplinary or other matters, i.e., in addition to treatment of patients." [] It did not escape our notice that the target of this analysis was the supervisory function of responsible direction. "Under § 2(11)," we noted, "an employee who in the course of employment uses independent judgment to engage in 1 of the 12 listed activities, including responsible direction of other employees, is a supervisor. Under the Board's test, however, a nurse who in the course of employment uses independent judgment to engage in responsible direction of other employees is not a supervisor." [] We therefore rejected the Board's analysis as "inconsistent with ... the statutory language," because it "rea[d] the responsible direction portion of § 2(11) out of the statute in nurse cases." [] It is impossible to avoid the conclusion that the Board's interpretation of "independent judgment," applied to nurses for the first time after our decision in *Health Care,* has precisely the same object. This interpretation of "independent judgment" is no less strained than the interpretation of "in the interest of the employer" that it has succeeded.

The Board contends, however, that Congress incorporated the Board's categorical restrictions on "independent judgment" when it first added the term "supervisor" to the Act in 1947. We think history shows the opposite. The Act as originally passed by Congress in 1935 did not mention supervisors directly. It extended to "employees" the "right to self-organization, to form, join, or assist labor organizations, [and] to bargain collectively through representatives of their own choosing...." Act of July 5, 1935, § 7, 49 Stat. 452, and it defined "employee" expansively (if circularly) to "include any employee," § 2(3). We therefore held that supervisors were protected by the Act. [] Congress in response added to the Act the exemption we had found lacking. The Labor Management Relations Act, 1947 (Taft–Hartley Act) expressly excluded "supervisors" from the definition of "employees" and thereby from the protections of the Act. § 2(3), 61 Stat. 137, as amended, 29 U.S.C. § 152(3). []

Well before the Taft–Hartley Act added the term "supervisor" to the Act, however, the Board had already been defining it, because while the Board agreed that supervisors were protected by the 1935 Act, it also determined that they should not be placed in the same bargaining unit as the employees they oversaw. To distinguish the two groups, the Board defined "supervisors" as employees who "supervise or direct the work of [other] employees ... , *and* who have authority to hire, promote, discharge, discipline, or otherwise effect changes in the status of such employees." [] The "and" bears emphasis because it was a true conjunctive: The Board consistently held that employees whose only supervisory function was directing the work of other employees were not "supervisors" within its test....

When the Taft–Hartley Act added the term "supervisor" to the Act in 1947, it largely borrowed the Board's definition of the term, with one notable exception: Whereas the Board required a supervisor to direct the work of other employees *and* perform another listed function, the Act permitted direction alone to suffice. "The term 'supervisor' means any individual having authority ... to hire, transfer, suspend, lay off, recall, promote, discharge, assign, reward, or discipline other employees, *or* responsibly to direct them, or to adjust their grievances." Taft–Hartley Act § 2(11), as amended, 29 U.S.C. § 152(11). Moreover, the Act assuredly did *not* incorporate the Board's current interpretation of the term "independent judgment" as applied to the function of responsible direction, since the Board had not yet developed that interpretation. It had had no reason to do so, because it had limited the category of supervisors more directly, by requiring functions *in addition* to responsible direction. It is the Act's alteration of precisely that aspect of the Board's jurisprudence that has pushed the Board into a running struggle to limit the impact of "responsibly to direct" on the number of employees qualifying for supervisory status—presumably driven by the policy concern that otherwise the proper balance of labor-management power will be disrupted.

It is upon that policy concern that the Board ultimately rests its defense of its interpretation of "independent judgment." In arguments that parallel those expressed by the dissent in *Health Care*, [] and which are adopted by Justice STEVENS in this case, the Board contends that its interpretation is necessary to preserve the inclusion of "professional employees" within the coverage of the Act. [] Professional employees by definition engage in work "involving the consistent exercise of discretion and judgment." § 152(12)(a)(ii). Therefore, the Board argues [] if judgment of that sort makes one a supervisor under § 152(11), then Congress's intent to include professionals in the Act will be frustrated, because "many professional employees (such as lawyers, doctors, and nurses) customarily give judgment-based direction to the less-skilled employees with whom they work." [] The problem with the argument is not the soundness of its labor policy (the Board is entitled to judge that without our constant second-guessing). It is that the policy cannot be given effect through this statutory text. See *Health Care, supra,* at 581, 114 S.Ct. 1778 ("[T]here may be 'some tension between the Act's exclusion of [supervisory and] managerial employees and its inclusion of professionals,' but we find no authority for 'suggesting that that tension can be resolved' by distorting the statutory language in the manner proposed by the Board.") Perhaps the Board could offer a limiting interpretation of the supervisory function of responsible direction by distinguishing employees who direct the manner of others' performance of discrete *tasks* from employees who direct other *employees,* as § 152(11) requires. Certain of the Board's decisions appear to have drawn that distinction in the past, see, *e.g., Providence Hospital,* 320 N.L.R.B. 717, 729 (1996). We have no occasion to consider it here, however, because the Board has carefully insisted that the proper interpretation of "responsibly to direct" is not at issue in this case.

What is at issue is the Board's contention that the policy of covering professional employees under the Act justifies the categorical exclusion of professional judgments from a term, "independent judgment," that naturally includes them. And further, that it justifies limiting this categorical exclusion to the supervisory function of responsibly directing other employees. These contentions contradict both the text and structure of the statute, and they contradict as well the rule of *Health Care* that the test for supervisory status applies no differently to professionals than to other employees. We therefore find the Board's interpretation unlawful. []

\* \* \*

Justice STEVENS, with whom Justice SOUTER, Justice GINSBURG, and Justice BREYER join, concurring in part and dissenting in part.

In my opinion, the National Labor Relations Board correctly found that respondent, Kentucky River Community Care, Inc., failed to prove that the six registered nurses employed at its facility in Pippa Passes, Kentucky, are "supervisors" within the meaning of the National Labor Relations Act. While we are unanimous in holding that the Court of Appeals set aside that finding based upon an incorrect allocation of the burden of proof, we disagree as to whether the Court of Appeals correctly concluded that the Board misinterpreted the provision of the NLRA excluding supervisors from the Act's coverage. Moreover, even if I agreed with the majority's view that the Board's interpretation was error, that error would not justify affirming the erroneous decision of the Court of Appeals.

I

In the proceedings before the Board, respondent relied heavily on the fact that two registered nurses (RNs) served as "building supervisors" on weekends, and on the second and third shifts. However, as the Regional Director who considered the evidence noted, the RNs received no extra compensation for serving as building supervisors and did not have keys to the facility. Instead, the only additional responsibility shouldered by the RNs when serving as building supervisors was that of contacting other employees if a shift was not fully staffed according to preestablished ratios not set by the RNs. However, the RNs had no authority to compel an employee to stay on duty or to come to work to fill a vacancy under threat of discipline.

With respect to the RNs' regular duties, while they might "occasionally request other employees to perform routine tasks," they had no "authority to take any action if the employee refuse[d] their directives."[1] In their routine work, they had no "authority to hire, fire, reward, promote or independently discipline employees or to effectively recommend such action. They did not evaluate employees or take any action which would affect their employment status." Indeed, the RNs, even when serving as "building supervisors," for the most part "work[ed] independently and by themselves without any subordinates."

Based on his evaluation of the evidence, the NLRB's Regional Director applied "the same test to registered nurses as is applicable to all other individuals in determining supervisory status." Under that test, he concluded that "only supervisory personnel vested with 'genuine management prerogatives' should be considered supervisors, and not 'straw bosses, leadmen, set-up men and other minor supervisory employees.'" [] He did, however, exclude from the bargaining unit 10 specific supervisors including the nursing coordinator.

Over the dissent of Judge Jones, the Court of Appeals set aside the Board's order. The panel majority first criticized the Board for ignoring its "repeated admonition" that the NLRB "'has the burden of proving that employees are not supervisors.'" After acknowledging that "whether an employee is a supervisor is a highly fact-intensive inquiry," that majority concluded that the RNs' duties as building supervisors involved "independent judgment which is not limited to, or inherent in, the professional training of nurses." The panel

---

1. The RNs did have the authority to file "incident reports, but so [could] any other employee." App. to Pet. for Cert. 51a.

majority also criticized the NLRB for interpreting the admittedly ambiguous statutory term "independent judgment" inconsistently with Sixth Circuit precedent.[2]

II

Although it is not necessary to do so to overturn the Court of Appeals' decision, the NLRB has asked us to reject the Sixth Circuit's interpretation of the term "independent judgment." In contrast to the Sixth Circuit, the NLRB interprets the term "independent judgment" as not including the exercise of ordinary professional or technical judgment in directing less-skilled employees to deliver services in accordance with employer-specified standards.[3] The Board's interpretation is a familiar one, which has been routinely applied in other employment contexts. Applying that interpretation, the NLRB has concluded that in some cases the employees in question are supervisors, and that in others they are not.

... To my mind, the Board's test is both fully rational and entirely consistent with the Act.

The term "independent judgment" is indisputably ambiguous, and it is settled law that the NLRB's interpretation of ambiguous language in the National Labor Relations Act is entitled to deference. []. ...

Moreover, since Congress has expressly provided that professional employees are entitled to the protection of the Act, there is good reason to resolve the ambiguities consistently with the Board's interpretation. At the same time that Congress acted to exclude supervisors from the NLRA's protection, it explicitly extended those same protections to professionals, who, by definition, engage in work that involves "the consistent exercise of discretion and judgment in its performance." [] As this Court has acknowledged, the inclusion of professional employees and the exclusion of supervisors necessarily gives rise to some tension in the statutory text. [] Accordingly, if the term "supervisor" is construed too broadly, without regard for the statutory context, then Congress' inclusion of professionals within the Act's protections is effectively nullified.[4] ....

* * *

[U]nder the Court's view, it is impermissible for the Board to attach a different weight to a nurse's judgment that an employee should be reassigned or disciplined than to a nurse's judgment that the employee should take a

---

**2.** "According to NLRB interpretations, the practice of a nurse supervising a nurse's aide in administering patient care, for example, does not involve 'independent judgment.' The NLRB classifies these activities as 'routine' because the nurses have the ability to direct patient care by virtue of their training and expertise, not because of their connection with 'management.'"

**3.** Oddly, the majority in this Court omits one element—namely, " 'in accordance with employer-specified standards.' " In so doing, it ignores a key nuance in the NLRB's position. That, however, is characteristic of the majority's treatment of the NLRB's position, which is at once more fact specific and far less categorical than the majority makes it out to be.

**4.** Moreover, so broad a reading seems contrary to congressional intent in enacting the supervisory exception. Rather, the definition of "supervisor" was intended to apply only to those employees with "genuine management prerogatives" so that those employees excluded from the Act's coverage would be "truly supervisory." S.Rep. No. 105, 80th Cong., 1st Sess., pp. 4, 19 (1947), 1 NLRB, Legislative History of the Labor Management Relations Act, 1947, pp. 410, 425 (1948).

patient's temperature, even if nurses routinely instruct others to take a patient's temperature but do not ordinarily reassign or discipline employees....

The Court further argues that the Board errs by not applying its limiting interpretation of the term "independent judgment" to all 12 functions identified by the statute as supervisory in nature. But of those 12, it is only "responsibly to direct" that is ambiguous and thus capable of swallowing the whole if not narrowly construed. The authority to "promote" or to "discharge," to use only two examples, is specific and readily identifiable. In contrast, the authority "responsibly to direct" is far more vague....

\* \* \*

### III

\* \* \*

... Given the Regional Director's findings that the RNs' duties as building supervisors do not qualify them as "supervisors" within the meaning of 29 U.S.C. § 152(11), and that they, "'for the most part, work independently and by themselves without any subordinates,'" it is absolutely clear that the nurses in question are covered by the NLRA.[11] The Court's willingness to treat them as supervisors even if they have no subordinates[12] is particularly ironic when compared to the Board's undisturbed decision to deny supervisory status to the other group of professionals employed by respondent—namely, the 20 rehabilitation counselors who supervise the work of 40 rehabilitation assistants.

Accordingly, while I join Part II of the Court's opinion, I respectfully dissent from its holding. I would reverse the judgment of the Court of Appeals.

### Notes and Questions

1. The Supreme Court majority may have found its decision in *Health Care & Retirement Corp.*, also a 5–4 majority, to be unusually clear, but the circuits have been split on the matter. See note 1 in the casebook. For discussion of *Kentucky River*, see Teresa R. Laidacker, 69 U. Cin. L. Rev. 1315 (2001).

2. In light of *Kentucky River*, does it appear that RNs and physicians will always be considered supervisory? The NLRB has continued to find that health care professionals are not supervisors in specific cases. The issue of whether a particular employee is a supervisor is highly fact sensitive. You might think that the Board is simply continuing to resist the majority, as Justice Scalia implies in his opinion. But see Beverly Health and Rehabilitation Services v. NLRB, 317 F.3d 316 (D.C.Cir.2003), holding that the NLRB properly accounted for the Supreme Court's decision in *Kentucky River* in concluding that licensed practical nurses

---

11. Nor do the RNs exercise any of the other supervisorial functions listed in § 152(11). They play no role in assigning staff to shifts on a permanent basis or in setting the staff-to-resident ratio. As noted above, the RNs, whether functioning in their ordinary capacity or as "building supervisors," do not have authority to hire, fire, reward, promote, or independently discipline employees, or to effectively recommend such action. Nor, for that matter, do they evaluate employees or take action that would affect their employment status.

12. Neither the licensed practical nurses nor the rehabilitation assistants report to the RNs.

were not supervisors and that in their direction of certified nurse assistants at Beverly's nursing home they exercised only routine authority that did not require independent judgment. See also, Maui Medical Group and Collective Bargaining Organization of the Hawaii Nurses Association, 2002 WL 561329 (N.L.R.B. Div. of Judges, 2002).

In the following case the Board, adopting the decision of the ALJ, held that the IV coordinator for a home health agency was not a supervisor. (Why does the Board adopt the opinion but include the first paragraph?)

## NURSES UNITED FOR IMPROVED PATIENT HEALTHCARE AND VNA CORPORATION

National Labor Relations Board.
338 NLRB No. 113, 2003 WL 1522895 (March 20, 2003).

In adopting the judge's finding that Marsha O'Roark is not a statutory supervisor, we conclude that the Charging Party/Employer failed to meet its necessary evidentiary burden of establishing that she is a supervisor under the Act. In so concluding, we do not rely on the judge's reference to the "degree of discretion" under NLRB v. Kentucky River Community Care, 532 U.S. 706 (2001). Finally, we disavow the judge's comparison of O'Roark's job to that of a dispatcher for a taxi or trucking company. Id.

[Ed. note: What follows is the ALJ opinion adopted as and included within the Board's decision.]

\* \* \*

O'Roark has been the IV clinical coordinator since 1995. The Employer argues that she is a supervisor because she assigns patients needing IV therapy to the field nurses case managers (the line employees who deliver the appropriate health care to the Employer's clients)....

O'Roark testified that in performing this function she relies primarily on the geographical proximity of the case manager to the patient and the case manager's work load. While she will occasionally consider a case manager's particular expertise, basically, according to her credible testimony, she considers all registered nurses to be equally competent (a matter not contested by the Employer).

The Employer failed to demonstrate that O'Roark's assignment of case managers is anything other than routine in nature. I cannot conclude that she actually exercises independent judgment in making this assignment. Given the Employer's daily average patient load of 900, someone must direct traffic. And such is O'Roark's principal function but making these assignments is essentially routine. The "degree of discretion" which O'Roark exercises is simply too minimal for her to be considered a supervisor. [ ] Cf. *NLRB v. Kentucky River Community Care*. O'Roark's job is analogous to that of a dispatcher for a taxi or trucking company who, absent exercising some supervisory function over the employees dispatched, are not considered by the Board to be statutory supervisors....

The Employer also contends that O'Roark regularly substitutes for the clinical manager. However, the record shows that such substitutions, on weekends and evenings, is limited and sporadic. I conclude that this factor is insufficient to establish that she is a supervisor. [ ]

The employer asserts, without supporting evidence, that she is paid $6000 to $8000 more than rank-and-file nurses, a fact which, if true would suggest that she is a supervisor. However, I find no evidence of her salary or how much higher it might be than the IV nurses.

Indicating that she is an employee is the fact that in 1996, after being employed as the IV coordinator, O'Roark earned an employee of the year award—an award for which supervisors are not eligible. While her duties could have changed in the intervening time, to include supervisory authority, there is no evidence they did. On balance, it appears that in her present position and predating the organizational campaign, O'Roark has been treated by the Employer as a rank-and-file employee.

Accordingly, I shall recommend that the challenge to her ballot be overruled.

### 3. *Concerted Action*

**Add, at p. 833, at the end of the Problem:**

#### *Problem: Changing Things, Continued*

Assume now that Nurse Jones called the local television station and gave an on-camera interview in which she expressed her concerns about how the staffing changes would affect patient care. Thereafter, several of the surgeons contacted hospital administration by letter and phone stating that they did not want Nurse Jones to be assigned to assist them in surgery. Others expressed anger at her remarks. After this episode, the hospital discharges Nurse Jones. What would the employer use as the reason for the discharge? What result would you expect should Jones challenge the dismissal as a violation of the NLRA? As a wrongful discharge?

See, St. Luke's Episcopal–Presbyterian Hospitals v. NLRB, 268 F.3d 575 (8th Cir.2001). In this case, the Eighth Circuit reversed the Board's finding that the discharge constituted an illegal discharge in violation of the NLRA. The Board had held that the reaction of coworkers was irrelevant. In contrast, the court finds that the discharge is appropriate, stating:

> Patient lives are at stake in hospital surgeries, and medical professionals are devoted to providing the highest quality patient care. Common sense teaches that patient care is directly affected by the ability of a team of physicians and nurses to work together in the confines of an operating room; that a hospital must not risk staffing the operating room with doctors and nurses who cannot work effectively together; and that surgeons cannot be expected to tolerate operating room staff who seem to be more interested in publicizing flaws in the process than in helping protect the patient.

How far does this statement go? The nurses at St. Luke's were in the middle of an organizing drive at the time that this occurred. What if the surgeons told hospital administration that they could not work with a particular nurse who was known for supporting unionization? What if Nurse Jones had not gone on television, but rather had called a state hotline to report her concerns, which angered the surgeons even more? What if she had testified against one of the surgeons in a malpractice case?

See also, Orchard Park Health Care Center, Inc. and Carol A. Gunnersen, 2003 WL 430502 (N.L.R.B. Div. of Judges, 2003) in which an NLRB administrative law judge holds that a certified nurse assistant and a registered nurse discharged for calling a state nursing home hotline were protected by the Act. In this case, the concerted action seems to be that the nurse dialed the phone and the CNA spoke.

# IV. DISCRIMINATION LAW

### Add, at p. 839, after note 1:

In Waddell v. Valley Forge Dental Associates, 276 F.3d 1275 (11th Cir.2001), the Eleventh Circuit held that a dental hygienist performed "exposure prone" activities and, therefore, posed a significant risk and a direct threat to the health of others. The court expressly refused to require the employer to provide any evidence of transmission of HIV in a similar context in determining whether a significant risk existed. The court stated that "this is not a somebody has to die first standard." By the same standard, could health care workers refuse to provide care to a patient who is HIV-positive? (See discussion in Chapter 11 of the casebook and these materials.) *Waddell* is clearly in the majority of cases in which health care professionals are performing "exposure prone" procedures.

On a related note, Mr. Waddell brought an action for wrongful disclosure of his health status against his primary care physician who had notified his employer without the patient's consent. Waddell v. Bhat, 257 Ga.App. 580, 571 S.E.2d 565 (2002). The Georgia court held that the need to provide such information to his employer and other health care providers outweighed Waddell's right to confidentiality. See also, Nelson v. Glynn–Brunswick Hospital Authority, 257 Ga.App. 571, 571 S.E.2d 557 (2002), holding that the medical director had no claim where a lab technician revealed the physician's post-needlestick HIV-positive test results to the lab director, who in turn informed the hospital administrator and legal counsel before informing the physician of the results of his own test. (See discussion of confidentiality in Chapter 5 of the casebook.)

### Add, at p. 839, at note 3:

The courts, led by the U.S. Supreme Court have continued to narrow the scope of "disability" under the ADA. Although *Bragdon* held that asymptomatic HIV was a disability under the ADA, the dissenters disagreed in part because the plaintiff had not proven that she intended to reproduce prior to her infection. In a case subsequent to *Bragdon*, the Fifth Circuit affirmed a district court ruling that an HIV-positive plaintiff was not disabled because the record showed that his wife had undergone a surgical sterilization procedure prior to his infection with HIV. Blanks v. Southwestern Bell Communications, 310 F.3d 398 (5th Cir.2002)

The Supreme Court has reinforced the need for a fact intensive, particularized analysis of the impact of the impairment in substantially limiting a major life activity. In Toyota Motor Manufacturing v. Williams, 534 U.S. 184, 122 S.Ct. 681, 151 L.Ed.2d 615 (2002), for example, the inability of an employee suffering from carpal tunnel syndrome to perform manual work-related tasks did not qualify her as disabled because it did not restrict any major life activities; and, therefore, her employer was not required to provide accommodations.

In Gowesky v. Singing River Hospital Systems, 321 F.3d 503 (5th Cir.2003), the court held that an emergency department physician who had contracted hepatitis C on the job was not disabled under the "regarded as disabled" provision of the ADA. (The plaintiff had not claimed that she was disabled.) The court explained:

> [T]he comments cited by Gowesky question her fitness to practice emergency room medicine, a professional calling in which routine exposure to blood and bodily fluids might allow the hepatitis C virus to spread. The supervisors' remarks, no matter how uninformed, do not suggest Gowesky was otherwise unable to work as a doctor in a less-exposed or -exposing environment. The EEOC regulations make plain that an inability to perform one particular job, as opposed to a broad range of jobs, does not constitute an impairment that substantially limits one's ability to work.

**Add, at p. 840, after note 4:**

In December 2001, the CDC issued a report on Surveillance of Healthcare Personnel with HIV/AIDS. The CDC reported that as of June 2001, 57 documented cases of occupational transmission of the virus had occurred in health care workers. The report is available at http://www.cdc.gov/ncidod/hip/BLOOD/hivpersonnel.html. The CDC has reported no new documented cases of seroconversion and one case of possible transmission from patient to health care worker as of the end of January 2003. The report also states that there are an additional 138 HIV-positive health care workers who report no risk factors for HIV and who report workplace exposure to the virus but who tested negative after the exposure. Surveillance indicates that the route of exposure makes a difference in whether the individual will become infected with the virus. The risk after needlestick or cut exposure to HIV-infected blood is 0.3% (99.7% of those who are exposed in that way do not become infected) and exposure of the mouth, eyes or nose to HIV-infected blood is 0.1%. Post-exposure prophylactic treatment does bring its own health risks, and so it is not recommended for the lowest-risk exposures (as defined by route of exposure and HIV status of patient).

The risk of a patient contracting HIV from a health care worker is even lower. There have been only six patients infected with HIV, and these are all reported from a single dentist before 1990. Studies conducted on 22,000 patients treated by 63 HIV-positive health care providers found no evidence of transmission from the providers, available at www.cdc.gov/hiv/pubs/faq/faq29.htm.

In contrast to the HIV virus, hospital-acquired (nosocomial) infections with other organisms infect approximately two million people every year. These infections are largely preventable and result from contact with an infected source, including health care workers who utilize poor infection control technique. One such nosocomial infection is staph aureus. In the United States, health care workers are not routinely tested to determine if they are carriers of the staph infection. Canada and some European countries routinely conduct surveillance of patients and health care workers and have been more successful in the control of drug-resistant staph aureus infections. See R. Rubin, et al., The Economic Impact of Staphylococcus aureus Infection in New York City Hospitals, 5 Emerging Infectious Diseases 1 (1999). The CDC does not recommend routine surveillance but recommends removal from patient care only for those workers connected epidemiologically with infected patients. CDC, Guidelines for Infection Control in Health Care Personnel, 1998, available at www.cdc.gov/ncidod/hip/guide/Infect-Control98.pdf.

The most common bloodborne infection in the U.S. is hepatitis C, and it is estimated that 3.9 million people in the U.S. have been infected. Of patients infected with hepatitis C, 70% will develop chronic liver disease with a death rate of approximately 3%. Hep C is responsible for forty percent of all chronic liver disease which is the tenth leading cause of death in adults. It is most commonly transmitted by people who do not feel ill and, therefore, do not know that they are infected. No recommendations restricting the duties of health care workers exist, and workers are only tested after they are exposed to blood or body fluids of patients. CDC, Recommendations for Prevention and Control of Hepatitis C Virus Infection and HCV–Related Chronic Disease, available at www.cdc.gov/ncidod/diseases/hepatitis/c_training/edu/6/.

Would these facts be relevant in a case of exclusion of a health care worker with HIV?

**Add at page 840, after note 6:**

In Clackamas Gastronenterology Associates, P.C. v. Wells, 123 S.Ct. 1673, (2003), the Supreme Court considered the issue of whether physicians who are director-shareholders in a professional corporation are "employees" within the definition of the ADA, noting that the definition is the same in each of the federal antidiscrimination statutes. The specific issue in this case, brought by a bookkeeper employee, was whether the physicians counted toward the minimum of 15 employees required for the application of the ADA (and Title VII) to an employer. The same definition of employee would also be applied in the case of a director-shareholder (or partner) who brought suit under these statutes. The Supreme Court noted a division in the circuits on the question of the appropriate test for employment status. Rather than focusing on the legal structure of a professional corporation (which the Court characterizes as a "new type of business entity" allowing the learned professions to adopt a corporate structure for their practice) and analyzing whether it is more like a partnership than a corporation as did the Ninth Circuit, the Court held that the "common-law element of control is the principal guidepost." The Court states that "an employer is the person, or group of persons, who owns and manages the enterprise" with the authority to hire and fire, assign tasks, supervise performance, and decide how profit and loss are distributed. The title of the position or the existence of a document entitled an "employment agreement" is not determinative. The Court observes that some of the District Court's findings of fact support a conclusion of employment status under the control test while others may not. The Court reversed the Ninth Circuit, which had held that the physicians were employees and that the practice was subject to the ADA, and remanded for an examination of employment status under the test articulated in this case.

7. Under the ADA, employers are explicitly allowed to exclude the disabled from the workplace when they pose a direct threat to the health or safety of "other individuals in the workplace." In Chevron v. Echazabal, 536 U.S. 73, 122 S.Ct. 2045, 153 L.Ed.2d 82 (2002), the Supreme Court considered a case of an oil refinery worker with hepatitis C who was refused employment because company doctors had concluded that occupational exposure to chemicals would result in an aggravation of his liver disease and pose a direct threat to himself. How might this apply in a health care setting? Could a recovering drug abuser be excluded because access to narcotics might heighten the risk of relapse?

# Chapter 13

# THE STRUCTURE OF THE HEALTH CARE ENTERPRISE

## II. FORMS OF BUSINESS ENTERPRISES AND THEIR LEGAL CONSEQUENCES

### B. GOVERNANCE AND FIDUCIARY DUTIES IN BUSINESS ASSOCIATIONS

Add, at p. 857, end of Note 3:

#### *Note on Actions by State Attorneys General Alleging Breaches of Fiduciary Duties*

State Attorneys General around the country have become increasingly active in challenging decisions of board members and officers of nonprofit health care organizations under various legal theories including breaches of fiduciary duties. These cases arise in a variety of contexts including change of control transactions, allegations of self-dealing and waste of charitable assets by insiders, and bankruptcies. See Michael W. Peregrine & James R. Schwartz, The Application of Nonprofit Corporation Law to Health Care Organizations (2002). The following are some examples of actions brought by Attorneys General in recent years:

*AHERF.* Before Enron, there was AHERF. The collapse of the Allegheny Health, Education, and Research Foundation (AHERF) was the nation's largest failure of a nonprofit health care corporation. Under the dominant leadership of its Chief Executive Officer, Sherif Abdelhak, AHERF grew rapidly, borrowed heavily, and collapsed precipitously. The many causes for AHERF's failure include poor business strategy, misleading and perhaps fraudulent accounting practices and financing arrangements, over-expansion, and unwise physician acquisitions. But the over-arching problem was the structure and performance of its governance system. The complex AHERF organization was governed by a parent board consisting of no less than thirty-five members. Ten other boards, having little overlapping membership, governed fifty-five corporations; each board was generally unaware of what other parts of the system were doing. Directors were chosen and dominated by Mr. Abdelhak and board meetings were, according to one analysis, "scripted affairs, intentionally staged to limit oversight and participation by board members ... Members received one thousand page briefing books and had little time to read them." See Lawton R. Burns et al., The Fall of the House of AHERF: The Allegheny Bankruptcy, 19 Health Affs. 7 (Jan/Feb 2000). Although the AHERF boards consisted of top-notch executives, all were extremely busy and unable to perform a broad oversight responsibility over the organization. In addition, the bylaws permitted many key decisions to be made by Mr. Abdelhak. Id. Over sixty lawsuits were filed, most alleging breaches of the duty of care and duty of loyalty by directors. A global settlement of almost all of the civil lawsuits ended with recovery by the Pennsylvania Attorney General of up to $35 million for losses to charitable endowment funds (the Attorney General had claimed restricted endowment funds had been diverted to system operation in violation of charitable trust law as well as other violations of state law). Criminal prosecutions also resulted in confinement for Mr. Abdelhak. See Editorial, AHERF Whimper, Pittsburgh Post–Gazette, Sept. 8, 2002, available at: www.post-gazette.com/forum/20020908edsharif0908p1.asp; Anatomy of a Bankruptcy (six part series published Jan. 17–Jan. 24, 1999) collected at www.post-gazette/com/aherf. The Attorney General's prosecution and its resulting recovery (which was funded primarily from director and officer insurance) stressed the role of nonprofit directors to safeguard assets and their responsibilities for effective oversight.

*Allina.* Following an investigation by the Attorney General of Minnesota, the Allina Health System, a large nonprofit integrated delivery system, entered into a Memorandum of Understanding (MOU) that required Allina to spin-off its HMO affiliate, Medica Health Plans, and adopt a variety of new policies dealing with problems involving conflicts of interest, expense reimbursement, executive compensation, third party contracting and other matters. See Memorandum of Understanding Between Allina Health System and Attorney General of Minnesota, available at *www.ag.state.mn.us/consumer/PDF/allina/MemUnder.pdf* . The allegations of the Attorney General included claims that Allina and its subsidiaries had wasted substantial corporate assets by abusing personal perquisites such as travel and entertainment, had not properly administered almost $50 million in consulting contracts, had acted contrary to the mission and purpose of Medica and had failed to negotiate and administer compensation contracts in the best interest of the nonprofit organization. In sum, it claimed that Allina had utilized "a significant amount of nonprofit assets for the personal benefit of executives." Id.

*Optima.* The Attorney General of New Hampshire undertook an extensive investigation of the operations of Optima Health, Inc. The report criticized Optima's decision to consolidate all acute care services at the Elliott Campus and to convert Catholic Medical Center into an out-patient facility. See New Hampshire Attorney General's Report on Optima Health (Mar. 10, 1998), available at www.state.nh.us/nhdoj/CHARITABLE/optima1.html. The report invoked the directors' fiduciary duties to the organization and cited a "duty of candor" to the community in regard to explaining and revealing its decisionmaking in connection with the consolidation and informing the community of the impact of such changes. The report concluded that the doctrine of *cy pres* may require court approval for such a consolidation and cessation of CMC's charitable functions. Ultimately, the parties unwound the affiliation agreement.

*Health Midwest.* The acquisition of Health Midwest by HCA, Inc., for $1.125 billion, the largest nonprofit acquisition in the history of the country, renewed the ancient border war between the states of Missouri and Kansas. With Health Midwest operating facilities and having corporate entities in both states, the Attorneys General of Kansas and Missouri both laid claim to a share of the charitable assets created by the conversion of the Health Midwest health care properties to for-profit status. A settlement with the Attorney General of Missouri resulted in an arrangement providing for division of the assets and control of the resulting foundation highly favorable to the state of Missouri. See Memorandum of Understanding between Attorney General of Missouri and Health Midwest, *www.ago.state.mo.us/lawsuits2003/012203healthmidwest.pdf*. The state of Kansas sued in state court to challenge the transaction, alleging, inter alia, that the compensation packages received by directors of Health Midwest constituted self-dealing, that the approval of the transaction on the terms provided were not an exercise of sound business judgment, and that the transaction should be reviewed under principles of charitable trust law instead of the corporate law standard. The Kansas court held that the corporate law standard applied to transactions by nonprofit organizations involving changes of control and found no breaches of fiduciary duties by the board of Health Midwest. Health Midwest v. Kline, 2003 WL 328845 (Kan.Dist.Ct.2003) (applying the business judgment rule and concluding that the board conducted a fair and reasonable examination of competing offers and that its conclusions were within the realm of discretion afforded by the rule). However, the court also concluded that the boards of certain subsidiary entities had not satisfied the business judgment rule standard in deciding to merge into a Missouri foundation with "little Kansas participation in governance and nebulous spending commitments to the citizens of Kansas" because they had not exercised their obligation to advance charitable goals and protect corporate assets pursuant to fiduciary duty and ultra vires principles. Id.

*Other cases.* Attorneys General have been active in a number of cases involving fiduciary obligations of nonprofit directors. See, e.g., Nathan Littauer Hospital v. Spitzer, 287 A.D.2d 202, 734 N.Y.S.2d 671 (2001) (challenge to affiliation between two hospitals involving substantial changes to corporate purposes; restatement of purposes and required compliance with Religious Directives for Catholic Health Care Facilities do not constitute change of magnitude sufficient to require judicial review under New York law). The Attorney General of Florida intervened to stop the plan by Intracoastal Health Systems to consolidate in-patient services at one of two hospitals it operated in Palm Beach County and terminate in-patient services at the other. Relying on charitable trust principles, the Attorney General filed suit claiming the nonprofit system's assets belong to the public and could not be reallocated without judicial approval. The case ultimately settled when a for-profit system agreed to buy both hospitals and continued to operate both for an extended period of time. See Non Profit Hospitals Settle AG's Suit, Agree to Sell Rather than Reorganize, 10 Health Law Reporter (BNA) at 443 (March 15, 2001).

**Add, at p. 861, after carryover paragraph:**

## MANHATTAN EYE, EAR AND THROAT HOSPITAL v. SPITZER

Supreme Court, New York County, New York, 1999.
186 Misc.2d 126, 715 N.Y.S.2d 575.

### FINDINGS OF FACT

*A. Manhattan Eye, Ear and Throat Hospital*

Established in 1869, originally located on East 34th Street, and then on East 41st Street, MEETH relocated to its present East 64th Street location in

1906, where it ultimately erected three buildings: the Old Hospital Building, the New Hospital Building and the Annex. At this location, it presently operates a highly sophisticated research and teaching (until it terminated its residency program on June 30, 1999), world-renowned, acute care specialty hospital, providing outpatient and inpatient medical services in three specialized areas: ophthalmology, otolaryngology, and plastic surgery. In February 1995, MEETH opened an Outpatient Extension Center in Harlem (the "Harlem Center"), which, unlike the 64th Street facilities, does not provide in patient care. Instead, it currently functions similarly to the outpatient clinic at 64th Street, and refers patients to 64th Street, for subspecialty clinics and surgery.

According to its Certificate of Incorporation, MEETH's corporate purposes are:

to establish, provide, conduct, operate and maintain a hospital in the City, County and State of New York for the general treatment of persons suffering from acute short-term illnesses; performing general plastic surgery; treating persons suffering from diseases of the eye, ear, nose or throat; and maintaining a school for post graduate instruction in the treatment of such illnesses, performing such surgery, and the treatment of such diseases, and conducting associated and basic research.

By all accounts, MEETH has outstandingly realized these corporate purposes. In order to fulfill its teaching purposes, it developed premier residency programs in the fields of ophthalmology and otolaryngology ("ENT"), as well as a premier fellowship program in aesthetic or plastic surgery. It has consistently been ranked among the top specialty hospitals in the United States. Its physicians have achieved world acclaim for their advancements in medical care and for their provision of acute care in these specialty areas. As to this there is no dispute.

[Changes in financing including reductions in Medicare and Medicaid revenues and the impact of managed care have impacted MEETH adversely.]

MEETH sought to cope with this changed landscape. In 1993, the hospital obtained approval to decertify beds and to establish six additional operating rooms for ambulatory surgery. In 1995, it opened its Harlem Center as a community outreach program, which also served to funnel patients to 64th Street. Dr. George A. Sarkar, Ph.D., J.D., MEETH's Executive Director, sent to the Board members a "proposed strategic plan," dated November 4, 1998, in which he discussed the "Sale or Lease of the Annex Building" and establishment of the proposed Brooklyn Extension Center ("Brooklyn Center"). Thereafter, in December 1998, MEETH applied to the State Department of Health ("DOH") for authorization to open the Brooklyn Center. In its application, MEETH explained that it "is a specialty hospital located . . . at east 64th Street." Although approved, the Brooklyn Center has not been opened.

Then in 1999 MEETH's Board of Directors abruptly decided to sell the 64th Street facility to MSKCC and Downtown; to terminate its residency programs; to close the Hospital; to transform the Harlem Center and the planned Brooklyn Center from extension centers to free standing Diagnostic and Treatment ("D & T") Centers; and to eventually add further D & T centers in the South Bronx. Following these decisions, MEETH entered into a nonbinding "Memorandum of Understanding" for a sponsorship agreement with New YorkPresbyterian Hospital ("NYPH"), under which NYPH would become MEETH's sole corporate member. Implementation of these plans necessitated the sale of the 64th Street facility, i.e., substantially all of the assets of MEETH, and led to this ligation.

### B. "Friends of MEETH" Letter

On October 22, 1998, the Board of Directors received a confidential memorandum, "Re: Crisis at MEETH," from "a group of physicians practicing at Manhattan Eye, [Ear] and Throat Hospital comprising substantially all of the members of the medical staff . . . an informal group known as the 'Friends of MEETH.'" This memorandum stated that there was a "crisis at MEETH," discussed a host of problems and recommended "that the Board of Directors, in keeping with its fiduciary responsibility to the Hospital, appoint an independent hospital consulting firm to examine the operations of MEETH in their entirety." Upon receipt of this memorandum, Mr. Lindsay C. Herkness, III, the Board President, contacted Dr. Sherrell Aston, Chairman of the Plastic Surgery Department, and requested that they meet "immediately." Mr. Herkness stated that "[the Friends of MEETH letter] is a bad document, a dangerous document, that could be harmful to both the physicians and the hospital" and asked Dr. Aston "to use [his] influence on the medical staff to withdraw it." When Dr. Aston refused, Mr. Herkness replied if "you guys give me a hard time and don't do that, I'm going to sell the hospital." Mr. Herkness did not deny that he made the remark. Rather, he testified that he did not "recall anything about selling the hospital. It was not on my mind."

[Although Mr. Herkness formed a Special Committee and the Board met to discuss the issues raised by the staff, no report or response from the Board was forthcoming.]

\* \* \*

### C. Decision to Monetize MEETH's Assets and to Sell the Hospital

#### 1. Retention of a Strategic Advisor

What occurred was that, [according to a MEETH report], there was "[a] bid from [MSKCC] to buy the entire hospital which came out of the blue in the middle of January of 1999." Mr. Whitman had learned of "the approach" from Mr. Herkness, and advised Mr. Herkness that "we have to consider it [the offer] and we would need a committee to do that," which caused Mr. Herkness to reconstitute the Special Committee into a Strategic Committee. Mr. Whitman also advised Mr. Herkness that a "financial advisor was necessary . . . because the board would need to have the offer analyzed from a financial point of view." This led to the retention of Shattuck Hammond Partners, a Division of Pricewaterhouse Coopers Securities, L.L.C. ("Shattuck Hammond"), an investment banking firm that provides services exclusively to the healthcare industry. According to Mr. Herkness, the offer from MSKCC was not what caused retention of Shattuck Hammond. Rather, he testified that the strategic advisors were retained after he received a draft of "Proposed 1999 Operating and Capital Budgets," dated January 15, 1999, which he described as "horrific." It is clear, however, that Shattuck Hammond was retained because of the MSKCC proposal.

On February 5, 1999, Mr. Herkness, with the approval of the Strategic Committee, entered into a written retention agreement with Shattuck Hammond to assist MEETH in evaluating its strategic options. The retainer agreement also authorized Shattuck Hammond to seek out parties "interested in entering into a Transaction with the Hospital," a task which seems irreconcilable with the determination of an appropriate strategic recommendation, a determination which should have come first.[1] The "transaction" referred to was defined in the retention agreement as "any merger, consolidation, reorganization, recapitalization, sale, business combination or other transaction pursuant to which the Hospital and/or any assets of the Hospital are involved in acquiring, being acquired by or combining with a third party."

MEETH agreed to pay Shattuck Hammond a retainer fee of $100,000, and agreed that "[u]pon the closing of a Transaction," it would pay a "Transaction Fee" of one percent (1%) of the "Aggregate Transaction Value." According to Mr. Herkness, he had been informed that this fee arrangement was "standard in the industry." The evidence confirms that there was an understanding that a sale was not only contemplated at the time Shattuck Hammond was retained, but was the actual expectation of the parties. Thus, Shattuck Hammond had a direct financial interest in an outcome which would require sale of the real estate. Significantly, while the fee arrangement was discussed by the members of the Strategic Committee, it does not appear to be the subject of any discussion by the Board. Indeed, neither Rozlyn Anderson, Esq., nor Mr. Underhill, both Board members, and not members of the Strategic Committee, was aware that if there was no transfer or acquisition of assets, Shattuck Hammond would not be entitled to the 1% transaction fee, although Ms. Anderson testified that had she known it would have been irrelevant.

### 2. *MEETH is Put Up For Sale*

On February 22, 1999, Mr. Herkness reported that he had appointed a Strategic Committee to assist in the review of "(1) whether MEETH can survive in today's medical and economic environment as an independent specialty care hospital; (2) what are the strategic options available; and (3) how should MEETH respond to the possible offers from Memorial Sloan Kettering Cancer Center ... and Mt. SinaiNYU Medical Center Health System [Mt. Sinai]." The Mt. Sinai possibility, as noted by various Board members, "would not involve the closure of the Hospital."

Shattuck Hammond's written report, which Mr. Herkness had described as a "fairness opinion," was presented. However, at trial he acknowledged that it is was not a "fairness opinion," which of course, as a financial advisor at a major brokerage firm, Mr. Herkness would have known is a term of art in the securities field. [ ] Shattuck Hammond described the "Hospital's ongoing mission.... 'to improve the quality of life for its patients'," and asked:

> Can the Board, Management and Medical Staff counteract market forces acting against the Hospital and does the Hospital have sufficient financial resources to sustainably support all aspects of the Hospital's current mission, role and business and charitable purposes?

---

**1.** Interestingly, at the time that this authorization was extended, the full Board had not even considered whether a sale of assets was necessary or strategically prudent.

Having posed this question, Mr. James S. Scibetta, a Shattuck Hammond director, concluded that the "business had no value, but the underlying real estate has considerable value" and "that probably one of the best things for the board to consider was to look at the real estate as a very valuable asset ... and see if it could use that as a way to capture additional resources for the board to sort of refocus its mission and do what the board had been discussing." Mr. Scibetta thought it "ridiculous" to contend that MEETH could remain independent. And he testified that "nobody would pay one dollar in order to just take over the business as is." It was this mindset, that the real estate was the only asset of MEETH with value, which determined the future course of events. As Mr. Scibetta put it, the Board wanted to "monetize the assets," rather than seek to preserve MEETH as its main priority.

Neither Shattuck Hammond nor the Board considered MEETH, itself, as having any ongoing economic value. Nor was there recognition or any discussion of the value of MEETH's name, which was considered by Mr. Morton P. Hyman, Chairman of Continuum Health Partners, Inc. (Continuum), to have "great value," and by Mr. Terrence M. O'Brien, Executive Vice President and Chief Operating Officer of Lenox Hill Hospital, to have "marquis value" as "one of the top hospitals in the country." Even Mr. Herkness conceded at trial that the name had "franchise value."

* * *

At the February 22nd meeting, Cushman & Wakefield submitted a "Restricted Appraisal Report," concluding that value of the 64th Street real estate "was in the range of $46 to $55 million, it being understood that an approximate 12 month marketing period would be required to attempt to realize such value in the real estate market." It was pointed out that the net proceeds would be reduced by "real estate brokerage commissions in the range of 2.3%." The fee arrangement with Shattuck Hammond was not discussed. The February 22nd meeting concluded with the nine board members present (two members had been excused) unanimously voting to sell the real estate to MSKCC or Mt. Sinai, or to "any other not-for-profit health care provider for a price as near as possible to $45 million," which was less than the Cushman & Wakefield appraisal. The Board also authorized filing of the requisite applications for regulatory and judicial approval.

[The Shattuck Hammond report concluded that the MSKCC sale would result in the MEETH surrendering its state hospital operating certificate and prohibit it from retaining the name "Manhattan Eye, Ear and Throat Hospital." The Court discusses prior expressions of interest in keeping MEETH as an acute care specialty hospital from the New York Eye and Ear Infirmary and Continuum. Neither was mentioned by the Board at the February 22 meeting or in the Shattuck Hammond Report.]

Thus, contrary to Mr. Scibetta's view that "nobody would pay one dollar in order to just take over the business as is," there was interest from other medical institutions in seeking to preserve MEETH as a worldclass teaching and research hospital, which were ignored by the Board in adopting the recommendations of Shattuck Hammond, its strategic advisor.

### 4. *March 22, 1999 Board Meeting: Mt. Sinai Offer Discussed*

On March 11, 1999, Mt. Sinai and MEETH entered into a thirty-day, binding agreement, which contained a noshop clause,[2] to sell the real estate for $46,000,000. Under this agreement, Mt. Sinai would continue to maintain MEETH's mission as an acute care specialty teaching hospital. This proposal was discussed at the March 22, 1999 meeting of the Executive Committee of the Board of Directors.

It was explained by the Strategic Committee that "such a transaction would bring a large critical mass and expertise to MEETH's existing operation, keep the Hospital's present services as well as add to them, ensure the continuance of the Residency Programs, and maintain all Hospital employees in their present or similar positions. This would allow MEETH to continue to run extension centers in underserved areas and fund research." This agreement between MEETH and Mt. Sinai lapsed before the next Board meeting.

### 5. *Board's Decision to Open the Bidding Up*

At its April 15, 1999, meeting, the Board was told by Mr. Scibetta that both MSKCC and Mt. Sinai had "backed away from their initial proposals and have indicated an interest only at a price substantially below the $46 million minimum amount . . . in the appraisal." Mr. Scibetta recommended that MEETH should "open up the process and inject some competitive forces into the negotiations." Because the Board "wanted to be able to offer [the properties] to real estate developers as well as to make sure that all of the potential bidders on the upper east side real estate [sic] would be approached," it voted to retain Cushman & Wakefield as its broker. Shattuck Hammond was to contact "likely not-for-profit hospital entities" and Cushman & Wakefield would seek to qualify "five or six of the most prominent and likely real estate buyers."

\* \* \*

On April 25, 1999, the New York Times reported that MEETH was for sale.

Thereafter, a scheduled annual Board meeting was held on April 29, 1999, at which time Mr. Scibetta said bids were expected to be received, beginning on April 30th, and he reiterated that Shattuck Hammond had determined "that the Hospital's business had no value." He also advised the Board that "[a]lthough Shattuck Hammond Partners tried to interest Mt. Sinai in taking over MEETH, Mt. Sinai was disinterested in keeping the business and only interested in the real estate aspect of the transaction, at a figure much lower than the appraisal." At this meeting, the Board voted to sell the hospital, at a price in excess of $40,000,000. There was no explanation for this decision to sell the real estate for *less* than its appraised value of $46 to $55 million. At this meeting, authorization to seek regulatory approvals was again provided. Moreover, the Board now realized that its sale and closure plan, leading to free standing D & T centers, would require an

---

**2.** MEETH agreed "not to solicit, initiate or encourage the submission by a third party of any competing proposal."

amendment to the Hospital's Certificate of Incorporation, and a proposed amendment was authorized, although never submitted.

Now, two months after the Board initially had voted to sell its real estate, the minutes for the first time identify, in the context of discussion of the New York Times article, that the Board had decided that "the Hospital was going back to its original mission of serving the poor in underserved areas, and redirecting its charitable assets to accomplish this goal." Other than the Shattuck Hammond report, which discusses the Hospital's "original" mission, there is no written record concerning this momentous decision. There had been no study concerning this so-called return to the "original mission" and no proposal or recommendation on the subject was provided to the Board for its review and deliberation. Notably, there was no management plan or recommendation discussing the need to return to this "original" mission, nor do prior Board minutes report any discussion held on the subject.

### 6. Board Accepts Downtown and MSKCC Offer

By the May 5, 1999 Board meeting, four separate proposals had been received, including a $41,000,000 bid from Downtown and MSKCC (and two proposals from real estate developers). According to this offer, MSKCC would open a breast cancer facility in the New Hospital Building, and the remaining real estate, to be purchased by Downtown, would be used as a building site for an apartment building. Mt. Sinai submitted two alternative proposals: (1) a $27,500,000 offer for the real estate, with the hospital closed; and (2) an offer to acquire the Hospital and its operations for "a very substantially reduced price." Because the second Mt. Sinai offer was "vague," the Board took a "short break" in its meeting during which Mr. Scibetta, at the Board's request, placed a telephone call to Mr. Barry Friedman, Mt. Sinai's President and Chief Financial Officer, who stated that Mt. Sinai would seek a "very reduced price," in the range of five to eleven million dollars, and would only commit to running MEETH for up to two or three years. This spur-of-the-moment telephone conversation persuaded the five Board members who were present that the MSKCC offer should be accepted "promptly." Somehow, this telephone call to Mr. Friedman had confirmed Shattuck Hammond's view that MEETH had no value, beyond the real estate it was "sitting" on, warranting acceptance of the MSKCC offer.

The Board took no further steps to seek a bidder which would save MEETH's longestablished mission. Instead it decided that "the most preferable offer" would be a combination of "fair and reasonable consideration" together with the involvement of a major tax exempt hospital. This sale would "provide the necessary funding for the Board's envisioned diagnostic and treatment centers and other hospital-type activities to be relocated to medically underserved areas in New York City." The Board then approved a sale to Downtown and MSKCC. That same day, Mr. Herkness executed a nonbinding letter of intent, without a noshop clause, to sell the real estate to Downtown and MSKCC. (On June 25, 1999, the parties entered into a "Real Property Contract for Sale" ["Contract"].)

The May 5th minutes record that after the decision to sell was approved, "[t]he Board *then* discussed the issue of closing the Hospital. The Board noted that *no* actual decision had been made to close the Hospital." (Emphasis added.) Previously, on April 29, 1999, the Board had terminated the residency program and authorized the President to prepare for possible hospital closure. However, even as of May 5th, as the minutes show, the Board did not seem to believe that it was actually closing the Hospital. One has to wonder exactly what the Board thought it was doing. Then, without a record of further discussion or Board authorization following this May 5th meeting, MEETH submitted a closure plan to the DOH on June 14, 1999, as an attachment to a letter from Dr. Sarkar, in which he also "requested issuance of a diagnostic and treatment center operating certificate for the existing Harlem facility." It was after this that Mr. Herkness sought (and obtained) "a resolution reaffirming the Hospital's intent to close the East 64th Street facility." This occurred at the July 26, 1999 Board meeting.

As of July 26th, the Board had neither received nor commissioned any study with regard to the Board's planned use of the sales proceeds to establish D & T centers, the necessity for such centers, or the viability of such centers. It was an idea in progress. It may be that written documentation, at this point, was not needed, if there had been any other type of evaluation; however, there was none. There had been no consultation with the medical staff or other medical experts or health care experts or anyone else concerning its feasibility or viability. Rather, Mr. Herkness testified that the "best feasibility study is five years of experience." It bears noting, however, that MEETH had no experience with free standing D & T centers. At best, this plan evolved from the Harlem Center, which was an extension center, and not a free standing center. Nonetheless, without such seemingly basic information, the decision to sell and close was made.

From these events, the conclusion is inescapable, based upon all the credible evidence, that the Board, recognizing MEETH's financial problems, certainly after the March 11, 1999 Mt. Sinai letter of intent lapsed, chose not to seek a solution that would preserve the Hospital, either itself, or in some sort of affiliation with a major medical institution that would be willing to try and preserve MEETH's historic purposes. Rather, the Board decided on a course of action which would lead to the sale and closure of the hospital, and then provide the Board with a substantial sum of money to allow it to take MEETH down the path to new, unstudied and unevaluated charitable purposes.

MEETH began to act, i.e., it terminated the residency program, upon the assumption that it would receive DOH approvals for closure and establishment of the D & T centers. It executed a letter evidencing its intent to sell to MSKCC, and chose to take steps to effectuate closure and receive regulatory approval for its plan, to enter into a contract for sale, and then to seek court approval under section 511 [Section 511 of the New York Not-for-Profit Law, governing sales of substantially all the assets of a corporation, is discussed infra]. This would have had the effect of presenting the court with what would have been essentially a fait accompli. To put it another way, if everything went as hoped for, MEETH would have been able to present the section 511 petition pertaining to an *already* closed hospital, with DOH approval for the D & T centers, and it would have asked the court to find "that the purposes of the corporation ... will be promoted." This would have effectively neutralized, or substantially compromised, any meaningful judicial role in the section 511 process. Indeed, under the scenario envisaged by

MEETH, denial of the petition would have been a pyrrhic victory for its opponents: the hospital would already be closed; under such circumstances, a court order could hardly have restored MEETH.

### E. *Alternative Proposals Designed to Preserve MEETH*

[The Court describes in detail MEETH's negotiations with two alternative purchasers. Continuum proposed to combine MEETH with NYEEI and thereby continue its mission as a hospital and continue operations of the Harlem Center while abandoning the plans to establish DET Centers. On July 13, 1999, Mr. Scibetta rejected the proposal stating that the board had "decided to sell the real estate." Lenox Hill also engaged in discussions with Mr. Herkness and Mr. Scibetta under which it would make certain investments in MEETH, with the latter becoming a subsidiary of Lenox, and continuing operation of the hospital in the New Hospital Building on East 64th Street. Although Lenox was asked to provide information, the MEETH similarly filed a petition for approval of the sale to MSKCC.]

### F. *MEETH'S Plan*

MEETH's plan is to sell a part of its real estate to MSKCC, one of the world's outstanding cancer treatment and research centers. MSKCC plans to convert the New Hospital Building to expand its breast cancer center. Undeniably, this would be an extremely worthwhile use. However, the issue under section 511 is not the buyer's planned use of the real estate, however worthy that use may be, but whether seller's use of the sale proceeds will promote its own corporate purposes. (E.g., Matter of St. Luke's Hospital, 33 Misc.2d 888, 228 N.Y.S.2d 25 [Sup.Ct., N.Y. County 1962].) The remaining real estate will be sold to Downtown, a real estate developer, which intends to erect an apartment building on the site.

Upon completion of the transaction, and following the hoped-for DOH approval, MEETH will close its existing specialty hospital. If further DOH approvals are obtained, MEETH will then convert the existing Harlem Center, and the already approved though-not-yet built Brooklyn center to the proposed D & T centers. In addition, as part of the transaction MEETH also has proposed entering into a sponsorship agreement with New York–Presbyterian Hospital.

\* \* \*

### CONCLUSIONS OF LAW

At issue is whether, as required under section 511(d) of the NotForProfit Corporation Law, MEETH has shown "to the satisfaction of the court," both that the "consideration and the terms of the transaction are fair and reasonable"[3] and that "the purposes of the corporation . . . will be promoted" by the sale of all or substantially all of the hospital's assets to Downtown and MSKCC. The few reported decisions dealing with this section have held that whether "the consideration and the terms of the transaction are fair and reasonable to the corporation" is to be evaluated at the time that the contract

---

**3.** This requirement was added in 1972 (L.1972, c. 961 § 6). Prior to this amendment, judicial decisions had required "fair market value" (e.g., Matter of St. Luke's Hospital, 33 Misc.2d 888, 891, 228 N.Y.S.2d 25 [Sup.Ct., N.Y. Cty., 1962]).

to sell is entered into. ... On the other hand, the cases hold that whether "the purposes of the corporation ... will be promoted" is to be evaluated "in light of conditions prevailing at the time the issue is presented to the court." ... Given my Findings of Fact, I conclude that MEETH has not satisfied either prong of section 511. Therefore I deny MEETH's petition to approve the proposed sale.

Before turning to section 511, there are several areas that warrant brief discussion. Not-for-profit corporations operate under legal regimes designed for traditional for-profit corporations.[4] However, fundamental structural differences between not-for-profit corporations and for-profit corporations render this approach incapable of providing effective internal mechanisms to guard against directors' improvident use of charitable assets. For example, in the forprofit context, shareholder power ensures that Boards make provident decisions, while in the not-for-profit context, this internal check does not exist. To put it another way, a nonprofit corporation has no "owners" or private parties with a pecuniary stake to monitor and scrutinize actions by the directors. This distinction is even more significant in the case of charitable corporations, such as MEETH, where there are no members, because the board is essentially self-perpetuating. [ ]

The Not-for-Profit Corporation Law addresses this lack of accountability by requiring court approval of fundamental changes in the life of a Type B charitable corporation, such as a disposition of all or substantially all assets, since there are no shareholders whose approval can be sought. The Attorney General is made a statutory party to such petitions, and his "active participation" is presumed. (See V. Bjorkland, [et al., New York Nonprofit Law and Practice]., § 82[a], p. 238). This is to ensure that the interests of the ultimate beneficiaries of the corporation, the public, are adequately represented and protected from improvident transactions. ...It is pursuant to this mandate that this court is called upon to review the sale of substantially all of MEETH's assets to MSKCC and Downtown.

A charitable Board is essentially a caretaker of the not-for-profit corporation and its assets. As caretaker, the Board "ha[s] the fiduciary obligation to act on behalf of the corporation ... and advance its interests" [ ]in "good faith and with that degree of diligence, care and skill which ordinarily prudent men would exercise under similar circumstances in like positions." (NPCL § 717[a] ). This formulation of the Board's duty of care is an "expansion" of the comparable section of the Business Corporation Law which does not contain the words "care" and "skill." ...

It is axiomatic that the Board of Directors is charged with the duty to ensure that the mission of the charitable corporation is carried out. This duty has been referred to as the "duty of obedience." It requires the director of a not-for-profit corporation to "be faithful to the purposes and goals of the organization," since "[u]nlike business corporations, whose ultimate objective is to make money, nonprofit corporations are defined by their specific objectives: perpetuation of particular activities are central to the raison d'être of the organization." (Bjorkland, *op. cit.*, § 114[a], at p. 414). Analysis of the

---

**4.** The NPCL was designed to reflect the Business Corporation Law as closely as the subject matter would permit. [ ]

duties of charitable directors more commonly arises in an action brought by the AG alleging breach of the duties owed to the corporation under NPCL §§ 112 and 720, and does not appear to have been discussed in any reported decision under section 511. But the duty of obedience, perforce, must inform the question of whether a proposed transaction to sell all or substantially all of a charity's assets promotes the purposes of the charitable corporation when analyzed under section 511.

In recent years, across the United States, there have been a series of transactions that, although certainly different from this petition, nevertheless resemble, in certain basics, MEETH's proposal. I am referring to the nationwide spate of conversions of nonprofit hospitals into for-profit hospitals which has caused a substantial output of commentary. [ ] It has also resulted in some twenty states enacting or considering legislation regulating such conversions. [ ] However, there has been no similar activity and little discussion in New York where such conversions are not permitted.

Nonetheless, the conversion analogy is analytically useful. This is because, absent the for-profit component, which of course is absent in a Section 511 petition, a conversion is conceptually similar to MEETH's petition, inasmuch as in both there is a charitable organization which alleges that it is incapable of continuing its primary mission of operating a hospital, seeks approval of the sale of all its assets, and plans to apply the sale proceeds towards a newly revised mission. As is relevant to the analysis, for example, legislation in one state requires that the attorney general examine the transaction to determine "(2) Whether the nonprofit hospital exercised due diligence in deciding to sell, selecting the purchaser, and negotiating the terms and conditions of the sale; (3) Whether the procedures used by the seller in making its decision, including whether appropriate expert assistance was used (were fair); (4) Whether conflict of interest was disclosed, including, but not limited to, conflicts of interest [of] board members ... and experts retained by the seller[;] [and] (5) Whether the seller will receive reasonably fair value for its assets." [ ] I believe this to be a clear and concise statement of factors which a court should be concerned with in evaluating a transaction under section 511 to sell all the assets. Indeed, they are in many respects mirrored in the AG's June 3, 1999 letter to MEETH, in essence agreed to by MEETH's counsel, in which the AG wrote "Elementary principles of corporate and fiduciary law require the Board, after it has decided to sell the hospital, to entertain all responsible proposals, not to favor any bidder over another in the process, and to treat all bidders and potential bidders identically and fairly."

I turn now to the first prong of section 511, which requires that "the consideration and terms of the transaction are fair and reasonable to the corporation." Because the sale of the real estate, as proposed, is inextricably interwoven with the closure of MEETH as it exists today, I believe that the transaction as a whole must be examined, not just the "fair market value" of the real estate. This transaction is unlike, for example Matter of Church of St. Francis De Sales, supra, a simple transaction which dealt only with the question of the value of a building being sold by the Church; there was no larger transaction involved. There do not appear to be reported decisions of more complex transactions, such as here, where implementing its decision to sell its real estate assets to MSKCC and Downtown would require the closing of MEETH and a fundamental change to its corporate purposes. The Board accepted Shattuck Hammond's conclusion that "the business [of MEETH] had no value," which I have found to be incorrect. Clearly MEETH, as a functioning acute care, specialty hospital, had value: major medical entities were willing to operate it and keep it open and guarantee the expenditure of substantial sums to do so. Thus, while it may be that the real estate was fairly valued, this is not enough. The transaction did not take into account MEETH's full value, and the NYPH proposal to establish a MEETH pavilion or building, with "plaques and/or signage," does not correct this since it does not necessarily contemplate preserving the business of MEETH, and therefore preserving the total assets of MEETH. Moreover, as I have also found, evidence at the hearing established that MEETH's name itself had significant value. Again under the terms of the proposed transaction, this value is not evaluated nor is it clear that it will be preserved. The Board disregarded these components of value when it decided to "monetize" its assets and sell the real estate. This is a fundamental flaw which leaves me unsatisfied that the terms and conditions of the proposed transaction are "fair and reasonable."

Under the second prong of section 511, which requires that "the purposes of the corporation ... will be promoted" (N–PCL § 511[d]), MEETH's petition fares no better. Unfortunately, there is lacking judicial precedent concerning a proposal of this magnitude.[5] While MEETH has argued that the proposal to abandon the acute care, teaching and research hospital component of its mission and to pursue the D & T centers does not require an amendment, this argument is belied by the Board's own action on April 29th, authorizing submission of an Amendment to its Certificate of Incorporation (although never submitted) expressly providing for the D & T centers. This is behavioral evidence that the Board knew that it was proposing a fundamental change in the corporation's mission, which indeed it was doing For generations MEETH's mission, as stated in its Certificate of Incorporation, was understood to be the operation of an acute care, specialty teaching and research hospital dedicated to "plastic surgery" and to the treatment of "persons suffering from diseases of the eye, ear, nose or throat." While it is certainly correct that the definition of "hospital" contained in section 2801(1) of the Public Health Law includes a diagnostic and treatment center, as MEETH now argues, it is sophistry to contend that this means that MEETH is not seeking a new and fundamentally different purpose, in light of the overwhelming evidence which demonstrates this is exactly what it is doing. The conclusion is inescapable that the proposed use of the assets involves a new and fundamentally different corporate purpose.

Before I turn to analysis of MEETH's failure to establish that the proposed transaction will further its corporate purposes as required by section 511, a prescient passage from one text is instructive:

> [A] hospital or clinic providing specialized services, that is so deeply in debt that its provision of services is seriously jeopardized, may wish to

---

**5.** There are reported decisions dealing with somewhat complicated sales. (E.g. Agudist Council of Greater New York v. Imperial Sales Co., 158 A.D.2d 683, 551 N.Y.S.2d 955 [2d Dept., 1990] [sale disapproved where services provided to senior citizens will be disrupted] and Church of God, 76 A.D.2d 712, 431 N.Y.S.2d 834). Such decisions generally deal with the impact of the sale of the assets on the existing mission, and do not involve a concomitant proposal to change or reprioritize the existing mission.

transfer its assets to another clinic or hospital providing basically the same services in return for assumption of its debt. The only alternative may be the protection of federal bankruptcy laws or a receivership under state law for the protection of creditors. [Bjorklund, *op. cit.*, § 8–2[b][3], at p. 243.]

While it may be appropriate, in certain cases, to solve financial difficulties by eliminating the organization's mission by selling its assets and then undertaking a new mission, the passage properly focuses attention upon the duty of obedience, which mandates that a Board, in the first instance, seek to preserve its original mission. Embarkation upon a course of conduct which turns it away from the charity's central and well-understood mission should be a carefully chosen option of last resort. Otherwise, a Board facing difficult financial straits might find sale of its assets, and "reprioritization" of its mission, to be an attractive option, rather than taking all reasonable efforts to preserve the mission which has been the object of its stewardship.

As has been documented in the Findings of Fact, the record is clear that this case is not a situation where the Board first made a reasoned and studied determination that there was a lack of need for MEETH as a hospital, or that the financial difficulties made it impossible to ensure the survival of MEETH. Rather, the credible evidence is that MEETH's decision to sell was impelled by MSKCC's offer, which caused the Board to recognize the value of the underlying real estate; then its realization that it could "monetize" this asset drove subsequent events.

The MSKCC offer initially drove the decision to retain a strategic advisor, Shattuck Hammond, which had a direct and substantial interest in a sale of the real estate, i.e., the 1% transaction fee. This arrangement, regardless of whether it was traditional in investment banking, as Mr. Hammond testified, resulted in a situation where the Board put its reliance upon a strategic advisor which had an actual interest in the recommendations of its strategic study. It is not necessary for me to conclude that this conflict of interest compromised the result; the fee arrangement certainly gives the appearance that the integrity of the process was flawed and that the Board had not obtained the assistance of a truly independent expert. Moreover, there does not appear to have been full disclosure to the Board of the potential for a conflict of interest in the expert. The evidence showed that two Board members were unaware of the percentage fee which was a part of Shattuck Hammond's retention. Additionally, there was no discussion or deliberation by the Board over the fact that its strategic advisor had a direct, and perhaps disabling, financial interest in the outcome of the strategic option it was recommending. Nor was there a decision by the Board to retain and rely upon Shattuck Hammond, notwithstanding this issue. The issue simply was never raised. As a result, it cannot be concluded with confidence that the Board received wholly disinterested advice. This becomes more troubling in view of the manner in which Shattuck Hammond dealt with bidders such as Continuum and Lenox Hill, which were not interested in purchasing the real estate, by providing misleading information concerning their offers, often omitting crucial details, and by asserting that the only realistic option was the sale of the real estate.

It is also clear that the MSKCC offer, which drove the decision to "monetize" the assets, drove the subsequent decisions to create a new or "reprioritized" mission, to prematurely terminate the residency programs, to seek approval to close the hospital, and virtually every other decision made by the Board, as I have detailed above.

This decision to "monetize" drove the need to change the corporate purposes, and these new or reprioritized purposes then became the basis for the argument that "purposes of the corporation ... will be promoted." A careful evaluation of whether there was a basis for changing the corporate purposes should have determined the need to sell, not vice versa. The total absence of any study beforehand, concerning the D & T centers, and the retention of healthcare experts, only after submission of the proposal to the DOH, and only to prepare a business plan "for fulfillment" or in "support" of the D & T proposal, not to independently evaluate the plan's feasibility, buttresses the conclusion that the sale drove the change in purpose. Indeed, the report submitted by Dr. Cicero and Mr. Kachmarick states that "[t]he following business plan describes how MEETH will achieve [its] goal, in keeping with its expanded mission statement." To argue that MEETH was returning to its original purposes without an iota of evidence that it made this fundamental determination prior to the decision to sell and close, cannot obscure the fact that this decision, of necessity, eliminated MEETH's historic mission, its historic raison d'être.

Moreover, the record also demonstrates that the Board failed to properly consider the various alternatives submitted which would have preserved MEETH's mission. The Board had concluded that these alternatives were the equivalent of "giving the keys away," and summarily rejected them.[6] However, the Board has no independent vitality. It appears that the Board confused preservation of the Hospital with preservation of the Board, when the appropriate calculus should be what is good for the Hospital is good for the Board. This is borne out by the testimony concerning Mr. Herkness' promise to consider the additional Lenox Hill materials, and his bringing the matter to vote without advising the Board of this commitment to Lenox Hill, which effectively foreclosed the Board from considering a proposal which would have preserved MEETH's mission. It is borne out by Mr. Scibetta's refusal to meet with Continuum in the presence of the AG, who is a statutory party to any section 511 petition, a decision acquiesced in by the Board. It also is borne out by the lack of interest in pursuing potential bidders who were willing to preserve MEETH. This conclusion is reinforced by the events on September 17, 1999 when Mr. Herkness inquired whether Continuum was willing to indemnify the Board and then refused to let Mr. Hyman [Continuum's representative] examine the MSKCC contract.

In sum, it is evident that this petition fails to meet the two pronged test of section 511. The terms of the transaction are not fair and reasonable to the corporation, inasmuch as no consideration was given to the value of MEETH

---

**6.** See Bjorklund, *op. cit.*, § 8–2[c], at p. 246, n. 58, discussing when a charitable "business" is being transferred, and in exchange the acquirer is assuming all liabilities and guaranteeing continuation of the seller services and noting that the "value (i.e., total assets transferred) may be much greater than the consideration (i.e., liabilities assumed)." Neither Continuum nor Lenox Hill was proposing this scenario, as was suggested by the "keys" metaphor.

as a going concern; rather, this value was disregarded. Moreover, evaluating the transaction at the time of the petition, it is clear that there has not been a showing that the sale will promote the purposes of the corporation. To the contrary, MEETH decided to sell, and then evolved its new or "reprioritized mission." There has been no reasoned determination that MEETH cannot continue to operate an acute care, specialty research and teaching hospital, as other medical institutions are proposing to do, and are willing to invest substantial sums to accomplish. MEETH instead chose to sell its real estate, to seek DOH approval to close its hospital, and then apply for judicial imprimatur of this plan. I conclude that this sales transaction should be disapproved.

## Notes and Questions

1. The MEETH Board retained a prominent, highly regarded investment-banking firm to advise it and help conduct negotiations. Why did the actions of the Board in reliance on this firm not fall under the protections of the Business Judgment Rule? What factors shape the directors' responsibilities when a financially troubled hospital is put up for sale? See Peregrine & Schwartz, supra ("*MEETH* should constitute a warning to directors/trustees of the importance of carefully considering the duty of obedience to purpose in the decisionmaking process, particularly when considering a change in the corporation's principle charitable purpose.") Note, however, that the fiduciary duties of corporate directors may shift when an entity is approaching bankruptcy. In such circumstances, the board may owe fiduciary duties to creditors of the corporation that may, in some circumstances, trump their obligations to the corporation itself. See Michael W. Peregrine et al., The Fiduciary Duties of Health Care Directors in the "Zone of Insolvency," 35 J. Health L. 227 (2002).

2. A further complication raised by the MEETH case is the overlapping and somewhat conflicting regulatory schemes that a corporation faces in change of ownership transactions. State law regulating hospital licensure may come into conflict with or pose strategic conundrums when considered in light of corporate fiduciary obligations under nonprofit law. See Scott Himes, The Collision of Healthcare and Corporate Law in a Hospital Closure Case, 34 J. Health L. 335 (2001).

## D. PROFESSIONALISM AND THE CORPORATE PRACTICE OF MEDICINE DOCTRINE

**Add, at p. 872, end of Note 2:**

The question of whether the holding in *Berlin* should be extended to other nonprofit health care organizations was addressed by the Illinois Supreme Court in Carter–Shields v. Alton Health Institute, 201 Ill.2d 441, 268 Ill.Dec. 25, 777 N.E.2d 948 (2002). The case involved a physician seeking to avoid application of a non-competition agreement she had signed with the Alton Health Institute, Inc. (AHI). AHI is a nonprofit corporation fifty-percent owned by St. Anthony's Health Systems, also a nonprofit corporation. Although not licensed as a hospital, St. Anthony's controlled two licensed hospitals in the area. The remaining fifty percent of AHI is owned by a partnership composed primarily of physician groups. The Court strongly reaffirmed the corporate practice of medicine doctrine, stating "the exercise of control or influence over the medical decisionmaking of a physician by a lay, unlicensed corporation results in a division of the physician's loyalty between the often divergent interests of the corporation and the patient." Id. at 957. However, it declined to extend its holding in *Berlin*, characterizing that decision as "carving out a narrow exception for an entity, such as a hospital, that must meet certain professional criteria established by the legislature." Id. Although AHI was a charitable nonprofit health care organization, it lacked a legislatively-determined role and was not subject to a similar regulatory oversight. The court also refused to view federal Medicare regulations governing kickbacks and conflicts of interests as sufficient to invoke the *Berlin* exception.

In states recognizing the corporate practice of medicine doctrine, what is the relationship between that doctrine's prohibitions and other statutes permitting physicians to organize their practice under a professional corporation form? In Pediatric Neurosurgery v. Russell, 44 P.3d 1063 (Colo.2002), the Supreme Court of Colorado held that the state's professional corporation statute did not abolish the corporate practice of medicine doctrine but carved out an exception allowing corporations to practice medicine while prohibiting them from doing anything that violates medical standards of conduct. The court went on to conclude that principles of respondeat superior would apply and a professional corporation could be held vicariously liable for the torts of its employee doctors acting in the course of their employment.

## III. INTEGRATION AND NEW ORGANIZATIONAL STRUCTURES
## WHERE'S WALDO—PART II

### A. THE CHANGING STRUCTURE OF THE MODERN HEALTH CARE ENTERPRISE

**Add, at p. 879, at the end of Note 2:**

*Continuing Disintegration.* The progression from integration and disintegration over the past decade was recently summarized by Mark Pauly and Lawton Burns:

> During the 1990's many hospitals pursued twin strategies of vertical and horizontal integration. Each type of integration assumed multiple forms. Vertical combination included acquisition of primary care physicians, strategic alliances with physicians in [PHOs and MSOs, and the development of HMOs]. Horizontal combinations included the formation of Multi-hospital systems mergers, and strategic alliances with neighboring hospitals to form local networks...
>
> While the form of integration varied across hospitals and markets, their economic performance, after a decade of experience, was genuinely uniform: Nothing worked.

Lawton R. Burns & Mark V. Pauly, Integrated Delivery Networks (IDNs): A Detour on the Road to Integrated Healthcare?, 21 Health Affs. 128 (July/Aug. 2002).

Examining both the *ex ante* justifications for integration and the performance of various systems in recent years, Burns and Pauly conclude that the integration phenomenon was built on faulty premises such as the inevitable spread of capitation payment and the ability of hospitals to "partner" with physicians and achieve economic savings, and that most participants ignored obstacles to realizing significant economies of scale and developing an appropriate regulatory infrastructure.

With the demise of capitation certain integrated structures have all but disappeared. For example, most HMOs sponsored by hospitals and multi-specialty groups have gone out of business or have been sold; national health plans have divested many of their staff model HMOs; and many large provider integrated networks have come unraveled. See James C. Robinson, The Future of Managed Care Organizations, 18 Health Affs. 7 (Mar./Apr. 1999). Observing the bankruptcies of hundreds of IPAs, physician groups have become extremely wary of accepting capitation. Consequently the popularity of organizing structures that developed to serve that method of payment have declined. See Deborah Gesensway, IPAs: Down—But Not Out—With Doctors, Am. Coll. of Physicians, Am. Soc'y of Internal Med. Observer (Sept. 2001), available at www.acponline.org*journals*news*Sep01*ipa.html. Despite consumer dissatisfaction with managed care, few predict a return to pure fee-for-service reimbursement or the end of IPAs and other horizontal forms of physician integration. Indeed, the increasing demand by employers and payers for data on quality and the shift of cost sharing onto employees may trigger renewed efforts among physicians to collaborate. See James C. Robinson, Physician Organizations in California: Crisis and Opportunity, 20 Health Affs. 81 (July/Aug. 2001).

## IV. TAX–EXEMPT HEALTH CARE ORGANIZATIONS

### A. CHARITABLE PURPOSES: HOSPITALS

**Add, at p. 896, Note 2:**

Recently, the IRS unsuccessfully attempted to establish that in addition to other requirements for satisfying the community benefit standard under 501(c)(3), hospitals must provide a significant amount of health care services to the indigent without any expectation of receiving payment for those services. The government also argued that the joint venture being challenged failed to satisfy the community benefit standard because it was not "controlled" by a "community board." St. David's Health Care System v. United States (text of opinion may be found *infra* this Supplement).

On March 9, 2001, the IRS issued a Field Service Advisory (FSA) regarding the issue of "whether a hospital whose stated policies are to provide health care services to individuals regardless of their ability to pay satisfies the charity care requirement of the community benefit standard under the operational test" of Section 501(c) 3.I.R.S., Field Serv. Advisory 2001–20030 (Mar. 9, 2001), 2001 WL 234018 (FSAs reflect internal advice from the IRS Assistant Chief Counsel to IRS field attorneys as to the factual criteria that revenue agents should consider when, for example, examining whether hospitals qualify for exempt status. They do not constitute legal precedent or formal guidance).

The Advisory concluded:

[A] hospital's mere assertions that it has a policy to provide health care services to the indigent is not sufficient to establish that the hospital meets the charity care requirement of the community benefit standard. Instead, the hospital also must show that it actually provided significant health care services to the indigent.

In addition, the FSA went on to provide some guidance as to how Service agents might address these issues:

Set forth below are a series of questions to address when developing the factual record on the charitable care policies and activities of a hospital.

1. Does the hospital have a specific, written plan or policy to provide free or low-cost health care services to the poor or indigent?

2. Under what circumstances may, or has, the hospital deviated for its stated policies on providing free or low-cost health care services to the poor or indigent?

3. Does the hospital broadcast the terms and conditions of its charity care policy to the public?

4. Does the hospital maintain and operate a full-time emergency room open to all persons regardless of their ability to pay?

5. What directives or instructions does the hospital provide to ambulance services about bringing poor or indigent patients to its emergency room?

6. What inpatient, outpatient, and diagnostic services does the hospital actually provide to the poor or indigent for free or for reduced charges?

7. Under what circumstances does the hospital deny health care services to the poor or indigent?

8. Does the hospital operate with the expectation of receiving full payment from all persons to whom it renders services?

9. How and when does the hospital ascertain whether a patient will be able to pay for the hospital's services?

10. What documents or agreements does the hospital require poor or indigent patients to sign before receiving care?

11. What is the hospital's policy on admitting poor or indigent patients as inpatients and outpatients?

12. Under what circumstances does the hospital refer poor or indigent individuals who require services to other hospitals in the area that do admit poor or indigent patients?

13. Does the hospital maintain separate and detailed records about the number of times, and circumstances under which, it actually provided free or reduced-cost care to the poor or indigent?

14. Does the hospital maintain a separate account on its books that segregates the costs of providing free or reduced-cost care to the poor or indigent? Does this account include any other items, such as write-offs for care to patients who were not poor or indigent?

## B. CHARITABLE PURPOSES: HEALTH MAINTENANCE ORGANIZATIONS

**Add, at p. 904, at end of Note 2:**

In IHC Health Plans, Inc. v. Comm'r, T.C. Memo 2001–246, 2001 WL 1103284 (U.S.Tax Ct.2001), the Tax Court upheld the revocation of tax exempt status for health plans sponsored by Intermountain Health Care. In concluding that the plans did not provide sufficient community benefit so as to qualify for a tax exemption as a 501(c)(3) charity, the court noted that, in contrast to the Sound Health Association HMO and the Geisinger HMO, petitioner did not own or operate its own medical facilities, employ (to any significant extent) its own physicians, or offer free medical care to the needy. In addition, it noted the absence of a reduced premium program and IHC's failure to provide free or low cost health care services apart from a few health care screenings. The Tax Court also noted that the record did not reveal why petitioner used community rating methodology for individual and small group employees while setting premiums for large group employees based on claims experience. It observed that "if the difference in treatment caused a disparity in premium costs there could be an inference that petitioner was benefiting larger employers." Id. The absence of community representation on the petitioner's board of trustees casts further doubt as to the existence of a community benefit. The court did not reach the question of whether petitioner's activities amounted to "commercial-type insurance" within the meaning of § 501m.

## C. CHARITABLE PURPOSES: INTEGRATED DELIVERY SYSTEMS (IDSS)

**Add, at p. 910, at end of Note 2:**

In the IHC Health Plans case, T.C. Memo 2001–246, 2001 WL 1103284 (2001), discussed *supra* this Supplement, the Tax Court rejected petitioner's claim that the health plans could qualify as an integral part of a tax-exempt affiliate. Despite "supervision and control" by the tax exempt affiliate over the plans, the latters' activities were not shown to constitute an unrelated trade or business if conducted by a tax exempt entity. The court also stressed that eighty percent of physician services received by health plan enrollees were provided by independent physicians lacking a "direct link" to the tax exempt affiliates. Noting that the IHC system operated a large number of hospitals and employed approximately four hundred primary care physicians and that the health plans provided no free or low cost services, the court "fail[ed] to see how petitioner's operations including its heavy reliance on independent physicians, would be essential or substantially related to Health Services exempt functions." Id.

## D. JOINT VENTURES BETWEEN TAX–EXEMPT AND FOR–PROFIT ORGANIZATIONS

**Add, at p. 931, after Note 2:**

### ST. DAVID'S HEALTH CARE SYSTEM v. UNITED STATES

United States District Court, W.D. Texas, Austin Division, 2002.
2002 WL 1335230.

#### ORDER

\* \* \*

Plaintiff St. David's Health Care System ("St.David's") brings this lawsuit to demand a refund of income taxes paid after the revocation of its tax exempt status by the Internal Revenue Service in 1996. St. David's first incorporated under Texas nonprofit law as a community-owned, not-for-profit hospital in 1925. In 1938, the IRS recognized St. David's as a tax-exempt organization under I.R.C. § 501(c)(3). St. David's charitable purposes were achieved through the ownership and operation of an acute-care hospital in Austin, Texas.

More recently, in 1996, St. David's entered into a limited partnership with HCA, Inc. (formerly known as Columbia/HCA Healthcare Corp.), a for-profit health care company that operates approximately 180 hospitals nationwide. St. David's contributed all of its hospital and medical assets, and HCA contributed its Austin-area hospitals and medical assets. The partnership has two general partners and two limited partners. The two general partners are St. David's and HCA's wholly-owned subsidiary, Round Rock Hospital, Inc. ("Round Rock"). Each general partner holds a ten percent interest, but Round Rock is the managing partner. The two limited partners include St. David's and HCA's wholly-owned subsidiary, Columbia/SDH Holding. St. David's ownership interest in the partnership as both a limited and general partner is 45.9%, leaving 54.1% ownership interest in the hands of the HCA entities.

In October 2000, the IRS issued a decision revoking St. David's tax exempt status retroactive to the partnership's formation in 1996. The stated reason for the revocation was that when St. David's entered into the partnership with HCA, it was no longer engaging in activities that primarily further a charitable purpose, as required under § 501(c)(3) of the Internal Revenue Code. Specifically, the IRS ruled that:

> St. David's participation in the Partnership does not permit it to act exclusively in furtherance of its charitable purposes and allows for greater than incidental benefits to HCA and its for-profit subsidiaries.

*Id.* In response to the decision to revoke St. David's tax-exempt status, St. David's has filed this suit.

## ANALYSIS

\* \* \*

As stated by the Magistrate Judge, the requirements for tax exemption under § 501(c)(3) are divided into two major tests: the organizational test and the operational test.

> "In order to be exempt as an organization described in section 501(c)(3), an organization must be both organized and operated exclusively for one or more of the purposes specified in such section. If an organization fails to meet either the organizational test or the operational test, it is not exempt."

26 C.F.R. § 1.501(c)(3)1(a) \* \* \* [T]he parties disagree as to whether St. David's was "operated exclusively for a charitable purpose" during the tax year 1996, as required by subpart (1).

\* \* \*

The only dispute between these parties centers around the "primary activities" prong [of the operational test].

> "An organization will be regarded as *operated exclusively* for one or more exempt purposes only if it engages primarily in activities which accomplish one or more of such exempt purposes specified in section 501(c)(3).

An organization will not be so regarded if more than an insubstantial part of its activities is not in furtherance of an exempt purpose."
26 C.F.R. § 1.501(c)(3)1(c)(1) (emphasis in original). Sadly, the last sentence of that section is a horrible amalgamation of negatives arranged like an inside joke prompting laughter only from seasoned and sadistic bureaucrats. In plain English, it means that an organization cannot be exempt while devoting a substantial portion of its activities to nonexempt purposes.

A list of exempt purposes is provided, which includes charity as an exempt purpose. 26 C.F.R. § 1.501(c)(3)1(d)(1)(i)(b). On the issue of whether or not St. David's has a charitable purpose, the government chooses to avert its eyes when Revenue Ruling 69–545 is raised. Specifically, the government turns its eyes to Revenue Ruling 56–185. The government says that "the promotion of health is not per se charitable" and relies on 56–185 for the proposition that an exempt hospital must be "operated to the extent of its financial ability for those not able to pay for the services rendered and not exclusively for those who are able and expected to pay and must not . . . refuse to accept patients in need of hospital care who cannot pay for such services." United States of America's Objections to the Report and Recommendation (Doc. No. 59), p. 5 (internal quotations omitted). However, Revenue Ruling 69–545 states, "In the general law of charity, the promotion of health is considered to be a charitable purpose." Revenue Ruling 69–545, 1969–2 C.B. 117, 118 (1969). The ruling does go on to say that more is required to be tax-exempt under 501(c)(3), but the promotion of health is clearly a charitable purpose.

The government also overlooks the final paragraph of 69–545, which expressly removes the requirement of giving care to patients without charge or at rates below cost. The government relies on this requirement as stated in Revenue Ruling 56–185, but this paragraph in 69–545 even cites that prior ruling when removing that requirement. There is therefore absolutely no issue as to whether St. David's has a charitable purpose, and any argument to the contrary appears at least mildly disingenuous.

Admittedly, the government has cited another court's opinion that 69–545 did not overrule 56–185, but merely provided an alternative test for determining tax-exempt status. See Eastern Kentucky Welfare Rights Org. v. Simon, 506 F.2d 1278, 1290 (D.C.Cir.1974). However, there are at least two problems with this statement as related to this case. First, 69–545, if it is merely an alternative test, it is far more relevant to this case than the 56–185 test because it is undisputed that St. David's has a generally accessible emergency room as required by the 69–545 test. The requirement of providing free or belowcost care is removed in specifically such a case, if not in others also. Second, it is difficult to view 69–545 as anything but an overruling of 56185 when the later ruling says that "56–185 is hereby modified . . ."

* * *

[T]he parties' dispute can be resolved by answering these two overlapping questions: First, is St. David's operated exclusively for charity, meaning that only insubstantial portions of its activities benefit private, nonexempt purposes? Second, is it operated for the community interest and not for a private interest, specifically, HCA? This is consistent with what was conveyed to St.

David's by the government when it revoked the tax-exempt status. See quotation in Factual Background portion of this Order, p. 2, supra.

As is often the case with statutes and regulations, these are but a starting point. They only begin to take a more definite shape after they have been applied to facts. Fortunately, these regulations have been applied to countless factual situations, and these situations guide the Court's decision. Revenue Ruling 69–545,[7] 1969–2 C.B. 117, is a seminal application of these regulations and is especially relevant to the facts in this case since it involves a similar hospital. It lists several important characteristics of a hospital, imaginatively referred to as "Hospital A," that now comprise what is referred to as the "community benefit" standard. The Court will list these characteristics in the order they appear in the Revenue Ruling, which is not indicative of relative importance.

First, Hospital A has a board of trustees comprised of "prominent citizens in the community." Second, all qualified physicians in the area have medical staff privileges, as the size and nature of its facility allows. Third, Hospital A operates an emergency room that does not deny treatment to anyone requiring emergency care. However, non-emergency care is given only to those who can pay for it, either themselves or via a third party. Those who cannot pay are referred to another hospital in the community that will serve them. Hospital A typically takes in more money than it spends, and that money is applied to expansion and replacement of existing facilities, etc. Finally, and most importantly, this Revenue Ruling holds that Hospital A is exempt from paying federal income taxes.

Having gotten past all of the detached rules and standards governing this case, there appear to the Court two things causing the government to revoke St. David's tax-exempt status. First, the government claims that St. David's is not controlled by a community board. Second, the government claims that HCA receives an impermissible private benefit.

## A. Community Board

In Revenue Ruling 69545, Hospital A had a community board, and this became a part of the community benefit standard. However, there is some dispute as to whether a community board is an absolute requirement, or just one point in favor of tax-exemption. Furthermore, there is some dispute as to what constitutes a community board. In this case, half of St. David's Board of Governors (the Board) is appointed by St. David's, and half by HCA.

### 1. Does the Community Benefit Standard Absolutely Require a Community Board?

The Court finds that, as a matter of law, the presence of a community board is a point in favor of exemption, but is not an absolute requirement for exemption. Going back to the original source of the community benefit standard, Revenue Ruling 69–545 never states that any one factor is an absolute requirement for exemption. Indeed, it lists several of the factors repeated here, then states, "These factors *indicate* that the use and control of Hospital A are for the benefit of the public . . ." Rev. Rul. 69–545, 19692 C.B.

---

**7.** This Court is not bound by this Revenue Ruling. However, the Court joins several others in finding that it is a correct and persuasive application of the law.

at 118 (emphasis added). This language suggests that the prongs of the community benefit standard are major factors but also that the absence of one is not absolutely dispositive of the question.

This finding is supported by other applications of the community benefit standard. The Court discussed Sound Health in which the HMO's board was made up of prominent members of the community, but they were selected only from the members of the HMO and in which the board was comprised of owners and was not selected from the community at large.

The government paints itself into a corner with its arguments in its response to the Magistrate's Report and Recommendation. It cites Revenue Ruling 83157, which held that a hospital that was identical to 69–545's Hospital A in every respect except for the fact that it had no emergency room. 83–157 held that this hospital was tax-exempt in spite of its lack of a generally accessible emergency room because a state agency determined that such an emergency room would unnecessarily duplicate other services provided in the community. The government actually writes that the Internal Revenue Service will "weigh all of the facts and circumstances" and the "absence of particular factors . . . or the presence of other factors will not necessarily be determinative. [ ]

The government later refers to the community benefit standard as "somewhat flexible," stating that "a core ingredient like control vested in a community board may not be omitted unless the presence of other factors render that ingredient unnecessary. Thus, by the government's own implicit admission, the individual factors of the community benefit standard laid out in 69–545 are not absolute requirements.

The government attempts to rely on Redlands Surgical Services, Inc. v. Commissioner, 113 T.C. 47 (1999), in which the Tax Court held that Redlands was not tax exempt. However, the facts of that case are only vaguely similar to this case. In *Redlands,* the surgery center deemed nonexempt operated no emergency room and provided no free care to indigents. As quoted by the government, the Tax Court stated that the surgery center was "largely unfettered by charitable objectives." Id., 113 T.C. at 92. As described fully below, the structure of this partnership precludes any genuine argument that St. David's is "unfettered by charitable objectives."

2. *Is St. David's Run by a Community Board?*

Even if a community board is an absolute requirement for 501(c)(3) tax exemption, St. David's Board satisfies the requirement. Although exactly half of the members are appointed by a for-profit entity, the purpose of a community board is more complex than giving wealthy self-styled philanthropists something to do on the rare occasion that they are not playing golf. The purpose of the community board is to ensure that the community's interests are given precedence over any private interests. Thus, if a board is structured to ensure such protection, it is clearly a community board.

The error of the government's position in arguing that St. David's board is not a community board is that it counts possible votes and discovers that members appointed by a nonprofit entity can only tie the members appointed by a for-profit entity, and then end the inquiry. Looking further reveals exceptional protections against running this hospital in pursuit of private interests. The partnership contract requires that all hospitals owned by the partnership operate in accord with the community benefit standard. Should the hospitals fail to meet that standard, St. David's has the unilateral right to dissolve the partnership. The chairmen's seat is reserved for a member appointed by St. David's and therefore great control over the board's agenda is exercised by St. David's. Even the day-to-day operations of the partnership are disproportionately impacted by the nonprofit entity, because St. David's has the power to unilaterally remove the Chief Executive Officer.

Voting strength is more than just a numbers game, and these provisions clearly protect the nonprofit, charitable pursuits as well as any community board could. The government seems focused on majority control, but the law is more concerned with control, regardless of whether its control springs from a majority or from a corporate structure. Even if it were slightly ambiguous as to whether the board was structured to protect the charitable purpose of the organization, the other factors from the community benefit standard are met with such overwhelming force as to carry the day for St. David's. Every hospital owned by the partnership provides emergency care without regard to the patient's ability to pay.

The government attempts to quibble about how St. David's differentiates between free care that is charity and free care that is bad debt. The Court thinks that is a silly and meaningless distinction for purposes of this case. When all who need emergency care are treated regardless of willingness or ability to pay, the function is charitable regardless of what the accountants discover later. The government uses the alleged fact that St. David's attempts to collect payment from all patients before determining whether the care rendered was charity care or bad debt to show that St. David's actually provides no charity care. This implicitly attempts to require St. David's to determine before rendering care whether to expect payment from that particular patient, a luxury allowed only to those privileged to live in a bubble constructed by theories without the rude pin prick of practicality that so frequently bursts such bubbles. Not surprisingly, the IRS offers no method by which that determination could be made, perhaps it could be based on skin color, the brand name of clothes worn by the patient upon entering the emergency room, or shaking a magic eight ball.

The IRS states that "a hospital does not dispense charity care merely because some of its patients fail to pay for the services rendered." [ ] While the Court will not argue with that as a general proposition, this does not preclude attempts at collecting payment before determining the care to be charitable. Knowing that the hospital will not be compensated for much of the care rendered can be sufficient even if it cannot predetermine which patients can pay and which cannot pay. When a hospital operates a generally accessible emergency room, it knows that it will not be paid for much of the care rendered. The statement cited by the IRS is more applicable to nonemergency care.

### B. *Private Benefit to HCA*

The IRS crystallizes the issue and governing standards for a private benefit in Objections to the Report and Recommendation (Doc. No. 59). The Court agrees that not all joint ventures between nonprofit and for-profit organizations are either per se exempt or per se nonexempt. Other factors must be considered. The standard under the operational test was set out in *Redlands,* and it focuses on control of the organization. The *Redlands* court stated,

> "To the extent that petitioner cedes control over its sole activity to forprofit parties having an independent economic interest in the same activity and *having no obligation to put charitable purposes ahead of profitmaking objectives,* petitioner cannot be assured that the partnerships will in fact be operated in furtherance of charitable purposes. In such a circumstance, we are led to the conclusion that petitioner is not operated exclusively for charitable purposes."

Redlands Surgical Services, Inc. v. Commission, 113 T.C. at 78 (1999) (emphasis added). Since the IRS accepts this as the governing law, the Court will use it for purposes of this case without deciding whether it is in fact the governing standard.

As discussed in detail above, it is difficult to imagine a corporate structure more protective of an organization's charitable purpose than the one at issue in this case. The purpose stated in Section 3.2 of the Partnership Agreement make the purpose clear, and the voting rules and rights of the nonprofit partner prevent any usurpation of that purpose by HCA. The government essentially argues that these protections are all basically irrelevant, but the truth of the matter is that St. David's has the power to ensure that the manager and CEO are to its liking. That, among other protections discussed above gives the nonprofit partner substantially more control than the for-profit partner, despite the facial 50–50 split in voting rights on the Board of Governors.

Upon application of all of these legal tests and standards to the undisputed facts of this case, it is clear that St. David's was exempt from federal income taxes under 501(c)(3) for the tax year 1996 as a matter of law, and therefore summary judgment must be granted.

## *Notes and Questions*

1. What factors distinguish the St. David's Health Care System whole hospital joint venture from the partnership arrangements in the Redland's Surgical Services case? Do the absence of an emergency room and the provision of free care to indigent patients distinguish the two cases sufficiently? Compare the two cases and Revenue Ruling 98–15 on the issue of control. See David M. Flynn & Duane Morris, St. David's Health Care System v. United States: District Court in Texas Rejects IRS "Whole Hospital" Joint Venture Positions, 15 Health Lawyer 45 (Sept. 2002)(" the St. David's case reduces, and may eliminate, concerns that the failure of an exempt participant to retain voting control over the management of a joint venture with a for-profit entity will be fatal to its exempt status so long as it retains other enforceable legal rights in the joint venture agreements permitting it to insure that the joint venture's activities will be consistent with and further its exempt purposes. This conclusion also appears to be consistent with the Tax Court's analysis in *Redlands*.")

2. Is the court correct in characterizing the distinction between charity care and bad debt as "silly and meaningless"? How would failure to distinguish the two concepts affect the incentives facing charitable institutions?

## E. RELATIONSHIPS BETWEEN PHYSICIANS AND TAX-EXEMPT HEALTH CARE ORGANIZATIONS

### 3. *Acquisition of Physician Practices by Exempt Organizations*

**Add, at p. 940, immediately before Problem: St. Andrew's Medical Center:**

*Caracci v. Commissioner.* Caracci v. Commissioner, 118 T.C. 379 (2002) is the first judicial opinion applying the intermediate sanctions provisions of the Internal Revenue Code. The Caracci family had operated their tax-exempt home health businesses, known as the Sta–Home Health Agency, very much as a family business. Family members were the sole members of the board of each of the tax exempt entities and also held all key employment positions. For these services, the Caracci family paid themselves what the tax court characterized as "executive level" compensation. After experiencing operating losses for three years, and facing the prospect that Medicare, the principal payer for Sta–Home patients, would shift from cost reimbursement to prospective payment, the Caracci's undertook to convert the entities to for-profit status by selling their assets to three S corporations which were controlled and operated by the Caracci family. Concluding that the S corporations paid inadequate consideration for the assets of the tax exempt entities, the Service asserted that the transaction resulted in an excess benefit transaction under § 4958 and sought to impose four items of relief:

1. A first tier (25%) and second tier (200%) excise tax on the Caracci family and the S corporations as "disqualified persons";

2. Organizational manager excise taxes (10% on family members who were directors and officers of the tax exempt entities);

3. Revocation of tax exempt status of the tax exempt entities (each of which remained in existence as shell corporations after the sale); and

4. Income tax on three Caracci family members because their S corporation shares became more valuable as a result of the bargain purchase of the assets of the tax exempt entities

In a 71–page opinion the Tax Court upheld the IRS's assessment of excise taxes but rejected revocation of the Sta–Home entities' tax exempt status. It also concluded that the total excess benefit to the disqualified persons was approximately $5 million. Several important lessons emerge from the court's holdings.

*Valuation.* Although the Caracci's tax advisor rendered an opinion at the time of the transaction and the family later obtained an appraisal from an expert appraiser with greater experience, the Tax Court sided with the Internal Revenue Service. Although the Sta–Home entities had lost money and had a negative cash flow, the court refused to conclude the entity was worthless, finding instead that the entities' intangible assets had considerable value. In addition, the Tax Court was influenced by the lack of objective contemporaneous evaluations and that fact that the entities themselves had no separate independent professional representation.

*Organizational Manager Tax.* Even though the Caracci family did not perform a thorough job in conducting the conversion, the IRS abandoned its claim for an organizational manager tax. The opinion, however, was rendered before the IRS issued its Final Regulations. See Treas. Reg. § 53.4958–1(d).

Nevertheless, the outcome may suggest that organizational managers will be subject to discipline only where serious derelictions occur.

*Revocation of Tax Exempt Status.* Although the sale stripped the tax-exempt entities of all their assets and those entities had long been inactive, the court refused to revoke their exemption under § 501(c)(3). The opinion implies that a single wrong is not sufficient to justify revocation of tax exempt status. Relying on the legislative history of § 4958, the court indicated that correction (e.g., by the return of property) would be the preferred remedy for excess benefit transactions.

*Imposition of first-tier and second-tier excise taxes.* The court imposed both first-tier and second-tier taxes jointly and severally on the disqualified persons. Because they had not yet corrected the transaction, no abatement was allowed.

The Opinion is noteworthy particularly because the Service had a strong case for revocation yet revocation was rejected by the court. The fact that only a single transaction was involved seemed dispositive. For a thorough analysis of this case, see James R. King, & David S. Boyce, Revocation of Tax–Exempt Status, Excise Taxes and Other Intermediate Sanctions Issues, Plus Income Taxes: How the Rules Have Changed after Caracci v. Commissioner, 36 J.H.Law 1 (2003).

# Chapter 14

# FRAUD AND ABUSE

## I. FALSE CLAIMS

### A. GOVERNMENTAL ENFORCEMENT

**Add, at p. 958, end of Note 9:**

The Office of Inspector General claims to have saved $21 billion in fiscal year 2002 based on estimates of audit disallowances, reduced costs resulting from IG recommendations, and the imposition of monetary penalties. Dep't. of Health and Human Services, Office of Inspector Gen., Semiannual Report to the Congress (Apr.–Sept. 2002) available at: www.oig.hhs.gov/publications/semiannual.html. The largest contribution came from the $875 million settlement with TAP Pharmaceutical Products resolving allegations that the company illegally marketed its prostate cancer drug Lupron. (Among the practices alleged were payments in various forms including travel, entertainment, debt forgiveness, consulting services, televisions, VCRs and free samples given to prescribing physicians and HMOs). See Kathleen McDermott, The Aftermath of United States v. TAP Pharmaceuticals, 6 Health Lawyers News 4 (April, 2002). Another notable target was one of the Medicare program's own carriers, General American Life Insurance Inc., which paid $76 million to resolve allegations that it had improperly handled claims and quality assurance reporting to maintain its high performance ratings.

**At p. 961, delete note 2 and insert at p. 962 after Note 5:**

### UNITED STATES EX REL. MIKES v. STRAUS

United States Court of Appeals, Second Circuit, 2001.
274 F.3d 687.

CARDAMONE, CIRCUIT JUDGE.

On this appeal we review a complaint asserting violations of the False Claims Act (Act) [ ] brought by a plaintiff employee against her former employers, who are health care providers. The appeal raises issues of first impression in this Circuit concerning the applicability of medical standards of care to the Act.

\* \* \*

## BACKGROUND

### A. Facts

In 1991 defendants Dr. Marc J. Straus, Dr. Jeffrey Ambinder and Dr. Eliot L. Friedman, physicians specializing in oncology and hematology, formed a partnership called Pulmonary and Critical Care Associates to extend their practice to include pulmonology, the branch of medicine covering the lungs and related breathing functions. In July of that year defendants hired plaintiff Dr. Patricia S. Mikes, a board-certified pulmonologist, to provide pulmonary and critical care services in defendants' offices in Westchester and Putnam Counties, New York. In September 1991 Mikes discussed with Dr. Straus her concerns relating to spirometry tests being performed in defendants' offices. Three months later, plaintiff was fired.

The parties dispute the reason for Mikes' termination. Plaintiff says she was fired because she questioned how defendants conducted their medical practice. Defendants declare that Mikes' employment agreement provided she was terminable-at-will, and that plaintiff had difficulty procuring privileges at area hospitals.

On April 16, 1992 Mikes commenced the instant litigation against defendants in the United States District Court for the Southern District of New York, asserting not only causes of action for retaliatory discharge and unlawfully withheld wages, but also a *qui tam* suit under the False Claims Act. She served the complaint on the United States Attorney who, on April 19, 1993, notified the district court that it declined its statutory right to substitute for Mikes in the prosecution of this litigation. [ ]

### B. Prior Proceedings

Plaintiff's *qui tam* cause of action under the Act alleged that defendants had submitted false reimbursement requests to the federal government for spirometry services. Plaintiff contended that defendants' failure to calibrate the spirometers rendered the results so unreliable as to be "false" under the Act. In addition, Mikes averred that spirometry is an eligible service under the Medicare statute, and that defendants submitted Medicare claims for reimbursement during the period relevant to this dispute—now said to be 1034 claims from 1986 through 1993—for a total Medicare payout of $28,922.89.

After the government declined to take over as plaintiff, Mikes served defendants with her complaint on December 22, 1993. [After the initial complaint was dismissed, Mikes filed an amended complaint which added the claim that that defendants improperly received Medicare reimbursement for referrals to Magnetic Resonance Imaging (MRI) facilities in which they held a financial interest which violated the anti-kickback provision of the Medicare statute and also violated the False Claims Act. Eventually the district court granted summary judgment in favor of defendants and, finding the MRI claim vexatious, awarded attorneys fees to defendants.]

### C. Spirometry

Before turning to a discussion of the law, it will be helpful to define spirometry—a subject that lies at the heart of this case—and plaintiff's allegations regarding defendants' performance of this diagnostic test. Spirometry is an easy-to-perform pulmonary function test used by doctors to detect both obstructive (such as asthma and emphysema) and restrictive (such as pulmonary fibrosis) lung diseases. The type of spirometers used by defendants measures the pressure change when a patient blows into a mouthpiece, thereby providing the doctor with on-the-spot analysis of the volume and speed by which patients can exhale. The spirometry equipment consists of readily transportable lightweight machines, and defendants apparently used at least one in each of their several offices.

Plaintiff's expert stated that spirometers are susceptible to inaccuracy through time and usage because they become clogged, causing false readings. Erroneous measurements may also arise from damage to the instrument through cleaning or disturbance during transport, or from variations in barometric pressure, temperature or humidity. Mikes claims that guidelines ... published by the American Thoracic Society (ATS guidelines), [which] set out the generally accepted standards for spirometry ... recommend daily calibration of spirometers ... Mikes maintains further that defendants' performance of spirometry did not conform to the ATS guidelines and thus would yield inherently unreliable data. She argues that defendants allowed medical assistants to perform spirometry tests when they were not trained in its proper administration. ...

Defendants insist that after plaintiff raised her concerns regarding the spirometer and its use in their practice, they told her to review exam results for inaccuracy, and to train the medical assistants in proper spirometric administration. Dr. Straus reports that plaintiff did not apprise the practice of any false readings in response to this directive, nor did she supervise the medical assistants. With this factual background, we turn to the law.

DISCUSSION

\* \* \*

*II. "Legally False" Certification Theory*

The thrust of plaintiff's *qui tam* suit is that the submission of Medicare reimbursement claims for spirometry procedures not performed in accordance with the relevant standard of care, that is, the ATS Guidelines—violates the False Claims Act. Mikes relies principally on the "certification theory" of liability, which is predicated upon a false representation of compliance with a federal statute or regulation or a prescribed contractual term. See Lisa Michelle Phelps, Note, Calling Off the Bounty Hunters: Discrediting the Use of Alleged Anti–Kickback Violations to Support Civil False Claims Actions, 51 Vand. L. Rev. 1003, 1014–15 (1998). This theory has also been called "legally false" certification. [ ] It differs from "factually false" certification, which involves an incorrect description of goods or services provided or a request for reimbursement for goods or services never provided.

Although the False Claims Act is "not designed to reach every kind of fraud practiced on the Government," United States v. McNinch, 356 U.S. at 599, 78 S.Ct. 950, it was intended to embrace at least some claims that suffer from legal falsehood. Thus, "a false claim may take many forms, the most common being a claim for goods or services not provided, or *provided in violation of contract terms, specification, statute, or regulation.*" S. Rep. No. 99–345, at 9, *reprinted in* 1986 U.S.C.C.A.N. 5266, 5274 (emphasis added).

Just as clearly, a claim for reimbursement made to the government is not legally false simply because the particular service furnished failed to comply with the mandates of a statute, regulation or contractual term that is only tangential to the service for which reimbursement is sought. Since the Act is restitutionary and aimed at retrieving ill-begotten funds, it would be anomalous to find liability when the alleged noncompliance would not have influenced the government's decision to pay. Accordingly, while the Act is "intended to reach all types of fraud, without qualification, that might result in financial loss to the Government,"[ ] it does not encompass those instances of regulatory noncompliance that are irrelevant to the government's disbursement decisions.

We join the Fourth, Fifth, Ninth, and District of Columbia Circuits in ruling that a claim under the Act is legally false only where a party certifies compliance with a statute or regulation as a condition to governmental payment. See United States ex rel. Siewick v. Jamieson Sci. & Eng'g, Inc., 214 F.3d 1372, 1376 (D.C.Cir.2000) ("[A] false certification of compliance with a statute or regulation cannot serve as the basis for a *qui tam* action under the [False Claims Act] unless payment is conditioned on that certification."); Harrison, 176 F.3d at 786–87, 793; United States ex rel. Thompson v. Columbia/HCA Healthcare Corp., 125 F.3d 899, 902 (5th Cir.1997); United States ex rel. Hopper v. Anton, 91 F.3d 1261, 1266–67 (9th Cir.1996).

We add that although materiality is a related concept, our holding is distinct from a requirement imposed by some courts that a false statement or claim must be material to the government's funding decision.[ ] A materiality requirement holds that only a subset of admittedly false claims is subject to False Claims Act liability.... We rule simply that not all instances of regulatory noncompliance will cause a claim to become false. We need not and do not address whether the Act contains a separate materiality requirement.

### A. *Express False Certification*

We analyze first plaintiff's argument that defendants' claims contained an express false certification. An expressly false claim is, as the term suggests, a claim that falsely certifies compliance with a particular statute, regulation or contractual term, where compliance is a prerequisite to payment.

Plaintiff contends that by submitting claims for Medicare reimbursement on HCFA–1500 forms or their electronic equivalent, defendants expressly certified that they would comply with the terms set out on the form. Form HCFA–1500 expressly says: "I certify that the services shown on this form were medically indicated and necessary for the health of the patient and were personally furnished by me or were furnished incident to my professional service by my employee under my immediate personal supervision." Both the form, which further provides "No Part B Medicare benefits may be paid unless this form is received as required by existing law and regulations," and the Medicare Regulations, see 42 C.F.R. § 424.32, state that certification is a precondition to Medicare reimbursement. We agree that defendants certified they would comply with the terms on the form and that such compliance was a precondition of governmental payment. Cf. United States ex rel. Piacentile v. Wolk, Civ.A.No. 93–5773, 1995 WL 20833, at *2–*3 (E.D.Pa. Jan.17, 1995) (finding False Claims Act violation where defendant altered Medicare Certificates of Medical Necessity without doctor's authorization, because the forms contained a certification that the claims represented the physician's judgment).

Yet plaintiff's objections to defendants' spirometry tests do not implicate the standard set out in the HCFA–1500 form that the procedure was dictated by "medical necessity." The term "medical necessity" does not impart a qualitative element mandating a particular standard of medical care, and Mikes does not point to any legal authority requiring us to read such a mandate into the form. Medical necessity ordinarily indicates the level—not the quality—of the service. * * *

This approach to the phrase "medically necessary"—as applying to *ex ante* coverage decisions but not *ex post* critiques of how providers executed a procedure—would also conform to our understanding of the phrase "reasonable and necessary" as used in the Medicare statute, 42 U.S.C. § 1395y(a)(1)(A) (1994) (disallowing payment for items or services not reasonable and necessary for diagnosis or treatment). * * *

Moreover, the section of the Medicare statute setting forth conditions of participation has separate provisions governing the medical necessity of a given procedure and its quality. [ ]This statutory design supports the conclusion that the medical necessity for a procedure and its quality are distinct considerations.

Inasmuch as Mikes challenges only the quality of defendants' spirometry tests and not the decisions to order this procedure for patients, she fails to support her contention that the tests were not medically necessary. ... Thus, plaintiff's cause of action insofar as it is founded on express false certification is without merit.

### B. *Implied False Certification*

#### 1. *Viability of Implied Certification Theory*

Plaintiff insists that defendants' submissions to the government for payment were impliedly false certifications. An implied false certification claim is based on the notion that the act of submitting a claim for reimbursement itself implies compliance with governing federal rules that are a precondition to payment. See Phelps, supra, at 1015. Foundational support for the implied false certification theory may be found in Congress' expressly stated purpose that the Act include at least some kinds of legally false claims, see S. Rep. No. 99–345, at 9, *reprinted in* 1986 U.S.C.C.A.N. 5266, 5274, and in the Supreme Court's admonition that the Act intends to reach all forms of fraud that might cause financial loss to the government, see Neifert–White Co., 390 U.S. at 232, 88 S.Ct. 959.

* * *

But caution should be exercised not to read this theory expansively and out of context. The Ab–Tech rationale, for example, does not fit comfortably into the health care context because the False Claims Act was not designed for use as a blunt instrument to enforce compliance with all medical regulations—but rather only those regulations that are a precondition to payment—and to construe the impliedly false certification theory in an expansive fashion would improperly broaden the Act's reach. Moreover, a limited application of implied certification in the health care field reconciles, on the one hand, the need to enforce the Medicare statute with, on the other hand, the active role actors outside the federal government play in assuring that appropriate standards of medical care are met. Interests of federalism counsel that "the regulation of health and safety matters is primarily, and historically, a matter of local concern." Hillsborough County v. Automated Med. Labs., Inc., 471 U.S. 707, 719, 105 S.Ct. 2371, 85 L.Ed.2d 714 (1985).

Moreover, permitting *qui tam* plaintiffs to assert that defendants' quality of care failed to meet medical standards would promote federalization of medical malpractice, as the federal government or the *qui tam* relator would replace the aggrieved patient as plaintiff.... For these reasons, we think a medical provider should be found to have implicitly certified compliance with a particular rule as a condition of reimbursement in limited circumstances. Specifically, implied false certification is appropriately applied only when the underlying statute or regulation upon which the plaintiff relies *expressly* states the provider must comply in order to be paid. See Siewick, 214 F.3d at 1376 (holding that court will "infer certification from silence" only when "certification was a prerequisite to the government action sought"). Liability under the Act may properly be found therefore when a defendant submits a claim for reimbursement while knowing—as that term is defined by the Act, see 31 U.S.C. § 3729(b)—that payment expressly is precluded because of some noncompliance by the defendant.

### 2. *Plaintiff's Allegations Under the Implied Theory*

Mikes asserts that compliance with § § 1395y(a)(1)(A) and 1320c–5(a) of the Medicare statute is a precondition to a request for federal funds and that submission of a HCFA–1500 form attests by implication to the providers' compliance with both of those provisions.

a. § 1395y(a)(1)(A). Section 1395y(a)(1)(A) of the Medicare statute states that "no payment may be made under [the Medicare statute] for any expenses incurred for items or services which ... are not *reasonable and necessary* for the diagnosis or treatment of illness or injury or to improve the functioning of a malformed body member." 42 U.S.C. § 1395y(a)(1)(A) (emphasis added). Because this section contains an express condition of payment—that is, "no payment may be made"—it explicitly links each Medicare *payment* to the requirement that the particular item or service be "reasonable and necessary." The Supreme Court has noted that this section precludes the government from reimbursing a Medicare provider who fails to comply.[ ] Since § 1395y(a)(1)(A) *expressly* prohibits payment if a provider fails to comply with its terms, defendants' submission of the claim forms implicitly certifies compliance with its provision.

Yet, Mikes' insistence that defendants' performance of spirometry was not reasonable and necessary is without support. As set forth in our discussion of express certification, the requirement that a service be reasonable and necessary generally pertains to the selection of the particular procedure and not to its performance. While such factors as the effectiveness and medical acceptance of a given procedure might determine whether it is reasonable and necessary, the failure of the procedure to conform to a particular standard of care ordinarily will not. [ ] Since plaintiff contends only that defendants' performance of spirometry was *qualitatively* deficient, her allegations that defendants falsely certified compliance with § 1395y(a)(1)(A) may not succeed.

b. § 1320c–5(a). Plaintiff's implied false certification claims rely more heavily upon § 1320c–5(a). That section does mandate a qualitative standard of care in that it provides

> It shall be the obligation of any health care practitioner ... who provides health care services for which payment may be made ... to assure, to the extent of his authority that services or items ordered or provided by such practitioner ...
>
> (1) will be provided economically and only when, and to the extent, medically necessary;
>
> (2) *will be of a quality which meets professionally recognized standards of health care;* and
>
> (3) will be supported by evidence of medical necessity and quality ... as may reasonably be required by a reviewing peer review organization in the exercise of its duties and responsibilities.

42 U.S.C. § 1320c–5(a) (emphasis added).

Mikes avers that the ATS guidelines comprise a "professionally recognized standard of health care" for spirometry, and that defendants' failure to conform to those guidelines violates the Medicare statute. She believes defendants, by submitting HCFA–1500 forms for spirometry tests that did not comply with the ATS guidelines, engaged in implied false certification. But plaintiff's allegations cannot establish liability under the False Claims Act because—unlike § 1395y(a)(1)(A)—the Medicare statute does not explicitly condition payment upon compliance with § 1320c–5(a).

Instead, § 1320c–5(a) simply states that "[i]t shall be the obligation" of a practitioner who provides a medical service "for which payment may be made ... to assure" compliance with the section. Hence, it may be seen that § 1320c–5(a) acts prospectively, setting forth obligations for a provider to be eligible to participate in the Medicare program.

* * *

The structure of the statute further informs us that § 1320c–5(a) establishes conditions of participation, rather than prerequisites to receiving reimbursement. The statute empowers peer review organizations to monitor providers' compliance with § 1320c–5(a). See 42 U.S.C. § 1320c–3(a) (1994). If a peer review organization determines that a provider has "failed in a substantial number of cases" to comply with the requirements of § 1320c–5(a) or that the provider has "grossly and flagrantly violated" the section, the organization may—after reasonable notice and an opportunity for corrective action— recommend sanctions. See id. § 1320c–5(b)(1) (1994 & Supp. V 1999). If the Secretary agrees that sanctions should be imposed, and further finds the provider unwilling or unable substantially to comply with its obligations, the Secretary may exclude the provider from the Medicare program. [ ]

The fact that § 1320c–5(b) permits sanctions for a failure to maintain an appropriate standard of care only where a dereliction occurred in "a substantial number of cases" or a violation was especially "gross[ ] and flagrant[ ]" makes it evident that the section is directed at the provider's continued eligibility in the Medicare program, rather than any individual incident of noncompliance. [ ] This conclusion is reinforced by the ultimate sanction provided by § 1320c–5(b)(1): exclusion of the provider from Medicare eligibility. Further, the section explicitly provides that the Secretary may authorize an alternate remedy—repayment of the cost of the noncompliant service to the United States—"as a condition to the continued eligibility" of the health care provider in the Medicare program. 42 U.S.C. § 1320c–5(b)(3). Accordingly, § 1320c–5(a) is quite plainly a condition of participation in the Medicare program.

Since § 1320c–5(a) does not expressly condition *payment* on compliance with its terms, defendants' certifications on the HCFA–1500 forms are not legally false. Consequently, defendants did not submit impliedly false claims by requesting reimbursement for spirometry tests that allegedly were not performed according to the recognized standards of health care.

Finally, our holding—that in submitting a Medicare reimbursement form, a defendant implicitly certifies compliance with § 1395y(a)(1)(A), but not § 1320c–5(a)—comports with Congress' purpose as discussed earlier in this opinion. Section 1395y(a)(1)(A) mandates that a provider's choice of procedures be "reasonable and necessary"; it does not obligate federal courts to step outside their primary area of competence and apply a qualitative standard measuring the efficacy of those procedures. The quality of care standard of § 1320c–5(a) is best enforced by those professionals most versed in the nuances of providing adequate health care.

### III. *Worthless Services Claim*

The government in its *amicus* brief and plaintiff at oral argument argue that the district court erred by not considering whether the defendants' submission of Medicare claims for substandard spirometry essentially constituted requests for the reimbursement of worthless services. An allegation that defendants violated the Act by submitting claims for worthless services is not predicated upon the false certification theory. Instead, a worthless services claim asserts that the knowing request of federal reimbursement for a procedure with no medical value violates the Act irrespective of any certification.

The Ninth Circuit's recent decision in United States ex rel. Lee v. SmithKline Beecham, Inc., 245 F.3d 1048 (9th Cir.2001), is the leading case on worthless services claims in the health care arena. In Lee, the relator alleged that defendant, an operator of regional clinical laboratories, falsified laboratory test data when test results fell outside the acceptable standard of error. Id. at 1050. The Ninth Circuit held that the false certification theory ... was only one form of action under the Act, and that the district court should have considered the distinct and separate worthless services claim. Lee, 245 F.3d at 1053. As the Ninth Circuit explained, "[i]n an appropriate case, knowingly billing for worthless services or recklessly doing so with deliberate ignorance may be actionable under § 3729 [of the False Claims Act], regardless of any false certification conduct." Id.

We agree that a worthless services claim is a distinct claim under the Act. It is effectively derivative of an allegation that a claim is factually false because it seeks reimbursement for a service not provided. In a worthless services claim, the performance of the service is so deficient that for all practical purposes it is the equivalent of no performance at all.

We nevertheless find no liability in the instant case because plaintiff makes no showing that defendants knowingly—as the Act defines that term—submitted a claim for the reimbursement of worthless services. We have adopted the Ninth Circuit's standard that the "requisite intent is the knowing presentation of what is known to be false" as opposed to negligence or innocent mistake. [ ]

Plaintiff fails to substantiate that defendants knew their Medicare claims for reimbursement were false. At best, plaintiff urges that defendants submitted Medicare claims knowing they did not conform to the ATS guidelines. This allegation alone fails to satisfy the standard for a worthless services claim. The notion of presenting a claim known to be false does not mean the claim is incorrect as a matter of proper accounting, but rather means it is a lie. *See id*. Defendants have presented such overwhelming evidence of their genuine belief that their use of spirometry had medical value, we conclude as a matter of law they did not submit their claims with the requisite scienter.

\* \* \*

Defendants have thus proffered ample evidence—most of which derives from disinterested non-party witnesses—supporting their contention that they held a good faith belief that their spirometry tests were of medical value. In light of this evidence, plaintiff's unsupported allegations to the contrary do not raise a triable issue of fact sufficient to bar summary judgment. [ ]

\* \* \*

### *Notes and Questions*

1. The *Mikes* opinion does not address the materiality of defendant's false claim. Consider the role materiality plays in the *Luckey* decision and evaluate whether plaintiffs should be required to prove that a false statement contained in a Medicare cost report would have affected the likelihood of payment. See United States v. Intervest Corp., 67 F.Supp.2d 637 (S.D.Miss.1999) (false statements about safe and sanitary conditions of housing units not material where government agency engaged in a pattern of making payments despite receiving reports of unsatisfactory conditions). An excellent analysis of the interrelationship of materiality and causation issues in the false certification cases is found in Joan H. Krause, Health Care Providers and the Public Fisc: Paradigms of Government Harm Under the Civil False Claims Act, 36 Ga.L. Rev. 121 (2001). Some courts have begun to question whether a qui tam action under the False Claims Act can ever lie where the alleged fraud rests on a violation of the anti-kickback law. See, e.g., United States ex rel. Barmak v. Sutter Corp., 2002 WL 987109 (S.D.N.Y. 2002) (citing Mikes and noting that the anti-kickback statute is a criminal statute that does not grant a private cause of action). But see United States ex rel. Pogue v. Diabetes Treatment Ctrs. of Am., Inc., 238 F.Supp.2d 258 (D.D.C.2002) (characterizing Mikes as the "most parsimonious application of the implied certification theory" and finding that the case law does not reject the theory).

2. Critics of doctrinal developments in false claims litigation have pointed to adverse effects on consumers and health care delivery. See Dayna Bowen Mat-

thew, An Economic Model to Analyze the Impact of the False Claims Act on Access to Healthcare for the Elderly, Disabled, Rural and Inner–City Poor, 27 Am. J.L. & Med. 439 (2001) (use by government and qui tam plaintiffs of false certification claims to fight against fraud is likely to have a disproportionately negative impact on the availability of healthcare to the poor); Joan H. Krause, "Promises to Keep": Health Care Providers and the Civil False Claims Act, 23 Cardozo L. Rev. 1363 (2002) (magnitude of penalties and imprecisely-defined concept of abuse may result in unchecked prosecutorial discretion which may expand the FCA to encompass legitimate transactions); Health Care Providers and the Public Fisc: Paradigms of Government Harm Under the Civil False Claims Act, 36 Ga.L.Rev. 121 (2001) ( False Claims Act is not applied to the health care industry in a manner consistent with either the law's own jurisprudence or current health care regulatory policy); Patrick Hooper, It's Time to Tone Down Rhetoric in "War" Against Fraud, 4 Health Care Fraud Rep. (BNA) 307 (2000) ("[t]he current health care environment is not unlike the politically charged investigations of other periods of our history"). On the broad discovery powers conferred on local U.S. Attorneys by the investigative subpoenas authorized by the Health Insurance and Portability and Accountability Act of 1996, see Paul W. Shaw & Stephanie Taverna Siden, Judicial Recognition and Enforcement of HIPAA Subpoenas, 14 The Health Lawyer 10 (June 2002).

### Add, at p. 963, end of carryover paragraph:

In the ongoing litigation against Columbia/HCA, the District Court for the District of Columbia held that a corporation may be liable under the False Claims Act for the acts of its employees or agents, even if the corporation receives no benefit from the fraudulent activity. The court based its departure from precedent by explaining that amendments to the False Claims Act in 1986 undermined the reasoning of earlier cases. United States ex rel. McCready v. Columbia/HCA Healthcare Corp., __ F.Supp.2d __, __, 2003 WL 912738, at *3 (D.D.C.2003) (corporation liable under FCA if employees are acting within the scope of their employment and to benefit the corporation).

## B. QUI TAM ACTIONS

### Add, at p. 965, end of Note 3:

The Fifth Circuit, sitting en banc, has reversed the panel decision in *Riley*, cited in the text, finding no violation of the Appointments Clause or other constitutional infirmities in qui tam litigation. *Riley*, 252 F.3d at 757–58.

In Cook County, Ill. v. United States ex rel. Chandler, __ U.S. __, 123 S.Ct. 1239, 155 L.Ed.2d 247 (2003), the Supreme Court held that local governments are "persons" subject to qui tam or whistleblower actions under the False Claims Act . Concluding that the increase from double to treble damages by the False Claims Amendments Act of 1986 served remedial purposes in addition to punitive objectives, the Court distinguished Vermont Agency, which had relied in part on the punitive character of damages provisions to hold that states were not persons subject to qui tam suits under the False Claims Act. Id. at 1242.

### Add, at p. 966, at end of Note 4:

Qui tam relators have been instrumental in uncovering fraudulent and erroneous billing practices. For example, dozens of hospitals have settled upcoding cases brought by Health Outcomes Technologies, Inc. as a qui tam relator involving alleged practices of assigning inaccurate DRG codes to patient discharges as a way to obtain higher federal reimbursements. See Tenet Announces Payment of $4.2 Million For Upcoding Allegations by Five Hospitals, 12 Health L. Rep. (BNA) at 231 (Feb. 13, 2003) (reporting $4.2 million settlement by Tenet Healthcare and settlements of dozens of claims involving upcoding of pneumonia DRGs). Qui tam relators have also gone after hospitals, including some prestigious academic medical centers that have allegedly defrauded Medicare by charging for millions of dollars worth of procedures involving experimental cardiac devices that were not properly reimbursable. DOJ Intervenes in FCA Case Against Duke, 11 Health L. Rep. (BNA) at 640 (May 2, 2002).

## II. MEDICARE AND MEDICAID FRAUD AND ABUSE

### E. STATUTORY EXCEPTIONS, SAFE HARBORS AND FRAUD ALERTS

**Add, at p. 987, immediately after carry-over paragraph:**

*Group Practices.* A safe harbor shelters payments (such as dividend or interest income) received in return for investment interests in group practices. 42 C.F.R. § 1001.952(p). It covers business arrangements having centralized decision-making, pooled expenses and revenues, and profit distribution systems "not based on satellite offices operating substantially as if they were separate enterprises or profit centers." Modeled on the Stark exception, it adopts that statute's definition of "group practice" and provides that income from ancillary services must meet the Stark definition of "in-office ancillary services."

*Specialty Services.* Another safe harbor protects specialty service referral agreements pursuant to which one party agrees to refer patients to the other party for the provision of specialty services in return for an agreement to refer that patient back provided the referral is medically appropriate, there is no payment between the parties or sharing or splitting of a global fee, and the only exchange of value between the parties is the remuneration they receive from third party payors or the patient for the services rendered. 42 C.F.R. § 1001.952(s).

**Add, at p. 992, after Note 3:**

The OIG issued 42 advisory opinions between January 1, 2001 and February 2003. Dep't of Health and Human Services, Office of Attorney Gen., Advisory Opinions, available at www.oig.hhs.gov/fraud/advisoryopinions/opinions.html. These opinions usually conclude that the proposed conduct falls within a safe harbor, can be undertaken with certain qualifications, or find prohibited remuneration but decline to subject the requester to sanctions. Some address "white hat" issues that may involve prohibited remuneration but are deemed not to present significant risk to Medicare program objectives See, e.g., Advisory Opinion No. 01–19 (Nov. 14, 2001) available at: www.oig.hhs.gov/fraud/docs/advisoryopinions/2001/ao01–19.pdf (involving a donation of free office space to an entity that provides free end-of-life services to patients with terminal illnesses). Although the vast majority of advisory opinions address whether a violation of the anti-kickback statute is present, a few discuss possible inducements to reduce or limit services. Waivers of co-payment are among the most frequently topics addressed, followed by proposed donations (including restocking of ambulance supplies) and joint ventures. In two recent opinions, the OIG indicated that the proposed conduct raised problems:

In Advisory Opinion No. 03–5 (Feb. 6, 2003) available, at: www.oig.hhs.gov/fraud/docs/advisoryopinions/2003/ao0305.pdf, the OIG disapproved an arrangement involving joint ownership of an ambulatory surgery center ("ASC") by a hospital and a multi-specialty physician group. In its assessment of the proposed arrangement, the OIG determined that: (a) the parties did not meet the ASC safe harbor because a number of physicians in the physician group did not intend to perform any procedures at the ASC; and (b) members of the physician group that do not perform surgeries as part of their practice would be in a position to benefit from referrals to the ASC, leading to an incentive for these physicians to refer to the ASC.

In another instance, the OIG's letter found an arrangement between a hospice and a nursing home may involve prohibited remuneration and subject the requester to sanctions. Advisory Opinion No.01–20 (Nov. 14, 2001) available at: www.oig.gov/fraud/docs/advisoryopinions/2001/ao01-20.pdf. The proposal involved a payment arrangement between a Medicare-certified hospice and certain nursing facilities for services provided to residents of such facilities who are eligible both for Medicaid and Medicare hospice benefits ("Dually Eligibles"). The hospice would pay the nursing facilities the full Medicaid nursing facility per diem rate for non-hospice patients, which covers pharmacy services, plus a separate payment for drugs used by Dually Eligibles in connection with their terminal illness.

**Add, at p. 992, before Problem:**

### *Note: Staff Privileges as Illegal Remuneration?*

Pursuant to a provision in HIPAA mandating that HHS annually solicit and consider proposals for new or modified safe harbor provisions under the anti-kickback statute, the American Medical Association requested guidance regarding the legality of certain practices in connection with the granting of hospital staff privileges. According to the AMA, an increasing number of hospitals are refusing to grant staff privileges to physicians who (1) own or have other financial interests in, or leadership positions with, competing healthcare entities, (2) refer to competing health care entities, or (3) fail to admit some specified percentage of their patients to the hospital. In response, the OIG issued a notice soliciting public comment on the following issues:

A. Are hospital staff privileges "remuneration"? ... What effect, if any [does the increased importance of managed care contracting] have on the determination whether staff privileges are remuneration? ... Under what circumstances do staff privileges have monetary value?

B. What are the implications of a hospital's denial of privileges to a physician who competes with the hospital? [Especially in circumstances in which physicians may be in a position to steer profitable business or patients to their own competing business through their control of referrals.]

C. Should the exercise of discretion by the privilege-granting hospital affect the analysis under the anti-kickback statute? [e.g., credentialing practices that give the privilege-granting hospital discretion to evaluate the "financial conflict" created by a physician's outside business interests] ... What factors other than the amount of business still being generated for the hospital might be used as the basis for the hospital exercising discretion in these kinds of arrangements? ... ...

D. Can privileges ever be conditioned on referrals, other than minimums necessary for clinical proficiency? [e.g. hospitals attempting to condition privileges on a physician's referral of a predetermined level of his or her hospital business to the hospital.] ...

E. What is the effect of credentialing restrictions that apply only to members of a group practice? ...

Department of Health and Human Services, Office of Inspector General, Solicitation of New Safe Harbors and Special Fraud Alerts, 67 Fed. Reg. 72894–01 (Dec. 9, 2002) (to be codified in 42 C.F.R. pt. 1001).

In response to this notice, a hospital association filed the following comments:

### Comments of Arizona Hospital and Healthcare Association to Office of Inspector General Regarding Development of Possible Guidance Addressing Certain Credentialing Practices

### File Code OIG–71–N

Janet Rehnquist, Inspector General

Office of Inspector General

\* \* \*

Dear Ms. Rehnquist:

These comments are filed on behalf of the more than one hundred hospital and health system members of the Arizona Hospital and Healthcare Association ("AzHHA") in response to the Office of Inspector General's ("OIG") request for comments on the development of possible guidance on the application of the anti-kickback statute, 42 U.S.C. § 1320a–7b(b) ("Anti–Kickback Law") on certain hospital credentialing arrangements for physicians. Specifically, the OIG has asked for comments on the legality under the Anti–Kickback Law of hospital credentialing policies that withhold medical staff membership and privileges to physicians (1) with ownership or other financial interests in competing health care facilities, (2) who refer to competing facilities, or (3) do not admit or treat a designated number of patients at the credentialing facility.

AzHHA appreciates the opportunity to provide these comments. AzHHA believes that the granting of medical staff membership and privileges by a hospital or other health care entity is not remuneration under the Anti–Kickback Law. While remuneration may exist in a limited range of situations where credentialing is directly linked to referral requirements or prohibitions that are intended to induce referrals and are not based upon legitimate quality of care, administrative and business concerns, AzHHA recommends that any OIG guidance in this area be carefully drawn in order to avoid potential criminal penalties for credentialing practices that respond to the evolving relationship of hospitals and physicians.

1. *The Nature of Physician and Hospital Relationships.*

   a. *Traditional Hospital Credentialing of Medical Staff Members.*

Medical staff credentialing by a hospital or health care facility establishes the right of a physician to treat his or her patients at that granting facility. The membership and credentialing process was intended historically to confirm the physician's fundamental medical competence.

\* \* \*

Medical staff membership often obligates physicians to assist the granting hospital with medical administrative functions, such as participation in medical staff meetings, peer review activities and participation in on-call rotations to provide emergency services at the facility. It does not, however, generally require that the physician use the facility.

\* \* \*

There are exceptions to the general practice that medical staff membership does not require use of the granting facility. Hospitals and health care providers may require that a physician perform a specific, limited number of procedures at the granting facility initially or on an annual basis in order to demonstrate current skill and qualification necessary for privileges. Hospitals may also require physicians to admit a certain number of cases annually in order to maintain "active" medical staff membership. This type of requirement addresses ongoing quality oversight and meets a hospital's administrative need to confirm that its active medical staff has a necessary familiarity with the hospital's operations and procedures.

Conversely, hospitals and health care entities may limit access to specific departments or services to certain physicians or physician groups in order to promote more efficient and reliable access to physician services, patient scheduling or efficient use of limited equipment or facilities. These "exclusive" arrangements are often used for hospital-based specialties, such as radiology, pathology and emergency department services.

### b. *Evolving Hospital and Medical Staff Relationships.*

The landscape that gave rise to the traditional hospital and physician relationship has altered dramatically. In the past, a physician would decide which hospital or facility to use based upon patient and physician preference. Now, a patient's choice of facility (and physician) often is guided by the managed care company or insurer with which the patient is enrolled.

\* \* \*

At the same time that physicians have access to alternative facilities for the provision of certain procedures and services, hospitals have an increased need for more structured relationships with physicians. For example, a general hospital providing emergency services must provide, under the Emergency Medical Treatment and Active Labor Act ("EMTALA"), the same scope of "staff and facilities available at the hospital . . ." [ ] The EMTALA provision that a hospital maintain an on-call roster of medical staff members to fulfill this obligation is based on the assumption that a hospital can require its medical staff to participate in on-call duty in order to make emergency care available.

This, however, is easier said than done: while physicians originally participated in emergency department on-call duty as part of a community obligation and a way to build a new practice, the burdens of on-call obligations have now eclipsed these benefits for many physicians. Physicians increasingly are refusing to participate in emergency department on-call schedules because of liability concerns, low (or no) reimbursement and the burden of interrupting already busy office practices and personal lives.

\* \* \*

The recent growth in physician-owned specialty hospitals is creating new conflicts of interest between physicians and hospitals. This is particularly true in Arizona, where the development of specialty "carve out" hospitals is fostered by the absence of certificate of need laws and a regulatory anomaly that requires only general hospitals to provide emergency services. Physicians are interested in developing special hospitals for many reasons, such as anticipated return on investment, the lack of on-call obligations, as well as perceived quality of care and efficiency benefits. These financial interests create a conflict of interest for the investing physician referring a patient for inpatient care. General hospitals face the very real threat that a physician investing in a special hospital will refer high reimbursement cases to the special hospital, while referring less favorable cases to the general hospital. This "cherry-picking" erodes the general hospital's ability to support essential community services, such as obstetrical, pediatric and emergency care. As a result, these hospitals may seek to limit medical staff membership to physicians who do not have a financial relationship with a specialty facility.

The implementation of a federal system for public reporting of hospital quality data also will impact the relationships between hospitals and physicians. ... As CMS and the public increasingly rely on quality indicator programs to evaluate hospitals, hospitals in turn will seek stronger, more effective means of working with physicians to address specific quality outcomes—and may have greater incentives to limit privileges to a core group of hospitalists, intensivists and key specialists who will participate in the development and implementation of protocols linked to quality measures rather than the large and loosely organized traditional medical staff.

*c. The Anti–Kickback Law.*

\* \* \*

[T]he Anti–Kickback Law casts a long shadow on hospitals and health care facilities as they respond to the rapidly evolving health care marketplace. In light of the changing nature of hospital and physician relationships and the need to foster innovation in this area, AzHHA respectfully recommends that the OIG narrowly focus its guidance not on medical staff or credentialing arrangements in general, but on the limited number of related requirements or arrangements that may create improper remuneration.

*2. Medical Staff Membership and Credentialing are Not Remuneration under the Anti–Kickback Law—or the Stark Law.*

AzHHA joins the American Hospital Association in its submission that the granting of hospital privileges to physicians has never been treated as remuneration under the Anti–Kickback Law. This position is correct and should not change.

*a. Medical Staff Credentialing Is Not Remuneration.*

Medical staff membership and privileges create a permissive relationship: a physician with privileges may use a facility, but is not required to do so. Credentialing alone does not convey any value (in cash or in kind) to a physician as contemplated by the Anti–Kickback Law. Any potential remuneration under the Anti–Kickback Law arises not out of the fact of credentialing, but from other relationships between a facility and a physician that might induce the physician to refer patients to that facility or otherwise generate business for the facility. The OIG has recognized this distinction between staff privileges and referral obligations in the safe harbor for practitioner recruitment, which allows a hospital to require that a recruited practitioner maintain staff privileges at the facility but prohibits any requirement that the practitioner make referrals to the facility.[1]

\* \* \*

The fact that the Stark Law includes no exception for medical staff membership or privileges indicates that neither Congress nor CMS intended privileges to constitute remuneration, and is consistent with the OIG's position to date. Any change in position by the OIG would require amendment to the Stark Law or the publication of additional regulatory provisions to avoid a landslide of unintended Stark Law violations.

### b. Managed Care Arrangements Do Not Transform Hospital Credentialing Into Remuneration.

Managed care arrangements do not change the conclusion that staff credentialing is not remuneration. In its request for comments, the OIG raised the concern that with the growth of managed care systems, especially in combination with a substantial local health care system, a physician's access to patients may depend on having privileges at a specific hospital. In reality, a physician's access to patients often depends on that physician's relationship with the managed care company, and whether the physician is included in the payor's approved physician panels. The managed care plan, in turn, may or may not contract with a specific hospital. As a result, it is the managed care company and its contracting or credentialing policies that controls the physician's access to patients—and just as importantly, the patient's access to a physician.

A hospital contracting with a managed care plan is not obligated to credential all physicians contracting with that plan.

\* \* \*

A managed care company, unlike hospitals and other facilities, can direct patients to a physician by including a physician on specific panels. Managed care credentialing is far closer to remuneration than hospital credentialing in providing patient access to a physician in exchange for the benefits requested, or requirements imposed, by the managed care company.

### c. Anti-Kickback Compliance Should Not Hinge on Market Analysis.

The request for comments raises the question of whether credentialing might have monetary value, and therefore constitute remuneration, if a particular facility has market power that could limit a physician's ability to provide care to a patient. This is the realm of state and federal antitrust regulation, not Anti-Kickback Law. It is difficult to imagine what criteria the OIG could establish that would reasonably allow health care facilities to determine whether they held market share to a degree that the granting of privileges constituted remuneration—and equally difficult for health care facilities to engage in new forms of credentialing and contracting in light of this uncertainty.

1. 42 C.F.R. § 1001.952(n).

The concept that remuneration may be determined by an extended market analysis casts doubt on a hospital or health care facility's ability to credential or close its medical staff for legitimate reasons. Health care facilities must maintain the right to limit privileges for quality of care, administrative and business reasons without fear that the action will violate the Anti–Kickback Law. For example, a hospital may seek to close its catheterization lab to one group in order to provide for constant and reliable coverage and medical management of this service. The action, however, may have financial impact on a physician who is not part of that group. While this situation may give rise to an antitrust claim, it should not be construed on its face as improper remuneration in violation of the Anti–Kickback Law. Similarly, an ambulatory surgical center owned by a group of physicians may refuse to allow other physicians access to the facility in order to meet certain administrative goals or to make sure that the owner physicians have sufficient operating and procedure room times to satisfy the requirement under the ambulatory surgery center safe harbor that one-third of each owner's procedures are performed at the center.[2] Depending upon the availability of other ambulatory surgery facilities in the area, this credentialing decision could have financial impact upon the requesting physician (and could result in an antitrust claim), but it should not constitute an Anti–Kickback Law violation.

3. *The Refusal of Privileges Based Upon a Physician's Financial Relationship with Competing Facility Does Not Violate the Anti–Kickback Law.*

A hospital or health care facility's refusal of privileges to a physician who owns an interest in or has a financial relationship with a competing facility is not a violation of the Anti–Kickback Law. As a matter of law, the privileges at issue are not remuneration; even if they were granted, there would be no obligation upon the physician to provide services at or refer patients to the hospital. The decision would have no impact on access to care, because the physician would be able to provide services at the competing facility. While selective contracting by a managed care company with either facility might affect patient access to services, this restriction is the result of the payor's contracting practices, not the hospital's credentialing practice.

In fact, this credentialing policy potentially would have the effect of limiting physician referrals to the hospital, rather than inducing additional referrals. Many hospitals, however, are willing to accept this result in order to limit significant conflicts of interest and to prevent physicians investing in competing facilities to cherry-pick profitable, healthier patients to a physician-owned facility while directing uninsured or underinsured complex cases to the general hospital. A community hospital may decide that its mission of delivering a full array of services to the community–including necessary but unprofitable services–is better served by foregoing possible referrals from a physician investing in a competing facility than by permitting these patient steering practices. By refusing privileges to physicians with conflicting ownership or financial interests, a hospital is acting in a manner wholly consistent with the Anti–Kickback Law, which is intended to protect patients and Federal reimbursement programs from physician referrals based upon economic self-interest rather than clinical judgment.

A credentialing policy that withholds membership from a physician with an ownership interest in a competing facility also addresses more traditional, but equally important, conflict of interest concerns. A physician investing in a facility may have conflicting fiduciary obligations if he or she serves on the governing

---

2. 42 C.F.R. § 1001.952(r)(3).

body or medical staff committees for another hospital. The conflict of interest is heightened when the physician has access to the policies, procedures, protocols and data of one hospital while holding an ownership interest in a competing facility. The ability of an investor physician to place more profitable patients at the owned facility while directing more complex, less profitable cases to another facility is an extreme, but realistic, illustration of conflicts of interest. Hospitals and health care facilities need to have the ability to establish privileging criteria that avoid these conflicts.

Hospital credentialing is not remuneration as intended under the Anti-Kickback Law, and AzHHA respectfully requests that the OIG not change this fundamental conclusion. The introduction of market analysis as a means to identify remuneration in the context of credentialing would create uncertainty in enforcement and compliance efforts; to the extent certain credentialing practices limit competition or access to essential facilities, there claims are properly addressed under the antitrust laws.

### *Notes and Questions*

What arguments would you make if you were assigned to write comments in this matter on behalf of the American Medical Association? How would you limit the scope of any rule you would propose? Compare the analysis that would be applied under antitrust law to instances in which hospitals deny staff privileges to doctors opening competing facilities (discussed infra Chapter 15 in this Supplement). What facts necessary to develop an antitrust case might not be required under a rule developed by the OIG? See also Mahan v. Avera St. Luke's, 621 N.W.2d 150 (S.D.2001) this Supplement, Chapter 12.

## III. STARK I & II: A TRANSACTIONAL APPROACH TO SELF-REFERRALS

### B. EXCEPTIONS

**Add, at p. 999, Immediately before Note on Stark I and II:**

#### *Note on Fair Market Value*

The meaning of "fair market value" is often critical for determining the legality of business arrangements under Stark and the Anti–Kickback law. For example, in United States ex rel. Goodstein v. McLaren Regional Medical Center, 202 F.Supp.2d 671 (E.D.Mich.2002), a qui tam action in which the government intervened, the issue was whether the defendant medical center had paid physicians illegal remuneration disguised as a lease agreement for the office building owned by the physicians' limited liability company. Because the physician defendants referred Medicare patients to the medical center and operated their practice out of the leased offices, and the payments allegedly violated both Stark and the anti-kickback statutes, the government asserted that false claims were involved. The court rejected the contention that the amount of rent paid was excessive, concluding that the lease agreement was an arms length transaction and that the lease rate set forth in the lease agreement was consistent with fair market value. Id. at 675. The court reasoned that the testimony of the experts used by defendants was sufficiently grounded on facts or data, was a product of reliable principles and methods, and reliably applied those principles to the facts in evidence. Id. at 679. Despite the fact that their appraisals were prepared in response to litigation, defendants won the "battle of experts" because of defects in the government's case, including the failure of its witnesses to consider certain comparables and their inconsistent application of valuation methodology. Moreover, the court held that the lease rate was not determined in a manner that took into account the value of potential patient referrals. Id. at 686. Do you find this holding controversial in view of the fact that the medical center had insisted on non-compete provisions and retained the right to vacate the leased space if the physician group ever moved out of the building (which the government had claimed "could have deprived [the medical center] of capturing a 'steady flow' of patient referrals)"?

In the context of hospitals acquiring physician practices, the future revenue stream from referrals by the acquired physicians is almost inevitably an important factor for a hospital deciding whether it will buy the practice. Yet the anti-kickback law squarely prohibits any excess payment that could be considered "remuneration" for such referrals. Hence, it is necessary to separate out the value of referrals before ascertaining the fair market value of the practice. In United States ex rel. Obert–Hong v. Advocate Health Care, 211 F.Supp.2d 1045, 1049 n. 2 (N.D.Ill.2002), a district court acknowledged the tension:

> We note that fair market value here may differ from traditional economic valuation formulae. Normally, we would expect the acquisition price to account for potential revenues from future referrals. Because the Anti-Kickback Act prohibits any inducement for those referrals, however, they must be excluded from any calculation of fair value here. See 42 C.F.R. §§ 1001.952(b) and (c) There is, nonetheless, some value that would be considered fair and would comply with the statute.

The court went on to find the complaint failed to allege any facts such as what assets were acquired, their purported value, or the amount actually paid, from which it could draw such an inference that the hospital's payment exceeded fair market value. Id. What, then, is the value of the practice to the hospital?

The court also rejected the claim that the requirement (in their employment contracts) that the doctors selling their practices refer their patients to defendant hospitals was, by definition, an inducement. It noted that both "the Stark and Anti-Kickback statutes are designed to remove economic incentives from medical referrals, not to regulate typical hospital-physician employment relationships ... [and] both statutes explicitly include employee exceptions." Id. at 1050.

**Add, at p. 1000, end of page:**

A district court has determined that HHS overstepped its authority when it included lithotripsy as a designated health service under Stark II, finding that such procedures are neither inpatient nor outpatient procedures within the meaning of the statute. Am. Lithotripsy Soc'y v. Thompson, 215 F.Supp.2d 23 (D.D.C.2002). Lithotripsy is a noninvasive procedure performed by urologists that breaks up kidney stones so they may pass through the urinary tract and out of the body. CMS requires that urologists performing lithotripsy procedures at ambulatory surgery centers must bill "under arrangement" with a hospital in order for physicians to receive reimbursement from Medicare for the technical fees associated with the procedure. The lithotripsy center typically provides all of the equipment and personnel to perform the procedure, including the lithotriptor itself, while the role of the hospital is limited to billing Medicare. By virtue of this billing role mandated by the "under arrangement" requirement, the hospital receives a large portion—up to 70%—of the Medicare technical fees for the lithotripsy services provided by the center, even though the lithotripsy center performs almost all of the work in delivering the services to patients. The district court noted that the role of the hospital was confined to billing and concluded that the required "under arrangement" contracts with *hospitals* did not convert lithotripsy into an inpatient or outpatient *hospital* service: "If it did, then any health service with a remote connection to a hospital would be an inpatient or outpatient hospital service." Id. at 33. The court also found exclusion of lithotripsy from Stark's reach consistent with the legislative purpose of the statute because the procedure was not one susceptible to overuse as there is no alternative available that is less invasive or less expensive. Id. at 36.

# Chapter 15

# ANTITRUST

## INTRODUCTION

**Add at p. 1008, after carry over paragraph:**

*FTC/DOJ Hearings on Antitrust and Health Care.* On February 26, 2003, the Federal Trade Commission and the Department of Justice commenced public hearings on the implications of competition law and policy for health financing and delivery. These broad ranging hearings, which will consider the "impact of competition law and policy on the cost, quality, and availability of health care, and the incentives for innovation in the field," should serve as a valuable resource for researchers and policymakers. They will also help inform future directions for enforcement of antitrust law in areas such as hospital mergers, monopolistic practices by payers, vertical integration, and state regulation of health care. The agencies will post materials and transcripts from the hearings at http://www.ftc.gov/ogc/healthcarehearings/index.htm

## I. CARTELS AND PROFESSIONALISM

### B. COLLECTIVE ACTIVITIES WITH JUSTIFICATIONS

#### 1. *Restrictions on Advertising and Dissemination of Information*

**Add, at p. 1034, after Note 2:**

In Viazis v. American Association of Orthodontists, 314 F.3d 758 (5th Cir. 2002), an orthodontist who designed and patented an orthodontic bracket advertised that braces utilizing his bracket were "faster, less expensive and potentially safer than other products." Defendant American Association of Orthodontists (AAO), suspended the Viazis's membership after finding his advertising violated the organization's Code of Professional Responsibility. The Fifth Circuit Court of Appeals, applying *California Dental*, concluded that the conduct was not per se illegal and that Viazis had failed to present sufficient evidence demonstrating the anti-competitive effects of the advertising restriction under either a quick look or rule of reason analysis. The fact that sales of plaintiff's brackets to orthodontists declined after sanctions were imposed by the AAO was insufficient to satisfy *California Dental's* requirement that plaintiff proffer "relevant data" as to market effect. The Court noted that there was no evidence that AAO coerced members into rejecting Viazis's brackets or that the decline in sales was attributable to anything other than the voluntary decisions of independent orthodontists.

Additional analysis, largely critical, of the California Dental opinion can be found in Timothy J. Muris, California Dental Association v. FTC: The Revenge of Footnote 17, 8 Sup. Ct. Econ. Rev. 265 (2000); Clark C. Havighurst, Health Care As A (Big) Business: The Antitrust Response, 26 J. Health Pol. Pol'y & L. 939 (2001); Thomas L. Greaney, A Perfect Storm on the Sea of Doubt: Physicians, Professionalism and Antitrust, 14 Loy. Consumer L. Rev. 481 (2001); Marina Lao, The Rule of Reason in Antitrust Restraints Among Professionals, 68 Antitrust L.J. 499 (2001). For a more favorable assessment, see William J. Kolasky, California Dental Association v. FTC: The New Antitrust Empiricism, 14 Antitrust 68 (Fall 1999).

**Add, at p. 1035, after Note 4:**

### Note on Information Dissemination by Physician Groups: Advocacy, Efficiency, or Cartelization?

In two notable advisory opinions, the FTC and Department of Justice expressed no objection to surveys to be undertaken by physician groups concerning managed care reimbursement for their services. Although the agencies have approved numerous proposals by providers to collect and share information, these plans are unique in that they rather explicitly focus on combating the perceived power of managed care.

*WSMA:* The Department of Justice indicated that it had no current intention of challenging the proposal by the Washington State Medical Association (WSMA) to conduct a fee and reimbursement survey of physicians and physician assistants and to publish the survey results. Letter from Charles A. James, Assistant Attorney General, Antitrust Division, U.S. Dept. of Justice to Jerry B. Edmonds (Sept. 23, 2002), available at: www.usdoj.gov/opa/pr/2002/September/01_at_542htm (Press Release). Under the plan, WSMA would survey its members to gather two categories of statistics: physician charges and insurer reimbursement for services. The Department's Business Review Letter noted that the plan complied with the DOJ/FTC Health Care Guidelines in that it will be managed by the WSMA professional staff, will utilize underlying data that is at least three months old at the time that the survey results are disseminated, and will aggregate the underlying data in a manner designed to prevent the identification and misuse of individual provider information. However, the letter went on to note that the portion of the survey involving insurer reimbursements might have the possibility of anticompetitive effects because the WSMA planned to identify average reimbursements paid by individual insurers. DOJ noted possible competitive concerns arising from the possibility that information could lead to boycotts or collusive pricing. Concluding, however, that the Department had no present intention of challenging the proposal, the letter cited as "mitigating factors": the procompetitive benefits of better information, the fact that no provider-specific information will be released, the unconcentrated structure of the physician market in Washington, obstacles to effective collusion resulting from the nature and timing of the data generated, and affirmative efforts by WSMA to educate its members about antitrust law.

*PriMed Physicians:* In February, 2003, the FTC issued a favorable advisory opinion concerning the proposed formation and operation of a "healthcare advocacy group" comprised of practicing physicians in the Dayton, Ohio, area. Letter from Jeffrey Brennan, Assistant Director, Bureau of Competition, Federal Trade Commission to Gregory G. Binford, Bensch Friedlander Coplan & Aronoff, LLP (Feb. 6, 2003) available at: www.ftc.gov/bc/adops/030206dayton.htm. The sponsor of the program is PriMed Physicians, a physician group practice with 55 physician employees. According to the advisory opinion, the organization will be open to all Dayton physicians and "thus may contain a majority of the area's practicing physicians." PriMed proposed to collect and publish (to physicians as well as to the public) the fees paid by named health plans for specific medical services. In its request to the FTC, PriMed described itself as an advocacy group designed to undertake "a campaign to inform and educate the general public" about the "ill effects and other consequences of the policies and procedures, including depressed reimbursement, by third party payers in Dayton." The Dayton market is dominated by two substantial managed care players, which together cover over half the privately insured population. Regarding potential risks to competition, the FTC Staff letter concluded:

> The likelihood that the survey actually would foster anticompetitive effects—through either express or tacit collusion—is reduced by Dayton's market structure for physician services, which we understand to be highly unconcentrated. According to information that you supplied, approximately 1,600 doctors practice medicine in Dayton, and most do so in solo practices or small groups.... In such a market, an exchange of price-related information is less likely to have anticompetitive effects by facilitating cartel behavior, because the unconcentrated structure usually is not conducive to effective tacit price coordination.

The FTC's advisory also noted that PriMed had structured its information-gathering in a way that minimized risk. Consistent with Statement 6 of the FTC/DOJ Policy Statements, the survey will be performed by an independent third party, and PriMed will not make disaggregated survey responses available to physicians, will not release compensation information by physician name, and will collect only payment data that are at least three months old.

Finally, the letter goes on to discuss the possible risk that the large managed care organizations could use the information to collude explicitly or tacitly to injure competition. It concludes that these payers may already have means to ascertain each others prices, in any event,

> The staff is not typically confronted with proposed activity that raises the theoretical, albeit unintended, risk of imposing competitive harm on the actors themselves. We conclude that, because physicians would be likely victims of any anticompetitive uses to which health plans could deploy the publicized data, and thus are in perhaps the best position to assess this risk, the physicians' participation in the survey presumably would corroborate your assertion that such an anticompetitive outcome is not likely.

Do the conclusions reached by the FTC and DOJ surprise you? Are the assurances provided by market conditions and the nature of the surveys sufficient to guard against potential harms? Should the charged environment and the parties' expressed intention to use the information for "advocacy" purposes affect the agencies' judgments?

### Note on Group Purchasing Organizations

The role of group purchasing organizations ("GPOs") in the health care system has come under increased scrutiny in the last year, as small manufacturers of medical devices have claimed that the contracting practices of the two largest GPOs, Premier and Novation, are anticompetitive. Barry Meier & Mary Williams Walsh, Senate Panel Criticizes Hospital Buying Groups, N.Y. Times, May 1, 2002, at C1. These manufacturers allege that they have been denied access to the decision makers at hospitals due to the exclusionary contracts negotiated by the largest GPOs. They assert that GPOs have effectively become gatekeepers that control access to member hospitals by virtue of exclusionary agreements. The claim is that large vendors pay elevated fees to the GPOs, which in turn establish incentives for hospitals not to purchase products from non-GPO vendors. Alleged anticompetitive harms flow from increasing the GPO's market power, increased entry barriers, and reduced incentives for innovation. A study by the General Accounting Office indicated that GPO prices "were not always lower and were often higher" than prices paid by hospitals negotiating with vendors directly. Group Purchasing Deals Give Hospitals No Edge on Prices GAO Tells Senate Panel, 11 Health L. Rep. (BNA) at 635 (May 2, 2002).

The GPOs respond that they only act on behalf of their member hospitals and lack both the incentive and ability to impair competition. They argue that the market in which GPOs operate is highly competitive with over 800 GPOs operating and most hospitals belonging to several GPOs. Further, most GPOs do not require members to purchase all supplies through their GPO contracts, and they assert that their practices are merely incentive arrangements encouraging members such as hospitals to purchase larger volumes through GPO contracts. See generally Federal Trade Commission, Health Care and Competition Law and Policy Workshop (Sept. 10, 2002), Tr. Pp. 48–140 available at www.ftc.gov/ogc/healthcare/20910trans.pdf; Tyco Accused of Using Dominant Position in Oximetry Market to Thwart Competition, 11 Health L. Rep. (BNA) at 827 (June 6, 2002) (describing allegations in Masino Corp. v. Tyco Health Care, group claiming monopolization by Tyco through use of rebates and provisions in GPO contracts to excludes competitors). See also Dept. of Justice & FTC Policy Statements on Health Care, Statement 7, available at www.ftc.gov/reports/hlth3s.htm#7.

### 2. *Private Accreditation and Professional Standard–Setting*

**Add, at p. 1043, end of Paragraph 5:**

See also Viazis v. American Association of Orthodontists, 314 F.3d 758 (5th Cir.2002) (finding no concerted action under § 1 of the Sherman Act where disciplinary action by professional association was followed by termination of plaintiff's marketing agreement with manufacturer; court analogized situation to terminations of distributorships following dealer complaints in manufacturer-distributor antitrust cases).

## II. HEALTH CARE ENTERPRISES, INTEGRATION AND FINANCING

### A. PROVIDER–CONTROLLED NETWORKS AND HEALTH PLANS

**Add, at p. 1072, end of Paragraph:**

*Physician Cartels or Davids Fighting Goliaths?* The Federal Trade Commission has continued to uncover collusive actions among physicians designed to raise fees for their services. In 2002 alone, the FTC reached settlements with five physician groups involving claims that the entities illegally combined to negotiate prices with managed care, without integrating their operations. Sys. Health Providers,. No. C–4064 (Oct. 24, 2002) (consent order), available at www.ftc.gov/os/2002/11/shpdo.pdf; R. T. Welter & Assocs., Inc. (Prof'ls in Women's Care),. No. C–4063 (Aug. 20, 2002) (proposed consent order), available at www.ftc.gov/os/2002/08/profwomenagree.pdf; Obstetrics and Gynecology Med. Corp. of Napa Valley, No. C–4048 (May 14, 2002) (consent order), available at: *www.ftc.gov/os/2002/05/obgyndo.pdf*; Physician Integrated Servs. of Denver, Inc., No. 4054 ( May 9, 2002) (proposed consent order), available at: www.ftc.gov/os/2002/05/pisdagreement.pdf; Aurora Assoc. Primary Care Physicians, L.L.C.,. No. 4055 (May 9, 2002) (proposed consent order), available at www.ftc.gov/os/2002/05/auroraagreement.pdf. The number of physicians involved in these cases ranged from eight in the Napa, California case to more than twelve hundred in the Dallas/Fort Worth, Texas matter. Each was settled by a consent decree pursuant to which physicians agreed to refrain from engaging in similar conduct in the future and to take other steps to ensure compliance with antitrust law. In one instance, the organization was dissolved pursuant to FTC order. In three cases, the FTC also obtained relief against consultants who were involved in coordinating the alleged legal conduct.

The AMA has sharply criticized the FTC's prosecutions in these matters, referring to "competition of physician Davids against health plan Goliaths," and asserting that the FTC had "unfortunately favored the big guys." Editorial, It's About Time: Insurers Facing Antitrust Scrutiny, Am. Med. News (Oct. 14, 2002), available at: www.ama-assn.org/sci-pubs/am-news/amn_02/edsa1014.htm. More recently, the AMA has published a study cataloguing the amount of concentration in managed care markets around the country. See Am. Med. Ass'n, Competition in Health Insurance: A Comprehensive Study of U.S. Markets (2nd ed. 2002); Statement of Jacqueline M. Dorrah to the Federal Trade Commission and the Department of Justice (Feb. 27, 2003). Responding to these claims, the Chairman of the Federal Trade Commission has pointed out that concentration levels in the five markets challenged by the agency in 2002 were quite low and did not evidence excessive payer concentration: "Bluntly stated, this conduct had everything to do with physician self interest and little or nothing to do with insurer monopsony power." Timothy J. Muris, Everything Old Is New Again: Health Care and Competition in the 21st Century, Remarks before the 7th Annual Competition in Health Care Forum, Chicago, Illinois (Nov. 7, 2002), available at www.ftc.gov/speeches/muris/murishealthcarespeech0211.pdf.

Do the absence of criminal enforcement and the murkiness of the distinction drawn by the law between permissible and impermissible conduct help explain the repeated instances of physicians crossing the FTC's line?

Add, at p. 1073, before Note on Physician Unions (or Replace pages 1067–71) with:

## FEDERAL TRADE COMMISSION, ADVISORY OPINION IN RE MEDSOUTH, INC.

(February 19, 2002).

\* \* \*

You have requested an advisory opinion relating to the proposal of MedSouth, Inc., a physician independent practice association located in Denver, Colorado, to integrate partially its member physicians' practices in the ways discussed below, and to enter into contracts with third-party payers for the sale of those physicians' services on a fee-for-service basis. Specifically, you request a statement whether the Commission staff would recommend a challenge to the proposed activities as a violation of Section 5 of the Federal Trade Commission Act.

Based on the information you provided as well as our independent inquiry, we have concluded that per se analysis would not be appropriate in evaluating MedSouth's proposed course of conduct, including its proposed joint negotiation of payer contracts. The program you have described appears to involve partial integration among MedSouth physicians that has the potential to increase the quality and reduce the cost of medical care that the physicians provide to patients. In addition, we have concluded that the joint contracting appears to be sufficiently related to, and reasonably necessary for, the achievement of the potential benefits to be regarded as ancillary to the operation of the venture.

### Description

MedSouth

MedSouth is an independent practice association (IPA) that includes competing primary care and specialist physicians who practice in the "South Denver/Arapahoe County" area of Denver, Colorado. It is a for-profit corporation owned by the physician practices of its members. All MedSouth physicians have a practice location in South Denver, and staff privileges at one of the three hospitals located in that area.

As we understand the facts based on the information you have submitted, MedSouth currently includes approximately 432 physicians in 216 practices. One hundred one of the physicians are primary care practitioners (PCPs) (family practitioners, general internists, and pediatricians); and 331 are specialists in 39 specialties and subspecialties. In general, the specialists in MedSouth are those to whom MedSouth PCPs most frequently refer. Until the year 2000, MedSouth had capitated risk contracts with payers that required most referrals to be made to other physicians in MedSouth. The referral patterns established under those contracts largely have continued. MedSouth estimates that its PCPs make 90% to 95% of their referrals to specialty physicians in MedSouth. MedSouth's specialists, however, also receive a large number of referrals from doctors outside the IPA.

MedSouth expects that a number of its current members will terminate their membership in the organization before it fully implements the proposed program and attempts to negotiate contracts, so that it will represent fewer physicians in negotiations with payers than currently are members.

\* \* \*

Contractual relationships between physicians and payers in the Denver area have undergone significant change in the past several years. Beginning in 1998 or 1999, Denver physicians established a number of financially-integrated IPAs that entered into capitated contracts with local HMOs. Many of these groups experienced significant financial difficulties under those contracts, and a number of the organizations declared bankruptcy. In the wake of this experience, payers and most physician groups, including Med-South, terminated their capitated contracts.[1] Some MedSouth physicians, however, wish to continue to practice on a partially-integrated basis with other members of the IPA.

**The Proposed Integration Program**

MedSouth proposes to implement a program that it believes will result in lower costs, higher quality, and more efficient delivery of its members' services. MedSouth has not yet placed the program into operation, or engaged in negotiation or contracting with insurance plans concerning the provision of physician services under the program. The essential features of the program, however, have been determined, and MedSouth has developed or is in the process of developing its various components. According to your letter, the proposed program has three major goals:

1. to integrate the provision of primary and specialty services so they are delivered in a coordinated fashion;[2]

2. to integrate these coordinated physician services with a clinical resource management program that involves sharing of patient clinical information, development and implementation of practice protocols, and oversight and reporting of physicians' performance relative to preestablished benchmarks, so as to improve patient outcomes, decrease use of physician resources, and provide MedSouth with a competitive advantage with respect to other physician practices in the area; and

3. to offer payers a network in which all physicians have agreed to participate and in which the physicians will work together to improve care and to compete with other physicians and physician groups.

MedSouth's physicians and its consultants, in conjunction with a health care information technology service provider and a national clinical laboratory company, have worked for over a year to develop the proposed program. It will have two major parts: (1) a web-based electronic clinical data record system that will permit MedSouth physicians to access and share clinical information relating to their patients; and (2) the adoption and implementa-

---

**1.** Our understanding is that when these capitated contracts were terminated, MedSouth members were in fact willing to contract with payers on an individual basis at prevailing market prices.

**2.** MedSouth's operating philosophy is that the quality and efficiency of patient care are maximized when the services of primary care and specialist physicians are integrated so that patients are cared for in a coordinated manner. In accordance with this outlook, primary and specialty care physicians are equally represented on MedSouth's Board of Directors. Also, two of MedSouth's four officers must be primary care doctors, while the other two must be specialists.

tion of clinical practice guidelines and performance goals relating to the quality and appropriate use of services provided by MedSouth physicians. All physicians contracting through MedSouth will be required to participate in these activities. With these systems, MedSouth believes it will be able to improve and standardize members' treatment of specific diagnoses and their fulfillment of standards of care; reduce medical errors and improve patient care outcomes; permit its members to provide their services more efficiently and to reduce the aggregate long-term cost of physician services; and demonstrate to payers, employers, and others that the integrated and coordinated delivery of services by primary care and specialist physicians can improve the quality and delivery of physician services.

The web-based clinical data record system is intended to permit MedSouth members rapidly to access and exchange clinical information relating to patients, including lab and radiological reports, transcribed patient records and office visit information, treatment plans, and prescription information. The doctors will be able to order prescriptions on-line, and at a future time will be able to determine whether the patient filled the prescription. The system can aggregate data from multiple doctors to show, for example, the trend of results on tests done at different times and places. In the future, data relating to hospital discharges and procedures also may be included. MedSouth expects this system to reduce duplicative testing and procedures, speed up treatment, decrease medical errors and adverse drug interactions, and facilitate communication and coordination of services among referring and referral physicians. Each practice will acquire the hardware necessary to use the system.

You stated that MedSouth also is developing: (1) clinical protocols covering the majority of MedSouth physicians' patient population; and (2) measurable performance goals relating to the quality and appropriate utilization of services that are linked to those protocols. The IPA proposes to secure members' commitment to adhere to those protocols in their office and hospital practices; review the performance of MedSouth physicians individually and collectively with respect to those goals; assist members in meeting the goals; and, if necessary, expel physicians who cannot or will not meet the goals. The physician participation agreement will specify the physicians' commitment to participate in all the network's programs; to adhere to the IPA's standards and protocols; and to implement the technology that permits MedSouth to report performance information to members and to third parties.

According to your letter, the clinical protocols were selected based on a review of available local and national guidelines and an assessment of the diagnoses encountered by MedSouth physicians where performance improvement would have the greatest positive effect on utilization and patient outcomes.

\* \* \*

Network utilization and quality goals or benchmarks are being developed based on the clinical protocols. Working in conjunction with its consultants, MedSouth is developing a computer-based infrastructure that will permit a committee to collect and analyze information on individual physicians' performance, and on the performance of the network as a whole, relative to the benchmarks. Much of the necessary information will be available on the electronic clinical information system.

\* \* \*

## Negotiation of Contracts

MedSouth proposes to offer the medical services of its participating members pursuant to this program to commercial third-party payers, and to negotiate and execute contracts under which MedSouth members would provide services to health plan enrollees. Thus, the IPA will seek to negotiate price and other contract terms on behalf of physician members of the network. It will retain a consultant to develop fee proposals for use in contract negotiations and, if necessary, to gather information from MedSouth physicians. The consultant will not disclose competitively sensitive information received from MedSouth physicians to other physicians in the network. Physician services will be paid for on a fee-for service basis. In addition, MedSouth intends to charge a network access fee to payers purchasing the package of services, that will support its operating and administrative costs. MedSouth will not be involved in claims processing or payment. Claims will be submitted by the physicians directly to the payers, and payment will be made directly to the physician providing the service. All MedSouth members will be required to provide services under those contracts, and to participate fully in MedSouth activities. MedSouth will not negotiate or execute such contracts on behalf of its members until all parts of the program are operational.

While MedSouth seeks to offer its members' services to payers as a package, you represent that it is intended to be, and will actually be, a non-exclusive network. The MedSouth Physician Participation Agreement will specifically state that physicians are not precluded from participating in other physician contracting organizations, or from contracting with payers independently. You have represented that customers not wishing to purchase the network services will be able to negotiate and contract with MedSouth physicians individually, and that MedSouth members will be advised by counsel that they may not reach agreements or understandings with competing physicians in the IPA to contract only through MedSouth, or exchange information about their prices or contracting strategies other than as they relate to MedSouth. In addition, you represent that MedSouth will be advised that it cannot state or suggest to payers that unless the payer reaches agreement with the IPA, its physicians will not participate in a payer's plan.

## Analysis

## Form of Analysis

The first question to be addressed is how MedSouth's proposed negotiation of fee-for-service contracts on behalf of its participating physicians should be analyzed. The information sharing and guidelines activities that MedSouth proposes to undertake, by themselves, are not inherently anticompetitive. Agreement by a group of physicians jointly to adopt an electronic patient record system that permits them more easily to communicate and share information about their patients, or to adopt and promote adherence to recognized, evidence-based practice guidelines or clinical protocols, would not normally raise serious concerns about anticompetitive effects.

Standing alone, however, joint negotiation of price terms by non-integrated, competing physicians would constitute an agreement among the physicians not to compete on price, and would be illegal per se. Per se treatment is inappropriate, however, and more elaborate analysis under the rule of reason is warranted, when the joint negotiation of price is reasonably related to an efficiency-enhancing integration of the participants' economic activity and is reasonably necessary to achieve the procompetitive benefits of that integration. How detailed that analysis should be depends, of course, on the circumstances. As the Supreme Court has ruled, truncated analysis under the rule of reason may be appropriate in some cases.

Efficiency-enhancing integration typically involves joint performance of one or more business functions of the participants in a way that potentially benefits consumers by expanding output, reducing price, or enhancing quality, service or innovation, and that could not reasonably be achieved by the participants individually. The integration must likely generate procompetitive benefits that enhance the participants' ability or incentives to compete, and thus offset any anticompetitive tendencies of the arrangement. Joint negotiation of prices is not "reasonably necessary" if the participants could achieve an equivalent or comparable efficiency-enhancing integration through practical means that provide significantly less restriction on competition.

We conclude that MedSouth's overall proposed course of conduct, as described in the information you have supplied, should not be accorded per se treatment. The program in which MedSouth proposes to engage appears to be capable of creating substantial partial integration of the participating physicians' practices, and to have the potential to produce efficiencies in the form of higher quality or reduced costs for patient care services rendered by network physicians. More elaborate analysis under the rule of reason, therefore, is warranted.

**Integration and Likely Efficiencies**

Taken as whole, the proposed program is designed to facilitate and increase communication and cooperation among MedSouth physicians, both in the treatment of individual patients and in modifying the regular practice patterns of members of the IPA. The collective development and implementation of the protocols and benchmarks has the potential to create significant integration and interdependence among the physicians in their rendering of medical services. The physicians have pooled their resources and expertise to identify common standards of care. Through their agreement to abide by those standards, the physicians have subjected themselves, to some extent, to the collective judgment of the group with respect to their patterns of practice; and they have agreed to make themselves individually and collectively accountable for their performance by making information about their achievement of goals, which are linked to those standards, available to customers.

Wide-spread attention has been given to the prospect that greater adherence to practice guidelines based on solid evidence can improve the quality, and in many cases reduce the cost, of medical care. Rigorous and effective implementation of the program proposed by MedSouth appears to have the potential to help the doctors render more appropriate, high-quality, and cost-effective care. Individual physicians acting independently do not appear capable of creating comparable efficiencies.

\* \* \*

The computer system facilitates both dissemination and implementation of these common standards and communications among MedSouth doctors relating to the care of particular patients. The system is intended thereby to reduce duplicative tests and procedures, promote better coordination of treatment, and speed up provision of referral services. Computerized prescribing and other data entry systems have the potential to reduce errors and adverse events. While any physician could achieve some of these benefits by investing in his/her own information system, adoption of the same system by a group of physicians who maintain referral relationships with one another can provide a number of additional benefits. Having compatible systems permits physicians in different practices who are caring for the same patients to communicate and share clinical information more easily. The cost of developing the system is spread over a larger number of practices, and those physicians who are less knowledgeable about information technology can benefit from the experience and interest of those who are more conversant with it. The existence of the system is likely to further cement referral relationships within the network and lead to closer working relationships among network physicians in the future, thus amplifying the benefits that result from the physicians' participation in the program. We note, however, that mere adoption of a common clinical information system by itself, without the other programs that MedSouth intends to implement, would not suffice to establish that otherwise competing members of a physician network have integrated their practices in a manner or to an extent that joint negotiation of prices could be deemed ancillary to an efficiency-enhancing joint venture.

## The Relationship of Joint Contracting to the Production of Efficiencies

The extent to which collective negotiation of prices is ancillary to this integration is a crucial question. Generally speaking, an agreement is ancillary to a competitor collaboration to the extent that it is subordinate to and reasonably necessary to accomplish the goals of the integration, unless the parties could have achieved similar efficiencies by practical, significantly less restrictive means.[3] It may be possible to develop an arrangement, apart from payment for the professional services of the network physicians, under which those physicians could be appropriately compensated for the costs entailed in providing programs of the type MedSouth intends to undertake. In this instance, however, we conclude that the price agreement embodied in joint negotiation of contracts for services to be provided subject to the entire proposed program appears to be reasonably related to the integration among

---

**3.** Health Care Statements at 71, 80; Competitor Collaboration Guidelines at § 3.36(b). See also Rothery Storage & Van Co. v. Atlas Van Lines, 792 F.2d 210, 224 (D.C.Cir.1986), cert. denied 479 U.S. 1033 (1987) ("The ancillary restraint is subordinate and collateral in the sense that it serves to make the main transaction more effective in accomplishing its purpose.... [T]he restraint imposed must be related to the efficiency sought to be achieved."); General Leaseways, Inc. v. National Truck Leasing Association, 744 F.2d 588, 595 (7th Cir.1984) (There must be an "organic connection between the restraint and the cooperative needs of the enterprise that would allow us to call the restraint a merely ancillary one....").

MedSouth members, and reasonably necessary for MedSouth to achieve the procompetitive benefits it seeks.

In order to establish and maintain the on-going collaboration and interdependence among physicians from which the projected efficiencies flow, the doctors need to be able to rely on the participation of other members of the group in the network and its activities on a continuing basis. This does not appear to be possible if contracting for the sale of services is done individually. The price for professional services rendered under health plan contracts needs to be established, and if it is done through individual negotiation and contracting, then no one can count on the full participation of the group's members. Whatever value the program has for consumers, beyond what would result from individual doctors computerizing their records and determining to follow particular guidelines, is significantly dependent on the doctors being able to function as a group within which patients are commonly referred.[4] In the absence of the group being able to assure continuing participation of its members in its contracts, some of the benefits are likely to go unrealized.

In addition, joint contracting may permit the network to allocate the returns among members of the network in a way that creates incentives for the physicians to make appropriate investments of time and effort in setting up and implementing the proposed program. According to your letter, it is important for MedSouth to be able to assure that the rewards from the program flow to the doctors in an equitable manner, so that some are not able to charge disproportionately high prices relative to other members, and thereby capture an excessive proportion of the value of the network's programs. It is unclear whether the proposed arrangement creates a level of interdependence and integration among each and every physician who currently is a member of MedSouth so as to make joint negotiation of their fees ancillary to operation of the venture. For example, MedSouth contains certain subspecialists who may or may not have enough patients referred by other MedSouth members to cause them either to be significantly involved in the design or implementation of protocols, or to have their practice patterns significantly affected by them. Because it is not clear at present how many of these physicians will remain members of the network when the program is fully operational, however, we have not attempted in this opinion to delineate more precisely which physician practices are integrated through the proposed program. Both MedSouth and the affected physicians would face significant

---

**4.** The situation here differs from that in Arizona v. Maricopa County Medical Society, 457 U.S. 332 (1982), where the decision of each doctor whether to accept the "maximum fee" as payment in full was essentially unrelated (except to the extent that the common agreement on prices eliminated competition among the participating doctors) to the decision of any other physician to do the same thing. While the organization performed some "peer review" of the necessity and appropriateness of care rendered to patients, it made no claim that the challenged agreement on prices was reasonably necessary to the efficient functioning of the review process. Brief for the United States as Amicus Curiae on Writ of Certiorari at 26. Moreover, it is highly unlikely that the type of peer review performed by the foundations for medical care in Maricopa created any significant interdependence or on-going cooperation among foundation members with respect to their clinical practices. The foundations for medical care of that era were community-wide organizations sponsored by local medical societies and designed to have broadly inclusive memberships. The peer review they performed was claims-based, retrospective review in order to determine whether the claim should be paid, reduced, or denied; the standards they used generally were designed simply to detect deviations from local community norms of practice. See, e.g., Egdahl, "Foundation for Medical Care," 288 New England J. Med. 491 (1973).

antitrust risk if MedSouth negotiated prices on behalf of physicians who are not sufficiently integrated with the venture through their participation in the activities that are expected to give rise to the efficiencies.

**Competitive Effects**

The fundamental concern of antitrust analysis is whether a given arrangement may have a substantial anticompetitive effect and, if so, whether that potential effect is offset by any procompetitive efficiencies resulting from the conduct. The central question is whether, taking into account both potential procompetitive and anticompetitive effects, the arrangement is likely to harm competition by increasing the ability or incentive of the participants to raise price above—or reduce output, quality, service, or innovation below the level that likely would prevail in the absence of the agreement. The ability and incentive of the participants to compete individually with one another and with their joint undertaking is an important part of the analysis.

Because the proposed program is yet to be implemented, it appears to be impossible at this point to predict the magnitude of anticompetitive or procompetitive effects that will flow from its actual operation. You were not able to obtain reliable information that would allow us to determine with any precision the relevant geographic markets for the services to be delivered through the network. However, the information available to us indicates that the MedSouth membership as presently constituted likely would be able to exercise significant market power, and thus to extract higher prices, if the doctors coordinate their actions outside the integrated group.

MedSouth currently has a large number of participating doctors who are concentrated in a distinct area of the city. In a number of specialties, they constitute half or more of the physicians with admitting privileges at the three hospitals in south Denver. Of particular significance with respect to the needs of local health plans that contract for physician services, MedSouth contains a substantial proportion of the internists and family practitioners in the south Denver area. For example, MedSouth's current members are 51% of the internists and 33% of the family practitioners at Swedish Hospital, and from 50% to 100% of the specialists in 19 other practice areas at that hospital. * * * As noted above, however, we do not know how many of these physicians will remain members of MedSouth after the venture is launched. A significant decrease in the number of MedSouth participating physicians would lessen the risk of anticompetitive harm.

It appears that access to some significant number of MedSouth doctors is necessary for health plans to have adequate networks to support a marketable product and to have enough conveniently located doctors to care for their current enrollees. [M]any practices in that area are full and some are closed to new patients. We have heard some evidence that waiting times for doctor appointments can be long and that it can be hard to find a doctor, particularly a primary care doctor. To date, however, in spite of that shortage, there appears to have been little new entry by physicians.

Doctors in other areas of the city do not appear to be realistic alternatives to many of the doctors located in south Denver, especially the PCPs. * * * Consequently, individual contracts with MedSouth members appear to be a principal alternative to a contract with the group as a whole. Health plans appear to be vulnerable to a threat by the group's members not to contract outside the group unless the plans pay higher than prevailing fees. Our experience in a number of markets suggests that actions of even relatively small groups of doctors can sometimes produce significant anticompetitive effects and consumer injury in the form of higher prices, fewer services, or reduced access to care.

In spite of MedSouth's explicit policy of "nonexclusivity," MedSouth members may have the incentive and the ability to agree not to contract independently of the venture. They have incentives to seek higher fees to recoup their investments in developing and implementing the proposed program. Negotiation of fee-for-service rates for the group will involve identification of price levels that could become the focal point for collusion on individual contracts. To the extent that the program creates greater communication and interdependence among the doctors, the easier it likely would be for them to coordinate their activities. Particularly in light of the doctors' existing referral arrangements, MedSouth members may be able to discipline members of the IPA who might be inclined to break ranks and contract independently. We cannot conclude with certainty that MedSouth's physicians actually will contract outside the IPA; nor can we conclude, at this early stage, that MedSouth's operation will restrict competition unreasonably. MedSouth plans to take steps to ensure that its physicians will in fact be available to contract independently with health plans. We recognize, further, that MedSouth physicians apparently did contract with health plans individually at prevailing market prices when the IPA's capitated contracts were terminated. We assume for purposes of this advisory opinion that your representations regarding the availability of MedSouth members to contract individually with health plans at competitive rates is accurate and will be borne out by the members' actual conduct.

In addition, we cannot now determine the extent to which the group will achieve the efficiencies that it expects. We are aware, however, that electronic record keeping and prescribing, and the application of evidence-based practice guidelines to regular clinical practice, are widely seen as potentially effective ways to increase the quality and efficiency of medical care. These practices may reduce errors, reduce the use of ineffective or counterproductive treatments, and increase the use of interventions that have been shown to be effective. We recognize the intention of MedSouth's leadership to achieve the goals they have established for the network, and the potential value of the means they have chosen to employ.

The information we have obtained in analyzing physician markets suggests that, in actual practice, it is often difficult to change physicians' established patterns of practice. Doing so does not result simply from the adoption of guidelines and benchmarks. Rather, the effectiveness of such programs depends upon a number of intangible factors, including the degree of commitment to the process by the members of the group and the effectiveness of its leadership. To change practice patterns requires an ongoing commitment of time, effort, and expertise, and it can be difficult to accomplish even when there are significant external incentives to do so. The experience of other physician groups indicates that it is harder to achieve implementation of this type of program in a large group, in the absence of direct financial risk relating to achievement of network goals, or where the physicians are not already closely connected to one another, and that each physician needs to have a significant number of patients subject to the system before it has an actual impact on his or her practice patterns.

The ultimate conclusion we draw in this advisory opinion turns in substantial measure on your representations concerning MedSouth's determination and ability to overcome these challenges. MedSouth has established efficiency goals and developed concrete plans to achieve them. We think a conclusion at this stage that MedSouth is unlikely to achieve the efficiencies it seeks is unwarranted. Nonetheless, the extent to which efficiencies actually are achieved would be an important factor in assessing the overall competitive effects of the proposed conduct.

## Conclusions

We conclude, on balance, that the proposed program appears to have the potential to improve the quality and effectiveness of health care services that are delivered to patients, and thus to provide important benefits to consumers. Given the prospective nature of the analysis inherent in an advisory opinion, we do not have any direct evidence of either efficiencies or competitive effects. Based on all the factors discussed above, we have concluded that we would not recommend a challenge to MedSouth fully implementing the program and then offering it to payers on a collective basis. As long as doctors are, in fact, willing to deal individually on competitive terms with payers who do not want the package product, as you represent will be the case, significant anticompetitive effects appear unlikely. If final physician participation in the group is significantly smaller than MedSouth's current membership, significant anticompetitive effects, likewise, may be unlikely. If, however, MedSouth's member physicians are able to use collective power to force payers to contract with the network or to pay higher prices, then absent evidence that substantial efficiency benefits outweighed likely anticompetitive effects, we likely would recommend that the Commission bring an enforcement action. As your letter recognizes, members of the network face an increased antitrust risk to the extent that they do not actually agree to contract with health plans independent of the network and at competitive prices, either when a payer prefers as an initial matter not to purchase the group product or when it has done so and then desires to return to individual contracting. Of course, concerted refusal by some or all of MedSouth's members to deal with payers outside of the IPA would appear to be unrelated to the joint venture presented in your request, and, thus, to be illegal per se. This office will monitor MedSouth's operations and the behavior of its physician members for indications that the proposed conduct is resulting in significant anticompetitive effects.

Sincerely yours,

Jeffrey W. Brennan
Assistant Director

### Add, at p. 1074, bottom of the page:

The Department of Justice settled its case against the Federation of Physicians and Dentists, prohibiting the Federation from serving as a third-party messenger in negotiations between physicians and health insurance plans and from making recommendations to physicians and discouraging them from making independent business judgments. See Federation of Physicians and Dentists, No. 98–475 (Nov. 6, 2002) (final judgment), available at www.doj.gov/atr.cases/f200600/200654.htm.

In 2002, there were numerous physician strikes or other work stoppages in protest of rising medical malpractice costs. Should these be regarded as boycotts under the antitrust law? Does the fact that these actions have a "political" objective immunize them from antitrust scrutiny? For an interesting parallel, see Superior Court Trial Lawyers Association v. FTC, 493 U.S. 411, 110 S.Ct. 768, 107 L.Ed.2d 851 (1990), in which the Supreme Court upheld the FTC's challenge to a group boycott by lawyers representing indigent clients in criminal matters in the District of Columbia. See also Charles Taylor, Over the Line? Feds Watch Doc Walkouts with Antitrust Concerns, Mod. Healthcare, at 12, available in 2003 WL 9135214 at *1.

Another labor-related antitrust issue is presented by a class action case challenging the National Resident Matching Program used to pair recent medical school graduates with residency programs. Plaintiffs allege the program restricts competition on wages and terms of employment by essentially forcing applicants to forfeit their right to negotiate. See Frances Miller & Thomas L. Greaney, The National Resident Matching Program and Antitrust Law, 289 JAMA 803 (2003).

**Add, at p. 1075, end of second paragraph:**

New Jersey has also adopted legislation immunizing collective bargaining from antitrust scrutiny under state law. See N.J. Stat. § 52:17B–196 (2002). No case law has addressed as yet the question of whether such laws will provide immunity from federal antitrust law under the State Action Doctrine. The Federal Trade Commission has filed comments with three state legislatures opposing proposed legislation immunizing collective bargaining and also contending that such laws may not afford immunity from federal antitrust laws. FTC Staff Opposes Ohio Bill To Allow Physician Collective Bargaining (Oct. 21, 2002), available at www.ftc.gov/opa/2002/10/physicians.htm; FTC Staff Opposes Washington State Proposal to Allow Physician Collective Bargaining (Feb. 14, 2002), available at: www.ftc.gov/opa/2002/02/washphys.htm; FTC Staff Opposes Alaska Proposal to Allow Physician Collective Bargaining (Jan. 31, 2002), available at: www.ftc.gov/opa/2002/01/alaskaphysicians.htm.

## *Notes and Questions*

1. Should clinical integration be treated on a par with financial integration for purposes of avoiding per se analysis? Is there a sufficiently precise definition of clinical integration contained in the FTC policy statements or the MedSouth decision to assure that physicians will align their efforts in a manner that improves efficiency and not direct them to raising prices? Does MedSouth adequately answer the question, required under Rule of Reason analysis, of why the price agreement is reasonably necessary to accomplish the procompetitive objectives of the plan?

2. Federal Trade Commissioner Thomas B. Leary has written a noteworthy article assessing the MedSouth opinion and raising some provocative questions. Thomas B. Leary, The Antitrust Implications of "Clinical Integration": An Analy-

sis of the FTC Staff's Advisory Opinion in MedSouth. 47 St. Louis U. L.J. 227 (2003). Leary questions whether counting physicians is an adequate measure of market power, given differentiation among physicians and the nature of the services they provide. He also doubts that efficiencies can be effectively measured using conventional antitrust tools. For example, does a decrease in output necessarily reflect less competition; might it indicate an improved use of resources (i.e., fewer unnecessary tests and services)? The article also raises the question of why MedSouth's arrangement should be non-exclusive. Isn't there an unacknowledged tension between the advisory letter's conclusions as to the necessity of joint contracting to promote efficiency (i.e., the need to assure that physicians are tightly bound to the plan) and its endorsement of the non-exclusive nature of the arrangement as lessening anticompetitive risks?

3. Some academic commentators have recently criticized antitrust doctrine for failing to explicitly account for quality. See William M. Sage & Peter J. Hammer, A Copernican View of Health Care Antitrust, 65 L. & Contemp. Probs. 241 (2002). A more radical critique of antitrust is provided by an economist who emphasizes the market imperfections endemic in health care and suggests that government control may yield better outcomes for consumers than reliance on competition. See Thomas Rice, The Economics of Health Care Reconsidered (1998).

**Add, at p. 1076:**

Erratum: twelfth line from the bottom of the page should read "The Court found no actual detrimental effect."

## B. EXCLUSIVE CONTRACTING

**Add, at p. 1084, after Note 3:**

### *Note on Monopolization by Hospitals*

In Surgical Care Center of Hammond v. Hospital Service District No. 1 of Tangipahoa Parish, 309 F.3d 836 (5th Cir.2002), the Fifth Circuit Court of Appeals confronted a fact setting that would make a great final exam question.

Surgical Care Center of Hammond is a limited liability company doing business as St. Luke's Surgicenter, an outpatient surgery clinic that opened in 1996 in Hammond, Louisiana. The Hospital Service District No. 1 of Tangipahoa Parish is a political subdivision of the State of Louisiana that operates North Oaks Medical Center, the largest hospital in the Hammond area. North Oaks offers a full range of inpatient and outpatient services, including outpatient surgery. Quorum Health Resources, Inc. manages the North Oaks facilities. St. Luke's brought this action against North Oaks and Quorum, alleging that their trade practices violated the Sherman Act [and state antitrust and consumer protection laws].

St. Luke's contends that North Oaks is attempting to monopolize the outpatient surgery market by exploiting its market power over inpatient care and, more specifically, by pressuring managed care companies to use North Oaks exclusively for both inpatient and outpatient care. [The "exclusive" contracts entitled HMO's or Preferred Provider organizations (PPO's) to up to a 25% discount of billed charges if the provider designated North Oaks as the sole provider of certain medical services, including outpatient surgery, within a designated geographic area.] According to St. Luke's, these exclusive agreements and the "tying" of inpatient and outpatient care are violations of both federal and state antitrust laws. St. Luke's also alleges that North Oaks refused to sign a patient transfer agreement with St. Luke's, refused to sign a blood type and cross match agreement, refused to lend medical equipment to St. Luke's, and engaged in various unfair employment practices.

After the issue of "state action immunity" was resolved, [the Fifth Circuit had previously held that the Louisiana legislature "did not make sufficiently clear an intent ... to insulate its creature of state government from the constraints of the Sherman Antitrust Act...." Surgical Care Ctr. of Hammond, L.C. v. Hospital Serv. Dist. No. 1 of Tangipahoa Parish, 171 F.3d 231, 232 (5th Cir.1999)(en banc)], the district court tried the case and entered judgment for the defendants on all claims. The district court concluded, first, that St. Luke's did not prove attempted monopolization of outpatient surgery under § 2 of the Sherman Act. According to the district court, St. Luke's evidence established neither predatory conduct by North Oaks nor a dangerous probability that North Oaks would achieve monopoly power in the outpatient surgery market. Second, the district court ruled that St. Luke's could not prevail on its conspiracy claim under § 2 of the Sherman Act because North Oaks and Quorum (*qua* principal and agent) are incapable of conspiring with one another to violate antitrust laws. Finally, the district court ruled that North Oaks was entitled to "discretionary act immunity" shielding it from liability under both the Louisiana Monopolies Act and the Louisiana Unfair Trade Practices Act. The district court did not address St. Luke's claims under § 1 of the Sherman Act because, prior to trial, the court ruled that St. Luke's complaint had not included § 1 claims and then denied St. Luke's request to amend its complaint. St. Luke's now appeals.

Unfortunately (for future exam takers), the Fifth Circuit disposed of the case on the narrow issue of whether plaintiff had met its burden of proving that defendant North Oaks had market power in a well-defined geographic market for inpatient services. Finding it did not, the court dismissed plaintiff's attempted monopolization, tying and exclusive dealing claims. Id. at 842. Nevertheless, the Hammond case represents an increasingly familiar pattern, as hospitals confront potential competition from their own doctors who are opening up surgicenters and other "carve out" facilities that will compete with them. Some hospitals have responded by withdrawing staff privileges from these physicians, while others have tried to "strike a deal" by agreeing to let the physicians joint venture with the hospital in its outpatient services. What potential antitrust claims do you see arising from these responses? For a discussion of a proposal to treat staff privilege determinations of this kind as illegal remuneration under the anti-kickback laws, see supra this Supplement, Chapter 14.

Hospitals often level the claim that physicians starting new facilities are engaging in "cherry picking", i.e. taking the most profitable services away from the hospital and leaving them with unprofitable services and the obligation to provide free care to the indigent. Is there any conceivable antitrust defense to the hospital's anticompetitive response based on the alleged "cherry picking" effect of its physicians' activities?

## Note on the FTC's Pharmaceutical Initiative

The FTC has devoted extensive enforcement resources at improving competition in the pharmaceutical sector. It has been particularly active in trying to prevent anticompetitive activities that inhibit entry of generic drugs, which usually have a substantial impact on prices. An important legislative development was the Hatch–Waxman Amendments to the Food, Drug and Cosmetic Act (FDCA), pursuant to which Congress sought to balance innovation and greater market access. Drug Price Competition and Patent Restoration Act of 1984, Pub. L. No. 98–417, 98 Stat. 1585 (1984) (codified as amended at 21 U.S.C. § 355 (2000)). The regulatory scheme for drug approvals requires that drug manufacturers must file information with the FDA pursuant to New Drug Applications (NDAs) specifying the patents that claim the drug products they intend to market. If it approves the new drug, the FDA lists the patents in an agency publication known as the Orange Book. When a generic drug manufacturer seeks to enter the market with a generic version of a branded drug, it generally files an "Abbreviate New Drug Application" (ANDA) which requires that the applicant file certain "certifications" regarding each patent listed in the Orange Book. A "Paragraph IV certification" asserts that the patent in question is invalid or not infringed and that the generic applicant seeks entry prior to the patent's expiration. If a patent holder brings an infringement suit against the generic applicant, the filing of that suit triggers an automatic 30–month stay of FDA approval of the generic drug. Unless the patent litigation is resolved in favor of the generic drug manufacturer, it cannot enter the market during this period. The Hatch–Waxman law provides 180 days of marketing exclusivity to the first generic drug manufacturer that files its application with the FDA and receives approval to market a particular generic drug prior to the expiration of the branded drug's products. After the 180 days, the FDA is free to approve subsequent generic applicants, assuming other regulatory requirements are met.

The FTC has uncovered and prosecuted a number of abuses of the Hatch–Waxman law, bringing cases against both branded and generic drug manufacturers. The Commission's first generation of pharmaceutical litigation focused on agreements between branded and generic drug manufacturers that allegedly delayed the entry of generic drugs. These agreements settled patent infringement litigation brought by the branded drug manufacturer against the generic drug manufacturer. Although settlement of patent infringement litigation can be efficient and pro-competitive, certain agreements can delay generic entry by "parking" the 180–day marketing exclusivity provided by the Hatch–Waxman Amendments. The FTC obtained consent judgments in two such cases. See Abbott Lab., No. C–3945 (May 22, 2000) (consent order), available at www.ftc.gov.os/2000/05/c3945.do.htm; Geneva Pharm., Inc., No. C–3946 (May 22, 2000) (consent order), available at www.ftc.gov/os/2000/05/c3946.do.htm; Hoechst Marion Roussel, Inc.,. No. D–9293 (May 8, 2001) (consent order), available at www.ftc.gov/os/2001/05/hoechstdo.htm. In a third case, Schering Plough Corp., the Commission entered a consent judgment against one firm; but an initial decision by an administrative law judge ruled against the Commission as to other parties and the case is currently pending before the Commission. See Shering Plough Corp.,. No. D–9297 (June 27, 2002) (initial decision), available at: www.ftc.gov/os/2002/07/scheringinitialdecisionp1.pdf.

The Commission's second-generation pharmaceutical cases involved unilateral action by branded drug manufacturers. The Commission alleged that improper Orange Book listing constituted anticompetitive abuse of the Hatch–Waxman process by creating the possibility of obtaining unwarranted 30–month stays of FDA approval of generic drug products. See Biovail Corp.,. No. C–4060 (Oct. 2, 2002) (consent order), available at: www.ftc.gov/os/2002/10/biovaildo.pdf. In private litigation, plaintiffs have claimed that fraudulent Orange Book listings violate the Sherman Act. See In re Buspirone, 185 F.Supp.2d 363 (S.D.N.Y.2002). The Commission's extended analysis of these issues can be found at: www.ftc.gov/os/2002/07/genericdrugstudy.pdf. A number of private treble damages actions have been brought by private parties and state attorneys general.

## D. MERGERS AND ACQUISITIONS

### 1. Hospital Mergers

**Add, at p. 1110, end of Note 5:**

*Hospital Mergers: The FTC's Response*

Federal and state enforcers have lost seven consecutive antitrust challenges to hospital mergers. The cause for these setbacks may include faulty doctrinal analysis by the courts, poor case selection by the agencies, and the subtle influence of the "managed care backlash" on judges who tacitly accept the notion that consolidation will aid consumers by "leveling the playing field" between hospitals and managed care. See Thomas L. Greaney, Whither Antitrust? The Uncertain Future of Competition Policy in Health Care, 21 Health Affs. 185(Mar./Apr. 2002). Many of these cases have turned on the government's failure to prove a localized geographic market for primary and secondary acute care hospital services. These outcomes have attracted considerable attention among economists who question the misuse of critical loss analysis and patient origin studies by the courts. See, e.g., Kenneth Danger & H.E. Frech, Critical Thinking about "Critical Loss" in Antitrust, 46 Antitrust L. Bull. 339 (2001); James Langenfeld and W. Li, Critical Loss Analysis in Evaluating Mergers, 46 Antitrust Bull. 299 (2001). But see Barry Harris and Joseph J. Simon, Focusing Market Definition: How Much Substitution is Enough?, 12 Research in L. & Economics 207 (1989).

Responding to its lack of success in court, the FTC has decided to conduct retrospective studies of the impact of horizontal hospital mergers in selected markets around the country, including some that were the subject of unsuccessful litigation by the government. In announcing the project, FTC Chairman Muris explained that the agency would gather information on consummated hospital mergers in concentrated markets to study whether they had resulted in anticompetitive harm, e.g. higher prices or lessened quality, as well as whether they had produced significant efficiencies. Timothy J. Muris, Everything Old is New Again, supra pg. 5. See also, David Balto & M. Geertsema, Why Hospital Merger Antitrust Enforcement Remains Necessary: A Retrospective of the Butterworth Merger, 34 J. Health L. 129 (2001); Jacqueline D. Scott, The FTC Staff's Prescription: Wrong for Healthcare in West Michigan, 34 J. Health L. 171 (2001). Chairman Muris also held out the possibility that the FTC might seek administrative remedies where mergers resulted in anticompetitive harm. Do you think it feasible to unwind a consummated merger? Even if it is, what problems do you foresee in obtaining relief that would reinvigorate hospital competition in a market?

# Part IV
# BIOETHICS

# Chapter 16

# HUMAN REPRODUCTION AND BIRTH

## I. WHEN DOES HUMAN LIFE BECOME A "PERSON"?

### B. LEGAL RECOGNITION OF THE BEGINNING OF HUMAN LIFE

#### 2. *Statutory Recognition*

**Add, at p. 1127, at the end of "2. Statutory Recognition":**

In 2002 the question of the status of the fetus for purposes of the criminal law arose in very different circumstances. Jaclyn Kurr was convicted of voluntary manslaughter when she knifed to death the father of the 17-week fetuses (there were twins) that she was carrying. In the midst of a fight over cocaine use, the father, who had a history of violently attacking Ms. Kurr, came at her and punched her twice in the stomach. She told him not to hit her any more because she was "carrying his babies." As he came at her again, she stabbed him. Although Michigan law recognizes that one may use deadly force in defense of another, the trial court refused her request for an instruction on "defense of others" on the grounds that the fetus was nonviable, and thus could not be an "other" for purposes of Michigan law.

The Michigan Court of Appeal reversed and held that "an individual may indeed defend a fetus from such an assault and may use deadly force if she honestly and reasonably believes the fetus to be in imminent danger of death or great bodily harm." People v. Kurr, 253 Mich.App. 317, 654 N.W.2d 651, 656 (2002). The court based its decision on the state policy of fetal protection that was explicit in Michigan's 1998 Fetal Protection Act.

> We conclude that in this state, the defense should also extend to the protection of a fetus, viable or nonviable, from an assault against the mother, and we base this conclusion primarily on the fetal protection act adopted by the Legislature in 1998. * * *
>
> *The plain language of these provisions shows the Legislature's conclusion that fetuses are worthy of protection as living entities as a matter of public policy.* * * * Moreover, in enacting the fetal protection act, the Legislature did not distinguish between fetuses that are viable, or capable of surviving outside the womb, and those that are nonviable. In fact, the Legislature used the term "embryo" as well as the term "fetus" [in the relevant statutory sections.] * * * . This definition clearly encompasses

nonviable fetuses. Moreover, the legislative analysis of the act indicates that, in passing the act, the Legislature was clearly determined to provide criminal penalties for harm caused to nonviable fetuses during assaults or negligent acts against pregnant women. [ ]

Because the act reflects a public policy to protect even an embryo from unlawful assaultive or negligent conduct, we conclude that the defense of others concept does extend to the protection of a nonviable fetus from an assault against the mother. We emphasize, however, that the defense is available *solely* in the context of an assault against the mother. Indeed, the Legislature has *not* extended the protection of the criminal laws to embryos existing outside a woman's body, i.e., frozen embryos stored for future use, and we therefore *do not* extend the applicability of the defense of others theory to situations involving these embryos.

People v. Kurr, 654 N.W.2d at 654 (italics in original). As you can imagine, the case has taken on political meaning, with right-to-life groups delighted with the recognition that the fetus is, in the words of legislative director of the National Right to Life committee, "a member of the human family." Right-to-choose groups were concerned about the decision, and one National Organization for Women chapter head suggested that "it's a slippery slope toward [outlawing] abortion."

### 3. *Common Law Recognition*

**Add, at p. 1130, at the end of "3. Common Law Recognition":**

In 2002 the Court of Appeals of Maryland was confronted with an action by a pregnant woman who lost her nonviable fetus in an automobile accident. Although Maryland law would not permit recovery in wrongful death for the death of the nonviable fetus, the plaintiff sought to recover for the injuries to her fetus as injuries to her own body, arguing that a nonviable fetus is a part of the mother. The Maryland court limited recovery to the injury to the mother but broadly defined that injury. In answering a certified question from the United States District Court, the Maryland Court of Appeals explained:

A pregnant woman who sustains personal injury as the result of a defendant's tortious conduct and who, as part of that injury, suffers the loss of the fetus may recover, in her own action for personal injuries, for any demonstrable emotional distress that accompanies and is attributable to the loss of the fetus. The distress recoverable in that action includes that arising from the unexpected termination of her pregnancy and the enduring of a miscarriage or stillbirth. Where a sufficient factual premise is shown, it may include compensation for (1) the depression, anguish, and grief that arises from the termination of the pregnancy, the manner in which the pregnancy was terminated, and from the miscarriage or stillbirth—the distress of not having been able to carry through to a successful completion of the pregnancy, of having to carry a fetus or a child which is destroyed by someone else's tortious conduct, of having to witness at the time of miscarriage or delivery the stillborn child or the fetal tissue that was to be her child—and (2) medical expenses reasonably incurred in the treatment of, and lost wages attendant to, that depression, anguish, or grief. It does *not* include, however, in the context of this case, pecuniary losses or solatium or loss of consortium damages recoverable under the wrongful death statute, whether or not that statute applies in the circumstance. The recovery, in other words, is for the psychic injury inflicted on the mother and not for her sorrow over the loss of the child. Recovery for that sorrow must be had, if at all, under the wrongful death statute.

Smith v. Borello, 370 Md. 227, 804 A.2d 1151, 1163 (2002).

In New York, the Appellate Division confronted a case in which the mother of a stillborn fetus attempted to show that the fetus had some brain activity before the stillbirth to justify an award of damages for the pre-stillbirth pain and suffering of the fetus. The court rejected the argument, maintaining the New York position that "no cause of action lies to recover damages on behalf of a stillborn fetus." Maher v. Yoon, 297 A.D.2d 361, 746 N.Y.S.2d 493 (2002).

## II. MEDICAL INTERVENTION IN REPRODUCTION

### A. LIMITING REPRODUCTION

#### 3. *Abortion*

**Add, at p. 1138, at the end of the page:**

There are few cases that have affected the American political landscape as much as *Roe v. Wade*. On January 22, 2003, many of those engaged in the abortion debates marked the thirtieth anniversary of this Supreme Court decision. Americans remain deeply divided on the issue, with polls showing the same split for the last fifteen years. For an interesting account of the celebrations and lamentations that attended the recognition that *Roe* had been law for three decades, see K. Zernike, Thirty Years After Roe v. Wade: New Trends But the Old Debate, New York Times, January 20, 2003, at A-1.

**Add, at p. 1157, at the end of note 1:**

Perhaps buoyed by the conservative victories at the polls in 2002, those wishing to restrict access to abortion are again seeking restrictive abortion legislation. Some of the state legislative battles are over the allocation of resources, including family planning and Medicaid resources. Some address proposed substantive changes in the law, though. For example, a handful of states have passed legislation requiring insurers to charge a separate and identifiable premium if a health insurance policy will cover abortion procedures, and more state legislatures are expected to debate this kind of legislation in the next couple of years.

Pro-choice advocates have also gone on the offensive in some state legislatures. Instead of merely opposing new restrictions on abortion, in some states advocates are supporting legislation that would make some procedures more easily available. For example, some state legislatures have debated proposals that would effectively require hospital emergency rooms to have emergency contraception available for women who have been assaulted. Whether such "emergency contraception" constitutes abortion remains a controversy. See the Note on page 1163 of the casebook.

**Add, at p. 1157, at the end of note 2:**

As this supplement goes to press in March of 2003, the Senate was considering new federal legislation to outlaw "partial birth abortions." The debate on the issue was complicated by a series of proposed amendments offered by pro-choice advocates, including one that would formally support the Supreme Court decision in Roe v. Wade, and one to provide more federal resources for family planning. Of course, the Constitutionality of any new federal law following *Stenberg* would depend on the language of the statute. While neither side in this debate seems willing to give an inch, most outside observers agree that any federal ban would be more symbolic than practically meaningful.

**Add, at p. 1159, at the end of note 5:**

In *A Woman's Choice–East Side Women's Clinic v. Newman*, 132 F.Supp.2d 1150 (S.D.Ind.2001), a trial court threw out an Indiana statute that required face-to-face counseling with a woman at least eighteen hours before that woman could be provided an abortion. Effectively, this statute imposed a two trip requirement on women seeking an abortion. The Indiana law was very similar to a provision of the Pennsylvania law that was upheld in *Casey*, but the Indiana federal court still found that it would place an undue burden on those seeking abortions. In reaching its conclusion, the court depended on post-*Casey* empirical studies that demonstrated that similar laws in Utah and Mississippi cut down the abortion rate in those states by ten percent.

The Seventh Circuit reversed in *A Woman's Choice—East Side Women's Clinic v. Newman*, 305 F.3d 684 (7th Cir.2002), finding that those studies were insufficient to support the trial court's conclusions. The Court of Appeals also noted that there was an emergency exception to the eighteen hour requirement. The United States Supreme Court denied certiorari in *A Woman's Choice–East Side Women's Clinic v. Brizzi*, ___ U.S. ___, 123 S.Ct. 1273, 154 L.Ed.2d 1026 (2003).

**Add, at p. 1160, at the end of Note 10:**

Legislation is now pending in Congress that would make it a crime to take a child across a state line to avoid parental consent or notification statutes.

**Add, at p. 1163, at the end of the first paragraph:**

In 2003 the Supreme Court determined that pro-life advocates do not obtain any property from another, and thus do not commit the federal crime of extortion under the Hobbs Act, when they use force or threats of force at abortion clinics to dissuade women from seeking abortion services. Whether the protesters had committed the crime of extortion was relevant to the underlying RICO claim filed by the National Organization of Women and others. *Scheidler v. NOW, Inc.*, ___ U.S. ___, 123 S.Ct. 1057, 154 L.Ed.2d 991 (2003).

### 4. Sterilization

**Add, at p. 1168, at the end of "4. Sterilization":**

One group, Children Requiring a Caring Community (Crack), also called Project Prevention, is now offering a cash payment (most recently, $200) to any drug addict who can prove that he or she has been sterilized or put on some long term contraceptive. The group was started by a woman who adopted four children who had been affected by prenatal drug abuse, and the bounty is paid upon proof of both addiction (an arrest record or doctor's note will do) and sterilization. The organization does not pay for the sterilization or long-term contraception itself. For a description of the program see C.M. Vega, Sterilization Offer to Addicts Reopens Ethics Issue, New York Times, January 6, 2003, at A–1.

Is there any ethical problem with this program? What is it? Who is being more paternalistic, those who want to encourage drug addicted people not to have children, or those who want to save these same poor, drug addicted people from considering this offer? Are there people our society should discourage from reproducing, or is that always improper? If so, are the drug addicted among those people? Are issues of race, ethnicity and gender relevant to your consideration of this issue? How?

## B. ASSISTING REPRODUCTION

### 3. *In Vitro Fertilization, Egg Transfer and Embryo Transfer*

**Add, at p. 1195, just before the Notes and Questions:**

For a complete list of current (2003) prices, fees and additional costs for IVF procedures at one multi-center clinic, see, *www.fertility-docs.com/fertility_fees.phtml*. For an account of the financial compensation available for egg vendors, see *www.eggdonor.com/edfinan.html*, which seeks women between 21 and 30 who are bright and attractive, have (or are pursuing) a college degree, are in excellent health, and have weight proportional to height. For a lively account of the journey of one Yale undergraduate who thought about becoming an egg vendor (at a substantial premium), see Jessica Cohen, Grade A: The Market for a Yale Woman's Eggs, The Atlantic Monthly, December 2002, at 74.

**Add, at p. 1203, at the end of the Davis case:**

### J.B. v. M.B.

Supreme Court of New Jersey, 2001.
170 N.J. 9, 783 A.2d 707.

PORITZ, C.J.

In this case, a divorced couple disagree about the disposition of seven preembryos that remain in storage after the couple, during their marriage, undertook in vitro fertilization procedures. We must first decide whether the husband and wife have entered into an enforceable contract that is now determinative on the disposition issue. If not, we must consider how such conflicts should be resolved by our courts.

I

A

J.B. and M.B. were married in February 1992. After J.B. suffered a miscarriage early in the marriage, the couple encountered difficulty conceiving a child and sought medical advice from the Jefferson Center for Women's Specialties. Although M.B. did not have infertility problems, J.B. learned that she had a condition that prevented her from becoming pregnant. On that diagnosis, the couple decided to attempt in vitro fertilization at the Cooper Center for In Vitro Fertilization, P.C. (the Cooper Center).

The in vitro fertilization procedure requires a woman to undergo a series of hormonal injections to stimulate the production of mature oocytes (egg cells or ova). The medication causes the ovaries to release multiple egg cells during a menstrual cycle rather than the single egg normally produced. The egg cells are retrieved from the woman's body and examined by a physician who evaluates their quality for fertilization. Egg cells ready for insemination are then combined with a sperm sample and allowed to incubate for approximately twelve to eighteen hours. Successful fertilization results in a zygote that develops into a four-to eight-cell preembryo. At that stage, the preembryos are either returned to the woman's uterus for implantation or cryopreserved at a temperature of–196 C and stored for possible future use.

A limited number of preembryos are implanted at one time to reduce the risk of a multiple pregnancy. Cryopreservation of unused preembryos reduces, and may eliminate, the need for further ovarian stimulation and egg retrieval, thereby reducing the medical risks and costs associated with both the hormone regimen and the surgical removal of egg cells from the woman's body. Cryopreservation also permits introduction of the preembryos into the uterus at the optimal time in the natural cycle for pregnancy. Egg cells must be fertilized before undergoing cryopreservation because unfertilized cells are difficult to preserve and, once preserved, are difficult to fertilize.

The Cooper Center's consent form describes the procedure:

> IVF [or in vitro fertilization] will be accomplished in a routine fashion: that is, ovulation induction followed by egg recovery, insemination, fertilization, embryo development and embryo transfer of up to three or four embryos in the stimulated cycle. With the couple's consent, any "extra" embryos beyond three or four will be cryopreserved according to our freezing protocol and stored at –196C. Extra embryos, upon thawing, must meet certain criteria for viability before being considered eligible for transfer. These criteria require that a certain minimum number of cells composing the embryo survive the freeze-thaw process. These extra embryos will be transferred into the woman's uterus in one or more future menstrual cycles for the purpose of establishing a normal pregnancy. The physicians and embryologists on the IVF team will be responsible for determining the appropriate biological conditions and the timing for transfers of cryopreserved embryos.

The consent form also contains language discussing the control and disposition of the preembryos:

> The control and disposition of the embryos belongs to the Patient and her Partner. You will be asked to execute the attached legal statement regarding control and disposition of cryopreserved embryos. The IVF team will not be obligated to proceed with the transfer of any cryopreserved embryos if experience indicates the risks outweigh the benefits.

Before undertaking in vitro fertilization in March 1995, the Cooper Center gave J.B. and M.B. the consent form with an attached agreement for their signatures. The agreement states, in relevant part:

> I, J.B. (patient), and M.B. (partner), agree that all control, direction, and ownership of our tissues will be relinquished to the IVF Program under the following circumstances:
>
> 1. A dissolution of our marriage by court order, unless the court specifies who takes control and direction of the tissues....

### B

The in vitro fertilization procedure was carried out in May 1995 and resulted in eleven preembryos. Four were transferred to J.B. and seven were cryopreserved. J.B. became pregnant, either as a result of the procedure or through natural means, and gave birth to the couple's daughter on March 19, 1996. In September 1996, however, the couple separated, and J.B. informed M.B. that she wished to have the remaining preembryos discarded. M.B. did not agree.

J.B. filed a complaint for divorce on November 25, 1996, in which she sought an order from the court "with regard to the * * * frozen embryos." In a counterclaim filed on November 24, 1997, M.B. demanded judgment compelling his wife "to allow the * * * frozen embryos currently in storage to be implanted or donated to other infertile couples." J.B. filed a motion for summary judgment on the preembryo issue in April 1998 alleging, in a certification filed with the motion, that she had intended to use the preembryos solely within her marriage to M.B. She stated:

> Defendant and I made the decision to attempt conception through in vitro fertilization treatment. Those decisions were made during a time when defendant and I were married and intended to remain married. Defendant and I planned to raise a family together as a married couple. I endured the in vitro process and agreed to preserve the preembryos for our use in the context of an intact family.

J.B. also certified that "there were never any discussions between the Defendant and I regarding the disposition of the frozen embryos should our marriage be dissolved."

M.B., in a cross-motion filed in July 1998, described his understanding very differently. He certified that he and J.B. had agreed prior to undergoing the in vitro fertilization procedure that any unused preembryos would not be destroyed, but would be used by his wife or donated to infertile couples. His certification stated:

> Before we began the I.V.F. treatments, we had many long and serious discussions regarding the process and the moral and ethical repercussions. For me, as a Catholic, the I.V.F. procedure itself posed a dilemma. We discussed this issue extensively and had agreed that no matter what happened the eggs would be either utilized by us or by other infertile couples. In fact, the option to donate [the preembryos] to infertile couples was the Plaintiff's idea. She came up with this idea because she knew of other individuals in her work place who were having trouble conceiving.

M.B.'s mother, father, and sister also certified that on several occasions during family gatherings J.B. had stated her intention to either use or donate the preembryos.

The couple's final judgment of divorce, entered in September 1998, resolved all issues except disposition of the preembryos.

* * *

### C

M.B. contends that the judgment of the court below violated his constitutional rights to procreation and the care and companionship of his children. He also contends that his constitutional rights outweigh J.B.'s right not to procreate because her right to bodily integrity is not implicated, as it would be in a case involving abortion. He asserts that religious convictions regarding preservation of the preembryos, and the State's interest in protecting potential life, take precedence over his former wife's more limited interests. Finally, M.B. argues that the Appellate Division should have enforced the clear agreement between the parties to give the preembryos a chance at life.

J.B. argues that the Appellate Division properly held that any alleged agreement between the parties to use or donate the preembryos would be unenforceable as a matter of public policy. She contends that New Jersey has "long recognized that individuals should not be bound by agreements requiring them to enter into family relationships or [that] seek to regulate personal intimate decisions relating to parenthood and family life." J.B. also argues that in the absence of an express agreement establishing the disposition of the preembryos, a court should not imply that an agreement exists. It is J.B.'s position that requiring use or donation of the preembryos would violate her constitutional right not to procreate. Discarding the preembryos, on the other hand, would not significantly affect M.B.'s right to procreate because he is fertile and capable of fathering another child.

* * *

### II

M.B. contends that he and J.B. entered into an agreement to use or donate the preembryos, and J.B. disputes the existence of any such agreement. As an initial matter, then, we must decide whether this case involves a contract for the disposition of the cryopreserved preembryos resulting from in vitro fertilization.

* * *

The consent form, and more important, the attachment, do not manifest a clear intent by J.B. and M.B. regarding disposition of the preembryos in the event of "[a] dissolution of [their] marriage." Although the attachment indicates that the preembryos "will be relinquished" to the clinic if the parties divorce, it carves out an exception that permits the parties to obtain a court order directing disposition of the preembryos. * * * Clearly, the thrust of the document signed by J.B. and M.B. is that the Cooper Center obtains control over the preembryos unless the parties choose otherwise in a writing, or unless a court specifically directs otherwise in an order of divorce.

* * *

We find no need for a remand to determine the parties' intentions at the time of the in vitro fertilization process. Assuming that it would be possible to enter into a valid agreement at that time irrevocably deciding the disposition of preembryos in circumstances such as we have here, a formal, unambiguous memorialization of the parties' intentions would be required to confirm their joint determination. The parties do not contest the lack of such a writing. We hold, therefore, that J.B. and M.B. never entered into a separate binding contract providing for the disposition of the cryopreserved preembryos now in the possession of the Cooper Center.

### III

In essence, J.B. and M.B. have agreed only that on their divorce the decision in respect of control, and therefore disposition, of their cryopreserved preembryos will be directed by the court. In this area, however, there are few guideposts for decision-making. Advances in medical technology have far outstripped the development of legal principles to resolve the inevitable disputes arising out of the new reproductive opportunities now available. For infertile couples, those opportunities may present the only way to have a biological family. Yet, at the point when a husband and wife decide to begin the in vitro fertilization process, they are unlikely to anticipate divorce or to be concerned about the disposition of preembryos on divorce. As they are both contributors of the genetic material comprising the preembryos, the decision should be theirs to make. [ ]

But what if, as here, the parties disagree. Without guidance from the Legislature, we must consider a means by which courts can engage in a principled review of the issues presented in such cases in order to achieve a just result. Because the claims before us derive, in part, from concepts found in the Federal Constitution and the Constitution of this State, we begin with those concepts.

### A

Both parties [and the amici] invoke the right to privacy in support of their respective positions. More specifically, they claim procreational autonomy as a fundamental attribute of the privacy rights guaranteed by both the Federal and New Jersey Constitutions. [The court then discusses the "fundamental nature of procreational rights," discussing both the *Baby M* and *Davis* cases.]

* * *

### B

We agree with the Tennessee Supreme Court [in *Davis*] that "ordinarily, the party wishing to avoid procreation should prevail." [ ] Here, the Appellate Division succinctly described the "apparent" conflict between J.B. and M.B.:

> In the present case, the wife's right not to become a parent seemingly conflicts with the husband's right to procreate. The conflict, however, is

more apparent than real. Recognition and enforcement of the wife's right would not seriously impair the husband's right to procreate. Though his right to procreate using the wife's egg would be terminated, he retains the capacity to father children.

[J.B. v. M.B., 331 N.J. Super. 223 at 232.]

In other words, M.B.'s right to procreate is not lost if he is denied an opportunity to use or donate the preembryos. M.B. is already a father and is able to become a father to additional children, whether through natural procreation or further in vitro fertilization. In contrast, J.B.'s right not to procreate may be lost through attempted use or through donation of the preembryos. Implantation, if successful, would result in the birth of her biological child and could have life-long emotional and psychological repercussions. * * *

### C

The court below "concluded that a contract to procreate is contrary to New Jersey public policy and is unenforceable." [ ] That determination follows the reasoning of the Massachusetts Supreme Judicial Court * * * wherein an agreement to compel biological parenthood was deemed unenforceable as a matter of public policy [citing *A.Z. v. B.Z.*]. The Massachusetts court likened enforcement of a contract permitting implantation of preembryos to other contracts to enter into familial relationships that were unenforceable under the laws of Massachusetts, i.e., contracts to marry or to give up a child for adoption prior to the fourth day after birth. * * *

As the Appellate Division opinion in this case points out, the laws of New Jersey also evince a policy against enforcing private contracts to enter into or terminate familial relationships. [The court then reviews the New Jersey law abolishing causes of action for breach of contract to marry, and analyzes the *Baby M* opinion.]

Enforcement of a contract that would allow the implantation of preembryos at some future date in a case where one party has reconsidered his or her earlier acquiescence raises similar issues [to those raised in *Baby M.*]. If implantation is successful, that party will have been forced to become a biological parent against his or her will.

* * *

We recognize that persuasive reasons exist for enforcing preembryo disposition agreements. * * * We also recognize that in vitro fertilization is in widespread use, and that there is a need for agreements between the participants and the clinics that perform the procedure. We believe that the better rule, and the one we adopt, is to enforce agreements entered into at the time in vitro fertilization is begun, subject to the right of either party to change his or her mind about disposition up to the point of use or destruction of any stored preembryos.

The public policy concerns that underlie limitations on contracts involving family relationships are protected by permitting either party to object at a later date to provisions specifying a disposition of preembryos that that party no longer accepts. Moreover, despite the conditional nature of the disposition provisions, in the large majority of cases the agreements will control, permitting fertility clinics and other like facilities to rely on their terms. Only when a party affirmatively notifies a clinic in writing of a change in intention should the disposition issue be reopened. Principles of fairness dictate that agreements provided by a clinic should be written in plain language, and that a qualified clinic representative should review the terms with the parties prior to execution. Agreements should not be signed in blank, * * * or in a manner suggesting that the parties have not given due consideration to the disposition question. Those and other reasonable safeguards should serve to limit later disputes.

Finally, if there is disagreement as to disposition because one party has reconsidered his or her earlier decision, the interests of both parties must be evaluated. Because ordinarily the party choosing not to become a biological parent will prevail, we do not anticipate increased litigation as a result of our decision. In this case, after having considered that M.B. is a father and is capable of fathering additional children, we have affirmed J.B.'s right to prevent implantation of the preembryos. We express no opinion in respect of a case in which a party who has become infertile seeks use of stored preembryos against the wishes of his or her partner, noting only that the possibility of adoption also may be a consideration, among others, in the court's assessment.

IV

Under the judgment of the Appellate Division, the seven remaining preembryos are to be destroyed. It was represented to us at oral argument, however, that J.B. does not object to their continued storage if M.B. wishes to pay any fees associated with that storage. M.B. must inform the trial court forthwith whether he will do so; otherwise, the preembryos are to be destroyed.

VERNIERO, J., concurring.

I join in the disposition of this case and in all but one aspect of the Court's opinion. I do not agree with the Court's suggestion, in dicta, that the right to procreate may depend on adoption as a consideration. [ ]

I also write to express my view that the same principles that compel the outcome in this case would permit an infertile party to assert his or her right to use a preembryo against the objections of the other party, if such use were the only means of procreation. In that instance, the balance arguably would weigh in favor of the infertile party absent countervailing factors of greater weight. I do not decide that profound question today, and the Court should not decide it or suggest a result, because it is absent from this case.

**Add, at p. 1204, at the end of note 4:**

How is J.B. v. M.B. different from Davis v. Davis? From A.Z v. B.Z.? Does the J.B. court permit a couple to enter into a binding agreement before the IVF is performed, or is that agreement always subject to reconsideration by a party who later decides that he or she does not want to become a parent? Do you believe that M.B.'s religious views are relevant? How should they be considered by the court?

If a deeply religious couple going through IVF were to ask you to draft an agreement that would assure that their fertilized ova would not be destroyed under any circumstances, could you help them? In Tennessee? New Jersey?

### 4. Surrogacy

**Add, at p. 1226, at the bottom of the page:**

## PRATO–MORRISON v. DOE
Court of Appeal of California, 2002.
103 Cal.App.4th 222, 126 Cal.Rptr.2d 509.

VOGEL, J:

\* \* \*

### FACTS

#### A.

In 1988, Donna Prato–Morrison and Robert Morrison were fertility clinic patients of the Center for Reproductive Health (CRH) at the University of California at Irvine (UCI). As part of the *in vitro* fertilization process, the Morrisons' eggs and sperm were entrusted to CRH with the intent that the resulting embryos would produce the child they hoped to conceive. No pregnancy was achieved and the Morrisons ultimately abandoned their efforts on the assumption that any remaining genetic material would be destroyed by CRH.

#### B.

In the mid–1990's, UCI learned stealing "had occurred—human eggs were taken from one patient and implanted in another without the consent of the donor." [ ] The Morrisons (and many others) sued CRH, UCI, and the doctors involved in the "egg stealing." The Morrisons' case was settled by the payment of money—but only after the Morrisons learned through the discovery process that their genetic material might not have been destroyed, that Judith and Jacob Doe (who were also patients of the CRH fertility clinic) *might have* (without the Does' knowledge) received the Morrisons' eggs, sperm, or embryos, and that (in December 1988) Judith Doe had given birth to twin daughters, Ida and Rose. The Morrisons claim they are the twins' genetic parents.

#### C.

In 1996, the Morrisons filed a "complaint to establish parental relationship," naming the Does as defendants, alleging that the Morrisons are the "biological and legal parents" of the twins, and asking for custody, visitation rights, and an award of attorney's fees. Between 1996 and 1999, the Morrisons attempted to obtain blood tests and DNA samples from the twins but the Does refused to provide them and these "negotiations" ultimately failed.

In 1999, the Morrisons filed an amended complaint in which they abandoned their quest for custody but reasserted their demands for blood tests and for visitation. At the Morrisons' request, a hearing was set to determine the Morrisons' right (1) to obtain DNA tests and (2) to have a mental health professional appointed to help determine "the commencement, frequency, degree of contact or visitation" the Morrisons should have with the twins.

\* \* \*

In April 2000, the Does asked the trial court (1) to seal the records of this case; (2) to issue protective orders "to ensure the privacy of the children in this potentially high-profile litigation, and to preclude deliberate or accidental disclosure of the existence of this litigation and the [Morrisons'] claims ... to the children"; and (3) to quash the Morrisons' petition on the grounds (among others) that (a) the Does are the "presumed natural and legal parents" of the twins, and (b) the Morrisons lacked standing to pursue a parentage action or to compel blood or DNA testing. [ ]

In support of their motions, the Does submitted declarations establishing that since 1983 they have lived together continuously as husband and wife, that in addition to the twins they have two older children (one from Jacob's former marriage, the other together), and that the twins were conceived because the Does had "actively tried to conceive with medical assistance, intending to use Jacob's sperm and anonymously and voluntarily donated ova." Judith Doe "became pregnant by [her] husband," gave birth to the twins, and remains a "full time mother." Jacob Doe was "neither impotent nor sterile" at the time the twins were conceived or at the time they were born, and he is their father (as well as the father of the Does' two older children). When Judith Doe gave birth to the twins, the Does "knowingly and joyously received the twins into [their] home and family. [They] have adored [the twins and have] reared them in [the Does'] culture and religion...." The Does "are the only parents that Ida and Rose have ever known." The Does objected to the release of any medical information to the Morrisons, pointed out that the Morrisons' claims had caused "great emotional stress" to the Does, and said the introduction of the Morrisons into the Does' "family life would be a monstrous intrusion."

In opposition to the Does' motion to quash, the Morrisons claimed they had standing to pursue this action because Donna Morrison is "a genetic mother." * * *

### D.

At a hearing held in June 2000, the family law court sustained the Does' objections to the Morrison's evidence and found that the Morrisons had failed to establish their status as "interested parties" entitled to pursue a parentage action. The court nevertheless continued the matter to afford the Morrisons an opportunity to present additional evidence.

As "additional evidence," the Morrisons submitted an unredacted copy of the handwritten list and a declaration from Teri Ord—who stated that she was employed from 1986 through and including 1988 by AMI Medical Center as an "In Vitro Fertilization Biologist" in charge of "the embryology lab at that facility." In that capacity, she states, she "participated" in "transfers of genetic materials obtained by the doctors [at UCI] from fertility patients. According to laboratory records, Donna [Morrison] was an infertility patient at AMI ... between March and May 1988, as was [Judith Doe]." Ord stated that, based on information contained in other clinical and laboratory records, she prepared the handwritten document in *1995* to show that, "between March and May of *1988*, patient '[Judith Doe]' received sixteen eggs from patient '[Donna Morrison].' Twenty-one eggs were extracted from [Donna Morrison], and five transferred into [Donna Morrison's] own fallopian tubes.

The remaining sixteen were transferred to [Judith Doe]," and the notations next to Judith Doe's name show that "a twin pregnancy resulted." (Emphasis added.) The Morrisons also submitted evidence that UCI's original clinical and laboratory records for its former patients were generally unavailable because they had been confiscated (in 1995) by the Federal Bureau of Investigation.

The Does objected to Ord's declaration and compilation as hearsay, and on the ground that it violated the Does' physician-patient privilege and their right to reproductive privacy. In October 2000, the family law court sustained the Does' evidentiary objections and granted their motion to quash. In April 2001, the court dismissed the Morrisons' action. The Morrisons appeal from the order of dismissal.

## DISCUSSION

### I.

The Morrisons contend their evidence is sufficient to establish Donna status as the genetic mother and, therefore, her standing to pursue a parentage action. We disagree.

"Any interested person may bring an action to determine the existence or non-existence of a mother and child relationship" [ ], but an unrelated person who is not a genetic parent is not an "interested person" within the meaning of [the relevant section]. [ ] The threshold question, therefore, is whether Ord's declaration and handwritten list were properly excluded by the trial court. If so, there is no evidence at all to suggest that Donna Morrison is the twins' genetic mother, or that either of the Morrisons is otherwise related to the twins.

The declaration and list were properly excluded as inadmissible hearsay that does not satisfy the requirements of the business record exception to the hearsay rule. As Ord concedes in her declaration, the list was compiled from other, non-identified clinical and laboratory records, and she does not attempt to establish her personal knowledge of the information stated on her list. She does not say she was a percipient witness to the transfers of genetic material, or that she made the entries in the original records. She admits the list was not made at or near the time of the events it purports to describe, but was in fact made almost eight years later. She offers no clue as to *why* the list was made. By Ord's own admission, her sources of information and method and time of preparation show a lack of trustworthiness and defeat the Morrisons' contention that the list comes within the business records exception to the hearsay rule. [ ]

To avoid this conclusion, the Morrisons contend the unavailability of the original records in itself makes Ord's statements and her list admissible. We disagree. When an original document is missing, secondary evidence offered to prove its content must be "otherwise admissible." [ ] Since the list and Ord's statements are inadmissible hearsay, they are not "otherwise admissible."
\* \* \*

Since Ord's declaration and list were properly excluded and since there is no other evidence suggesting a genetic link between the Morrisons and the Does' twins, the Morrisons had no standing to pursue their parentage action.

## II.

The Morrisons contend they should be allowed to "discover" whether the twins were born "as a result of the theft of their genetic materials," and that their rights as alleged biological parents ought to trump the Does' rights as presumed parents. We disagree.

The Morrisons' "rights" were vindicated when they accepted an undisclosed amount of money to resolve their lawsuit against CRH, UCI, and the individuals involved in the misuse of the Morrisons' genetic materials. The rights still at issue are not the Morrisons' rights. They are the rights of the Does and their twins to be free from the interference of strangers who have no standing to pursue their demands for blood tests or visitation rights, and the Morrisons cannot alter the focus of this issue by characterizing the Does' rights as mere privacy interests that may, under appropriate circumstances, give way to greater rights. [ ]

The trial court found, and we agree, that the dismissal of this action is in the best interests of the children. More to the point, we conclude that, had the Morrisons presented proof of a genetic link to the twins sufficient to establish their standing to pursue a parentage action, it would not be in the best interests of the twins to have the Morrisons intrude into their lives, or to be subjected to the blood tests and "mental health" evaluation suggested by the Morrisons. Because the twins are now almost 14 years old, their relationship with their presumed parents is considerably more palpable than the possibility of a new relationship with a previously unknown biological parent, and the Morrisons will not be allowed to disrupt the Does' "family in order to satisfy the [alleged] biological [parents'] unilateral desire, however strong, to turn their genetic connection into a personal relationship." [ ]

Simply put, the social relationship established by the Does and their daughters is more important to the children than a genetic relationship with a stranger.[ ][10]

The order of dismissal is affirmed. * * *

### Notes on Prato–Morrison v. Doe

1. Should the Morrisons be recognized as "interested parties" under the California statute? How does the court know that the Morrisons are unrelated persons who are not "genetic parents" of the twins in the absence of DNA testing? Under the circumstances of this case, given the fraud of the fertility clinic, is there any other way that the Morrisons could develop admissible evidence of their genetic parentage? Shouldn't the production of some evidence—even if it is not admissible—be enough to justify the order of DNA testing? Why doesn't the court simply require the DNA testing, so that there will be no doubt as to the genetic parentage of the twins?

2. Why does the fact that the Morrisons accepted a damage award from the fertility clinic cut off their claims of parentage? Did that damage award amount to

---

**10.** We join the chorus of judicial voices pleading for legislative attention to the increasing number of complex legal issues spawned by recent advances in the field of artificial reproduction. Whatever merit there may be to a fact-driven case-by-case resolution of each new issue, some over-all legislative guidelines would allow the participants to make informed choices and the courts to strive for uniformity in their decisions. ( *In re Marriage of Buzzanca* [ ]; *Johnson v. Calvert*[ ].)

a purchase of the rights to the children by the clinic? Why should it have any effect on the relationship between the Morrisons and the Does (who were not a party to the Morrisons lawsuit against the clinic)?

3. Would the result in this case be the same if the Morrisons had discovered the twins shortly after their birth, instead of eight years later? If they had discovered the mix-up during the pregnancy? Should the result be the same?

4. In the last full paragraph of the opinion the court refers to the "best interests of the children." Is the court applying the "bests interests" standard to resolve this case? Does this paragraph suggest that the Morrisons could not establish legal parentage to Ida and Rose even if they *could* produce proof—DNA evidence, for example—that they are the genetic progenitors of the twins? Is this an appropriate use of this standard?

5. How terrible would it be for Ida and Rose to find out that their social parents are not their genetic parents? Would it be worse for them to make this discovery than it is for adopted children who make this discovery? Might it be in their interest to get this information, or would the disruption of the Does' household be so harmful that it would outweigh any benefit to the girls?

6. The girls themselves were not represented in this litigation. Should the court have appointed a guardian ad litem to represent their interests? Could the court do that without telling them about the litigation, and thus undercutting the very status quo that the Does fought so hard to maintain?

### 5. Cloning

**Add, at p. 1235, after the NBAC Report, add:**

### *Note on Reproductive and Therapeutic Cloning and Stem Cell Research*

The controversy over cloning became more focused when Congress debated bills to outlaw the practice in 2003. While almost everyone agrees that there is no justification for *reproductive cloning*—i.e., cloning designed to create a human being—the propriety of *therapeutic cloning*—i.e., cloning designed to develop stem cells that would be useful in research and for treatment purposes—remains more controversial.

Both forms of cloning may require somatic cell nuclear transfer, a process in which the nucleus of an unfertilized human ovum is removed and replaced with the nucleus from an adult cell. The resulting ovum cell, which has the full complement of human genetic material, is then stimulated so that it will divide and form a pre-embryo. In *therapeutic cloning*, some cells from the pre-embryo are removed for purposes of medical research or treatment. These stem cells have the potential to develop into almost any human cells, and they may be useful in repairing almost any human tissue. In *reproductive cloning*, the pre-embryo would be placed in a uterus to develop into a human being.

Reproductive cloning became a matter of immediate concern in 2002 when a company—Clonaid—claimed that it had cloned a human being. Clonaid was founded in 1997 by Rael, the spiritual leader of the Raelian Movement, which claims that a human extraterrestrial race used DNA and genetic engineering to scientifically create all life on Earth. Clonaid officials believe that Dolly, who recently died, was killed in an effort to cast doubt on the safety of the cloning enterprise. For an interesting look at Clonaid, the Raelians, and pictures of allegedly cloned human beings, see www.clonaid.com. While there are few who accept Clonaid's bizarre claims, the publicity that attended them created widespread concern over reproductive cloning.

Because of the scientific promise shown by stem cell research, on the other hand, many people who support legislation banning reproductive cloning vigorously oppose placing any limitations upon therapeutic cloning. However, because this research requires that a pre-embryo, which could develop into a human being, be the subject of research, the process is viewed by some as requiring an act that kills a potential human being.

As this supplement goes to press, the House has approved and sent to the Senate a bill imposing civil and criminal sanctions on both reproductive and therapeutic cloning. A similar bill failed in the Senate in 2002, but the Senate had become more conservative in the interim. Those in Congress who support stem cell research have offered alternative bills, which would outlaw reproductive cloning but permit therapeutic cloning. The President has expressed his opposition to all forms of human cloning, and he has permitted federal funds to be used for stem cell research only when the research is done on stem cell lines already available.

## III. FETAL MATERNAL DECISIONMAKING

**Add, at p. 1247, at the end of "b. criminal remedies," add:**

Prosecutors continue to look for ways to impose criminal liability on women whose drug use during pregnancy have adverse consequences on their fetuses or children. In December of 2002 a Kansas judge dismissed child endangerment charges that had been filed against a woman who took drugs before giving birth to her child on the side of Interstate 35. The prosecutor argued that earlier Kansas cases holding that a fetus could not be the victim of a crime should not govern this case because in this case the perpetrator of the crime—the mother—knew that her fetus would be born alive. The mother's motion to dismiss another charge, causing a child to be a child in need of care, was denied. See T. Rizzo, Judge Dismisses One Charge Against Woman Who Gave Birth Along I-35, Kansas City Star, December 11, 2002, at 1.

**Add, at p. 1247, at the end of "c. Civil Commitment and Court Ordered Protective Custody," add:**

In 2002 an Arkansas state judge ordered the state to take custody of a neglected fetus when he sent the mother to jail for criminal contempt of an order not to use drugs. The trial judge, whose order was opposed by the state Human Services Department, added a suggestion that the pregnant woman undergo a tubal ligation after the baby is born. See T. Shurley, Custody Ruling on Fetus Irks Officials; State Lacks Authority to Assume Fetal Care, Arkansas Democrat-Gazette, December 17, 2002, at 11.

# Chapter 17

# LEGAL, SOCIAL AND ETHICAL ISSUES IN HUMAN GENETICS

## I. INTRODUCTION

**Add, at p. 1253:**

The Governor of the State of Virginia issued a formal apology for the state's program of forced sterilization that was conducted as part of the eugenics movement of the early part of the twentieth century. About 8,000 low-income, uneducated and mentally retarded Virginians were sterilized as part of a eugenics program in that state between 1924 and 1979. Thirty states engaged in such programs, and 65,000 individuals nationwide were involuntarily sterilized. Calling the program a "shameful effort," the Governor stated that "the state government never should have been involved."

For a ten-year perspective on shifting emphases in public policy relating to genetics, see Frances H. Miller, Foreward: Phase II of the Genetics Revolution: Sophisticated Issues for Home and Abroad, 28 Am.J.L. & Med. 145 (2002), introducing a symposium issue of the Journal. Public health issues in genetics are highlighted in a symposium published in volume 30 of the Journal of Law, Medicine & Ethics (Summer 2002).

## II. LEGAL RESPONSES TO PRIVACY, CONFIDENTIALITY, CONSENT AND DISCRIMINATION

### A. FOCUS ON PRIVACY

**Add, at p. 1262:**

Another model statute for privacy of genetic information is offered in Model Act for Genetic Privacy and Control (MAGPAC), 88 Iowa L. Rev. 121 (2002).

### B. FOCUS ON DISCRIMINATION

**Add, at p. 1270, after Note 4:**

In 2002, Burlington Northern Santa Fe Railroad (BNSF) agreed to pay 36 workers up to $2.2 million in settlement of a claim brought by the EEOC on behalf of the employees under the Americans with Disabilities Act. This was the first action ever brought by the EEOC concerning employment-based genetic testing.

The company also agreed it will no longer use genetic tests in required medical examinations of current employees, will provide additional ADA training to its medical and claims staff, and will require senior management review of all significant medical policies and practices. In an earlier court order granting a preliminary injunction against the company, BNSF "admit[ed] that it requested certain employees who claimed that they had developed work-related carpal tunnel syndrome to submit an evaluative 34-item medical examination conducted by outside health-care providers and that one item of that examination was a blood test for a genetic marker." The company denied that the testing violated the ADA, although the EEOC found that it did.

According to the EEOC's brief submitted in support of the preliminary injunction, employees were tested without their knowledge and had not been informed that blood tests would include genetic testing. (Plaintiff's brief, Civ. No. 01–4013, U.S.N.D., Iowa, February, 2001) The employees had received notification that the company required the employee to undergo medical examination, including laboratory testing, to prove whether the carpal tunnel syndrome was a work-related injury, but they had not been told that the genetic testing would be included. (Presumably, the testing was done as a potential defense to employee claims under the FELA that the syndrome was a compensable work-place injury.)

The genetic testing came to light when an employee's spouse (who was a nurse) asked why blood tests were being performed to ascertain whether the carpal tunnel syndrome experienced by her husband was work-related. The EEOC's brief claims that the employee was told he would be terminated if he did not submit to the genetic test. In response to the EEOC's petition, BNSF agreed to the entry of the District Court's order that the company cease testing immediately and protect the medical information and physical samples already in its possession.

BNSF was testing for the presence of a rare genetic condition called Hereditary Neuropathy with liability to Pressure Palsies (HNPP). The company that performed the testing states in its testing protocol that carpal tunnel syndrome may be a manifestation of HNPP. (See website http://www.athenadiagnositcs.com) One estimate is that HNPP occurs in 2 to 5 of 100,000 individuals. Nelis E, et al., Estimation of the mutation frequencies in Charcot–Marie–Tooth disease type 1 and hereditary neuropathy with liability to pressure palsies: a European collaborative study. *Eur J. Hum. Genet.* 4:25–33 (1996), cited in http://geneclinics.org

The claim that the testing itself violated the ADA relied on the statute's limitations on testing current employees. An employer may test current employees only where the testing is job-related or a matter of business necessity. In interpreting this standard, the EEOC has issued guidance indicating that the standard requires that the employer have a reasonable belief that the employee's ability to perform the job will be impaired or that the employee poses a direct threat in the workplace. At least some of the BNSF employees had been released as work ready and were working at the time of the testing.

In statements concerning the settlement, BNSF maintained that the testing did not violate the ADA. The president-CEO of BNSF said, "at no time did the company use, or intend to use, any genetic test to screen out asymptomatic employees. We are pleased with the commission's acknowledgment, that BNSF did not engage in genetic screening of asymptomatic employees for any employment action, which should correct any public misimpression about this matter."

One of the Commissioners of the EEOC stated: "While the EEOC did not find that BNSF had used genetic tests to screen out employees, employers should be aware of the EEOC's position that the mere gathering of an employee's DNA may constitute a violation of the ADA." 7/12/02 Genomics & Genetics Wkly. 12 (2002 WL 9237499) (The Commissioner's statement references testing of current employees only rather than prospective employees who have received conditional job offers. The EEOC Compliance Manual, cited in note 4 on page 1270, would apply in the latter case.)

Is the Commissioner correct in asserting that the ADA's prohibition on testing of employees unless the test is job-related or a matter of business necessity would make all genetic testing of current employees a violation of the Act?

Assuming that Burlington Northern were a federal agency, how would its actions fare under Executive Order 13145 on page 1260 of the text?

Was there any breach of confidentiality of genetic information under the California statute on page 1258 of the text?

Would BNSF's actions be illegal under the following Missouri statute? Would the employees be able to sue under this statute?

## MISSOURI STATUTES TITLE XXIV.
## BUSINESS AND FINANCIAL INSTITUTIONS

375.1306. Genetic information or test results, discrimination—penalty

1. An employer shall not use any genetic information or genetic test results of an employee or prospective employee to distinguish between, discriminate against, or restrict any right or benefit otherwise due or available to such employee or prospective employee. The requirements of this section shall not prohibit:

(1) Underwriting in connection with individual or group life, disability income or long-term care insurance;

(2) Any action required or permissible by law or regulation;

(3) Action taken with the written permission of an employee or prospective employee or such person's authorized representative; or

(4) The use of genetic information when such information is directly related to a person's ability to perform assigned job responsibilities.

2. Any person who violates the provisions of this section shall be fined not more than five hundred dollars for each violation of this section.

For a sophisticated analysis of the Burlington Northern settlement, genetic testing and employment, see Anita Silvers and Michael Ashley Stein, An Equality Paradigm for Preventing Genetic Discrimination, 55 Vand. L. Rev. 1341 (2002).

For a very interesting and accessible discussion of the issues raised in workplace genetic testing, see Cynthia Nance, Paul Miller, and Mark Rothstein, Discrimination in Employment on the Basis of Genetics: Proceedings of the 2002 Annual Meeting, Association of American Law Schools, 6 Emp.Rights and Emp.Policy Journal 57 (2002).

In that discussion, Mark Rothstein asks: "Is it that the genetic information is really not very accurate, that it's not predictive at all, and that employers will be unfairly making mistakes by excluding certain people from employment? ... The other possibility is that we're concerned about genetic discrimination because genetic information is, in fact, predictive, but nevertheless we still shouldn't allow employers to use genetic information because it violates some public policy." Does framing the issue in this way make a difference in your analysis of the following statement by a lawyer who represents employers?

> What if an employer could use DNA testing to show that carpal tunnel syndrome or other ergonomic conditions are genetically predetermined and thus, not work-related? The employer's ability to successfully contest workers' compensation claims would be bolstered, to say the least.

> Or suppose an employer could use genetic tests to ascertain which employees are prone to back injuries, so that those employees could be assigned to less physically demanding jobs. Provided such assignments don't result in lower wages or fewer promotional opportunities, workplace genetic testing could be a win-win. Workplace injuries would be reduced, lowering employers' work-related injury costs. Condon McGlothlen, Genetic testing: the solution to ergonomics claims?, CTD News, Aug. 1, 2002 (2002 WL 16418453)

## C. CREATING DNA DATABASES

**Add, at p. 1274, after Note 5:**

The private-public joint venture that established the Icelandic DNA database described in note 5 in the text is now over two years old. A central purpose of the project was to diversify Iceland's "cod economy," and the agreement explicitly anticipated commercial development of the country's DNA database.

Jamaica Potts describes the foundation of the database: the homogeneity of Iceland's population as a result of a series of natural disasters that decimated and isolated the population for the past millenium; the nation's cultural commitment to excellent genealogy, which provides accurate family trees; and the presence of comprehensive health records on individuals. In 1998, the Icelandic parliament enacted legislation providing that health records are not owned by patients, health care providers, or companies; and this provided the legal basis for the consolidation of these health records into a national database.

The development of the national health database has been controversial in Iceland. Potts reports that ethicists in that country threatened litigation, and approximately one-third of Icelandic physicians are withholding medical records on patients. The Icelandic Medical Association has been opposed to the creation of the national health database, but finally reached a compromise with deCode by establishing a set of principles and mechanisms to govern the project. As part of this compromise, the "opt out" process was strengthened, and 7% of Iceland's population of just over 750,000 have opted out of the project. In part because of the degree of opposition, the health records database is not complete.

Professor Potts provides a detailed analysis of the agreement between the Icelandic government and deCode, the private joint venturer. The company pays an annual fee of approximately $700,000 for the license, which expires after 12 years; bears all of the expenses of developing and maintaining the health records database; pays for the expenses of the government oversight mechanism; and shares the profits of any product developed as a result of the Icelandic information, although the share is capped at $1.4 million. Finally, all of the database work must be done in Iceland itself, and the database is "tethered" to Iceland for purposes of control, oversight, and development. Roche, the pharmaceutical firm, has entered into a joint venture with deCode, under which medications developed through the project will be provided to Iceland without charge.

Jamaica Potts, At Least Give the Natives Glass Beads: An Examination of the Bargain Made Between Iceland and deCode Genetics with Implications for Global Prospecting, 7 Va. J. Law & Tech. 8 (2002).

### *Problem: Creating the Treasure Trove*

The Icelandic experience has direct application to the United States. On January 21, 2003, the Governor of Utah announced a new joint venture called GenData—a not-for-profit corporation formed by the state, the University of Utah and the Huntsman Cancer Foundation.

The project combines databases now held by the three partners and creates a database that will form the foundation for medical research. The joint public-private project also will allow researchers to link to state databases such as the state's cancer registry. The Governor said that the project is enriched in Utah because of the wealth of genealogical information maintained in that state.

The database at the University was begun approximately 20 years ago with the support and cooperation of members of the Church of Jesus Christ of Latter-day Saints, who provided family medical history for the good of research. One news article reported that "few DNA codes" are included in the database, and instead it consists primarily of family medical histories, genealogy records, the state's vital statistics records, driver's licenses and so on. The executive director of the Huntsman Cancer Foundation said that "knowing the genetic cause of disease is important, but also knowing the interaction of environment and other population factors could play a huge role in improved science."

The leaders of the project said the information is entirely confidential. In his State of the State address, the Governor asked the legislature to "build into law an impenetrable wall of privacy protection." The legislature had already appropriated over $3 million for the project.

The Governor also stated that the project will attract venture capital and pharmaceutical and medical research organizations "from all over the world" to the state of Utah. The Governor declared that the project would create a "scientific treasure." Joe Bauman and Amy Joi Bryson, "Leavitt Announces Utah Genetics Project," Deseret News B03 (1/22/03); Troy Goodman, "State Invests in Database for Biotech," Salt Lake Trib. A1 (1/22/03).

Assume that you are a member of the Utah legislature, what approach will you take in your next legislative session to respond to this development? What definition of "genetic information" will you use, if any? Would you attach nondiscrimination provisions to your privacy provisions, and, if so, what would be the scope of these prohibitions? Will you require consent from Utah citizens for inclusion in the database? Will you instead use presumed consent and allow individuals to opt out? How do you make sure that the state and its citizens reap the profits of the results of this effort? Do you remember your first-year property law–who owns the information in the database? Any medical tissue that is used in the project? Any products that are developed as a result? Refer to Moore v. Regents of the University of California at page 386 in the casebook for one approach to these property questions. See also, note 4 at page 1274 of the text for a discussion of the use of stored tissue for research.

## III. GENETIC SCREENING

**Add, at p. 1277, at the end of Note 6:**

See, Symposium on Genetics and the Just Society, 39 San Diego Law Review (Summer 2002), for a good collection of articles on this issue organized around responses to Allen Buchanan et al., From Chance to Choice: Genetics and Justice (2000).

**Add, at p. 1278, at the beginning of the Problem:**

New York, Wisconsin, and Massachusetts have all added mandatory screening for CF to their mandatory genetic screening programs for newborns. As reported in American Political Network, May 29, 2002.

**Add, at p. 1279:**

Much of the driving force for the mapping of the human genome and the enormous investment in genetic research is the promise of the development of drugs genetically tailored to individual persons ("pharmacogenetics" or "pharmacogenomics") and the development of gene therapy in which a vector delivers a "new" gene to correct serious malfunction. It is common to find in discussions of the potential negative effects of genetic testing the assertion of the great positive effect to come in terms of these interventions. Most of this promise still lies in the far future.

Like all of the developments in genetic research, the realization of that promise will bring its own challenges. The availability of genetic therapy, for example, raises issues of payment for what will at first be an experimental treatment and is most likely to remain a financially dear treatment. The potential for gene therapy also raises the same issues of health and illness with which we begin the casebook. (See also note 6 on page 1277 of this Chapter.) If you want to follow particular protocols in gene therapy, you may want to review regularly Gene Therapy Weekly, which is available on Westlaw.

Cystic fibrosis is one of the diseases in which the prospects for gene therapy have been the most intensely researched. See, U. Griesenbach et al., Gene Therapy Progress and Prospects: Cystic Fibrosis, 9 Gene Therapy 1344 (2002), reporting on the 18 clinical trials of gene therapy for CF that had been conducted since 1989 and describing the difficulties that have arisen in delivering the gene.

Gene therapy (more specifically, experiments in gene therapy) has suffered two serious setbacks. In 1999, Jesse Gelsinger died as a result of an experimental genetic intervention in which an adenovirus was used as a vector to deliver a gene to his liver to correct a liver disorder. The virus injected directly into his liver unexpectedly infiltrated several other organs and caused widespread inflammation which ultimately was fatal. After the death of the patient, the scientists injected the vector into mice and found the same reaction. A Valuable Lesson in Gene Therapy, Gene Therapy Weekly, Feb. 8, 2001. Most of the discussion following Jesse Gelsinger's death focused on the conduct of research in the United States rather than on gene therapy as a subset of medical research. The physicians involved had financial interests in the success of their experimental therapy and had failed to report to the NIH adverse reactions in other patients. The case is discussed in more detail in this supplement in Chapter 20.

In October 2002, it was discovered that one of five boys treated with experimental gene therapy for SCID (severe combined immunodeficiency, the "bubble boy" disease) had developed leukemia as a result of the therapy. Later, another boy developed the same disease. This occurred only six months after the researchers had reported in the New England Journal of Medicine that the replacement of a defective gene with a functional one had produced apparently healthy immune systems 30 months after the intervention. The authors at that time had stated that the therapy should be tested in a larger cohort of patients. Hacein–Bey–Abina et al., Sustained Correction of X–Linked Severe Combined Immunodeficiency by ex Vivo Gene Therapy, 346 NEJM 1185 (April 18, 2002). This episode with SCID, combined with Jesse Gelsinger's case, has raised significant fundamental issues in the foundation of the science of gene therapy relating to the vectors that are used to deliver the genetic material.

# Chapter 18

# DEFINING DEATH

## III. THE "DEAD DONOR" RULE AND EXPANDING CLASSES OF ORGAN DONORS—ANENCEPHALIC INFANTS AND "NON–HEART BEATING" DONORS

**Add, at p. 1302, at the end of the first full paragraph:**

Despite the results of a study that suggested that organs from non-heart-beating donors were as useful for transplant as those from brain dead donors, the use of non-heart beating donors has remained controversial in the United States and around the world. Although the district attorney who threatened to prosecute the transplant team that obtained organs from non-heart-beating donors has been replaced, the replacement has taken the same position. This controversy seems to be dividing the bioethics community in the same way that the abortion controversy has divided it. Those who support the practice are more likely to be utilitarian defenders of patient autonomy (and pro-choice), while those who oppose it often come from the ranks of pro-life advocates. See Harlan Spector, Misgivings Again About Organ Donations; How Do We Decide When Life Really Ends?, Cleveland Plain Dealer, November 27, 2002, A–1. See also Wesley Smith, The Ethics of Organ Donation; Mere Boosterism Won't Be Enough to Encourage This Ultimate Charitable Act, Weekly Standard, May 28, 2001, p. 24.

The same issues that have been discussed in the United States have arisen elsewhere when there is a proposal to begin to harvest organs from non-heart-beating organ donors. See, for example, S. Crompton, A Heartbeat Away, The Times (London), March 10, 2003, at 10 (United Kingdom).

# Chapter 19

# LIFE AND DEATH DECISIONS

## IV. THE "RIGHT TO DIE"—PATIENTS WITHOUT DECISIONAL CAPACITY

### B. DETERMINING THE PATIENT'S CHOICE

#### 2. Decisionmaking in the Absence of a Governing Statute

*b. The Role of the Courts and the Burden of Proof in Cases Involving the Decision to Forego Life-sustaining Treatment*

**Add, at p. 1392, after the Court of Appeal opinion in *Wendland*:**

The California Supreme Court reversed the decision of the Court of Appeal in late 2001. Review the following opinion from a unanimous court and ask just how it differs from the opinion of the Court of Appeal. The result is different, of course—but is the rule that emerges?

### CONSERVATORSHIP OF WENDLAND
Supreme Court of California, 2001.
26 Cal.4th 519, 28 P.3d 151, 110 Cal.Rptr.2d 412.

WERDEGAR, J.

In this case we consider whether a conservator of the person may withhold artificial nutrition and hydration from a conscious conservatee who is not terminally ill, comatose, or in a persistent vegetative state, and who has not left formal instructions for health care or appointed an agent or surrogate for health care decisions. Interpreting the Probate Code in light of the relevant provisions of the California Constitution, we conclude a conservator may not withhold artificial nutrition and hydration from such a person absent clear and convincing evidence the conservator's decision is in accordance with either the conservatee's own wishes or best interest.

The trial court in the case before us, applying the clear and convincing evidence standard, found the evidence on both points insufficient and, thus, denied the conservator's request for authority to withhold artificial nutrition and hydration. The Court of Appeal, which believed the trial court was required to defer to the conservator's good faith decision, reversed. We reverse the decision of the Court of Appeal.

## I. FACTS AND PROCEDURAL HISTORY

On September 29, 1993, Robert Wendland rolled his truck at high speed in a solo accident while driving under the influence of alcohol. The accident injured Robert's brain, leaving him conscious yet severely disabled, both mentally and physically, and dependent on artificial nutrition and hydration. Two years later Rose Wendland, Robert's wife and conservator, proposed to direct his physician to remove his feeding tube and allow him to die ... Robert's mother and sister ... objected to the conservator's decision. This proceeding arose under the provisions of the Probate Code authorizing courts to settle such disputes.

Following the accident, Robert remained in a coma, totally unresponsive, for several months. During this period Rose visited him daily, often with their children, and authorized treatment as necessary to maintain his health.

Robert eventually regained consciousness. His subsequent medical history is described in a comprehensive medical evaluation later submitted to the court. According to the report, Rose "first noticed signs of responsiveness sometime in late 1994 or early 1995 and alerted [Robert's] physicians and nursing staff." ... At his highest level of function between February and July, 1995, Robert was able to do such things as throw and catch a ball, operate an electric wheelchair with assistance, turn pages, draw circles, draw an 'R' and perform two-step commands." For example, "[h]e was able to respond appropriately to the command 'close your eyes and open them when I say the number 3.' ... He could choose a requested color block out of four color blocks. He could set the right peg in a pegboard. He remained unable to vocalize. Eye blinking was successfully used as a communication mode for a while, however no consistent method of communication was developed."

Despite improvements made in therapy, Robert remained severely disabled, both mentally and physically. The same medical report summarized his continuing impairments as follows: "severe cognitive impairment that is not possible to fully appreciate due to the concurrent motor and communication impairments ..."; "maladaptive behavior characterized by agitation, aggressiveness and non-compliance"; "severe paralysis on the right and moderate paralysis on the left"; "severely impaired communication, without compensatory augmentative communication system"; "severe swallowing dysfunction, dependent upon non-oral enteric tube feeding for nutrition and hydration"; "incontinence of bowel and bladder"; "moderate spasticity"; "mild to moderate contractures"; "general dysphoria"; "recurrent medical illnesses, including pneumonia, bladder infections, sinusitis"; and "dental issues."

After Robert regained consciousness and while he was undergoing therapy, Rose authorized surgery three times to replace dislodged feeding tubes. When physicians sought her permission a fourth time, she declined. She discussed the decision with her daughters and with Robert's brother Michael, all of whom believed that Robert would not have approved the procedure even if necessary to sustain his life. Rose also discussed the decision with Robert's treating physician, Dr. Kass, other physicians, and the hospital's ombudsman, all of whom apparently supported her decision. Dr. Kass, however, inserted a nasogastric feeding tube to keep Robert alive pending input from the hospital's ethics committee.

Eventually, the 20-member ethics committee unanimously approved Rose's decision. In the course of their deliberations, however, the committee did not speak with Robert's mother or sister. [They] learned, apparently through an anonymous telephone call, that Dr. Kass planned to remove Robert's feeding tube [and] applied for a temporary restraining order to bar him from so doing, and the court granted the motion ex parte.

Rose immediately thereafter petitioned for appointment as Robert's conservator. In the petition, she asked the court to determine that Robert lacked the capacity to give informed consent for medical treatment and to confirm her authority "to withdraw and/or withhold medical treatment and/or life-sustaining treatment, including, but not limited to, withholding nutrition and hydration." [Robert's mother and sister] (hereafter sometimes objectors) opposed the petition. After a hearing, the court appointed Rose as conservator but reserved judgment on her request for authority to remove Robert's feeding tube. * * *

After [a 60 day observation period] elapsed without significant improvement in Robert's condition, the conservator renewed her request for authority to remove his feeding tube. The objectors asked the trial court to appoint independent counsel for the conservatee. The trial court declined, and the Court of Appeal summarily denied the objectors' petition for writ of mandate. We granted review and transferred the case to the Court of Appeal, which then directed the trial court to appoint counsel. [ ] Appointed counsel, exercising his independent judgment [ ], decided to support the conservator's decision. * * *

* * *

The [consequent] trial generated the evidence set out above. The testifying physicians agreed that Robert would not likely experience further cognitive recovery. Dr. Kass, Robert's treating physician, testified that, to the highest degree of medical certainty, Robert would never be able to make medical treatment decisions, walk, talk, feed himself, eat, drink, or control his bowel and bladder functions.

* * *

Robert's wife, brother and daughter recounted preaccident statements Robert had made about his attitude towards life-sustaining health care. Robert's wife recounted specific statements on two occasions. The first occasion was Rose's decision whether to turn off a respirator sustaining the life of her father, who was near death from gangrene. Rose recalls Robert saying: "I would never want to live like that, and I wouldn't want my children to see me like that and look at the hurt you're going through as an adult seeing your father like that." On cross-examination, Rose acknowledged Robert said on this occasion that Rose's father "wouldn't want to live like a vegetable" and "wouldn't want to live in a comatose state."

After his father-in-law's death, Robert developed a serious drinking problem. After a particular incident, Rose asked Michael, Robert's brother, to talk to him. When Robert arrived home the next day he was angry to see Michael there, interfering in what he considered a private family matter. Rose remembers Michael telling Robert: "I'm going to get a call from Rosie one day, and you're going to be in a terrible accident." Robert replied: "If that ever happened to me, you know what my feelings are. Don't let that happen to me. Just let me go. Leave me alone." ... Robert's daughter Katie remembers him saying on this occasion that "if he could not be a provider for his family, if he could not do all the things that he enjoyed doing, just enjoying the outdoors, just basic things, feeding himself, talking, communicating, if he could not do those things, he would not want to live."

\* \* \* Specifically, the court found the conservator "ha[d] not met her duty and burden to show by clear and convincing evidence that conservatee Robert Wendland, who is not in a persistent vegetative state nor suffering from a terminal illness would, under the circumstances, want to die. Conservator has likewise not met her burden of establishing that the withdrawal of artificially delivered nutrition and hydration is commensurate with conservatee's best interests. \* \* \* Based on these findings, the court granted the objectors' motion for judgment [ ], thus denying the conservator's request for confirmation of her proposal to withdraw treatment. The court also found the conservator had acted in good faith and would be permitted to remain in that office. Nevertheless, the court limited her powers by ordering that she would "have no authority to direct ... [any] health care provider to remove the conservatee's life sustaining medical treatment in the form of withholding nutrition and hydration." [ ]

The conservator appealed this decision. The Court of Appeal reversed. In the Court of Appeal's view, "[t]he trial court properly placed the burden of producing evidence on [the conservator] and properly applied a clear and convincing evidence standard. However, the court erred in requiring [the conservator] to prove that [the conservatee], while competent, expressed a desire to die in the circumstances and in substituting its own judgment concerning [the conservatee's] best interests \* \* \* ." Instead, the trial court's role was "merely to satisfy itself that the conservator had considered the conservatee's best interests in good faith \* \* \* ." \* \* \* We granted review of this decision.

## II. DISCUSSION

### A. *The Relevant Legal Principles*

\* \* \*

#### 1. *Constitutional and common law principles*

One relatively certain principle is that a competent adult has the right to refuse medical treatment, even treatment necessary to sustain life. The Legislature has cited this principle to justify legislation governing medical care decisions [ ], and courts have invoked it as a starting point for analysis, even in cases examining the rights of incompetent persons and the duties of surrogate decision makers [ ]. This case requires us to look beyond the rights of a competent person to the rights of incompetent conservatees and the duties of conservators, but the principle just mentioned is a logical place to begin.

That a competent person has the right to refuse treatment is a statement both of common law and of state constitutional law. [The court then discussed the development of this right in common law, depending on informed consent and other cases.]

The Courts of Appeal have found another source for the same right in the California Constitution's privacy clause. * * *

Federal law has little to say about the competent person's right to refuse treatment, but what it does say is not to the contrary. The United States Supreme Court spoke provisionally to the point in *Cruzan* [where the Court] acknowledged that "a competent person['s] * * * constitutionally protected liberty interest in refusing unwanted medical treatment may be inferred" [ ] from prior decisions holding that state laws requiring persons to submit to involuntary medical procedures must be justified by countervailing state interests. The "logic" of such cases would, the court thought, implicate a competent person's liberty interest in refusing artificially delivered food and water essential to life. [ ] Whether any given state law infringed such a liberty interest, however, would have to be determined by balancing the liberty interest against the relevant state interests, in particular the state's interest in preserving life. [ ]

In view of these authorities, the competent adult's right to refuse medical treatment may be safely considered established, at least in California.

The same right survives incapacity, in a practical sense, if exercised while competent pursuant to a law giving that act lasting validity. For some time, California law has given competent adults the power to leave formal directions for health care in the event they later become incompetent; over time, the Legislature has afforded ever greater scope to that power. * * *

Effective July 1, 2000, the Health Care Decisions Law [ ] gives competent adults extremely broad power to direct all aspects of their health care in the event they become incompetent.... Briefly, and as relevant here, the new law permits a competent person to execute an advance directive about "any aspect" of health care. Among other things, a person may direct that life-sustaining treatment be withheld or withdrawn under conditions specified by the person and not limited to terminal illness, permanent coma, or persistent vegetative state. A competent person may still use a power of attorney for health care to give an agent the power to make health care decisions [ ], but a patient may also orally designate a surrogate to make such decisions by personally informing the patient's supervising health care provider. [ ] Under the new law, agents and surrogates are required to make health care decisions "in accordance with the principal's individual health care instructions, if any, and other wishes to the extent known to the agent." [ ]

All of the laws just mentioned merely give effect to the decision of a competent person, in the form either of instructions for health care or the designation of an agent or surrogate for health care decisions. Such laws may accurately be described, as the Legislature has described them, as a means to respect personal autonomy by giving effect to competent decisions: * * *

In contrast, decisions made by conservators typically derive their authority from a different basis—the *parens patriae* power of the state to protect incompetent persons. Unlike an agent or a surrogate for health care, who is voluntarily appointed by a competent person, a conservator is appointed by the court because the conservatee "has been adjudicated to lack the capacity to make health care decisions."

* * *

2. *[The Probate Code]*

[The court then analyzed the history of the relevant Probate Code provision.]

### B. *The Present Case*

This background illuminates the parties' arguments, which reduce in essence to this: The conservator has claimed the power under [the Probate Code] to direct the conservatee's health care providers to cease providing artificial nutrition and hydration. In opposition, the objectors have contended the statute violates the conservatee's rights to privacy and life under the facts of this case if the conservator's interpretation of the statute is correct.[10]

\* \* \*

1. *The primary standard: a decision in accordance with the conservatee's wishes*

The conservator asserts she offered sufficient evidence at trial to satisfy the primary statutory standard, which contemplates a decision "in accordance with the conservatee's \* \* \* wishes \* \* \* ." [ ] The trial court, however, determined the evidence on this point was insufficient. The conservator did "not [meet] her duty and burden," the court expressly found, "to show by clear and convincing evidence that [the] conservatee ... , who is not in a persistent vegetative state nor suffering from a terminal illness would, under the circumstances, want to die." \* \* \*

The conservator argues the Legislature understood and intended that the low preponderance of the evidence standard would apply. Certainly this was the Law Revision Commission's understanding [in drafting the statute]. \* \* \*

The objectors, in opposition, argue that [the relevant section] would be unconstitutional if construed to permit a conservator to end the life of a conscious conservatee based on a finding by the low preponderance of the evidence standard that the latter would not want to live. We see no basis for holding the statute unconstitutional on its face. We do, however, find merit in the objectors' argument. We therefore construe the statute to minimize the possibility of its unconstitutional application by requiring clear and convincing evidence of a conscious conservatee's wish to refuse life-sustaining treatment when the conservator relies on that asserted wish to justify withholding life-sustaining treatment.... [W]e see no constitutional reason to apply the higher evidentiary standard to the majority of health care decisions made by conservators not contemplating a conscious conservatee's death.

\* \* \*

Notwithstanding the foregoing, one must acknowledge that the primary standard for decisionmaking set out in [the Probate Code] does articulate

---

**10.** The conservator argues that a conservator's decision to withdraw life support does not entail state action and, thus, cannot implicate the conservatee's constitutional rights. State action, however, is of no concern because the state constitutional right to privacy (Cal. Const., art. I, § 1), one of the traditional sources of a patient's right to autonomy and bodily integrity, protects against private conduct and is sufficiently broad to justify our conclusion. [ ] A conservatee's right to life (Cal. Const., art. I, § 1), which coincides here with the state's interest in protecting life, also supports the conclusion and enjoys some protection against private conduct, as illustrated by the laws prohibiting homicide and expressing legislative disapproval of mercy killing, assisted suicide, and euthanasia [ ].

what will in some cases form a constitutional basis for a conservator's decision to end the life of a conscious patient: deference to the patient's own wishes. This standard also appears in the new provisions governing decisions by agents and surrogates designated by competent adults. [ ] As applied in that context, the requirement that decisions be made "in accordance with the principal's individual health care instructions * * * and other wishes" [ ] merely respects the principal-agent relationship and gives effect to the properly expressed wishes of a competent adult. Because a competent adult may refuse life-sustaining treatment [ ], it follows that an agent properly and voluntarily designated by the principal may refuse treatment on the principal's behalf unless, of course, such authority is revoked. [ ]

The only apparent purpose of requiring conservators to make decisions in accordance with the conservatee's wishes, when those wishes are known, is to enforce the fundamental principle of personal autonomy. The same requirement, as applied to agents and surrogates freely designated by competent persons, enforces the principles of agency. A reasonable person presumably will designate for such purposes only a person in whom the former reposes the highest degree of confidence. A conservator, in contrast, is *not* an agent of the conservatee, and unlike a freely designated agent cannot be presumed to have special knowledge of the conservatee's health care wishes.* * * While it may be constitutionally permissible to assume that an agent freely designated by a formerly competent person to make all health care decisions, including life-ending ones, will resolve such questions "in accordance with the principal's ... wishes" [ ] one cannot apply the same assumption to conservators and conservatees .[ ] For this reason, when the legal premise of a conservator's decision to end a conservatee's life by withholding medical care is that the conservatee would refuse such care, to apply a high standard of proof will help to ensure the reliability of the decision.

The function of a standard of proof is to instruct the fact finder concerning the degree of confidence our society deems necessary in the correctness of factual conclusions for a particular type of adjudication, to allocate the risk of error between the litigants, and to indicate the relative importance attached to the ultimate decision. [ ] Thus, "the standard of proof may depend upon the 'gravity of the consequences that would result from an erroneous determination of the issue involved.' "[ ] The default standard of proof in civil cases is the preponderance of the evidence. [ ] Nevertheless, courts have applied the clear and convincing evidence standard when necessary to protect important rights.

We applied the clear and convincing evidence standard, for example * * * to ensure that a conservator's decision to authorize sterilization of a developmentally disabled conservatee was truly in the latter's best interests. We have also applied the clear and convincing evidence standard to findings necessary to terminate parental rights [ ] and to findings supporting the discipline of judges [ ] The Courts of Appeal have required clear and convincing evidence of a person's inability to provide for his or her personal needs as a prerequisite to the appointment of a conservator [ ] and of a conservatee's incompetence to accept or reject treatment as a prerequisite to permitting involuntary electroconvulsive therapy [ ]. Similarly, the United States Supreme Court has applied the clear and convincing evidence standard in cases implicating fundamental liberty interests protected by the Fourteenth Amendment, such as proceedings to terminate parental rights [ ], to commit to a mental hospital [ ], and to deport [ ].

In this case, the importance of the ultimate decision and the risk of error are manifest. So too should be the degree of confidence required in the necessary findings of fact. The ultimate decision is whether a conservatee lives or dies, and the risk is that a conservator, claiming statutory authority to end a conscious conservatee's life "in accordance with the conservatee's ... wishes" [ ] by withdrawing artificial nutrition and hydration, will make a decision with which the conservatee subjectively disagrees and which subjects the conservatee to starvation, dehydration and death. This would represent the gravest possible affront to a conservatee's state constitutional right to privacy, in the sense of freedom from unwanted bodily intrusions, and to life. * * * Certainly it is possible, as the conservator here urges, that an incompetent and uncommunicative but conscious conservatee might perceive the efforts to keep him alive as unwanted intrusion and the withdrawal of those efforts as welcome release. But the decision to treat is reversible. The decision to withdraw treatment is not. The role of a high evidentiary standard in such a case is to adjust the risk of error to favor the less perilous result. * * *

In conclusion, to interpret [the Probate Code] to permit a conservator to withdraw artificial nutrition and hydration from a conscious conservatee based on a finding, by a mere preponderance of the evidence, that the conservatee would refuse treatment creates a serious risk that the law will be unconstitutionally applied in some cases, with grave injury to fundamental rights. Under these circumstances, we may properly ask whether the statute may be construed in a way that mitigates the risk. * * * Here, where the risk to conservatees' rights is grave and the proposed construction is consistent with the language of the statute, to construe the statute to avoid the constitutional risk is an appropriate exercise of judicial power.

* * *

One amicus curiae argues that "[i]mposing so high an evidentiary burden [i.e., clear and convincing evidence] would ... frustrate many genuine treatment desires—particularly the choices of young people, who are less likely than older people to envision the need for advanced directives, or poor people, who are less likely than affluent people to have the resources to obtain formal legal documents." But the Legislature has already accommodated this concern in large part by permitting patients to nominate surrogate decision makers by orally informing a supervising physician [ ] and by giving effect to specific oral health care instructions [ ]. To go still farther, by giving conclusive effect to wishes inferred from informal, oral statements proved only by a preponderance of the evidence, may serve the interests of incompetent persons whose wishes are correctly determined, but to do so also poses an unacceptable risk of violating other incompetent patients' rights to privacy and life, as already explained. To the argument that applying a high standard of proof in such cases impermissibly burdens the right to determine one's own medical treatment, one need only repeat the United States Supreme Court's response to the same assertion: "The differences between the choice made *by* a competent person to refuse medical treatment, and the choice made *for* an incompetent person by someone else to refuse medical treatment, are so obviously different that the State is warranted in establishing rigorous procedures for the latter class of cases which do not apply to the former class." *Cruzan [ ]*

\* \* \*

In the case before us, the trial court found that the conservator failed to show "by clear and convincing evidence that conservatee Robert Wendland, who is not in a persistent vegetative state nor suffering from a terminal illness would, under the circumstances, want to die." The conservator does not appear to challenge the trial court's finding on this point; her challenge, rather, is to the trial court's understanding of the law. For these reasons, we need not review the sufficiency of the evidence to support the finding. Nevertheless, given the exceptional circumstances of this case, we note that the finding appears to be correct.

\* \* \*

### 2. *The best interest standard*

Having rejected the conservator's argument that withdrawing artificial hydration and nutrition would have been "in accordance with the conservatee's \* \* \* wishes" [ ], we must next consider her contention that the same action would have been proper under the fallback best interest standard. Under that standard, "the conservator shall make the decision in accordance with the conservator's determination of the conservatee's best interest. In determining the conservatee's best interest, the conservator shall consider the conservatee's personal values to the extent known to the conservator." [ ] The trial court, as noted, ruled the conservator had the burden of establishing that the withdrawal of artificially delivered nutrition and hydration was in the conservatee's best interest, and had not met that burden.

Here, as before, the conservator argues that the trial court applied too high a standard of proof. This follows, she contends, from [the Probate Code], which gives her as conservator "the *exclusive* authority" to give consent for such medical treatment as she "in good faith based on medical advice determines to be necessary" \* \* \* . Based on these statements, the conservator argues the trial court has no power other than to verify that she has made the decision for which the Probate Code expressly calls: a "good faith" decision "based on medical advice" and "consider[ing] the conservatee's personal values" whether treatment is "necessary" in the conservatee's "best interest."[ ] The trial court, as noted, rejected the conservator's assessment of the conservatee's best interest but nevertheless found by clear and convincing evidence that she had acted "in good faith, based on medical evidence and after consideration of the conservatee's best interests, including his likely wishes, based on his previous statements." This finding, the conservator concludes, should end the litigation as a matter of law in her favor.

\* \* \*. To be sure, the statute provides that "the conservator shall make the decision in accordance with *the conservator's determination* of the conservatee's best interest." [ ] But the conservator herself concedes the court must be able to review her decision for abuse of discretion. This much, at least, follows from the conservator's status as an officer of the court subject to judicial supervision. While the assessment of a conservatee's best interest belongs in the first instance to the conservator, this does not mean the court must invariably defer to the conservator regardless of the evidence.

In the exceptional case where a conservator proposes to end the life of a conscious but incompetent conservatee, we believe the same factor that principally justifies applying the clear and convincing evidence standard to a determination of the conservatee's wishes also justifies applying that standard to a determination of the conservatee's best interest: The decision threatens the conservatee's fundamental rights to privacy and life. * * *

We need not in this case attempt to define the extreme factual predicates that, if proved by clear and convincing evidence, might support a conservator's decision that withdrawing life support would be in the best interest of a conscious conservatee. Here, the conservator offered no basis for such a finding other than her own subjective judgment that the conservatee did not enjoy a satisfactory quality of life and legally insufficient evidence to the effect that he would have wished to die. On this record, the trial court's decision was correct.

## III. CONCLUSION

For the reasons set out above, we conclude the superior court correctly required the conservator to prove, by clear and convincing evidence, either that the conservatee wished to refuse life-sustaining treatment or that to withhold such treatment would have been in his best interest; lacking such evidence, the superior court correctly denied the conservator's request for permission to withdraw artificial hydration and nutrition. We emphasize, however, that the clear and convincing evidence standard does not apply to the vast majority of health care decisions made by conservators under [the Probate Code]. Only the decision to withdraw life-sustaining treatment, because of its effect on a conscious conservatee's fundamental rights, justifies imposing that high standard of proof. Therefore, our decision today affects only a narrow class of persons: conscious conservatees who have not left formal directions for health care and whose conservators propose to withhold life-sustaining treatment for the purpose of causing their conservatees' deaths. Our conclusion does not affect permanently unconscious patients, including those who are comatose or in a persistent vegetative state [ ], persons who have left legally cognizable instructions for health care [ ], persons who have designated agents or other surrogates for health care [ ], or conservatees for whom conservators have made medical decisions other than those intended to bring about the death of a conscious conservatee.

The decision of the Court of Appeal is reversed.

### Notes and Questions on the California Supreme Court opinion in Wendland

1. How, exactly, does the Supreme Court rule differ from the rule proposed by the Court of Appeal? They each propose a "clear and convincing evidence" standard—but for what material fact(s)? Does either court use this evidentiary standard as a surrogate for what is really a different substantive rule? Do the two courts merely disagree on the strength of the evidence actually presented to the trial court in this case?

2. The California Supreme Court would support the Court of Appeal analysis in the case of an unconscious patient. Of course, Robert Wendland was unconscious for some time before he emerged from the coma. Could Rose have decided

to terminate life-sustaining medical treatment if she had acted before he regained consciousness? Might the *Wendland* case encourage families to act quickly to discontinue life-sustaining treatment to protect the patient from the harsh rule–virtually forbidding termination of treatment–that would apply if the patient should regain the tiniest amount of consciousness?

Perhaps the California Supreme Court meant to exempt only the "permanently unconscious" from the *Wendland* rule, not any "unconscious" patient. Can we ever be sure that a patient is "permanently unconscious"? What tests should physicians apply to make this diagnosis?

3. Are you convinced that the rule that applies to those who are comatose ought to be different from the rule that applies to those with some consciousness (but no decisional capacity)? What is the justification for this distinction? Is it that a conscious patient may gain enjoyment from life, while an unconscious patient can not? Is it relevant, then, that a conscious patient may also suffer pain while a patient in persistent vegetative state can not? Ultimately, does the California Supreme Court rest on any argument other than the traditional default position that we should err on the side of life?

4. Some of Rose's supporters argued that if physicians "may not follow a surrogate's instruction to withdraw life-sustaining treatment unless the evidence of the patient's wishes satisfies a 'clear and convincing' standard of proof, many physicians will refuse to do so without judicial approval." 110 Cal.Rptr.2d at 437 (referring to briefs filed by amici). Is there a risk that the Wendland case will chill physicians from appropriately recognizing surrogates' decisions, and that physicians will require family members (and other surrogates) to get court orders before they are willing to withdraw life-sustaining treatment? The California Supreme Court was not worried:

> [T]his will not be a valid concern, as we have already explained, in the case of patients who have personally appointed agents or surrogates for health care decisions or left formal instructions for health care, nor in the vast majority of health care decisions, i.e., those less weighty than the decision to withdraw life-sustaining treatment from a conscious patient. The constitutional considerations on which we rely justify applying the clear and convincing evidence standard only when a conservator seeks to withdraw life-sustaining treatment from a conscious, incompetent patient who has not left legally cognizable instructions for health care or appointed an agent or surrogate for health care decisions.

Id. at 438. Are you convinced that the Wendland rule will not affect "the vast majority of health care decisions"?

5. Should Robert Wendland's mother and sister have had standing to challenge the decision of his conservator? Who else should have standing to commence a judicial action seeking to review a decision to terminate life-sustaining medical treatment? All relatives? Health care providers? Health care institutions? Patient advocacy groups? Right-to-life or Right-to-Die advocacy groups? Who should be able to join such litigation as a party?

# V. THE "RIGHT TO DIE"—CHILDREN AND NEWBORNS

## B. NEWBORNS

**Add, at p. 1421, just above the Problem:**

National attention has been drawn to the issue of the appropriate treatment of seriously ill newborns once again as a consequence of a high profile Texas lawsuit in which parents sought damages against a health care institution (but not individual health care providers) for failing to follow the parents' instructions to withhold life-sustaining treatment.

### HCA, INC. v. MILLER

Court of Appeals of Texas, 2000.
36 S.W.3d 187, review granted by the Texas Supreme Court.
sub nom. *S.A.M. v. HCA, Inc.*, (Tex. Jan. 31, 2002)

Edelman, J.:

HCA, Inc. [and other institutional defendants] (collectively "HCA") appeal a judgment entered in favor of Sidney Ainsley Miller ("Sidney"), by and through her next friend, Karla H. Miller, and Karla H. Miller ("Karla") and J. Mark Miller ("Mark"), individually (collectively, the "Millers"). Among other things, HCA contends that a health care provider is not liable in tort for administering urgently needed life-sustaining medical treatment to a newborn infant contrary to the pre-birth instructions of her parents not to do so. After a lengthy struggle with the difficult issues presented, we conclude that HCA is not liable under the facts of this case, reverse the judgment of the trial court, and render a take-nothing judgment.

### Background

Although the tragic circumstances of this case are far more numerous, those pertinent to this appeal can be summarized as follows. Early on August 17, 1990, Karla was admitted to Woman's Hospital of Texas (the "hospital") with symptoms of premature labor. An ultrasound revealed that her fetus, weighing approximately 629 grams, had an estimated gestational age of 23 weeks. In addition, Karla was feared to have an infection that could endanger her life. Dr. Jacobs, Karla's attending obstetrician, and Dr. Kelley, a neonatologist, informed the Millers that if the baby were born alive and survived, she would suffer severe impairments.[2] Accordingly, the Millers orally requested that no heroic measures be performed on the baby after her birth. Dr. Kelley recorded the Millers' oral request in the medical records, and Dr. Jacobs informed the nursing staff that no neonatologist would be needed at delivery.

However, after further consultation, Dr. Jacobs concluded that if the Millers' baby was born alive and weighed over 500 grams, the medical staff

---

**2.** Mark testified that medical personnel at the hospital indicated to him that they had never had such a premature child live and that anything they did to sustain life on such an infant would be guesswork on their part. They further told him that every year for the past five years, the weights of children being born successfully had gotten lower, but they were still learning.

would be obligated by law and hospital policy to administer life-sustaining procedures even if the Millers did not consent to it. Dr. Jacobs explained this to Mark who verbally reiterated his and Karla's desire that their baby not be resuscitated.

Sidney was born late that night. The attending neonatologist, Dr. Otero, determined that Sidney was viable and instituted resuscitative measures. Although Sidney survived, she suffers, as had been anticipated, from severe physical and mental impairments and will never be able to care for herself.

The Millers filed this lawsuit against HCA, asserting: (1) vicarious liability for the actions of the hospital in: (a) treating Sidney without consent; and (b) having a policy which mandated the resuscitation of newborn infants weighing over 500 grams even in the absence of parental consent; and (2) direct liability for failing to have policies to prevent such treatment without consent. Based on the jury's findings of liability[5] and damages, the trial court entered judgment in favor of the Millers in the amount of $29,400,000 in past and future medical expenses, $13,500,000 in punitive damages, and $17,503,066 in prejudgment interest.

**Existence of Tort Duty**

Among other things, HCA challenges the imposition of tort liability against it in this case on the ground that it did not owe the Millers the tort duties that the Millers claim HCA breached. In particular, HCA argues that it could not be liable for battery or negligence in treating Sidney without the consent and against the instructions of the Millers because the doctor and hospital personnel who resuscitated Sidney were legally obligated to do so and because the Millers had no right to withhold life-sustaining medical treatment from Sidney. Because this issue is dispositive of the appeal, we address it first.

Although this issue has implications which extend well beyond the facts of this case, the parties have cited, and we have found, no authority which directly addresses it. A resolution of the issue requires us to find a juncture between three fundamental but competing legal and policy interests.

On the one hand, Texas law expressly gives parents a right to consent to their children's medical care. [ ] Thus, unless a child's need for life-sustaining medical treatment is too urgent for consent to be obtained from a parent or other person with legal authority (the "emergency exception"), a doctor's treatment of the child without such consent is actionable even if the condition requiring treatment would eventually be life-threatening and the treatment is otherwise provided without negligence. [ ] Obviously, the logical corollary of a right of consent is a right not to consent, *i.e.*, to refuse medical treatment. *See*

---

**5.** Liability was predicated on the jury's findings that: (1) the hospital performed resuscitative treatment on Sidney without Karla's or Mark's consent; and (2) the (unspecified) negligence of both the hospital and Columbia/HCA Healthcare Corporation proximately caused the occurrence in question. According to the Millers' brief, this negligence consisted of: (a) failing to have a policy that precluded treatment on a patient without consent; and (b) formulating and implementing a policy that required treatment without consent.

\* \* \*

In addition, although the Millers contend that the resuscitation performed on Sidney itself contributed to her impairment, they do not assert that the liability imposed against HCA was predicated on negligence in the *manner* that the resuscitation was performed but only in that it was performed at all, *i.e.*, without their consent and against their instructions.

\* \* \*

*Cruzan* [ ]. In addition, in Texas, the Advance Directives Act * * * allows parents to withhold or withdraw life-sustaining medical treatment from their child where the child's condition has been certified in writing by a physician to be terminal, *i.e.*, incurable or irreversible and such that even providing life-sustaining treatment will only temporarily postpone death. [ ]

On the other hand parents have a legal duty to provide needed medical care to their children. [ ] Thus, the failure of a parent to provide such care is a criminal offense when it causes injury or impairment to the child.

The third competing legal and policy interest is that of the state, acting as *parens patriae*, to guard the well-being of minors, even where doing so requires limiting the freedom and authority of parents over their children.[ ] In addition, the state's authority over children's activities is broader than over like actions of adults. [ ] In other words, parents are not free to make all decisions for their children that they are free to make for themselves. [ ] Thus, for example, in Texas, the rights and duties of a parent are subject to a court order affecting those rights and duties, including an order granting a governmental entity temporary conservatorship of a child with authority to consent to medical treatment refused by the child's parents. [ ] Notably, however, it is not the health care provider who has the right or obligation to seek such court intervention, but the appropriate governmental agency, which the provider must notify in order for intervention to be sought pursuant to the State's interest in protecting the child. [ ]Therefore, until ordered to do otherwise by a court of competent jurisdiction, a health care provider's obligation is generally to comply with a patient's (or parent's) refusal of medical treatment. [ ]

But does a parent have a right to deny urgently needed life-sustaining medical treatment to their child, *i.e.*, to decide, in effect, to let their child die? In Texas, the Legislature has expressly given parents a right to withhold medical treatment, urgently needed or not, for a child whose medical condition is certifiably terminal, but it has not extended that right to the parents of children with non-terminal impairments, deformities, or disabilities, regardless of their severity. In addition, although the Act expressly states that it does not impair or supersede any legal right a person may have to withhold or withdraw life-sustaining treatment in a lawful manner, the parties have cited, and we have found, no other statutory or common law authority allowing urgently needed life-sustaining medical treatment to be withheld from a non-terminally ill child by a parent. To infer that parents have a general common law right to withhold such treatment from a non-terminally ill child would, in effect, mean that the Legislature has afforded greater protection to children who are terminally ill than to those who are not. On the contrary, if anything, the state's interest in preserving life is greatest when life *can* be preserved and then weakens as the prognosis dims. [ ]

More importantly, to infer that parents have a common law right to withhold urgently needed life-sustaining treatment from non-terminally ill children would pose imponderable legal and policy issues. For example, if parents *had* such a right, would it apply to otherwise healthy, normal children or only to those with some degree of abnormality? If the latter, which circumstances would qualify, which would not, and how could any such distinctions be justified legally? [ ] In light of the high value our law places on preserving human life, and especially on protecting the life and well-being of minors, we perceive no legal basis or other rationale for concluding that Texas law gives parents a common law right to withhold urgently needed life-sustaining medical treatment from children in circumstances in which the Act does not apply. * * *

Having recognized, as a general rule, that parents have no right to refuse urgently-needed life-sustaining medical treatment to their non-terminally ill children, a compelling argument can be made to carve out an exception for infants born so prematurely and in such poor condition that sustaining their life, even if medically possible, cannot be justified. To whatever extent such an approach would be preferable from a policy standpoint to having no such an exception, and to whatever extent such an approach is available to the Legislature or a higher court, we do not believe it is an alternative available to this court because: (1) a sufficient record does not exist in this case to identify where to "draw the line" for such an exception; and, more importantly, (2) it is not within the province of an intermediate appellate court to, in effect, legislate in that manner.

* * *

In a situation where non-urgently needed or non-life-sustaining medical treatment is proposed for a child, a court order is needed to override a parent's refusal to consent to the treatment because a determination of such issues as the child's safety, welfare, and best interest can vary under differing circumstances and alternatives. By contrast, where life-sustaining medical treatment is urgently needed, time constraints will often not permit resort to the courts. Where the need for such treatment can be anticipated before it becomes acute, the circumstances might allow the parents to remove the child from the health provider's care; and, under existing legal principles, the treatment cannot lawfully be provided without consent before the need for it becomes acute in any event. However, where the need for life-sustaining medical treatment is or becomes urgent while a non-terminally ill child is under a health care provider's care, and where the child's parents refuse consent to that treatment, we do not believe that a court order is necessary to override that refusal because no legal or factual issue exists for a court to decide regarding the provision of such treatment. * * *

In this case, the Millers had a right to refuse urgently needed life-sustaining medical treatment for Sidney only to the extent that her condition was certifiably terminal and other requirements of the Act were satisfied. Although there was considerable doubt that Sidney would be born alive at all and that, if and when born alive, she could be kept alive, there is no evidence that her condition before or after birth was (or could have been) certified as terminal. In addition, the record is clear that at the time Sidney was born, her need for life-sustaining procedures was urgent. Following her birth, Sidney's condition proved, with the efforts of her doctors, not to be terminal. Under these circumstances, the Millers had no right to deny the urgently needed life-sustaining medical treatment to Sidney, and no court order was needed to overcome their refusal to consent to it.

Based on the foregoing, we sustain HCA's contentions that it did not owe the Millers a tort duty to: (a) refrain from resuscitating Sidney; (b) have no policy requiring resuscitation of patients like Sidney without consent; and (3) have policies prohibiting resuscitation of patients like Sidney without consent.

* * *

Amidei, J., dissenting:

I respectfully dissent.

* * *

I disagree with the majority's conclusion that under these circumstances, a court order is not necessary to override the parents' refusal to consent because no legal or factual issue existed for the court to decide regarding the provision of such treatment. The court must decide the most important issue: What is in the best interest of the child? A court decision in favor of the resuscitation would afford the physician and hospital the consent necessary to treat the newborn infant. In the interest of justice, having a court hear the matter would have provided an impartial tribunal without any conflict of interest or appearance of conflict of interest to decide the matter.

* * *

The majority repeatedly refers to "urgently needed life sustaining treatment" and to the "emergency exception" without explaining how we can hold the "emergency exception" applies without a jury finding on the issue. I would hold as a matter of law there was no emergency. * * *

Appellants had alternative courses available to them early on. Particularly, the course of withholding life support (no resuscitation), as first suggested by the Millers' doctors, and with which the Millers agreed, could have been accomplished by a simple change of doctors. Another doctor holding a different opinion could have delivered the baby and not applied resuscitation. The appellants did not suggest to the Millers they could change doctors. There was ample time during which the appellants met and decided their chosen course of action without obtaining the Millers' consent. The urgency, if any, was due to the appellants' indecision and delay. Eleven hours elapsed after the Millers informed their doctors they wanted to take their original advice and not resuscitate the baby, if born alive. The appellants decided there was going to be resuscitation and performed it knowing the Millers were there and available to consult regarding the consent. This was not a medical emergency which excuses not having a consent. A true medical emergency is where a doctor must operate and no one is available to give the proper consent. The Millers were present in the hospital at all times leading up to the birth and resuscitation, but appellants chose not to try to change the Miller minds, change doctors, or try to obtain a court order. Anytime a group of doctors and a hospital administration has the luxury of multiple meetings to change the original doctors' medical opinions, without taking a more obvious course of action, there is no medical emergency.

In the event there was no emergency as a matter of law, it was still the appellant's burden to plead and prove as a defense an emergency or circumstances requiring the immediate resuscitative procedure without consent of the Millers. [ ] No defense questions were submitted to the jury. Specifically no question as to an emergency which would excuse having no consent was requested. [ ] Appellant's have not raised any issue regarding an emergency jury question on appeal. Therefore, we cannot consider whether an emergency existed which would imply consent and, in effect, deem the issue in favor appellants. Appellants waived the issue.

The resulting conflict could have and should have been avoided by the appellants. Appellants were not entitled to immunity or a deemed finding that an emergency existed to excuse obtaining a consent. I would overrule appellants' issues, and affirm the trial court.

### Notes and Questions on HCA, Inc. v. Miller

1. The Supreme Court of Texas granted review of the divided decision of the Court of Appeals and heard argument in April of 2002. As this Supplement was prepared in early 2003, fourteen months after review was granted, the case was still pending in that court.

2. The Miller baby was 23 weeks gestation and weighed 1 pound, 2 ounces. While a few babies born at this level of development and with this weight live normal lives, others die very quickly. Many are in between–they live with impairments that range from very mild to very severe. Sidney Miller has cerebral palsy. She is almost completely blind, very severely retarded, and she will never be able to care for herself. She cannot walk or talk. For a description of the dilemma faced by her parents at her birth, see D. W. Linden and M. W. Doron, Eyes of Texas Fasten on Life, Death and the Premature Infant, New York Times, April 30, 2002, p. F5.

3. Should there be a cut-off below which premature babies are not provided intensive treatment? How would you establish that line? Gestational age? Weight? Medical prognosis, considering both of those factors? Should the fact that a newborn *can* be kept alive be enough to assure that the newborn is provided all available care, whatever the parents might want? Instead, should we require that there is a chance that the newborn will lead a "normal life" before the parents' decision to forgo life-sustaining treatment at birth is overruled? What is a "normal life"? What if there is only a 10% chance of a "normal life"? A one percent chance? A one-tenth of one percent chance?

4. What does it mean to describe a newborn infant as "terminal"? This term can be confusing when it is used to describe someone reaching the end of a long life; it is more difficult to apply it to a newborn. If a newborn is likely to die from birth anomalies—but not for years—is that newborn "terminal"? What if the newborn is likely to die in months? Weeks? If a newborn would die in the absence of highly invasive life-sustaining treatment, but could be kept alive for a year through the use of that machinery, is the newborn "terminal"? Might you want to define "terminal" differently for newborns than you do for others?

5. If you were consulted as counsel by someone in the position of the Miller family, what would you say? If the parents were committed to making sure that their baby did not go through the decade of medical intervention that Sidney received, what advice would you give them? Should you report them to the state child protective services office as parents about to medically neglect their child? On the other hand, could you seek a declaratory judgment that the hospital is not permitted to keep the infant alive against the wishes of the parents? How would you draft the complaint? The proposed order? Would it be appropriate for you to

advise the parents that they should leave the country if they do not want all available medical resources used to keep their newborn alive?

6. How much of the Miller case is a result of the court's analysis of the underlying health care decision-making issue, and how much is driven by the fact that the case is a medical malpractice damages action? Would the analysis be the same if the issue came up in an action for injunctive relief or declaratory judgment?

## VII. PHYSICIAN ASSISTED DEATH

### B. LEGISLATION TO SUPPORT PHYSICIAN ASSISTED DEATH— "DEATH WITH DIGNITY" INITIATIVES

**Add, at p. 1456, just before the Notes and Questions:**

The Fifth Annual Report on the operation of the Death with Dignity Act was released in March of 2003. The full text of that report is available at the new state Death with Dignity Act web site, http://www.ohd.hr.state.or.us/chs/pas.htm. The "Results" section of this report summarizes the way in which the Act was applied during its first five years in effect. In this report, "PAS" refers to physician assisted suicide.

### FIFTH ANNUAL REPORT ON OREGON'S DEATH WITH DIGNITY ACT

Oregon Department of Human Services, Office of Disease Prevention and Epidemiology.
March 6, 2003.

\* \* \*

**Results:**

\* \* \*

Both the number of prescriptions written and the number of Oregonians using PAS have increased over the five years that PAS has been legal in Oregon. In 2002, 58 prescriptions for lethal doses of medication were written by 33 physicians. This compares to 44 prescriptions written in 2001, 39 in 2000, 33 in 1999 and 24 in 1998. Thirty-six of the patients who received prescriptions during 2002 died after ingesting the lethal medication and 6 were alive on December 31, 2002. In addition, two patients who received their prescriptions during 2001 died in 2002 after ingesting lethal medications for a total of 38 PAS deaths during 2002. This compares to 21 deaths in 2001, 27 deaths in 2000, 27 deaths in 1999, and 16 deaths in 1998.

Patients participating in 2002 were similar to those in previous years except that more males and persons without a college degree used PAS [ ]. Similar to previous years, most patients (84%) choosing PAS had cancer.

During 2001, a total of 30,128 Oregonians died. Thus, patients ingesting lethal medications in 2002 represented an estimated 13/10,000 total Oregon deaths. By comparison, 2001 patients represented 7/10,000 deaths, 2000 and 1999 PAS patients, 9/10,000 deaths, and 1998 PAS patients represented 6/10,000 deaths.

### Patient Characteristics

The characteristics of the 129 PAS patients who died in 1998–2002 differed in several ways from the 42,274 Oregonians who died from the same underlying causes. An inverse relationship exists between age and participation with younger patients more likely to use PAS than older patients [ ]. Although based on relatively few deaths (four), Asian residents were three times more likely to use PAS than were non-hispanic whites. Divorced Oregonians were almost twice as likely to use PAS than their married counterparts. As educational attainment increases, so too does the likelihood of a terminally ill Oregonian choosing to use PAS; compared to those without a high school diploma, college graduates were 6.5 times more likely to use PAS. Finally, the type of terminal illness was related to use of PAS; residents with cancer and amyotrophic lateral sclerosis (ALS) were more likely to use PAS.

During 2002, all patients died at home and all but one had some form of health insurance [ ]. As in previous years, most (92%) of the patients who used PAS in 2002 were enrolled in hospice care. The median length of the patient-physician relationship was 11 weeks.

### Physician Characteristics

The prescribing physicians of patients who used PAS during 2002 had been in practice a median of 18.5 years. Their medical specialties included: internal medicine (29%), oncology (45%), family medicine (24%), and other (5%). [Note: the sum of the percentages do not equal 100 because some physicians had two specialities.]

Prescribing physicians were present while 13 (34%) of the 38 patients ingested the lethal medications. Among the remaining 25 patients, attendant status was known for 23. Of these individuals, 78% ingested the medication in the presence of another health care provider/volunteer.

No physicians were reported to the Oregon Board of Medical Examiners in 2002.

### Lethal Medication

[This section discussed the actual medication prescribed under the Act. Until 2001, most lethal prescriptions were written for secobarbital. When production of this drug was stopped in May of 2001, physicians turned primarily to pentobarbital.]

### Complications

During 2002, after ingesting the prescribed medication, one patient coughed and gagged for 10–15 seconds, expectorating some clear mucoid material and another patient vomited; the first patient died 13 minutes after ingesting the opiate while the other died two hours later. Three patients lived more than six hours after drinking the lethal medication: one participant, who had impaired digestion, lived 14 hours; another, with a complete bowel obstruction, lived nine hours; and a third lived 12 hours for unknown reasons. * * * No patient regained consciousness after taking the medications.

**End of Life Concerns**

Physicians were asked if, based on discussions with patients, any of six end-of-life concerns might have contributed to the patients' requests for lethal medication [ ]. In nearly all cases, physicians reported multiple concerns contributing to the request. Four patients (10%) were reported to have one end-of-life concern, 12 (32%) had two concerns, 12 (32%) had three concerns, 7 (18%) had four concerns, and three (8%) had five concerns. The most frequently reported concerns included losing autonomy (84%), a decreasing ability to participate in activities that make life enjoyable (84%), and losing control of bodily functions (47%).

**Comments:**

During the five years since legalization, the number of prescriptions written for physician-assisted suicide and the number of terminally-ill patients taking lethal medication has increased. However, even with this increase the number has remained small compared to the total number of deaths in Oregon, with fewer than 1/8 of one percent of Oregonians dying by PAS. This proportion is consistent with numbers from a survey of Oregon physicians. Overall, smaller numbers of patients appear to use PAS in Oregon compared to the Netherlands. However, as detailed in previous reports, our numbers are based on a reporting system for terminally-ill patients who legally receive prescriptions for lethal medications, and do not include patients and physicians who may act outside the law.

That educated patients are more likely to choose PAS is consistent with findings that Oregon patients with at least a college degree are more likely to be knowledgeable about end-of-life choices.

Over the last five years the rate of PAS among patients with ALS in Oregon has been substantially higher than among patients with other illnesses. This finding is consistent with other studies. In the Netherlands, where both PAS and euthanasia are openly practiced, one in five ALS patients died as a result of PAS or euthanasia. A study of Oregon and Washington ALS patients found that one-third of these patients discussed wanting PAS in the last month of life . It is not known with certainty why ALS patients appear to be more likely to be interested in choosing PAS than other terminally ill patients.

Over the five years, physicians have consistently reported that concern about loss of autonomy and participation in activities that make life enjoyable have been important motivating factors in patient requests for lethal medication across all five years. Interviews with family members during 1999 corroborated physician reports. These findings were supported by a recent study of hospice nurses and social workers caring for PAS patients in Oregon .

The availability of PAS may have led to efforts to improve end-of-life care through other modalities. While it may be common for patients with a terminal illness to consider PAS, a request for PAS can be an opportunity for a medical provider to explore with patients their fears and wishes around end-of-life care, and to make patients aware of other options. Often once the provider has addressed patients' concerns, they may choose not to pursue PAS. The availability of PAS as an option in Oregon also may have spurred

Oregon doctors to address other end-of life care options more effectively. In one study Oregon physicians reported that, since the passage of the Death with Dignity Act in 1994, they had made efforts to improve their knowledge of the use of pain medications in the terminally ill, to improve their recognition of psychiatric disorders such as depression, and to refer patients more frequently to hospice.

**Add, at p. 1457, at the end of Note 4:**

In part as a result of the narrow defeat of the Maine measure, during the next legislative session both supporters and opponents of physician assisted death joined to support a number of bills improving the quality of end-of-life care in that State. See note 5. The question of physician assisted death itself has not moved off the legislative radar screen, though. In 2002 the Hawai'i House of Representatives passed an Oregon-like bill that came within a couple of votes of passing the Senate. More legislative action—on Oregon-like bills and compromise end-of-life care bills—is expected in other states in 2003 and 2004.

**Add, at p. 1457, at the end of Note 5:**

Federal and state policy may conflict on one kind of palliative care—the use of marijuana. Some cancer patients, patients with glaucoma, AIDS patients, patients with multiple sclerosis, those with migraine headaches and others find that they can obtain relief from some of the symptoms of the disease–or from some of the side effects of the treatments for the disease–through the use of marijuana. In particular, some cancer patients find that marijuana helps them overcome the nausea that follows the use of many chemotherapeutic agents. While several states have now legalized the use of marijuana under such circumstances, the manufacture and distribution of marijuana, a schedule I drug, is still a felony under the Federal Controlled Substances Act. Whether the Federal law outlawing such manufacture and distribution effectively trump the new state laws that permit its use under controlled circumstances, and under medical prescription, was resolved by the Supreme Court in 2001. For a full discussion of this issue, see the next section of this supplement.

**Add, at p. 1458, at the end of Note 6:**

Indeed, the new Attorney General, John Ashcroft, reversed the Department of Justice position on the issue of the application of the Controlled Substances Act in late 2001. He set federal government machinery in motion to prosecute those who prescribed or dispensed medications under the Death with Dignity Act. Within a day Oregon sought relief from the Attorney General's decision in the United States District Court, and a private action also seeking an injunction against the Ashcroft position was filed shortly thereafter on behalf of an Oregon oncologist. The District Court immediately restrained the United States from enforcing the new interpretation of the Controlled Substances Act, and on April 17, 2002, permanently enjoined its enforcement, in part because no federal agency is authorized "to establish a national medical practice or act as a national medical board." Oregon v. Ashcroft, Civil 01–1647–JO (D. Or., April 17, 2002). As this supplement goes to press in early 2003, the issue is pending in the Ninth Circuit.

Add, at p. 1459, at the end of the Chapter:

## VIII. REGULATION OF END–OF–LIFE CARE: THE CASE OF MEDICAL MARIJUANA

### UNITED STATES v. OAKLAND CANNABIS BUYERS' COOPERATIVE

Supreme Court of the United States, 2001.
532 U.S. 483, 121 S.Ct. 1711, 149 L.Ed.2d 722.

JUSTICE THOMAS delivered the opinion of the Court.

The Controlled Substances Act, [ ] prohibits the manufacture and distribution of various drugs, including marijuana. In this case, we must decide whether there is a medical necessity exception to these prohibitions. We hold that there is not.

I

In November 1996, California voters enacted an initiative measure entitled the Compassionate Use Act of 1996. Attempting "to ensure that seriously ill Californians have the right to obtain and use marijuana for medical purposes," [ ] the statute creates an exception to California laws prohibiting the possession and cultivation of marijuana. These prohibitions no longer apply to a patient or his primary caregiver who possesses or cultivates marijuana for the patient's medical purposes upon the recommendation or approval of a physician. [ ] In the wake of this voter initiative, several groups organized "medical cannabis dispensaries" to meet the needs of qualified patients. [ ] Respondent Oakland Cannabis Buyers' Cooperative is one of these groups.

The Cooperative is a not-for-profit organization that operates in downtown Oakland. A physician serves as medical director, and registered nurses staff the Cooperative during business hours. To become a member, a patient must provide a written statement from a treating physician assenting to marijuana therapy and must submit to a screening interview. If accepted as a member, the patient receives an identification card entitling him to obtain marijuana from the Cooperative.

In January 1998, the United States sued the Cooperative * * * in the United States District Court for the Northern District of California. Seeking to enjoin the Cooperative from distributing and manufacturing marijuana, the United States argued that, whether or not the Cooperative's activities are legal under California law, they violate federal law. Specifically, the Government argued that the Cooperative violated the Controlled Substances Act's prohibitions on distributing, manufacturing, and possessing with the intent to distribute or manufacture a controlled substance. [ ] Concluding that the Government had established a probability of success on the merits, the District Court granted a preliminary injunction. [ ]

The Cooperative did not appeal the injunction but instead openly violated it by distributing marijuana to numerous persons [ ]. To terminate these violations, the Government initiated contempt proceedings. In defense, the Cooperative contended that any distributions were medically necessary. Marijuana is the only drug, according to the Cooperative, that can alleviate the severe pain and other debilitating symptoms of the Cooperative's patients. [ ] The District Court rejected this defense, however, after determining there was insufficient evidence that each recipient of marijuana was in actual danger of imminent harm without the drug. [ ] The District Court found the Cooperative in contempt and, at the Government's request, modified the preliminary injunction to empower the United States Marshal to seize the Cooperative's premises. Although recognizing that "human suffering" could result, the District Court reasoned that a court's "equitable powers [do] not permit it to ignore federal law." [ ] Three days later, the District Court summarily rejected a motion by the Cooperative to modify the injunction to permit distributions that are medically necessary.

The Cooperative appealed both the contempt order and the denial of the Cooperative's motion to modify. Before the Court of Appeals for the Ninth Circuit decided the case, however, the Cooperative voluntarily purged its contempt by promising the District Court that it would comply with the initial preliminary injunction. Consequently, the Court of Appeals determined that the appeal of the contempt order was moot. [ ]

The denial of the Cooperative's motion to modify the injunction, however, presented a live controversy * * *. Reaching the merits of this issue, the Court of Appeals reversed and remanded. According to the Court of Appeals, the medical necessity defense was a "legally cognizable defense" that likely would apply in the circumstances. [ ] Moreover, the Court of Appeals reasoned, the District Court erroneously "believed that it had no discretion to issue an injunction that was more limited in scope than the Controlled Substances Act itself." [ ] Because, according to the Court of Appeals, district courts retain "broad equitable discretion" to fashion injunctive relief, the District Court could have, and should have, weighed the "public interest" and considered factors such as the serious harm in depriving patients of marijuana. [ ] Remanding the case, the Court of Appeals instructed the District Court to consider "the criteria for a medical necessity exemption, and, should it modify the injunction, to set forth those criteria in the modification order."[ ] Following these instructions, the District Court granted the Cooperative's motion to modify the injunction to incorporate a medical necessity defense.[2]

The United States petitioned for certiorari to review the Court of Appeals' decision that medical necessity is a legally cognizable defense to violations of the Controlled Substances Act. Because the decision raises

---

**2.** The amended preliminary injunction reaffirmed that the Cooperative is generally enjoined from manufacturing, distributing, and possessing with the intent to manufacture or distribute marijuana, but it carved out an exception for cases of medical necessity. Specifically, the District Court ordered that "the foregoing injunction does not apply to the distribution of cannabis by [the Cooperative] to patient-members who (1) suffer from a serious medical condition, (2) will suffer imminent harm if the patient-member does not have access to cannabis, (3) need cannabis for the treatment of the patient-member's medical condition, or need cannabis to alleviate the medical condition or symptoms associated with the medical condition, and (4) have no reasonable legal alternative to cannabis for the effective treatment or alleviation of the patient-member's medical condition or symptoms associated with the medical condition because the patient-member has tried all other legal alternatives to cannabis and the alternatives have been ineffective in treating or alleviating the patient-member's medical condition or symptoms associated with the medical condition, or the alternatives result in side effects which the patient-member cannot reasonably tolerate."
[ ]

significant questions as to the ability of the United States to enforce the Nation's drug laws, we granted certiorari. [ ]

## II

The Controlled Substances Act provides that, "except as authorized by this subchapter, it shall be unlawful for any person knowingly or intentionally ... to manufacture, distribute, or dispense, or possess with intent to manufacture, distribute, or dispense, a controlled substance." [ ] The subchapter, in turn, establishes exceptions. For marijuana (and other drugs that have been classified as "schedule I" controlled substances), there is but one express exception, and it is available only for Government-approved research projects [ ]. Not conducting such a project, the Cooperative cannot, and indeed does not, claim this statutory exemption.

The Cooperative contends, however, that notwithstanding the apparently absolute language * * *, the statute is subject to additional, implied exceptions, one of which is medical necessity. According to the Cooperative, because necessity was a defense at common law, medical necessity should be read into the Controlled Substances Act. We disagree.

As an initial matter, we note that it is an open question whether federal courts ever have authority to recognize a necessity defense not provided by statute. * * *

We need not decide, however, whether necessity can ever be a defense when the federal statute does not expressly provide for it. In this case, to resolve the question presented, we need only recognize that a medical necessity exception for marijuana is at odds with the terms of the Controlled Substances Act. The statute, to be sure, does not explicitly abrogate the defense. But its provisions leave no doubt that the defense is unavailable.

Under any conception of legal necessity, one principle is clear: The defense cannot succeed when the legislature itself has made a "determination of values." [ ] In the case of the Controlled Substances Act, the statute reflects a determination that marijuana has no medical benefits worthy of an exception (outside the confines of a Government-approved research project). Whereas some other drugs can be dispensed and prescribed for medical use, [ ] the same is not true for marijuana. Indeed, for purposes of the Controlled Substances Act, marijuana has "no currently accepted medical use" at all. [ ]

[The Court then describes the structure of the Controlled Substances Act and points out that the fact that Congress, not the Attorney General, classified marijuana as a schedule I drug, is legally irrelevant. A schedule I drug "has no currently acceptable medical use in treatment in the United States" and "has a high potential for abuse."]

\* \* \*

The Cooperative further argues that use of schedule I drugs generally—whether placed in schedule I by Congress or the Attorney General—can be medically necessary, notwithstanding that they have "no currently accepted medical use." According to the Cooperative, a drug may not yet have achieved general acceptance as a medical treatment but may nonetheless have medical benefits to a particular patient or class of patients. We decline to parse the statute in this manner. It is clear from the text of the Act that Congress has made a determination that marijuana has no medical benefits worthy of an exception.

Finally, the Cooperative contends that we should construe the Controlled Substances Act to include a medical necessity defense in order to avoid what it considers to be difficult constitutional questions. In particular, the Cooperative asserts that, shorn of a medical necessity defense, the statute exceeds Congress' Commerce Clause powers, violates the substantive due process rights of patients, and offends the fundamental liberties of the people under the Fifth, Ninth, and Tenth Amendments. As the Cooperative acknowledges, however, the canon of constitutional avoidance has no application in the absence of statutory ambiguity. Because we have no doubt that the Controlled Substances Act cannot bear a medical necessity defense to distributions of marijuana, we do not find guidance in this avoidance principle. Nor do we consider the underlying constitutional issues today. Because the Court of Appeals did not address these claims, we decline to do so in the first instance.

For these reasons, we hold that medical necessity is not a defense to manufacturing and distributing marijuana.[7] The Court of Appeals erred when it held that medical necessity is a "legally cognizable defense." [ ]. It further erred when it instructed the District Court on remand to consider "the criteria for a medical necessity exemption, and, should it modify the injunction, to set forth those criteria in the modification order." [ ]

### III

The Cooperative contends that, even if the Controlled Substances Act forecloses the medical necessity defense, there is an alternative ground for affirming the Court of Appeals. This case, the Cooperative reminds us, arises from a motion to modify an injunction to permit distributions that are medically necessary. According to the Cooperative, the Court of Appeals was correct that the District Court had "broad equitable discretion" to tailor the injunctive relief to account for medical necessity, irrespective of whether there is a legal defense of necessity in the statute. [ ] To sustain the judgment below, the argument goes, we need only reaffirm that federal courts, in the exercise of their equity jurisdiction, have discretion to modify an injunction based upon a weighing of the public interest.

We disagree. Although district courts whose equity powers have been properly invoked indeed have discretion in fashioning injunctive relief (in the absence of a statutory restriction), the Court of Appeals erred concerning the factors that the district courts may consider in exercising such discretion.

---

**7.** Lest there be any confusion, we clarify that nothing in our analysis, or the statute, suggests that a distinction should be drawn between the prohibitions on manufacturing and distributing and the other prohibitions in the Controlled Substances Act. Furthermore, the very point of our holding is that there is no medical necessity exception to the prohibitions at issue, even when the patient is "seriously ill" and lacks alternative avenues for relief. Indeed, it is the Cooperative's argument that its patients are "seriously ill," [ ], and lacking "alternatives," [ ]. We reject the argument that these factors warrant a medical necessity exception. If we did not, we would be affirming instead of reversing the Court of Appeals.

Finally, we share Justice Stevens' concern for "showing respect for the sovereign States that comprise our Federal Union." [ ]. However, we are "construing an Act of Congress, not drafting it." [ ] Because federal courts interpret, rather than author, the federal criminal code, we are not at liberty to rewrite it. Nor are we passing today on a constitutional question, such as whether the Controlled Substances Act exceeds Congress' power under the Commerce Clause.

[The Court described the limits on the District Court's exercise of discretion, and pointed out that the lower courts could not ignore policy determinations of Congress in exercising such discretion.]

In this case, the Court of Appeals erred by considering relevant the evidence that some people have "serious medical conditions for whom the use of cannabis is necessary in order to treat or alleviate those conditions or their symptoms," that these people "will suffer serious harm if they are denied cannabis," and that "there is no legal alternative to cannabis for the effective treatment of their medical conditions." [ ] [T]he balance already has been struck [by Congress] against a medical necessity exception. Because the statutory prohibitions cover even those who have what could be termed a medical necessity, the Act precludes consideration of this evidence. It was thus error for the Court of Appeals to instruct the District Court on remand to consider "the criteria for a medical necessity exemption, and, should it modify the injunction, to set forth those criteria in the modification order."

\* \* \*

JUSTICE BREYER took no part in the consideration or decision of this case.

JUSTICE STEVENS, with whom JUSTICE SOUTER and JUSTICE GINSBURG join, concurring in the judgment.

Lest the Court's narrow holding be lost in its broad dicta, let me restate it here: "We hold that medical necessity is not a defense to *manufacturing* and *distributing* marijuana." \* \* \*

\* \* \*

Apart from its limited holding, the Court takes two unwarranted and unfortunate excursions that prevent me from joining its opinion. First, the Court reaches beyond its holding, and beyond the facts of the case, by suggesting that the defense of necessity is unavailable for anyone under the Controlled Substances Act. [ ] Because necessity was raised in this case as a defense to distribution, the Court need not venture an opinion on whether the defense is available to anyone other than distributors. Most notably, whether the defense might be available to a seriously ill patient for whom there is no alternative means of avoiding starvation or extraordinary suffering is a difficult issue that is not presented here.

[Justice Stevens also questioned the majority's suggestion that whether necessity is a defense to any federal statute is an "open question".]

The overbroad language of the Court's opinion is especially unfortunate given the importance of showing respect for the sovereign States that comprise our Federal Union. That respect imposes a duty on federal courts, whenever possible, to avoid or minimize conflict between federal and state law, particularly in situations in which the citizens of a State have chosen to "serve as a laboratory" in the trial of "novel social and economic experiments without risk to the rest of the country." [ ] In my view, this is such a case.[3] By passing Proposition 215, California voters have decided that seriously ill

---

3. Cf. Feeney, Bush Backs States' Rights on Marijuana: He Opposes Medical Use But Favors Local Control, Dallas Morning News, Oct. 20, 1999, p. 6 A. 1999 WL 28018944 (then-Governor Bush supporting state self-determination on medical marijuana use).

patients and their primary caregivers should be exempt from prosecution under state laws for cultivating and possessing marijuana if the patient's physician recommends using the drug for treatment. This case does not call upon the Court to deprive *all* such patients of the benefit of the necessity defense to federal prosecution, when the case itself does not involve *any* such patients.

An additional point deserves emphasis. This case does not require us to rule on the scope of the District Court's discretion to enjoin, or to refuse to enjoin, the possession of marijuana or other potential violations of the Controlled Substances Act by a seriously ill patient for whom the drug may be a necessity. * * *

I join the Court's judgment of reversal because I agree that a distributor of marijuana does not have a medical necessity defense under the Controlled Substances Act. I do not, however, join the dicta in the Court's opinion.

### *Notes and Questions on United States v. Cannabis Buyers' Cooperative*

1. Marijuana has long been at the center of both medical and cultural battles. It was not illegal anyplace in the United States until 1915 when it was outlawed—ironically, given the site of current legal concerns—in California. It became subject to the federal law in the Marijuana Tax Act of 1937, which effectively outlawed the drug in the United States. There was further federal action in 1951 and 1956, and it is now regulated under the 1970 Controlled Substances Act. This Act divides drugs into five schedules. While the classification of most drugs is an administrative action, marijuana has been placed in schedule I, the most restricted list, by Congress itself. Under the Controlled Substances Act, a schedule I drug (1) has no currently accepted medical use, (2) is not safe for medical use, and (3) has a high potential for abuse. 21 U.S.C.A. section 812. Under Federal law, its use is permitted only for research (not therapeutic) purposes approved by the United States. See J. R. Conboy, Smoke Screen: America's Drug Policy and Medical Marijuana, 55 Food and Drug L.J. 601 (2000).

2. Eight states have approved statutes permitting the use of medical marijuana through the voter initiative process, and one state has promulgated such a statute through the normal legislative process. Thus, the medical use of marijuana is now legal, under some circumstances, in nine states—Alaska, Arizona, California, Colorado, Hawaii, Maine, Nevada, Oregon and Washington. Given that all but two of these states (Colorado and Maine) are in the Ninth Circuit, it is not really a surprise that the Ninth Circuit has been the first federal appellate court to see these issues. While there is some variation in these statutes, an early typical statute–and the one to give rise to the most litigation–is the California Compassionate Use Act of 1996:

**Use of Marijuana for Medical Purposes**

**Cal Health & Saf. Code § 11362.5 (2003)**

(a) This section shall be known and may be cited as the Compassionate Use Act of 1996.

(b)(1) The people of the State of California hereby find and declare that the purposes of the Compassionate Use Act of 1996 are as follows:

(A) To ensure that seriously ill Californians have the right to obtain and use marijuana for medical purposes where that medical use is deemed appropriate and has been recommended by a physician who has determined that the person's health would benefit from the use of marijuana in the treatment of cancer, anorexia, AIDS, chronic pain, spasticity, glaucoma, arthritis, migraine, or any other illness for which marijuana provides relief.

(B) To ensure that patients and their primary caregivers who obtain and use marijuana for medical purposes upon the recommendation of a physician are not subject to criminal prosecution or sanction.

(C) To encourage the federal and state governments to implement a plan to provide for the safe and affordable distribution of marijuana to all patients in medical need of marijuana.

(2) Nothing in this section shall be construed to supersede legislation prohibiting persons from engaging in conduct that endangers others, nor to condone the diversion of marijuana for nonmedical purposes.

(c) Notwithstanding any other provision of law, no physician in this state shall be punished, or denied any right or privilege, for having recommended marijuana to a patient for medical purposes.

(d) Section 11357, relating to the possession of marijuana, and Section 11358, relating to the cultivation of marijuana, shall not apply to a patient, or to a patient's primary caregiver, who possesses or cultivates marijuana for the personal medical purposes of the patient upon the written or oral recommendation or approval of a physician.

(e) For the purposes of this section, "primary caregiver" means the individual designated by the person exempted under this section who has consistently assumed responsibility for the housing, health, or safety of that person.

3. There is a great deal of evidence that marijuana is useful as a therapeutic agent in some cases, but there is also some evidence that marijuana is a regularly abused drug that is also "gateway" drug for other drug use. For a summary of the medicinal value of marijuana see L. Grinspoon and J. Bakalar, Marihuana as Medicine, A Plea for Reconsideration, 273 JAMA 1875 (1995), and Conboy, supra note 1. In 1999 the Institute of Medicine of the National Academy of Sciences published the report of their year-long investigation of the therapeutic value of marijuana, concluding that "cannabinoid drugs" had potential value for pain relief, control of nausea and vomiting and appetite stimulation, especially for patients with some forms of cancer, AIDS, multiple sclerosis, and other identified condition. It also found the drugs to be potentially valuable as a palliative care agent for those treated with various forms of chemotherapy. See Institute of Med., Marijuana and Medicine (J. Joy et al, eds., 1999). Who should balance the potential medical need for marijuana with the potential social costs of the increased availability of this drug? Does Congress have that power? Do the state legislatures? The courts? Individual doctors?

4. As the *Cannabis Buyers' Cooperative* case suggests, the United States has interpreted federal policy to be the discouragement of all use of marijuana, whatever state law may say about this subject. In 1996, after Arizona and California became the first two states to formally legalize the use of medical marijuana, the Office of the National Drug Control Policy consulted with the Drug Enforcement Agency, the Department of Justice and other federal agencies. It

then issued a policy aimed at discouraging physicians from mentioning the potential use of marijuana to their patients. Specifically, the policy provided that any physician who recommended or prescribed any schedule I controlled substance would put his DEA registration (and, thus, his authority to prescribe any controlled substance) at risk. The federal policy was challenged by patients and physicians who sought an injunction against its enforcement. The plaintiffs based their arguments on the free speech clause of the First Amendment, while the government argued that the physicians' recommendation of marijuana use would constitute aiding or abetting the violation of the Controlled Substances Act, or the participation in a conspiracy to violate that federal law. The trial court granted an injunction and ordered the government (1) not to threaten to remove the DEA license from physicians who recommended medical marijuana to their patients and (2) not to threaten to investigate physicians solely on the grounds that they recommended medical marijuana. *Conant v. Walters,* 309 F.3d 629 (9th Cir.2002).

This issue eventually made its way to the Ninth Circuit which based its conclusion on the First Amendment rights of the physicians to openly discuss all medical options with their patients. As the court pointed out,

> The government's policy in this case seeks to punish physicians on the basis of the content of doctor-patient communications. Only doctor patient conversations that include discussions of the medical use of marijuana trigger the policy. Moreover, the policy does not merely prohibit the discussion of marijuana; it condemns expression of a particular viewpoint, i.e., that medical marijuana would likely help a specific patient. Such condemnation of particular views is especially troubling in the Furst Amendment context.

309 F.3d at 637. In his concurring opinion, Judge Kozinski depended upon the result on the patients' First Amendment right to hear that medical advice. As he pointed out, "Those immediately and directly affected ... are the patients, who will be denied information crucial to their well-being, and the State of California, whose policy of exempting certain patients from the sweep of its drug laws will be thwarted. 309 F.3d at 640 (Kozinksi, J., concurring).

5. In the *Cannabis Buyer's Cooperative* case, the majority explicitly leaves open the question of "whether the Controlled Substances Act exceeds Congress' power under the Commerce clause." Does it? In this Act, does Congress effectively regulate the practice of medicine within a state? Does it have the power to do so? How might Congress have authority to regulate the use of marijuana that is grown within a state for use by patients certified under the state law? Would cannabis cooperatives be legal if they sold only locally produced marijuana?

6. Are there other Constitutional issues that might be raised against the federal government's policy of enforcing the Controlled Substances Act in the manner in which it has chosen? For example, is the federal government "commandeering" the resources of the states to serve a federal purpose with which those states may disagree, in a way that is inconsistent with the rule announced in New York v. United States, 505 U.S. 144, 112 S.Ct. 2408, 120 L.Ed.2d 120 (1992) and Printz v. United States, 521 U.S. 898, 117 S.Ct. 2365, 138 L.Ed.2d 914 (1997)? In the Conant case, issued after *Cannabis Buyers' Cooperative* was decided by the Supreme Court, concurring Judge Kozinski thought that it was. See Conant, 309 F.3d at 645–46.

7. The part of the federal law that was vindicated in *Cannabis Buyers' Cooperative* addresses only the manufacture and distribution of marijuana. Could a state license the use of marijuana without authorizing its manufacture or distribution? Did California do so in the statute reprinted above? Might a state statute avoid the application of the Controlled Substances Act if it provided for physicians to recommend (but not prescribe) marijuana for patients who would then be licensed to cultivate a sufficient supply for their own medical use?

8. Over the past decade the use of medical marijuana has become an issue outside of the United States, too. The concurring opinion in the *Conant* case also provided insight into the development of the law in the United Kingdom and in Canada:

> At about the time the IOM study got underway, the British House of Lords—a body not known for its wild and crazy views—opened public hearings on the medical benefits and drawbacks of cannabis. Like the IOM, the Lords concluded that "cannabis almost certainly does have genuine medical applications, especially in treating the painful muscular spasms and other symptoms of MS and in the control of other forms of pain." Select Comm. on Sci. & Tech., House of Lords, Sess. 1997–98, Ninth Report, *Cannabis: The Scientific and Medical Evidence: Report* § 8.2 (Nov. 4, 1998)[ ]. The Lords recommended that the British government act immediately "to allow doctors to prescribe an appropriate preparation of cannabis, albeit as an unlicensed medicine." *Id.* § 8.6.
>
> In June 2001, Canada promulgated its Marihuana Medical Access Regulations after an extensive study of the available evidence. *See* Marihuana Medical Access Regulations, SOR 2001–227 (June 14, 2001)[ ]. The new regulations allow certain persons to cultivate and possess marijuana for medical use, and authorize doctors to recommend and prescribe marijuana to patients who are suffering from severe pain, muscle spasms, anorexia, weight loss or nausea, and who have not found relief from conventional therapies. *See* Office of Cannabis Med. Access, Health Canada, *Medical Access to Marijuana—How the Regulations Work* [ ].

309 F.3d at 641–42. In March of 2003 Canada began holding immigration hearings in the cases of several Americans who claimed refugee status because they were denied access to necessary medical care—medical marijuana—in their home country. Should they be granted refugee status and be allowed to remain where they can get access to therapeutic doses of marijuana?

9. To what extent is the battle over medical marijuana just a reprise of the American culture war of the 1960s? To what extent is this a confrontation between those who approve of the values of those who used marijuana forty years ago, and those who detest those values and thought that every indicia of them had been destroyed? A legislator's general position on these cultural issues is very highly predictive of what that legislator's views will be on this medical issue, too.

10. Apply the various theories of ethics and bioethics to the question of the legalization of medical marijuana. What would a utilitarian do? A Kantian? A person attempting to follow the requirements of natural law? A law and economics believer? A critical legal studies advocate?

## Problem: Drafting Medical Marijuana Legislation

Draft a bill for your state legislature that would permit the medical use of marijuana but would not increase the abuse of marijuana. If your state already has such legislation, draft a bill to amend it to make it most effective in light of the *Cannabis Buyers' Cooperative* case. Write your bill so that it is consistent with the requirements of the Federal law, including the Controlled Substances Act, but would still permit the use of medical marijuana when that is recommended (or would you say prescribed?) by a physician. What legal problems do you face? How do you overcome them?

How would you draft the bill to assure yourself of the most political support? Remember—while voters seem to like medical marijuana initiatives, only one state legislature has passed such a bill. Why are state legislatures so reluctant to act? How will medical interest groups react? Patient advocacy groups? Religious groups? Who will oppose your bill? Is there a way to increase the chance that it will be supported by state prosecutors, police, and other public safety groups? Is there a way to make such legislation consistent with the "war on drugs"?

Who would be able to possess medical marijuana under your bill? How much would they be able to possess? Where would they be able to get a supply? For what symptoms would it be available?

# Chapter 20

# INTERDISCIPLINARY DECISIONMAKING IN HEALTH CARE: REGULATION OF RESEARCH INVOLVING HUMAN SUBJECTS, ETHICS COMMITTEES, AND ADVISORY COMMITTEES

## I. REGULATION OF RESEARCH UPON HUMAN SUBJECTS

### C. CURRENT REGULATION OF RESEARCH UPON HUMAN SUBJECTS IN THE UNITED STATES

**Add, at p. 1490, at the end of note 13:**

The issue of researcher conflicts of interest has become more apparent during the last few years. Two major lawsuits brought on behalf of research subjects—both ultimately settled for large amounts—alleged that the researchers and their institutions had substantial economic interests in the success of research involving human subjects. Both were filed by Alan Milstein, a New Jersey trial lawyer who has also filed other actions against researchers.

The first resulted from the death of Jesse Gelsinger, an otherwise healthy 18–year old who was enticed to serve as a research subject in a gene therapy trial conducted by Dr. James Wilson at the University of Pennsylvania. Both Dr. Wilson and the University had very substantial interests in Genovo, which produced the therapy that was being tested. Eventually the research was halted, but both Dr. Wilson and the University still made millions from their investment. The suit named the University, the researchers, a consulting bioethicist, and the institutional review board and its members, among other defendants.

The second was filed on behalf of subjects at the Fred Hutchinson Cancer Center in Seattle, which is one of the world's premier bone-marrow transplant venues. This action, filed on behalf of the 82 human subjects who participated in "Protocol 126," named the institution, the Genetic Systems corporation, and several physicians, including one former Nobel Prize winner, among its defendants. Genetic Systems, which owned the right to use some of the drugs tested, had given stock to the research physicians and to the Fred Hutchinson Cancer Center.

For an account of these cases, see D. Wilson and D. Heath, Class Action Filed Against "The Hutch," Seattle Times, March 27, 2001, A–1, and J. Washburn, Informed Consent, Washington Post, December 30, 2001, Magazine p. 16.

**Add, at p. 1490, after the final note:**

## Note: Liability Arising out of Research Involving Human Subjects

Over the past few years there has been a dramatic increase in actions seeking damages from physician researchers and institutional sponsors of research involving human subjects. Among the most famous cases are the two cases described in the preceding note—the Gelsinger case and the case against "The Hutch." The same plaintiff's attorney who filed those actions also has filed one against the University of Oklahoma and its research establishment and the manufacturer of the anthrax vaccine that was tested on soldiers during the Gulf War. See J. Washburn, supra. In addition, there have been large judgments entered against hospitals doing research on poor pregnant women in Tampa, and the FDA collected over a million dollars in fines from a company that engaged in unsafe and fraudulent research. See A. Dembner, Lawsuits Target Medical Research Patient Safeguards, Boston Globe, August 12, 2002, A–1.

While some of these lawsuits are ordinary medical malpractice lawsuits, many also include claims that there was inadequate legal or ethical oversight of the research, and they seek damages for injury to the subjects' "dignitary interest." In particular, there is a claim that some of the conduct of the researchers violates the Nuremberg Code, found on page 1463, the Declaration of Helsinki, found on page 1464, and other international agreements and statements of ethical standards. See J. Washburn, supra. Is it fair to hold researchers to those standards, and to award damages when those standards are violated? Is it appropriate to use research standards that arose out of the Nazi atrocities to guide contemporary American research involving human subjects?

**Add, at p. 1490, after the note above:**

## D. REFORMING THE SYSTEM TO PROTECT RESEARCH PARTICIPANTS

Over the past several years the Institute of Medicine, on commission of the Department of Health and Human Services, performed a comprehensive assessment of the system in place to protect research subjects in the United States. Their most recent and most general report was released in late 2002, and parts of the Executive Summary are reprinted here. Throughout the report the Committee refers to "human research participant protection programs"—HRPPPs—which would replace the current IRB system. If the recommendations of the Committee were adopted, it would provide for a substantial change in the oversight of research involving human subjects (soon to be called "human research participants").

## COMMITTEE ON ASSESSING THE SYSTEM FOR PROTECTING HUMAN RESEARCH PARTICIPANTS OF THE INSTITUTE OF MEDICINE, RESPONSIBLE RESEARCH: A SYSTEMS APPROACH TO PROTECTING RESEARCH PARTICIPANTS*

(D.D. Federman et al., eds, 2003).

### Executive Summary

\* \* \*

#### STATEMENT OF THE PROBLEM

As recently detailed by the National Bioethics Advisory Commission (NBAC), many highly regarded groups have assessed the strengths and weaknesses of the national system for ensuring the ethical protection of volunteer research participants. Proposals for reform have been presented to the public, the Executive Branch of the federal government, and Congress. However, a fact that has repeatedly confounded this committee's deliberations is the lack of data regarding the scope and scale of current protection activities. This absence of information seriously handicaps an objective assessment of protection program performance and needs and the development of useful policy directions. Nonetheless, the evidence is abundant regarding the significant strains and weaknesses of the current system, and this committee has reached the conclusion that major reforms are in order.

First, significant doubt exists regarding the capacity of the current system to meet its core objectives. Although all stakeholders agree that participant protection must be of paramount concern in every aspect of the research process, a variety of faults and problems in the present system have been noted. The common finding is that dissatisfaction with the current system is widespread.

Second, it has been shown that IRBs are "under strain" and "in need of reform" [ ]. The complexity of the issues, the variability in the research settings, the limitations of funding options, the demands of investigators and participants for access to research, and the accountability for institutional compliance have magnified and complicated IRBs' responsibilities. This heavy burden has made it difficult both to recruit knowledgeable IRB members and to allow them sufficient time for the necessary ethical reflection.

Third, the existing regulatory framework \* \* \* cannot adequately respond to the complex and ever-changing research environment, with weaknesses related to gaps in authority, structure, and resources. \* \* \*

#### MAJOR RECOMMENDATIONS

The major recommendations of this report aim to ensure the protection of every research participant. The committee envisions a three-part strategy to achieve this goal, including refocusing the mission of the IRB on the thorough ethical review and oversight of research protocols; recognizing research partic-

---

\* © 2003, National Academy of Sciences. Reprinted with permission.

ipants' contributions and integrating them into the system; and maintaining high standards for and continuing review of HRPPP performance. * * *

*Protect Every Research Participant*

The protection of research participants is fundamental and should remain paramount to any research endeavor. * * *

* * *

The specific structure of a protection program is secondary to its performance of several essential functions. These functions include:

1) comprehensive review of protocols (including scientific, financial conflict of interest, and ethical reviews),

2) ethically sound participant-investigator interactions,

3) ongoing (and risk-appropriate) safety monitoring throughout the conduct of the study, and

4) quality improvement (QI) and compliance activities.

**Recommendation: Adequate protection of participants requires that all human research be subject to a responsible Human Research Participant Protection Program (HRPPP) under federal oversight. Federal law should require every organization sponsoring or conducting research with humans to assure that all of the necessary functions of an HRPPP are carried out and should also require every individual conducting research with humans to be acting under the authority of an established HRPPP.** *(Recommendation 2.1)*

**Establish Accountability Within an Ethical Research Culture**

* * *

**Recommendation: The authority and responsibility for research participant protections should reside within the highest level of the research organization. Leaders of public and private research organizations should establish a culture of research excellence that is pervasive and that includes clear lines of authority and responsibility for participant protection.** *(Recommendation 2.2)*

Establishing the appropriate research culture will require ongoing efforts to educate researchers, research administrators, IRB members, and participants about research ethics and participant protection issues, as well as continuous QI activities. The Office for Human Research Protections (OHRP), with input from a variety of scholars in science and ethics, should coordinate the development and dissemination of core education elements and practices for human research ethics for those conducting and those overseeing such research. The individual research organization is responsible for ensuring that its personnel are educated about their responsibilities and expected conduct [ ]. The sponsor also shares some responsibility for ensuring that the research organization it engages employs only qualified personnel and has the resources to conduct the study. The stimulation of a high-quality research culture is one area in which the committee believes that developing accreditation programs may offer a significant contribution by focusing an organization's attention on QI and specific resource needs. * * *

*Provide Sufficient Resources*

\* \* \*

*Refocus Institutional Review Board Mission on Ethical Review of Protocols*

As the demands on the research oversight system have grown, so has the reliance upon IRBs to accomplish all protection tasks. This is a disservice to research participants, because IRBs, which are intended to focus on the ethical review and oversight of proposals, find it exceedingly difficult to both manage the increasing volume of protocol actions and ensure the safety of research volunteers, particularly when these boards are often under-resourced.

\* \* \*

To reflect this refocused role, the committee recommends moving away from the term "Institutional Review Board," which conflates institutional interests with those of participants, and suggests adopting a more functionally appropriate term.

**Recommendation: The Institutional Review Board (IRB), as the principal representative of the interests of potential research participants, should focus its full committee deliberations and oversight primarily on the ethical aspects of protection issues. To reflect this role, IRBs should be appropriately renamed within research organizations' internal documents that define institutional structure and policies. The committee suggests the name "Research Ethics Review Board" (Research ERB).** *(Recommendation 3.1)*

From this point forward in this report, the term "Research ERB" will be used in the context of the committee's envisioned HRPPP, and the term "IRB" will be reserved for comments regarding the existing protection framework.

All members of the Research ERB should have a core body of knowledge, and a critical mass of the membership, either scientist or nonscientist, should possess a specialized knowledge of human research ethics. The research organization's goal should be to create or associate with a Research ERB in which unaffiliated members, nonscientists, and those who represent the local community and/or the participant perspective comprise at least 25 percent of the membership [ ]. Although the committee recognizes that identifying this increased proportion of willing and able unaffiliated and nonscientist individuals will be difficult and that they will require additional training, the proportional shift is important to the integration of the participant or community and could help insulate Research ERBs from potential conflicts of interest at the organizational level.

Further, as modern IRBs have tended to become larger and to reflect a broader range of scientific expertise, some IRB deliberations have tended to be dominated by the scientific perspective, increasing the potential to marginalize the perspectives of nonscientist members and those who focus on ethics-based concerns [ ]. Therefore, the refocused Research ERB's deliberative objective should aim for consensus rather than majority control [ ]. No protocol should be approved without three-quarters of the voting members concurring. Just as a vote of unanimity would effectively give a veto to a single dissenting committee member, allowing a simple majority to approve a protocol in the face of substantial minority opinion can too easily suppress responsible ethical opinions.

*Distinguish Scientific, Conflict of Interest, and Ethics Review Mechanisms*

The scientific and ethical review of protocols should be equally rigorous. Therefore, each review requires distinct, although overlapping, expertise. Research ERBs that are constituted to emphasize the ethical dimensions of protocol review should not be expected to have a primary membership with the range of knowledge and skills needed to adequately assess the scientific and technical merits of every protocol under their purview. Although the in-depth scientific evaluation of proposals is fundamental to the comprehensive ethics review of any protocol, the Research ERB need not conduct the initial scientific review. Instead, summaries of the scientific review should be submitted to the Research ERB as a component of its ethics-focused deliberations.

Furthermore, there is a need to ensure that no financial or other interests on the part of the investigator, research organization, or the Research ERB (as a body or as individual members) will distort the conduct of research with human participants. While there are non-financial self-interests intrinsic to the pursuit of research questions, the frequency and complexity of potential financial conflicts of interest in research are expanding, and the federal government and relevant professional and industry groups should continue to consider their potential ramifications and pursue rigorous policies for handling them [ ]. A process for scrutinizing potential financial conflicts of interest in any protocol is vital to the subsequent evaluation of participant risks and benefits by the Research ERB [ ].

Despite the need for review from three distinct perspectives (scientific, ethical, and financial conflict of interest), the interrelated nature of these perspectives requires that a *single* body be vested with the authority to make final protocol determinations and be accountable for those determinations. This body is and should remain the Research ERB. The focused reviews of scientific merit and potential financial conflicts of interest should inform the ethics review process for each protocol [ ].

**Recommendation: Research organizations and research sponsors should ensure that Human Research Participant Protection Programs utilize distinct mechanisms for the initial, focused reviews of scientific and financial conflicts of interest. These reviews should precede and inform the comprehensive ethical review of research studies by the Research Ethics Review Board (Research ERB) through summaries of the relevant findings submitted to the Research ERB for full board consideration.** *(Recommendation 3.2)*

*Emphasize Risk–Appropriate Protection*

\* \* \*

*Increase Program Productivity*

The effective oversight and management of the rapidly expanding number of multisite studies, particularly in the high-risk clinical domain, is an area of substantial concern [ ]; full-scale IRB review of protocols by all participating organizations does not necessarily increase participant protection. Therefore, the committee encourages the streamlining of multisite trial review, recommending one primary scientific review committee and one primary Research ERB assume the lead review functions, subject to acceptance by the local committees and boards at participating sites [ ].

\* \* \*

### Recognize and Integrate Participant Contributions

As stated in this committee's first report, participants and their representatives should be meaningfully included in the review and oversight of research to ensure that pertinent concerns are heard and that researchers conduct studies that meet participant needs [ ]. \* \* \*

### Revitalize Informed Consent

Informed consent should be an ongoing process that focuses not on a written form or a static disclosure event, but rather on a series of dynamic conversations between the participant and the research staff that should begin before enrollment and be reinforced during each encounter or intervention (see Box 4.3). Multidisciplinary approaches should be tailored to individual differences in participant education and learning capabilities.

**Recommendation: The informed consent process should be an ongoing, interactive dialogue between research staff and research participants involving the disclosure and exchange of relevant information, discussion of that information, and assessment of the individual's understanding of the discussion.** *(Recommendation 4.1)*

The informed consent conversation(s), as well as the written consent document, should not be obscured by language designed mainly to insulate the institution from liability. Rather, the process should ensure that participants clearly understand the nature of the proposed research and its potential risks and benefits to them and society.

**Recommendation: Forms signed by individuals to provide their legally valid consent to participate in research should be called "consent forms" rather than "informed consent forms." Research Ethics Review Boards should ensure that the focus of the informed consent process and the consent form is on informing and protecting participants, NOT on protecting institutions.** *(Recommendation 3.4)*

### Increase System Accessibility

\* \* \*

To ensure that information about all clinical trials is available, the committee proposes the creation of a comprehensive and soundly structured clinical trials registry for use by the public. Material submitted to Research ERBs could serve as the backbone of this registry. The committee believes that although the challenges and resource requirements involved in such an undertaking are significant, clinical trials are of such public concern that the effort should be pursued [ ].

## Compensate Participants for Research–Related Injury

Despite decades of discussion on the ethical obligation to compensate participants for research-related injury, little information is available regarding the number of such injuries and the cost of providing compensation for them [ ]. In the face of real potential for diminished public trust in the research community, providing reasonable compensation for legitimate instances of research harm is critical to restoring credibility.

\* \* \*

The responsibility for no-fault compensation programs should fall initially on the institution or organization accountable for conducting the research, and its terms should be specified in the documentation accompanying the participant's agreement to participate. The committee supports the findings of the many reports addressing this topic—that a comprehensive research participant protection system should include a compensation mechanism for medical and rehabilitative costs [ ]. The committee further believes that the next step in this process should be to pilot test mechanisms to provide remuneration for lost work time.

**Recommendation: Organizations conducting research should compensate any research participant who is injured as a direct result of participating in research, without regard to fault. Compensation should include at least the costs of medical care and rehabilitation, and accrediting bodies should include such compensation as a requirement of accreditation.** *(Recommendation 6.8)*

## Maintain Vigilance

\* \* \*

## Collect National Level Data About the System

\* \* \*

## Enhance Safety Monitoring

The safety of research volunteers must be guaranteed from the inception of a protocol, through its execution, to final completion and reporting of results. Continual review and monitoring of risk-prone studies is needed to ensure that emerging information has not altered the original risk-benefit analysis. Therefore, risk-appropriate mechanisms are needed to track protocols and study personnel; provide assurances that data are valid and collected according to applicable practices (e.g., Good Clinical Practice); and ensure that participants' safety, privacy, and confidentiality are protected throughout a study. Protection measures should be monitored by various means at all levels to ensure that consent has been properly given and that all adverse events have been identified and appropriately reported by the investigator to the relevant institutional body, sponsor, and federal agency(ies).

**Recommendation: Research organizations and Research Ethics Review Boards should have written policies and procedures in place that detail internal oversight and auditing processes. Plans and resources for data and safety monitoring within an individual study**

should be commensurate with the level of risk anticipated for that particular research protocol. *(Recommendation 5.1)*

\* \* \*

*Continuously Improve Quality*

\* \* \*

**Recommendation: Research sponsors should initiate research programs and funding support for innovative research that would develop criteria for evaluating program performance and enhancing the practice of quality improvement.** *(Recommendation 6.2)*

As observed in this committee's first report, accreditation programs represent one promising approach to assessing the protection functions of research organizations in a uniform and independent manner, and may serve as a useful stimulus for QI programs [ ]. \* \* \*

*Manage Potential Conflicts of Interest*

Confidence about the current system of participant protection is undermined by the perception that harm to research participants may result from conflicts of interest involving the researcher, the research organization, and/or the research sponsor. This concern is particularly acute regarding financial conflicts of interest, as the relationships between the academic and private research enterprises continue to evolve. Therefore, mechanisms for identifying, disclosing, and resolving conflicts of interest should be strengthened, especially those involving financial relationships [ ].

Strong organizational leadership and the promotion of an ethically based research culture (possibly complemented through appropriate accreditation standards) may help avoid the need for management policies regarding potential self-interests; however, a dedicated conflict of interest review process will remain essential. \* \* \*

In the committee's view, because the Research ERB lacks the necessary resources or authority to ensure the appropriate management of potential conflicts of interest, the responsibility for assessing and managing financial conflicts of individuals (investigators, research staff, and Research ERB members) should lie with the research organization [ ]. Likewise, organizations should ensure that an independent, external mechanism is in place for the evaluation of potential institutional conflicts [ ]. In both instances, conflict of interest information should be communicated in a timely and effective manner to the Research ERB, which should make the final assessment with regard to ensuring participant protections.

\* \* \*

*Periodically Assess the National System*

\* \* \*

CONCLUDING REMARKS

Policy makers and the scientific community should ensure that the interests and dignity of every research participant are diligently protected throughout the research process. * * * The recommendations offered within this report are intended to guide HRPPPs and policy makers as they work to guarantee that research participants' safety and rights are protected throughout their involvement in any research study and that the national research enterprise is worthy of the public's trust and continued support.

## *Notes and Questions on Proposed Reform*

1. What are the biggest changes in the current IRB system recommended by the Institute of Medicine Committee? Is it a bold proposal that would substantially reform the system, or a mere tinkering with the current system?

2. Who would be required to act to institute the changes that have been recommended? Which would require Congressional action, which could be done by federal administrative agencies, and which would be accomplished by changes at local institutions?

3. Current regulations apply only to federally funded research (and, effectively, to other research conducted by those institutions which receive federal funds). The amount of privately funded medical research has increased substantially, and much research is not covered by current federal regulations. The proposal would extend coverage to virtually all research with human participants in the United States, even research that is privately funded and conducted at research centers that receive no government funding of any kind. Is that extension of federal regulatory authority warranted as a matter of policy? Does the federal government have authority to regulate research in this way?

4. The Committee would separate the ethics issues that arise out of research protocols (reserved for "Research ERBs") from the scientific issues and issues surrounding potential financial conflicts, which would be reviewed through separate processes. Is it possible to separate out these kinds of review? Is it a good idea?

5. The review process would also be changed in other ways. "Unaffiliated members, nonscientists, and those who represent the local community and/or the participant perspective" must make up at least a quarter of the Committee, and a three-quarters super majority would be required to approve protocols. Does this make sense? Will this be enough to break the hold that many believe scientists maintain on IRBs?

6. The adoption of the Committee recommendations will require that institutional research bureaucrats learn a new set of names and acronyms. The current IRB system will become the "human research participant protection programs," or HRPPPs. Subjects will become participants "to reflect [the Committee's belief] that the optimal functioning of research oversight programs necessitates the meaningful integration of research participants and their perspectives." IRBs themselves will become Research Ethics Review Boards, or Research ERBs.

7. An earlier Committee report had suggested accreditation of IRB programs, and in late 2002 the National Committee for Quality Assurance (the "NCQA"), a private non-profit which accredits other health care enterprises, announced standards for its Human Research Protection Accreditation Program, or HRPAP. What are the advantages and disadvantages of having HRPPPs (or

Research ERBs, or IRBs, for that matter) accredited by a non-governmental entity?

8. Is it appropriate to institute a no-fault compensation scheme into the regulation of research with human participants? What should be the relationship between that compensation system and the tort system, which has been applied with vigor to compensate injured subjects of research over the past few years?

9. Critics of the Committee claim that it is too timid in its recommendations. They are especially concerned that it continues to allow research institutions to appoint their own IRBs (or Research ERBs). Is this an inherent conflict? One critic argues that the Committee "disingenuously recommended entrusting 'the responsibility for ensuring that protective rules are followed' to 'the leadership of the organization doing the study.'" See M. Kranish and A. Dembner, Panel Urges Changes in Research on Humans, Boston Globe, October 4, 2002, p. A–2. What is the alternative? Could a government agency establish and appoint members to Research ERBs at private institutions? Should Research ERBs be identified with individual institutions at all, or should there be centralized review of research protocols?

## *Problem*

You are counsel to a University Hospital that does a substantial amount of research with human participants. You have been asked by your Representative in the United States House of Representatives to write a short memorandum telling her which of these recommendations she should support, and which she should oppose, in order to advance the research work of the hospital. How would you answer that question? What would you want to know about the research now being conducted at your hospital? What else would you want to know? How would you suggest that your Representative fill in the details that the Committee left open?

†